EVIDENCE

OBJECTIVE

Seventh Edition

MICHAEL H. GRAHAM
Professor of Law
Deans Distinguished Scholar
University of Miami Law School

Exam Pro®

WEST
ACADEMIC
PUBLISHING

Exam Pro Series is a trademark registered in the U.S. Patent and Trademark Office.

© West, A Thomson business, 2002, 2006, 2008
© 2011 Thomson Reuters
© 2015, 2018 LEG, Inc. d/b/a West Academic
© 2021 LEG, Inc. d/b/a West Academic
     444 Cedar Street, Suite 700
     St. Paul, MN 55101
     1-877-888-1330

Printed in the United States of America

ISBN: 978-1-68467-696-5

Table of Contents

SPECIFIC SUBJECT MATTER REVIEW

HEARSAY EXAMS

COMPREHENSIVE EXAMS

SPECIFIC SUBJECT MATTER REVIEW ANSWER KEY

HEARSAY EXAMS ANSWER KEY

COMPREHENSIVE EXAMS ANSWER KEY

APPENDICES

EVIDENCE

OBJECTIVE

Seventh Edition

SPECIFIC SUBJECT
MATTER REVIEW

SPECIFIC SUBJECT MATTER REVIEW

TRUE-FALSE QUESTIONS

1. **Relevance and the Exclusion of Relevant Evidence: Fed.R.Evid. 401–403**

___1. Circumstantial evidence must possess plus value to be relevant.

___2. Fact of consequence is synonymous with material proposition.

___3. Fact of consequence includes evidence constituting impeachment of a witness.

___4. Evidence of background is relevant.

___5. Evidence that tends to establish the proposition it is offered to prove may nevertheless be inadmissible under Rule 401.

___6. Evidence creating a risk of unfair prejudice will be excluded under Rule 403.

___7. Surprise and waste of time are trial concerns balanced against probative value under Rule 403.

___8. A party can ordinarily refuse to accept an offer by an opponent to stipulate to a fact and introduce evidence establishing such fact for its fair and legitimate weight.

___9.   Evidence that a jury might consider for a purpose other than the purpose for which it is received in spite of a limiting instruction creates a risk of unfair prejudice.

___10.   Misleading refers to the risk of the jury improperly evaluating the probative value of a particular item of evidence.

2. Competency of Lay Witnesses: Fed.R.Evid. 601–606

___1.   In a diversity action brought in federal court, it is possible that a defendant in a negligence case will be incompetent to testify as to the accident.

___2.   Pursuant to Rule 601, every two year old child is competent to testify.

___3.   Under the Federal Rules of Evidence an attorney representing a litigant is a competent witness in the same trial.

___4.   A judge may not testify at any trial in the district in which he or she presides.

___5.   Lack of personal knowledge affects only weight, not admissibility.

___6.   A juror may attack a verdict on the basis of an experiment conducted by a fellow juror with the results reported and discussed during jury deliberation.

___7.   A juror may attack a verdict on the grounds that a fellow juror was drunk during jury deliberation.

___8.   A juror may attack a verdict on the basis of the bailiff telling members of the jury during the deliberation that he was surprised the defendant had gotten out of jail so soon after his prior robbery conviction.

___9.   A partner of the lawyer trying a case is always incompetent to testify.

___10.   The requirement of personal knowledge is decided alone by the trial court pursuant to Rule 104(a).

3.   **Direct Examination: Fed.R.Evid. 106, 611(c), 612, 615**

___1.   Leading questions are usually permitted on direct examination.

___2.   If the prosecution calls the mother of the defendant to testify as an occurrence witness, the prosecution will most likely be able to conduct the direct examination using leading questions.

___3.   A question is not leading unless it calls for a yes or no answer.

___4.   The use of leading questions will rarely result in reversible error.

___5.   It is more likely that counsel will be permitted to lead a child on direct than an adult witness.

___6.   A witness who testifies to a fact may never have his recollection refreshed on this point.

___7.   If counsel has in his possession a document that might refresh the witness' recollection, a leading question to refresh recollection is never proper.

___8.   A leading question employed to refresh recollection on a non-critical matter may be asked in open court before the jury.

___9.   Counsel may write out on a piece of paper "You idiot, I told you to say Harry said ' * * * * ' ", and show it to a witness who claims he lacks recollection as to what Harry said.

___10.   Writings used to refresh recollection must be shown upon request to opposing counsel who may then introduce it for the purpose of the jury evaluating credibility.

___11.   An adverse party may require a party to introduce along with a writing just introduced another writing which ought in fairness be considered contemporaneously.

___12.   Another portion of an oral conversation can be inquired of on cross-examination but the party introducing a portion of the communication on direct cannot be required to introduce that other portion on direct examination.

___13.   The prosecution may have the lead law enforcement officer remain at counsel table in spite of the fact that this person will be a witness in the case and "The Rule" has been invoked.

___14.   The expert who will be a witness in the case may not remain in the courtroom to advise counsel when "The Rule" has been invoked.

___15.   A witness who on his own violates "The Rule" is likely to be precluded from testifying.

4.   Hearsay Definition: Fed.R.Evid. 801(a)–(d)

For each of the fact patterns that follow, the question asks whether the evidence is hearsay as defined in Rules 801(a)–(d) of the Federal Rules of Evidence. To signify that the evidence is hearsay answer "T." To signify that the evidence does not fall within the definition of hearsay contained in Rules 801(a)–(d) of the Federal Rules of Evidence answer "F." Assume that all necessary foundations have been offered, that the evidence is relevant, that no privilege is applicable, etc. In short, focus solely upon the hearsay issue. Thus if a statement, for example, is relevant as a "verbal act," or for its "effect upon listener," the correct answer to whether the statement is "Hearsay" is "F." The correct answer for a statement that meets the requirements of either Rule 801(d)(1), prior statements by witness, or Rule 801(d)(2), admission by party-opponent, is also "F."

Appendix A contains a comprehensive textual explanation of the Federal Rules of Evidence approach to the definition of hearsay including the defining as not hearsay some but by no means all prior statements by declarants who testify at the trial or hearing, Rule 801(d)(1), and admissions of a party-opponent as set forth in Rule 801(d)(2). Appendix A is extremely useful reading for all students trying to distinguish hearsay from not hearsay out of court statements.

   ___1.   To prove that two people, X and Y, are engaged, Z, their friend, is called to testify that he heard X ask Y, "Will you marry me?" and Y answered "Yes."

   ___2.   To prove that X was a good gardener, a party offers evidence that just before he went on a month-long European vacation, he gave X all of his house plants to take care of.

   ___3.   Prosecution for bestiality. The prosecution calls a witness to testify that he saw the defendant kissing his horse.

   ___4.   Will contest. Plaintiff testifies that the testator was his father.

   ___5.   Action to recover the price of a car sold to defendant. To prove the car was paid for, defendant offers the testimony of a witness who claims to have heard defendant say to plaintiff, "Here is $5,000 in payment for the car." Plaintiff remained silent.

___6.   Prosecution of D for running a house of prostitution. D denies that her establishment was a house of prostitution. The prosecution calls W, a police officer, who testifies that while he was at the scene arresting D, he answered the phone and the caller on the other end said, "Make me an 8:30 with Candy tonight."

___7.   To prove that D had a motive to kill V, P offers the testimony of D's ex-wife that she saw D lose over $10,000 to V in a poker game one night before the murder.

___8.   Same as above, only instead the ex-wife's testimony will be that the day before the murder V came to D's ex-wife's apartment looking for D and told D's ex-wife that D owed him $10,000 from a poker game and that he had better pay up soon. (The ex-wife will also testify that she did not tell D about the incident with V.)

___9.   Same as above, only instead the ex-wife's testimony will be that the night before the murder, D told her that "that S.O.B. V had just cheated him out of $10,000."

___10.   Prosecution for assault with a deadly weapon. To prove defendant acted reasonably in self-defense, the defendant testifies that a bartender told him, "Jake (the victim) was in here looking for you an hour ago with blood in his eye and a rod in his pocket. He says you cheated him at cards."

___11.   Product liability action against the manufacturer of a tire that blew out, causing injuries. To prove that the tire was defectively designed, plaintiff offers a report written by a government agency which investigated the type of tire involved in the accident and which concluded that the tire was defectively designed.

___12.   To prove that the car brakes were defective, D had them fixed the day after the accident.

___13.   To prove that M is an unfit mother in a child custody suit, the father offers the testimony of the children's social worker that when she was visiting with the children in her office, the mother walked in, and the children immediately began crying and ran to hide behind the curtains.

___14. Same as above, only the father offers the testimony of the family's neighbor that on several occasions she heard the mother yell at the children, "You are just a bunch of spoiled brats who can't behave properly; I'll teach you."

___15. Personal injury action. To prove the extent of injuries she suffered, plaintiff introduces a copy of her hospital record.

___16. Action on life insurance contract. To prove the insured is dead, plaintiff offers a death certificate.

___17. A police officer testifies that the bank teller, who have already testified but is still under subpoena, picked the defendant out of a line-up as the person who held up the bank.

___18. Personal injury action that requires retrial. Plaintiff died between the trials. To prove the plaintiff had the green light, W testifies that at the first trial, plaintiff testified that he had the green light.

___19. To show that P was in pain after an accident, a nurse will testify that he was screaming and moaning when admitted to the hospital.

___20. Shareholder action against a corporate board for taking irresponsible action in passing a particular resolution. To prove that the resolution was *not* passed by the board, defendants call W, who testifies that she was present at the meeting and that fewer than half of the board members raised their hands after the chairman asked all in favor of the resolution to do so.

___21. X always leaves the house key under the back door mat when she leaves the house. To prove that she was in the house at a particular time, Z will testify that he was unable to find the key under that mat.

_____22.   Divorce action. To prove adultery the husband testifies that he overheard a friend in the men's locker room describe a birthmark that the husband's wife has on an intimate part of her anatomy. The wife has testified that only her husband knew of the mark.

_____23.   To show that X was ill on a certain day, W offers to testify that on that date X complained to her that he had a pain in his chest.

_____24.   Action for breach of contract. To prove the making of the contract, the plaintiff introduces evidence that the defendant's secretary told her mother, "The boss just made a great deal for a gross of widgets."

_____25.   On the issue of what time it was, evidence that "Hal," the witness's talking watch, said, "The time is ten-twenty p.m."

_____26.   To prove the value of a recently purchased car, the receipt for the purchase price, given at the sale by seller is offered.

_____27.   Paternity suit. The mother takes the stand and when asked to identify the father, she points to the defendant.

_____28.   To prove D's provocation for assaulting Y, D calls his friend X to testify that he heard W, D's wife, tell D that "Y raped me."

_____29.   Defamation action by P against D. P alleges that D stood up in front of a large group and called P a "heavy drinker." D claims that she did not call P a "heavy drinker." At trial, D takes the stand and testifies that she called P a "heavy *thinker*" in front of that group.

___30. Prosecution for corporate piracy. To show that defendant stole the formula for plastic scissors, the prosecution offers a note in defendant's handwriting, setting forth a formula, found in defendant's possession identical to the actual formula for plastic scissor in plaintiff's possession.

___31. To prove paternity, P calls Z, a family friend, to testify that D, the defendant, referred to the child as "my son."

___32. Action for breach of contract. The plaintiff, to show the existence of the contract, introduces a letter from plaintiff to defendant that states, "I accept your offer to sell one hundred widgets."

___33. To prove that D was V's assailant and murderer, P calls V's doctor to testify that the police brought D to the hospital where V had been taken after the stabbing. When V opened her eyes and saw D, she shrunk back with a terrified look on her face and immediately lapsed into unconsciousness, never to awaken again.

___34. To prove that he could not possibly have taken the jewelry that he is now on trial for stealing, D offers the testimony of the housekeeper of V (the owner of the allegedly stolen jewelry who lives in Los Angeles) that two days before the alleged robbery in New Orleans, where V was attending a convention, V told her that he was planning to leave his jewelry at home because he didn't want it to get stolen in New Orleans.

___35. On the issue of who has the right of way, evidence that a sign facing D as he approached the intersection read "Yield Right of Way."

___36. To prove that X knew that a resolution had been passed by a corporate board, W testifies that he told X that the resolution had passed.

___37.   Prosecutor for attempted bribery. A police officer testifies that the defendant said to him "If you don't give me a ticket, I will give you $100 cash money."

___38.   Grand theft prosecution. The owner of the store is called to testify to the items that the defendant took, but on the stand is unable to recall all of them. The prosecutor shows him a copy of the police report in which the items found on the defendant are listed. The witness says, "Oh, yes. Now I remember." He then testifies as to the remainder of the stolen items.

___39.   Employee's action for breach of an employment contract. Plaintiff had worked as an engineer for defendant's firm. Defendant claims that plaintiff was fired because of incompetence. To prove that he was competent, plaintiff offers a letter written to him by one of defendant's clients in which the client asked him to conduct a complex engineering survey.

___40.   Prosecution of D for battery upon V. To prove that she acted in self-defense, D testifies that the day before the fight, X told her that V was out to kill D for stealing V's boyfriend.

___41.   On the issue of whether the plaintiff had a temperature, plaintiff's doctor offers to testify that the thermometer he used on plaintiff read 105°.

___42.   On the same issue, the plaintiff's mother offers to testify that the plaintiff said, "I feel hot and feverish."

___43.   On the same issue, the nurse offers to testify that the doctor wrapped the plaintiff in wet blankets (a standard treatment for fever).

___44.   On the same issue, plaintiff offers to testify, "The doctor told me I had a temperature."

___45. On the same issue, plaintiff offers to testify, "I felt hot and feverish."

___46. On the same issue, plaintiff's doctor offers to testify, "The nurse told me the thermometer is registering 105°."

___47. Prosecution of D for assault. The prosecution calls W, the alleged victim, and asks him if his attacker is in the courtroom. W responds by pointing to the defendant.

___48. Malpractice action for a botched nose job. To prove damages, the plaintiff testifies that for weeks after the accident, his fellow workers referred to him to his face as "Hose-Nose."

___49. To prove that it was warm outside on a certain day, X calls a witness who testifies that when she was at the ball park on that day, many fans were in short sleeve shirts and shorts.

___50. Action for breach of contract. To prove the breach, plaintiff testifies that the defendant told him, "You can take your contract and cram it."

5.   Hearsay Definition and Exceptions: Fed.R.Evid. 801–807

For each of the fact patterns that follow, the first question asks whether the evidence is hearsay as defined in Rules 801(a)–(d) of the Federal Rules of Evidence. To signify that the evidence is hearsay answer "T." To signify that the evidence does not fall within the definition of hearsay contained in Rules 801(a)–(d) of the Federal Rules of Evidence answer "F." Thus if a statement for example is relevant as a "verbal act" or for its "effect upon listener," the correct answer to whether the statement is "Hearsay" is "F." The correct answer for a statement that meets the requirements of either Rule 801(d)(1), prior statements by witness, or Rule 801(d)(2), admissibility by party-opponent is also "F." The second question with respect to each of the fifty sets of facts asks whether the evidence is admissible pursuant to a hearsay exception contained in either Rule 803, 804 or 807 or as multiple level hearsay pursuant to Rule 805 of the Federal Rules of Evidence. Of course, if the answer to the first question in the set is "F", i.e., not hearsay, then the answer to the second question is always "T", i.e., admissible. With respect to the residual exception,

Rule 807, assume that notice has been provided, Rule 807(b), and that the requirement of Rule 807(a)(2) is satisfied, i.e., concentrate solely upon whether the statement "is supported by sufficient guarantees of trustworthiness," Rule 807(a)(1). Assume that all necessary foundations have been offered, that the evidence is relevant, that no privilege is applicable, etc. In short, focus solely upon the hearsay issue.

Appendix A contains a comprehensive textual explanation of the Federal Rules of Evidence approach to the definition of hearsay including the defining as not hearsay some but by no means all prior statements by declarants who testify at the trial or hearing, Rule 801(d)(1), and admissions of a party-opponent as set forth in Rule 801(d)(2). Appendix A is extremely useful reading for all students trying to distinguish hearsay from not hearsay out of court statements.

- To prove the license number of the car involved in a hit-and-run accident, P offers the testimony of a witness as to the content of a crumpled slip of paper on which appears the number EE2468 along with the testimony of a man that, though he cannot now recall the number of the car, he did, while the number was fresh in his mind, shortly after seeing the accident, write the number down on the piece of paper offered in evidence.

  ___1.   Hearsay?

  ___2.   Admissible?

- To prove the license number of the car involved in a hit-and-run accident, P offers a photograph of a retreating automobile bearing the license number EE2468 and the testimony of a woman that she took the photograph offered in evidence of the accident car as it left the scene, and that the photograph is accurate.

  ___3.   Hearsay?

  ___4.   Admissible?

- P v. D. To prove the way in which an industrial accident happened, P offers a motion picture taken by Y of P reenacting the accident.

  ___5.   Hearsay?

  ___6.   Admissible?

- P v. D. To prove that P was able to get around after the accident, D offers a motion picture taken by Y of P reenacting the accident.

  ___7.   Hearsay?

  ___8.   Admissible?

- To prove that T lacked testamentary capacity on January 1, 2011, testimony of Y that on several occasions during December and January T had told Y that she (T) was Michael Jordan.

  ___9.   Hearsay?

  ___10.   Admissible?

- P v. D. As tending to prove title to Blackacre in defendant (D) by adverse possession under claim of title, D offers the testimony of W that plaintiff (P) said to his sister, "I've been down to the town meeting, and D is telling everyone that he owns Blackacre."

    ___11.   Hearsay?

    ___12.   Admissible?

- P v. D. To prove that A was an agent of D, P offers the testimony of W that A said, "I am an agent of D."

    ___13.   Hearsay?

    ___14.   Admissible?

- Issue, whether testator's will is a forgery. X is sole legatee. The party claiming forgery calls W to testify that testator, two days before the date of the alleged will complained to the police that X was threatening to kill him.

    ___15.   Hearsay?

    ___16.   Admissible?

- P v. D. On the issue of P's knowledge that D was in the city, D offers X's testimony that Z said to P, "D is in the city," to which P responded "No way".

    ___17.   Hearsay?

    ___18.   Admissible?

- The testimony above is offered to prove that D was in the city.

    ___19.   Hearsay?

    ___20.   Admissible?

- P v. D. To prove that D was present in the city, D offers W's testimony that P said, "I know that D is in the city."

    ___21.   Hearsay?

    ___22.   Admissible?

- Prosecution of D for killing V. Plea of self-defense. On the issue of D's fear of V, WI testifies that he heard W2 say to D, "V has knifed three people in the last year."

    ___23.   Hearsay?

    ___24.   Admissible?

- Same as above except the evidence is offered to prove V was the aggressor.

    ___25.   Hearsay?

    ___26.   Admissible?

- P sues for damages arising out of an automobile accident. P calls W, who testifies that X, D's employee, was driving D's truck at the time of the collision and that the day after the collision he (W) heard X say to D, "I'm sorry, boss, I just didn't see the light."

___27.   Hearsay?

___28.   Admissible?

- State v. D. To prove that V's assailant was D, testimony by Y that at the police line-up V, separated from the suspect by one-way glass, pointed his index finger at D in response to a question, "Do you see the man who did it?" V is unavailable at trial.

___29.   Hearsay?

___30.   Admissible?

- P v. D. To prove that D accepted P's offer, P offers his (P's) testimony that D said in response to the offer, "All right, P, it's a deal."

___31.   Hearsay?

___32.   Admissible?

- State v. D for killing V. To prove that D had a motive for killing V, the State offers the testimony of Y that he (Y) had told D that he (Y) saw V rape D's sister.

___33.   Hearsay?

___34.   Admissible?

- To prove that P was driving too quickly for conditions, the defendant calls X to testify that several signs had been placed on the road traveled by P immediately prior to the accident stating "Slow, repairs ahead."

___35.   Hearsay?

___36.   Admissible?

- P v. D. W1 testifies for P that D's car was going "over fifty miles an hour." Solely to impeach W1, D offers the testimony of W2 that W1 said a day after the accident that D was going "slow."

___37.   Hearsay?

___38.   Admissible?

- The evidence above is offered by D to prove that he (D) was going slowly.

___39.   Hearsay?

___40.   Admissible?

- Same as above except W2 is a police officer with no present recollection of W1's statement, so D offers W2's accident report, written the day after the accident, containing W1's statement to prove that D was going slowly.

___41.   Hearsay?

___42. Admissible?

- State v. D. To prove that D's house is a house of prostitution, testimony of Y that he (Y) saw many women who (D stipulated) were prostitutes entering and leaving the place.

  ___43. Hearsay?

  ___44. Admissible?

- P v. D Corporation. To prove that D Corporation mailed out certain literature, P offers the testimony of Y that D's president said that D Corporation mailed out the literature.

  ___45. Hearsay?

  ___46. Admissible?

- P v. D. To prove that D paid P for a piano, D calls Y, who testifies that he saw D hand P some cash and heard D at the time say, "OK, this is in full payment for the piano."

  ___47. Hearsay?

  ___48. Admissible?

- P v. D. D wants to prove that on a certain day AOL stock closed at 30. D testifies that on the afternoon of that day he telephoned P and said to him, "P, I've just seen on my computer that AOL closed at 30."

  ___49. Hearsay?

  ___50. Admissible?

- In a civil action between P and D, one of the issues is whether X was present in Chicago on November 20, 2020. X is available at the trial. P calls W who testifies that on November 19 he visited X at X's home in New York and X shows him an airline ticket with X's name typed on it for a trip from New York to Chicago on November 20, 2020.

  ___51. Hearsay?

  ___52. Admissible?

- Same issue as above except that P offers a reimbursement voucher signed by X that X submitted to his company-employer covering expenses of "my trip to Chicago, November 20, 2020."

  ___53. Hearsay?

  ___54. Admissible?

- Same issue as above except that P calls W to testify that W heard X tell Y on November 19, 2020 that "I plan to go to Chicago tomorrow."

  ___55. Hearsay?

  ___56. Admissible?

- Same issue as above except that P calls W to testify that on November 21, 2020, X told W, "Yesterday I was in Chicago."

___57.   Hearsay?

___58.   Admissible?

- P v. D. To prove that P was over forty years old in 2020, D offers a 2018 hospital record of P containing an entry: "Patient gives age as 42."

___59.   Hearsay?

___60.   Admissible?

- P v. D. To prove that the accident was caused by a defective tire, D offers the testimony of Y that he (Y) told P just before the trip that "D's tire is about ready to blow."

___61.   Hearsay?

___62.   Admissible?

- P v. D. To prove that P in riding with D assumed the risk, D offers the testimony of Y that he (Y) told P just before the trip that "D's tire is about ready to blow."

___63.   Hearsay?

___64.   Admissible?

- P v. D. To prove that an accident was caused by a blowout, P offers his own testimony that he and D were riding in the car and that just before the crash, he (P) shouted at D, "My God, one of your back tires has blown out!"

___65.   Hearsay?

___66.   Admissible?

- P v. D's executor. On the issue of D's testamentary capacity, P offers testimony that on the day before the will was executed, D walked around "barking like a dog."

___67.   Hearsay?

___68.   Admissible?

- As tending to show that D had a revolver in his possession, the State offers the testimony of W that, as D passed W's house, W called her husband's attention to a revolver sticking out of D's pocket.

___69.   Hearsay?

___70.   Admissible?

- P v. D. To prove P's damages, P calls Y, who testifies that P, still pinned in the demolished car, said, "My leg hurts something awful!"

___71.   Hearsay?

___72.   Admissible?

- P v. D. To prove that P was conscious soon after the wreck, D calls Y, who testifies that P, still pinned in the demolished car, said, "My leg hurts something awful!"

  ___73. Hearsay?

  ___74. Admissible?

- On the issue of D's guilt of the crime of killing V, W testifies that D fled the scene immediately after V's murder.

  ___75. Hearsay?

  ___76. Admissible?

- On the issue of witness W1's prejudice against defendant (D), W2 testifies for P that W1 said to D in an angry tone, while D remained silent, "Well, at least I've never stolen money from my employer like you have."

  ___77. Hearsay?

  ___78. Admissible?

- On the issue whether D stole money from his employer, plaintiff offers the evidence in 77.

  ___79. Hearsay?

  ___80. Admissible?

- On the issue whether plaintiff (P) had cancer, D calls N (a nurse), who testifies that E, a doctor, gave P X-ray treatments.

  ___81. Hearsay?

  ___82. Admissible?

- As above but N testifies instead that she heard E tell P that P had cancer.

  ___83. Hearsay?

  ___84. Admissible?

- As above but instead of using N's testimony, D offers in evidence the hospital record containing a notation made by E to the effect that he had found a malignant tumor in P.

  ___85. Hearsay?

  ___86. Admissible?

- As above except that the hospital record contains a notation by the receiving physician to the effect that P, on entering the hospital, said that he had "a cancerous tumor."

  ___87. Hearsay?

  ___88. Admissible?

- P's administrator v. D. To prove that D in fact received a deed to Blackacre from P, D offers the testimony of Y that D said during the relevant period, "Blackacre is mine. I've got papers from P to prove it."

  ___89. Hearsay?

  ___90. Admissible?

- P's administrator v. D. To prove that D in fact received a deed to Blackacre from P, D offers the testimony of Q that P once said, "Blackacre now belongs to D. I delivered the deed to him yesterday."

  ___91. Hearsay?

  ___92. Admissible?

- To prove that X had heard of the firm of Credit Bureau, testimony by Y that X once said, "I subscribe to the Credit Bureau monthly."

  ___93. Hearsay?

  ___94. Admissible?

- To prove that Q was bankrupt, testimony by X that "the latest Credit Bureau report indicated that Q was bankrupt."

  ___95. Hearsay?

  ___96. Admissible?

- To prove that D acted in good faith in foreclosing a mortgage on Q's property, a Credit Bureau report received by D shortly before the foreclosure indicated that Q was having financial troubles.

  ___97. Hearsay?

  ___98. Admissible?

- To prove that Q was bankrupt introduction of a copy retained by Q of an annual financial report of Q filed with the Securities and Exchange Commission.

  ___99. Hearsay?

  ___100. Admissible?

6. Authentication and Identification: Fed.R.Evid. 901–903

___1. If a person in the chain of custody has a motive to alter, substitute, or change the condition of a particular item, it is more likely the court will exclude the item of evidence for an improper chain of custody if that person fails to testify.

___2. A fax received in reply to a telephone call cannot constitute reply doctrine authentication.

___3. Familiarity acquired by a lay witness for the purpose of litigation to authenticate handwriting is permissible.

___4. If both the prosecutor and the defense submit transcripts of a recorded conversation, it is the trial judge's responsibility, Rule 104(a), to determine which is accurate.

___5. A break in the chain of custody means that a fungible item cannot be received in evidence.

___6. A sufficient foundation of authentication is established by evidence that an e-mail which purports to be sent by X contains a reference to an e-mail the proponent of the evidence previously sent to X.

___7. An item purporting to be a newspaper is admissible to establish Elm Street was widened in the spring of 2020.

___8. Transcripts of sound recordings constitute the evidence of the conversation.

___9. A certified copy of a public record may be employed to establish that a California driver's license has not been issued to Notowana Sims.

____10.   The voice of a person must have been heard prior to the relevant incident to be identified by an occurrence witness in court.

7.   The Original Writing (Best Evidence) Rule: Fed.R.Evid. 1001–1008

____1.   Whether a particular writing is an original is ultimately for the jury to determine under Rule 104(b).

____2.   The objection "The document speaks for itself," is interposed to prevent counsel on cross-examination from questioning the witness concerning the content of an original writing introduced into evidence.

____3.   A photograph of a truck involved in an accident bearing lettering stating that the truck is owned and operated by Big Jim Thompson is secondary evidence properly admitted under the original writing rule.

____4.   The fact that an original document was created by the cut and paste method may create a circumstance where it would be unfair to admit a duplicate in lieu of the original.

____5.   Rule 1006 governing the use of a chart, summary, or calculation to present the content of voluminous writings, recordings, or photographs that cannot be conveniently examined in court permits the jury to consider evidence that could not otherwise be properly brought to their attention.

____6.   Former testimony must be proven through the original transcript produced by the court reporter or it must be shown to be unavailable.

___7.   According to the Advisory Committee an ordinary print from a negative showing an accident scene testified by an occurrence witness to fairly and accurately depict the accident scene shortly after the accident happened does not bring into play the Original Writing Rule.

___8.   A notice to produce requires the opposing party to produce in court the document designated or face contempt of court.

___9.   A party upon objection can always require that an opponent introduce an original or show that it is unavailable rather than introduce a copy thereof.

___10.   An original is unavailable if located outside of the territorial jurisdiction of the trial court.

8.   Opinions and Expert Testimony: Fed.R.Evid. 701–706

___1.   A police officer with specialized training may opine that X was at fault in the accident.

___2.   A person may not testify as an expert unless he has prior experience working with the particular item, matter, or product involved in the litigation.

___3.   Testimony by an expert that a particular quantity of drugs were possessed for the purpose of distribution violates Rule 704.

___4.   Testimony by an expert that a particular quantity of drugs where possessed by the defendant with an intent to distribute violates Rule 704.

___5.   Everybody may testify that the room smelled of limburger cheese.

___6.   Civil plaintiffs have overall benefited by the replacement of *Frye* with *Daubert/Kumho/*Rule 702 in the federal court.

___7.   Neither a lay nor expert witness may testify that the defendant is correct and should win.

___8.   Regular, customary, and ordinary is the definition of reasonably relied upon as employed in Rule 703.

___9.   A person with no formal education may still qualify as an expert in a particular field.

___10. A doctor may disclose the opinion of a consulting physician not otherwise admitted into evidence relating to the condition of the patient in her testimony to the jury because such an opinion is reasonably relied upon by an expert in the field.

___11. A lay witness may testify that it was bitter cold outside that day.

___12. Expert testimony is precluded as "not helpful" if the jury has a general understanding of the matter under consideration.

___13. A lay witness may not testify that he thinks the man was carrying a gun but is not 100% positive.

___14. General acceptance of an explanative theory still plays a part in the *Daubert/Kumho/*Rule 702 gatekeeping determination.

___15.   A lay witness may testify that a person appeared nervous as she approached the microphone.

___16.   An expert for the defense but not the prosecution may testify as to whether the accused lacked the capacity to have a premeditated intent to commit a homicide.

___17.   A lay witness may testify that Bob assaulted Sam in the bar.

___18.   Gatekeeping under *Daubert/Kumho*/Rule 702 requires the trial court to find the presence of sufficient assurances of correctness of the explanative theory as actually applied to facts, data, or opinions sufficiently established to exist.

___19.   A woman leaving the scene of a robbery may be described by a witness as elegantly dressed in black.

___20.   The *Daubert* decision of the United States Supreme Court makes the employment of the *Frye* standard unconstitutional in state court.

___21.   Under *Daubert/Kumho*/Rule 702 failure to have published a publishable explanative theory espoused by the expert bars its utilization in court.

___22.   An expert may not be paid on a contingent fee basis.

___23.   An expert witness may not testify that X "could be" the cause of Y.

___24.   An expert may testify that a child is telling the truth in his testimony at trial.

___25.   If the court appoints an expert witness, the court must permit the jury to be told when the expert witness testifies at trial that the expert witness was appointed by the court.

9.   Character, Habit and Routine Practice: Fed.R.Evid. 404–406, 412–415

___1.   A limiting instruction should accompany evidence admitted pursuant to Rule 404(b)(2).

___2.   Evidence that a car stolen in another county was used two weeks later in a bank robbery is inextricably intertwined evidence falling outside the scope of Rule 404(b)(1).

___3.   Rule 404(b)(2) lists all of the other purposes for which other crimes, wrongs, or other acts evidence is admissible.

___4.   When character evidence is an essential element in a case, specific instances of conduct become admissible along with reputation and opinion testimony.

___5.   The prosecution in its case in chief can offer opinion testimony that the pertinent character of the victim for honesty was good.

___6.   If the accused offers character evidence in the form of reputation testimony as to the bad character of the victim for the pertinent trait of peacefulness, then the prosecution can offer opinion character testimony that the accused character for peacefulness was bad.

___7.   Character evidence of carelessness is inadmissible in a civil case.

___8.   Mailing of letters will ordinarily qualify as a routine practice of an organization.

___9.   An offer to stipulate by the accused greatly reduces probative value and thus virtually assures that the other crimes, wrongs, or acts evidence will be ruled inadmissible under Rule 403 when offered by the prosecution.

___10.   If the accused offers character evidence in the form of opinion testimony that his character for peacefulness was good, the prosecution may offer character evidence in the form of specific instances of conduct and reputation testimony that the accused character for peacefulness was bad.

___11.   Modus operandi and common design are not synonymous.

___12.   The presence of an eyewitness makes habit testimony of an individual inadmissible.

___13.   For other crimes, wrongs, or acts evidence to be admissible, the proponent must present clear and convincing evidence of the events existence.

___14.   Proof of habit of an individual may be in the form of opinion testimony.

___15.   Character forms an essential element in a litigation alleging negligent hiring and evidence of specific instances of conduct is admissible to prove character when character is an essential element.

___16.   On cross-examination of a character witness whether testifying in the form of reputation or opinion, inquiry is allowable into relevant specific instances of conduct.

___17.   The accused may offer evidence of a pertinent trait of his character through reputation testimony and specific instances of conduct.

___18.   Evidence constituting the charged crime itself is subject to the notice requirement of Rule 404(b)(2).

___19.   Turning back of an odometer, not illegal when done by the defendant, can nevertheless qualify as other crimes, wrongs, or acts evidence.

___20.   At common law, on cross-examination a reputation witness was cross-examined as to specific instances of conduct of the principle witness starting with the words, "Are you aware."

___21.   Evidence in the form of reputation or opinion as to an alleged victim's character with respect to sexual matters is not admissible in a criminal case.

___22.   A criminal defendant is entitled to show that an alleged victim's pregnancy was the result of sexual behavior with another person.

___23.   In a civil case, evidence of sexual predisposition of an alleged victim under Rule 412 is never admissible.

___24.   In a criminal case in which the defendant is accused of child molestation, evidence of other crimes, wrongs, or acts committed by the defendant is admissible to prove the character of the defendant in order to show action in conformity therewith.

___25.   Rule 413(a) states that "(a) In a criminal case in which the defendant is accused of sexual assault, the court may admit evidence that the defendant committed any other sexual assault. The evidence may be considered in any matter to which it is relevant," which means that Rule 403 is inapplicable.

10.   Real and Demonstrative Evidence, Experiments and Views

___1.   Most experiments are conducted in open court before the trier of fact.

___2.   The photographer is not required to authenticate a photograph.

___3.   Courtroom demonstrations employing tangible items such as scale model cars are not permitted.

___4.   A greater degree of accuracy is often required of models and computer animations than other types of demonstrative evidence.

___5.   Real evidence is always direct evidence.

___6.   Experiments purporting to recreate the incident in question will be subjected by the court to a strict substantiality of conditions requirement.

___7.   The Advisory Committee to the Federal Rules of Evidence asserts that a photograph of an intersection testified by a witness in court to fairly and accurately represent the intersection at the relevant time is admitted as illustrative rather than substantive evidence.

___8.   Real evidence provides the trier of fact with the opportunity to draw a relevant first hand sense impression.

___9.   Views by the trier of fact are limited to observations of real property.

___10.   The fact that a photograph of an intersection is taken three months after the accident precludes admissibility.

___11.   The Federal Rules of Evidence provide that a court may not permit the giving of testimony by witnesses at a view.

___12.   A videotape of a nighttime burglary of a jewelry store will be admitted as substantive evidence rather than illustrative evidence.

___13.   A party by offering to stipulate to what is depicted in a photograph can effectively prevent the photograph from being received in evidence.

___14.   Before permitting a jury view, the trial judge should determine whether the use of demonstrative aids such as diagrams, photography, or computer animation is preferable to the jury view.

___15.   Gruesome photographs of victims of crimes are usually excluded on objection under Rule 403 on the grounds of unfair prejudice.

11.   Cross-Examination

A.   Leading Questions; Scope and Expert: Fed.R.Evid. 611(b)(c)

___1.   On cross-examination leading questions are always permitted.

___2.   Counsel cross-examining a witness always wishes to attack the credibility of the witness if possible.

___3.   When a party calls a witness identified with an adverse party, interrogation on direct examination can be by leading questions.

___4.   If a witness is called by a party as a hostile witness, the opposing party may never cross-examine that witness employing leading questions.

___5.   The scope of cross-examination is limited to the subject matter of the litigation and matters affecting credibility.

___6.   The cross-examiner may develop additional relevant evidence on cross-examination within the subject matter on direct examination that does not affect negatively on the credibility of the witness.

___7.   The purpose of ordinarily permitting leading questions on cross-examination but not direct examination is to save time.

___8.   A witness may be examined beyond the scope of subject matter of the direct examination as of right although leading questions may not be employed.

___9.   A criminal defendant by testifying as a witness in this case on any matter under Rule 611 waives his privilege against self-incrimination as to all relevant matters.

___10. Cross-examination is the greatest legal engine ever invented for the discovery of truth.

___11. Objections to the extent of cross-examination permitted by the trial judge are more likely to lead to reversal on appeal in criminal versus civil cases.

___12.   The criminal defendant's equal protection rights are
         implicated in a trial court's decision to preclude further
         cross-examination addressed to the untrustworthy
         partiality of a government witness.

___13.   The convenience of the witness is a significant reason
         why a trial court may permit cross-examination beyond
         the scope of direct examination.

___14.   A criminal defendant by testifying on a motion to
         suppress becomes subject to cross-examination on all
         issues in the case.

___15.   In an ordinary automobile accident case, the scope of
         direct of an occurrence witness is extremely likely to
         encompass all relevant evidence possessed by the
         witness with respect to the litigation as a whole.

**B.   Modes of Impeachment; Collateral and Non-
         Collateral Matters; Good Faith Basis**

___1.   Modes of impeachment seek to attack the weight to be
         given to a witness's testimony by questioning her
         sincerity.

___2.   The use of leading questions is a mode of impeachment.

___3.   Factors that are relevant in determining the
         competency of a witness, factors that also underlie the
         rule against hearsay, also are essential in determining
         the credibility of a witness.

___4.   Demeanor of a witness may properly be considered by
         the trier of fact in assessing credibility.

___5.   Alcohol use at the time of an event is more likely to be permitted to be shown to affect the credibility of the witness than the witness's alcohol addiction.

___6.   Defense counsel has a right to know the current name used and place of residence of all prosecution witnesses.

___7.   A matter which is considered collateral may not be inquired of on cross-examination.

___8.   Questions directed to establishing untrustworthy partiality of a witness on cross-examination raise a non-collateral matter.

___9.   If a witness denies on cross-examination the truth of a question raising a non-collateral matter, then the examiner must always introduce extrinsic evidence to establish the truth of the matter asserted in the question.

___10.   A good faith basis is required of the underlying matter contained in a question for it to be permitted to be asked on cross-examination.

C.   Prior Inconsistent Statements: Fed.R.Evid. 613

___1.   For a prior inconsistent statement to be admitted as substantive evidence under Rule 801(d)(1)(A) counsel must also comply with Rule 613.

___2.   For an admission of a party-opponent to be employed on cross-examination of a party, counsel must also comply with Rule 613.

___3.   For an excited utterance to be employed on cross-examination of a witness, counsel must also comply with Rule 613.

___4.   A written statement must be shown upon request to opposing counsel but not the witness prior to it being employed to impeach.

___5.   A prior inconsistent statement, by establishing that the witness had said something inconsistent at an earlier time, asks the jury to question whether the witness's current testimony is worthy of belief.

___6.   A failure to mention a material matter when making an earlier statement does not constitute an inconsistent statement.

___7.   A prior statement is inconsistent with the witness's trial testimony if a person who believed the truth of the facts testified to would be unlikely to have made the prior statement.

___8.   Prior lack of recollection is not inconsistent with testimony in court that X occurred.

___9.   Under Rule 613(b), it is not required that a witness be cross-examined as to time, place, persons present, and content of the prior statement before extrinsic evidence of a non-collateral inconsistent statement is introduced.

___10.   The traditional common law foundation is most often in practice presented on cross-examination of a witness testifying in the federal court in spite of Rule 613.

___11.   Failure to give a cautionary or limiting instruction when a prior inconsistent statement is admissible solely to impeach is always plain error.

___12. In presenting extrinsic evidence of a non-collateral prior inconsistent statement, leading questions presenting the content of the statement may be employed.

___13. If a witness admits the making of a non-collateral prior inconsistent statement, extrinsic evidence establishing that the prior inconsistent statement was made will rarely be offered.

___14. If a witness does not admit making a collateral prior inconsistent statement, extrinsic evidence is not admissible.

___15. Examining counsel is not required by Rule 613 to permit the witness to offer an explanation on cross-examination when examined as to an alleged prior inconsistent statement.

D. Untrustworthy Partiality; Bias, Interest, Corruption, Coercion

___1. Ordinarily counsel will lay a foundation on cross-examination with respect to matters raising an implied or express charge of untrustworthy partiality.

___2. On cross-examination, counsel may inquire as to statements made by the witness raising the specter of untrustworthy partiality but may not inquire directly of the witness's feelings or beliefs on the matter.

___3. Bias is a collateral matter, i.e., extrinsic evidence evidencing bias is inadmissible.

___4. The criminal defendant is entitled to wide latitude in examining a prosecution witness on the issue of untrustworthy partiality.

___5.   A good faith basis is required for the question, "You were promised that you wouldn't have to serve jail time if you testified against my client in this case, weren't you?" but not for the question, "Were you made any promises by the prosecution with respect to your testimony?"

E.   Conviction of a Crime: Fed.R.Evid. 609

___1.   Prior conviction impeachment is essential to make the jury realize that a criminal defendant may not testify truthfully on the witness stand.

___2.   A misdemeanor conviction for petty larceny may never be employed to impeach a witness' character for truthfulness.

___3.   Shoplifting is a crime of dishonesty or false statement.

___4.   A trial judge is obligated to rule definitively on a motion in limine seeking an order barring the use of a prior conviction to impeach the accused if he testifies.

___5.   Evidence of a prior conviction is admissible under Rule 609 to show character for not being law abiding for the inference that the accused committed the crime for which on trial.

___6.   Prior acts of violence are particularly probative of whether a witness will testify truthfully in court.

___7.   The pendency of an appeal may not be established when a witness other than the criminal defendant is impeached by means of a prior conviction.

___8.   The "mere fact" method of prior conviction impeachment has generally found favor in the federal courts.

___9.   Prior conviction impeachment rests upon the premise that a person who has been shown to be willing to violate a serious law of society possesses a general character to be untruthful from which the jury may infer untruthfulness of the witness in testifying in the matter at hand.

___10.   If a witness denies he was the one convicted, the prosecution must establish the fact of conviction and that the witness was in fact the person convicted through extrinsic evidence.

___11.   Embezzlement is a crime of dishonesty or false statement.

___12.   In practice, where employed, the "mere fact" method tends to favor the prosecution over the criminal defendant.

___13.   Prior convictions, even those involving dishonesty or false statement, over ten years old may not be employed to impeach a witness.

___14.   Impeachment by means of a prior conviction may raise in the mind of the jury the "bad man" inference in spite of the giving of a cautionary and/or limiting instruction.

___15.   Under Rule 609, successful completion of probation without incident will preclude the use of the underlying conviction to impeach.

___16.   Introduction by the criminal defendant on his direct examination of the fact of a prior conviction definitively ruled admissible to impeach by the trial court on a motion in limine does not waive the right to assert the error of the trial judge's motion in limine ruling on appeal.

___17.   A crime of dishonesty or false statement may always be employed to impeach without satisfaction of a discretionary balancing test.

___18.   Failure to give a limiting instruction is more likely to be plain error where the prior conviction is similar to the crime for which the accused is on trial.

___19.   A juvenile adjudication of the criminal defendant in the instant case may never be employed to impeach.

___20.   Prior conviction impeachment is a collateral matter.

___21.   Every pardon issued by President Clinton or any other President makes the conviction inadmissible to impeach.

___22.   A criminal defendant may be impeached by evidence of a conviction that was punishable by death or imprisonment in excess of one year if Rule 403 is satisfied.

___23.   Armed robbery is a crime of dishonesty or false statement.

___24.   The fact that the crime for which an accused was convicted is identical to the crime for which he is on trial makes it more likely that the trial court will permit the prior conviction to be used to impeach.

___25.   The criminal defendant through anticipatory disclosure may testify to having been convicted of a particular offense in a particular court, on a particular date, but may not testify to having pled guilty on that occasion.

F.   **Prior Acts of Misconduct: Fed.R.Evid. 608(b)(1)**

___1.   The giving of testimony by any witness does not waive her privilege against self-incrimination when examined with respect to matters which relate only to credibility.

___2.   Rule 608(b)(1) specifically provides that prior acts of misconduct probative of untruthfulness are admissible on direct examination.

___3.   Only specific instances of conduct that constitute criminal activity are sufficiently probative of untruthfulness to be inquired of on cross-examination.

___4.   Cross-examination as to an arrest for filing false income tax returns is likely to be permitted by the trial court under Rule 608(b)(1).

___5.   Inquiry into a specific instance of conduct probative of untruthfulness is a collateral matter.

G.   **Character for Truthfulness or Untruthfulness: Fed.R.Evid. 608**

___1.   Character evidence in the form of reputation or opinion testimony as to character for truthfulness is admissible to support the credibility of every witness.

___2.   Contradiction of the witness by other evidence constitutes a sufficient direct attack on character for truthfulness to permit character evidence in the form of reputation or opinion evidence to be admitted to rebut.

___3.   A character witness testifying in the form of reputation testimony theoretically should be cross-examined using the form, "Do you know that. . . . ?"

___4.   If the opinion character witness denies on cross-examination being aware of a rumor of a specific instance of conduct probative of untruthfulness, extrinsic evidence establishing both the existence of the rumor and the character witness's awareness thereof is admissible.

___5.   The extent of the relationship between a character witness testifying in the form of opinion and the witness about whose character he is testifying is a proper subject of cross-examination.

___6.   The character of every witness may be attacked by testimony in the form of reputation or opinion testimony as to character for truthfulness.

___7.   A showing of bias constitutes a sufficient direct attack on character for truthfulness to permit character evidence in the form of reputation or opinion evidence to be admitted to rebut.

___8.   A reputation witness testifying as to character for truthfulness may be asked whether he would believe the witness as to whose character he is supporting when such witness is testifying under oath.

___9.   An opinion witness testifying as to character for truthfulness may be asked whether knowledge of a particular fact not involving the incident at hand would result in the witness changing his testimony as to the character of the principal witness.

___10.   An opinion witness as to character for truthfulness may not be cross-examined as to whether he is aware that the principal witness was convicted of tax evasion in Birmingham, Alabama, in 2017.

___11.   If the character of a witness for truthfulness has been attacked in such a manner as to trigger the right to support such a witness's character for truthfulness, specific instances of conduct along with reputation or opinion evidence becomes admissible.

___12.   A reputation witness as to character for truthfulness may not be asked whether he has heard that the principal witness was arrested last week for armed robbery.

___13.   Testimony as to the reputation of a witness as to his character for truthfulness may be based upon never having heard his reputation discussed under circumstances indicating that the witness would have heard of negative comments had they existed.

___14.   A question implying either coercion or corruption constitutes a sufficient direct attack on character for truthfulness to permit character evidence in the form of reputation or opinion evidence to be admitted to rebut.

___15.   Character for truthfulness at the time of the event forming the subject matter of the litigation is the relevant inquiry.

12.   Relevant Evidence and Social Policy: Fed.R.Evid. 407–411

___1.   An alteration made to a product design occurring between the time of sale of the product alleged to be defective and unreasonably dangerous in the lawsuit and the time of injury is barred by Rule 407.

___2.   Evidence of a subsequent remedial measure while not admissible to prove negligence is always admissible to impeach.

___3.   A change in an instruction manual may be a subsequent remedial measure barred by Rule 407.

___4.   If defendant's expert says that the way the company protected against the kind of accident that occurred was by far the best approach to the problem, the expert may be impeached by evidence of a subsequent remedial measure.

___5.   A statement by a driver as he exits his car stating, "It's my fault, I'll take care of your damages." is not barred by Rule 408.

___6.   Completed comprises when offered by third parties on the issue of fault are admissible.

___7.   Statements made during compromise negotiations are admissible on the issue of fault unless accompanied by qualifying phrases such as "without prejudice."

___8.   Statements made in compromise negotiations are not admissible to impeach.

___9.   A statement offering to pay hospital expenses resulting from an injury is inadmissible even if a statement disputing liability or amount of damages does not accompany.

___10.   Statements of fault or fact accompanying an offer to pay medical expenses are admissible.

___11.   A withdrawn plea of guilty may not be employed to impeach the defendant when a party in a subsequent litigation.

___12.   An unexpressed subjective intent to negotiate a plea will suffice to preclude admissibility of any statements made to an attorney for the prosecuting authority.

___13.   An unwithdrawn plea of guilty is not admissible in a later action against the criminal defendant.

___14.   Statements to law enforcement officials during plea negotiations fall within the ban to admissibility of plea bargaining statements erected by Rule 410.

___15.   The fact that an investigator testifying to a witness's statement is employed directly by an insurance company having a policy applicable to the matter at hand is admissible to impeach.

13.   Privileges: Fed.R.Evid. 501

___1.   To the extent State law supplies the rule of decision in civil actions and proceedings privileges are to be determined by State law.

___2.   If a husband and wife consult the same attorney, their statements to the attorney made in the presence of the other spouse are not protected by the lawyer-client privilege with respect to claims by third parties.

___3.   The presence of a law student clerking in an attorney's office at a meeting with the client will waive the lawyer-client privilege.

___4.   The lawyer-client privilege includes communications by the lawyer that directly or indirectly reveal the substance of a client's confidence.

___5.   A statement by the client to its attorney that the attorney should advise XYZ Corporation that the client is prepared to act in a particular way is not protected by the attorney-client privilege.

___6.   A husband can preclude his wife from testifying against him in a criminal case.

___7.   The husband-wife confidential communication privilege survives termination of the marriage by death or divorce.

___8.   An informant's identity is likely to be required to be disclosed to the criminal defendant where the informer arranged a narcotics sale even though he is not present at the sale.

___9.   Voluntary disclosure of privileged information waives the privilege with respect to all communications between the client and lawyer.

___10.   To the extent possible the assertion of a claim of privilege should be made outside the jury's presence.

___11.   The "subject matter test" refers in the law of privilege to scope of the husband-wife testimonial privilege.

___12.   A party does not waive a privilege where the confidential communication is overheard through a secret listening device.

___13.   When a client and his lawyer meet with another lawyer and his client concerning a matter of common interest, any communication made at that meeting falls within the lawyer-client privilege in any dispute that may subsequently arise between the two clients.

___14.   A communication relevant to an issue between parties who claim through the same deceased client does not fall within the lawyer-client privilege.

___15.   Privileges serve an important public purpose and are thus liberally created and construed.

___16.   Federal courts recognize a husband-wife confidential communication privilege.

___17.   Client for purpose of the lawyer-client privilege does not include unincorporated associations.

___18.   In a civil action, the fact that a witness has exercised her privilege against self-incrimination may be commented upon by a party.

___19.   The Federal Rules of Evidence in Rule 501 precluded federal courts from creating additional common law privileges.

___20.   An attorney's statements to an expert retained solely to assist in trial preparation falls within the lawyer-client privilege.

___21.   Federal courts recognize a psychotherapist patient privilege.

___22.   A pre-existing document by virtue of being forwarded to an attorney for the purpose of receiving legal advice acquires a privileged status.

___23.   Federal courts recognize an accountant-client privilege.

___24.   Trade secrets are privileged and thus are not subject to being ordered by the court to be disclosed.

___25.   The presence of a third party in an elevator will bar a statement made by a client to a lawyer from being protected by the lawyer-client privilege.

___26.   The testimonial husband-wife privilege continues to exist so long as there is no divorce even if the marriage is an utter sham.

___27.   A communication to an attorney intended to be publicly disclosed is not confidential.

___28.   A representative of a corporate client that may speak to a lawyer and have his or her communication fall within the lawyer-client privilege is limited to those persons having authority to act upon the advice rendered pursuant thereto.

___29.   Even if a wife has previously disclosed the content of her anticipated testimony to others, she may not over her objection be made to testify against her husband in a criminal case.

___30.   A statement may be protected by the lawyer-client privilege even though the person providing legal advice is not in fact an attorney.

___31.   The Federal Rules of Evidence provide for a psychotherapist-patient privilege.

___32.   Federal courts recognize a parent-child confidential communication privilege.

___33.   The husband-wife testimonial privilege permits a wife to refuse to testify against her husband in civil and criminal cases.

___34.   A parent may accompany a minor child to a meeting with the child's lawyer to discuss the child's lawsuit for personal injuries sustained without waiving the lawyer-client privilege.

___35.   Federal courts recognize a priest-penitent privilege.

14.   Burden of Proof and Presumptions: Fed.R.Evid. 301–302

___1.   The plaintiff bears the burden of pleading and the burden of proof on most matters in part because the plaintiff is the party seeking change.

___2.   A presumption in a criminal case may not shift the burden of persuasion to the criminal defendant.

___3.   Satisfaction of the burden of going forward in the ordinary civil case requires the introduction of clear and convincing evidence.

___4.   The Morgan theory of presumptions shifts the burden of producing evidence but not the burden of persuasion.

___5.   An inference and a presumption are not synonymous.

___6.   With respect to insanity in the federal court the accused bears the burden of persuasion of clear and convincing evidence.

___7.   The introduction of prima facie evidence creates a presumption.

___8.   A conclusive presumption operating against the criminal defendant is unconstitutional.

___9.   A presumption is a conclusion as to the existence of a
          particular fact reached by considering other facts in the
          usual course of human reasoning.

___10.   Burden of proof encompasses the burden of production
          and the burden of persuasion.

___11.   The bursting bubble theory of presumptions is
          mandated by Rule 301 in civil cases unless otherwise
          provided by a federal rule of evidence or Act of Congress.

___12.   The Morgan theory of presumptions helps the party who
          must establish the basic facts more than the Thayer
          bursting bubble theory.

___13.   A presumption is not evidence.

___14.   A criminal presumption is an instructed inference
          highlighting to the jury the propriety of drawing a
          factual inference they might otherwise be naturally less
          likely to draw.

___15.   Under the Thayer "bursting bubble" theory the jury
          should never be instructed in terms of a presumption.

___16.   The burden of persuasion in an ordinary civil suit is best
          described as requiring proof by a preponderance of the
          evidence.

___17.   In a civil case, the effect of a presumption respecting a
          fact which is an element of a claim or defense as to which
          State law supplies the rule of decision is determined in
          accordance with State law.

___18.   The burden of production is satisfied by evidence which
          when viewed most favorable to the burdened party will

permit the trier of fact to reasonably find that the burden of persuasion has been satisfied.

___19.   A presumption in a criminal case permits but does not require the trier of fact to find another fact to be true.

___20.   The Thayer "bursting bubble" theory of presumptions shifts the burden of proof.

___21.   Clear and convincing evidence is a more difficult burden of persuasion to satisfy than beyond a reasonable doubt.

___22.   The Thayer "bursting bubble" theory of presumptions provides that in civil cases when the basic facts are established, the presumed fact must be taken as established unless and until the opponent introduces evidence sufficient to support a finding by a reasonable trier of fact of the nonexistence of the presumed fact.

___23.   A conclusive presumption fails to meet the definition of a presumption as employed in Rule 301.

___24.   The Thayer bursting bubble theory of presumptions is no longer employed in the federal courts.

___25.   A prima facie case requires that a directed verdict be entered unless rebutted.

15.   **Judicial Notice: Fed.R.Evid. 201**

___1.   Adjudicative facts may be judicially noticed if not subject to reasonable dispute.

___2.   The state of Alabama is required to take judicial notice of the judicial decisions of the highest court in Albania.

___3.   A high degree of indisputability is required before a
          court may take judicial notice of a legislative fact.

___4.   If the trial court judicially notices an adjudicative fact
          in a criminal case, the trial court must instruct the jury
          that it may, but is not required to, accept the fact
          judicially noticed as conclusive.

___5.   An opportunity to be heard as to the propriety of a court
          taking judicial notice may be provided after judicial
          notice has been taken.

___6.   The fact that The Miami Herald newspaper has a large
          circulation may be judicially noticed by a trial court in
          Miami, Florida.

___7.   The state of Alabama is required to take judicial notice
          of a statute of the state of Mississippi as well as Acts of
          Congress.

___8.   Judicial notice of both the facts of the case and the law
          governing the case is governed by Rule 201.

___9.   A trial judge in New York City may judicially notice that
          males are easily frightened by loud noises having grown
          up on a farm in Arkansas.

___10.   Judicial notice may not be taken for the first time on
          appeal.

___11.   The number of world championships won by the New
          York Yankees is properly the subject of judicial notice as
          a fact not subject to reasonable dispute in that it is
          capable of accurate and ready determination by resort
          to sources whose accuracy cannot reasonably be
          questioned, Rule 201(b)(2).

___12.   Judicial notice of adjudicative facts is inapplicable when the judge alone is making the factual determination pursuant to Rule 104(a).

___13.   The average annual rainfall for Miami, Florida is properly judicially noticed by a court in Miami, Florida as a fact generally known within the territorial jurisdiction of the trial court, Rule 201(b)(1).

___14.   A trial court may take judicial notice of an adjudicative fact on its own motion.

___15.   An adjudicative fact judicially noticed by the trial court in a civil case is conclusively established.

16.   **Judge and Jury Participation: Fed.R.Evid. 611(a), 614**

___1.   Federal judges very rarely exercise their common law authority to sum up the evidence for the jury.

___2.   It is within the discretion of the trial judge to permit a witness for the defendant to be called as a witness and examined even though plaintiff's case in chief is still in progress.

___3.   If the trial court calls a witness to testify, counsel must object before the witness is examined or waive the objection for purposes of appeal.

___4.   Trial courts frequently call lay witnesses on its own motion.

___5.   The trial court may question a witness to clarify a confused factual issue.

17.   Rulings on Admissibility: Fed.R.Evid. 103–106, 602

___1.   A formal exception to an adverse ruling made to an objection must be recorded to preserve the matter for review on appeal.

___2.   If a general objection is sustained, it will be upheld on appeal if a correct specific objection that could not be obviated could have been interposed.

___3.   Violation of a "structural" constitutional right may never be harmless error.

___4.   A motion in limine refers to any motion made prior to the trial commencing.

___5.   The "rule of completeness" applies also to writings offered solely for the purpose of impeachment.

___6.   "Door opening" only opens the door to evidence that would otherwise be admissible later in the trial in any event.

___7.   The objection lack of foundation applies solely to matters of conditional relevancy, Rule 104(b).

___8.   The objection "lack of foundation" preserves the question of relevancy for appeal.

___9.   The motion in limine is an important tool in planning trial strategy.

___10.   An answer which is non responsive may not be stricken if otherwise admissible.

___11.   A motion in limine may be employed to obtain a ruling that a matter be first raised at trial with the court before being exposed to the jury in any form.

___12.   Transcripts of a deposition of an unavailable witness admitted into evidence will ordinarily accompany the jury during its deliberations.

___13.   A motion to strike will almost invariably be accompanied by a curative instruction.

___14.   Trial counsel objecting to testimony being elicited on cross-examination is likely to object on the ground of lack of foundation if unsure of the appropriate specific objection.

___15.   Conditional relevancy applies the same in criminal and civil cases.

___16.   A substantial right is affected by error that had a material effect upon or substantially swayed the deliberations of the jury.

___17.   A limiting instruction rests upon the almost invariable assumption of the law that jurors follow their instructions.

___18.   A specific ground must always be stated for an objection to preserve error for appeal.

___19.   When a matter is for the court alone to decide, the rules of evidence, except for those concerning privilege, are inapplicable.

___20.   The "rule of completeness" applies to oral statements as well as other parts or any other writing or recorded statement which ought in fairness be considered contemporaneous with the evidence being offered.

____21. The specific objection "hearsay" will not preserve the objection "improper character evidence" for appeal.

____22. On direct examination counsel is required to employ narrative questions first and can employ specific inquiries only to bring out details that were omitted in the narrative response.

____23. Error affecting a substantial right of a party requires reversal on appeal.

____24. The trial court in its discretion may admit evidence upon a representation of counsel that counsel will later in the trial introduce evidence sufficient to support a finding of the fulfillment of a condition to admissibility.

____25. A motion to strike may be accompanied by a request to the court to instruct the jury to disregard the objected to evidence.

____26. A "definitive" ruling by the court on a motion in limine means that the losing party need not renew an objection at trial to preserve the issue for appeal.

____27. The trial court has no discretion as to the form of an offer of proof; all that is required is that it be made known to the court with particularity the substance of what the witness would testify to if permitted to do so.

____28. The determination as to whether a statement is admissible as an excited utterance is a matter of conditional relevancy, Rule 104(b).

___29. What comes through the door once opened rests in the sound discretion of the trial court.

___30. Ordinarily, the attorney making an offer of proof may do so without having the witness whose testimony has been excluded actually testify outside the presence of the jury.

___31. Personal knowledge is a specific application of the concept of conditional relevancy, Rule 104(b).

___32. Plain error analysis applies in criminal cases only.

___33. The trial court under Rule 104(a) alone determines whether a document is authentic.

___34. A limiting instruction is ordinarily considered sufficient to permit evidence admissible against less than all parties to be admitted into evidence.

___35. A party waives the right to employ the remainder of a writing on cross-examination if it fails to invoke the rule of completeness when the writing is first referred to on direct examination of the witness.

___36. A curative instruction is given by the trial judge to the jury as part of his instructions to the jury as to the law governing the case.

___37. A general objection raises only the ground of unfair prejudice.

___38. A learned treatise employed by an expert on direct examination may not accompany the jury during its deliberations.

___39.   A "definitive" ruling on a motion in limine becomes the law of the case and may not be changed by the trial judge.

___40.   Failure to give the jury a limiting instruction with respect to crimes, wrongs, or other acts evidence, Rule 404(b)(2), is plain error.

___41.   Even if a party introduces evidence sufficient to support a finding of the fulfillment of a condition, it is possible that following the introduction of evidence by the opponent the proponent's evidence will be struck by the court.

___42.   "Door opening" may operate together with the "rule of completeness" to permit the introduction of otherwise inadmissible evidence.

___43.   Admission of evidence cannot be assigned as error if a ruling was reserved by the court but never made.

___44.   *Daubert/Kumho*/Rule 702 gatekeeping is for the court alone under Rule 104(a).

___45.   The objection "non responsive" is available to both the party inquiring and the opposing party.

___46.   Violation of the confrontation clause is subject to harmless error analysis.

___47.   Where the substance of the evidence is not apparent from the context, failure to make an offer of proof precludes raising the correctness of the exclusionary ruling on appeal.

___48.   A trial court's ruling that does not affect a substantial right will not result in a reversal on appeal.

___49.   If a party whose objection to the introduction of evidence was overruled by the trial court in advance of trial with a "definitive" ruling introduces the evidence objected to itself at trial to remove the sting, i.e., anticipatory disclosure, that party waives the right to raise on appeal that the trial court's ruling on the motion in limine was in error.

___50.   Harmless error is error that does not affect a substantial right.

18.   Confrontation Clause: *Crawford* to *Clark*

___1.   The confrontation clause precludes admissibility of all hearsay statements made by an unavailable declarant in a criminal case.

___2.   The confrontation clause requires that the trial court determine whether a statement made by an unavailable declarant in a criminal case is either firmly rooted or possesses particularized guarantees of trustworthiness.

___3.   A statement is "testimonial" under the confrontation clause wherever circumstances would lead an objective witness reasonably to believe that the statement would be available for use at a later trial.

___4.   A statement is "testimonial" under the confrontation clause whenever it is made to a police officer, other law enforcement personnel, or a judicial officer.

___5.   A statement is "testimonial" under the confrontation clause whenever circumstances would lead an objective witness reasonably to believe that the statement would be available for use at trial *and* the statement was made to a police officer, law enforcement personnel or a judicial officer.

___6.   "Testimonial" statements are inadmissible in a criminal case if the declarant is not available for cross-examination at trial if no prior opportunity for cross-examination has been provided.

___7.   A statement made casually to a friend is a "nontestimonial" statement the admissibility of which is not affected by the confrontation clause.

___8.   A given statement may be both "testimonial" in part and "nontestimonial" in part.

___9.   A statement is "nontestimonial" if made on a 911 call seeking emergency assistance in connection with an ongoing event.

___10.   A statement made to a police officer, other law enforcement personnel, or judicial officer is "testimonial" if the primary purpose of the investigation is to establish or prove past events potentially relevant to later criminal prosecution.

___11.   Testimony by a supervisor, new to the job, presenting a laboratory report of a forensic test conducted prior to the supervisor's employment satisfies the confrontation clause.

___12.   Testimony by a supervisor who signed the certification after observing the forensic laboratory test detailed in the laboratory report satisfies the confrontation clause.

___13.   Bob, a police officer, is standing in front of a large apartment building in uniform speaking to his friend, John, an accountant in private practice.

Sam, a fourteen year old boy, comes running out of the front entrance to the apartment building. Sam, who does not later testify at trial, sees Bob and John, runs full speed up to them and screams in a loud excited voice:

(1)   "Oh my God!!! My dad is beating the hell out of my mom. They're in apartment 5201. Help, please help!!!"

or

Sam instead screams in a loud excited voice:

(2)   "Oh my God!!! My father just threw my mother over the balcony on the 52nd floor. That son of a bitch is just sitting on the couch crying. Come arrest the bastard!!!"

With respect to each of the following, is the statement of Sam "testimonial":

a)   Sam's statement is illustration (1) to John?

b)   Sam's statement is illustration (1) to Bob?

c)   Sam's statement is illustration (2) to John?

d)   Sam's statement is illustration (2) to Bob?

19.   **Selected Federal Rules of Evidence Amendments: Fed.R.Evid. 404, 408, 606, 609, 801(d)(1)(B), 803(6), 803(7), 803(8), 803(10), 803(16) and 804(b)(3)**

___1.   In a civil case, when the central issue is essentially criminal, evidence of a person's character or a trait of character is admissible pursuant to Rule 404(a) for the purpose of proving action in conformity therewith on a particular occasion.

___2.   In a criminal case, evidence of a pertinent trait of character of the alleged victim of the crime is always admissible pursuant to Rule 404(a)(2) when offered by the accused.

___3.   An offer or acceptance of a compromise of any civil claim is excluded under Rule 408 in a criminal case if offered against the criminal defendant as an admission of fault.

___4.   Conduct or statements made in compromise negotiations regarding the claim are admissible under Rule 408 when offered in a criminal case provided that the negotiations related to a claim by a public office or agency in the exercise of regulatory, investigative, or enforcement authority.

____5.   Statements made in compromise negotiations are admissible when offered to impeach through a prior inconsistent statement or contradiction.

____6.   Under Rule 804(b)(3) corroboration is required only with respect to exculpatory statements against penal interest offered by the defendant.

____7.   Rule 408 does not require the exclusion of any evidence otherwise discoverable merely because it is presented in the course of compromise negotiations.

____8.   A juror pursuant to Rule 606(b) may testify that the jurors were operating under a misunderstanding about the consequences of the result they agreed on or that the jury misapplied a jury instruction.

____9.   Rule 609(a)(2) provides that evidence that a witness has been convicted of a crime is automatically admissible for impeachment, subject to a ten year time limitation, regardless of the punishment if it readily can be determined that establishing the elements of the crime required proof or admission of an act of dishonesty or false statement by the witness.

____10.   Evidence that a witness was convicted of a crime of violence, such as murder, is not automatically admissible for impeachment, even if the witness acted deceitfully in the course of committing the crime.

____11.   A prior consistent statement if related to or supportive of a denial or explanation offered in response to impeachment of the witness by an alleged prior inconsistent statement is admissible solely for corroborative purposes.

___12.   The burden is on the opponent of admission of a statement offered as a business record under Rule 803(6) to show that the source of information or the method or circumstances of preparative indicate lack of trustworthiness.

___13.   With respect to evidence that a matter is not included in a business record offered pursuant to Rule 803(7), the burden is on the proponent to show that the sources of information or other circumstances support the trustworthiness of the evidence.

___14.   In a criminal case, a prosecutor who intends to offer a certification as to the absence of a public record or entry must provide written notice of that intent at least 14 days before trial, and the defendant does not object in writing within 7 days of receiving the notice—unless the court sets a different time for the notice or the objection.

___15.   In both a civil and criminal case a statement in a document prepared in 1988 and whose authenticity is established is admissible as a hearsay exception pursuant to Rule 803(16).

HEARSAY EXAMS

HEARSAY EXAMS
TRUE-FALSE EXAM I

Instructions

For each of the fact patterns that follow, the first question asks whether the evidence is hearsay as defined in Rules 801(a)–(d) of the Federal Rules of Evidence. To signify that the evidence is hearsay answer "T." To signify that the evidence does not fall within the definition of hearsay contained in Rules 801(a)–(d) of the Federal Rules of Evidence answer "F." Thus if a statement, for example, is relevant as a "verbal act," or for its "effect upon listener," the correct answer to whether the statement is "Hearsay" is "F." The correct answer for a statement that meets the requirements of either Rule 801(d)(1), prior statements by witness, or Rule 801(d)(2), admission by party-opponent, is also "F." The second question with respect to each of the one hundred sets of facts asks whether the evidence is admissible pursuant to a hearsay exception contained in either Rule 803, 804 or 807 or as multiple level hearsay pursuant to Rule 805 of the Federal Rules of Evidence. Of course, if the answer to the first question in the set is "F", i.e., not hearsay, then the answer to the second question is always "T", i.e., admissible. With respect to the residual exception, Rule 807, assume that notice has been provided, Rule 807(a)(1), and that the requirement of Rule 807(a)(2) is satisfied, i.e., concentrate solely upon whether the statement "is supported by sufficient guarantees of trustworthiness," Rule 807(a)(1). Assume that all necessary foundations have been offered, that the evidence is relevant, that no privilege is applicable, etc. In short, focus *solely* upon the hearsay issue.

Appendix A contains a comprehensive textual explanation of the Federal Rules of Evidence approach to the definition of hearsay including the defining as not hearsay some but by no means all prior statements by declarants who testify at the trial or hearing, Rule 801(d)(1), and admissions of a party-opponent as set forth in Rule 801(d)(2). Appendix A is extremely useful reading for all students trying to distinguish hearsay from not hearsay out of court statements.

- Prosecution for auto theft. The prosecution, to prove that defendant stole the car rather than rented it, introduces a printout from a car rental company showing that the car was never rented to the defendant.

  ___1.　Hearsay?

  ___2.　Admissible?

- To prove that a race car was in safe condition, a party offers evidence that before the driver got in the car and took off, she walked around the car twice, looking closely at some critical spots.

  ___3.   Hearsay?

  ___4.   Admissible?

- Personal injury action. To refute a claim that the road was rain-slicked, the plaintiff calls a witness from the weather bureau who testifies that the agency has a computer attached to a rain gauge in such a fashion that the date and time of any measurable precipitation is recorded in the computer. The plaintiff then introduces a computer printout that shows no rain on the day of the accident.

  ___5.   Hearsay?

  ___6.   Admissible?

- On the issue whether P has adversely possessed Beigeacre, W offers to testify that for the past twenty years P has said, "I own Beigeacre."

  ___7.   Hearsay?

  ___8.   Admissible?

- A confession of a co-conspirator naming the defendant as the head of a drug smuggling ring is introduced to prove defendant's guilt.

  ___9.   Hearsay?

  ___10.   Admissible?

- To prove that D, now deceased, was competent to execute his will the legatees under the will offer the testimony of J that two days after the will was executed he heard D deliver a lecture on the application of calculus to the prediction of stock market performance.

  ___11.   Hearsay?

  ___12.   Admissible?

- Same as above only the legatees offer the testimony of G, D's bridge partner, that shortly after the will was executed D told him that "I [D] have never been more healthy and alert in my life."

  ___13.   Hearsay?

  ___14.   Admissible?

- Same as above only the legatees offer the testimony of H, the appointments secretary to the governor, that shortly after the will was executed the governor scheduled and attended a meeting with D to consult with him on several sensitive political issues.

  ___15.   Hearsay?

  ___16.   Admissible?

- To impeach a police officer who testified that the defendant confessed to the crime, the defense offers the police officer's prior statement that it was another person who had confessed.

    ___17. Hearsay?

    ___18. Admissible?

- Murder prosecution. To prove guilt, the prosecution introduces a tape recording of defendants confession to the crime.

    ___19. Hearsay?

    ___20. Admissible?

- Personal injury action. To prove damages, a witness testifies that at the scene the plaintiff screamed, "Aaaaaaaagh!"

    ___21. Hearsay?

    ___22. Admissible?

- Robbery prosecution. Before the grand jury, a police officer testifies that they were chasing the masked robber but lost sight of him. Ten minutes later, a bystander pointed to a nearby garage. They entered and found the defendant sitting in a car and the mask in a garbage can.

    ___23. Hearsay?

    ___24. Admissible?

- To prove defendant is honest he introduces the fact his employer promoted him from inventory clerk to cashier.

    ___25. Hearsay?

    ___26. Admissible?

- Commitment proceeding. To show that Sam was crazy, the plaintiff offers his statement, "I am John Wayne."

    ___27. Hearsay?

    ___28. Admissible?

- Prosecution for embezzlement. To show motive, the prosecution calls a neighbor who testifies that she heard the defendant's wife shouting during an argument, "When are you going to stop playing the ponies? You'll never win."

    ___29. Hearsay?

    ___30. Admissible?

- Will contest. To prove the will is a forgery, plaintiff introduces the out-of-court statement of the defendant's girlfriend to the defendant, "Well, at least I never forged a will." The defendant replied, "What the hell are you talking about?"

    ___31. Hearsay?

___32.   Admissible?

- To prove that X was an honest person, that his employer bonded all of his employees except X.

___33.   Hearsay?

___34.   Admissible?

- Will contest. To prove that the testator was incompetent, the contestants offer the statement of his wife: "Bob Harris thinks he's the Pope."

___35.   Hearsay?

___36.   Admissible?

- Action on an insurance contract. To prove the insured did not die immediately after impact, his statement, "I'm alive," is offered.

___37.   Hearsay?

___38.   Admissible?

- Action for personal injuries. Plaintiff testifies that when a witness at the scene of the accident stated, "Joe ran the red light," Joe (the defendant) said nothing.

___39.   Hearsay?

___40.   Admissible?

- Action for personal injuries. The witness testifies that defendant ran the red light. Defendant offers evidence that the same witness said at the scene to a police officer investigating the accident, "Sam (the plaintiff) ran the red light," to prove plaintiff was negligent.

___41.   Hearsay?

___42.   Admissible?

- To prove that X loved Y, that X transferred substantial amounts of money to Y.

___43.   Hearsay?

___44.   Admissible?

- Evidence that the witness who at trial says he doesn't recall seeing the accident at a deposition stated that "the truck ran the red light," to prove plaintiff was negligent.

___45.   Hearsay?

___46.   Admissible?

- To prove an intention to sell a ring rather than to give a ring to Sarah, his wife, Clifford's earlier signing of a criminal complaint against Sarah for adultery.

___47.   Hearsay?

___48.   Admissible?

- Murder prosecution. To prove the defendant's guilt, the prosecution introduces evidence that when the police entered the victim's apartment where the body was found, the victim's parrot was screeching, "Don't shoot."

___49. Hearsay?

___50. Admissible?

HEARSAY EXAMS
TRUE-FALSE EXAM II

Instructions

For each of the fact patterns that follow, the first question asks whether the evidence is hearsay as defined in Rules 801(a)–(d) of the Federal Rules of Evidence. To signify that the evidence is hearsay answer "T." To signify that the evidence does not fall within the definition of hearsay contained in Rules 801(a)–(d) of the Federal Rules of Evidence answer "F." Thus if a statement, for example, is relevant as a "verbal act," or for its "effect upon listener," the correct answer to whether the statement is "Hearsay" is "F." The correct answer for a statement that meets the requirements of either Rule 801(d)(1), prior statements by witness, or Rule 801(d)(2), admission by party-opponent, is also "F." The second question with respect to each of the one hundred sets of facts asks whether the evidence is admissible pursuant to a hearsay exception contained in either Rule 803, 804 or 807 or as multiple level hearsay pursuant to Rule 805 of the Federal Rules of Evidence. Of course, if the answer to the first question in the set is "F", i.e., not hearsay, then the answer to the second question is always "T", i.e., admissible. With respect to the residual exception, Rule 807, assume that notice has been provided, Rule 807(b), and that the requirement of Rule 807(a)(2) is satisfied, i.e., concentrate solely upon whether the statement "is supported by sufficient guarantees of trustworthiness," Rule 807(a)(1). Assume that all necessary foundations have been offered, that the evidence is relevant, that no privilege is applicable, etc. In short, focus *solely* upon the hearsay issue.

Appendix A contains a comprehensive textual explanation of the Federal Rules of Evidence approach to the definition of hearsay including the defining as not hearsay some but by no means all prior statements by declarants who testify at the trial or hearing, Rule 801(d)(1), and admissions of a party-opponent as set forth in Rule 801(d)(2). Appendix A is extremely useful reading for all students trying to distinguish hearsay from not hearsay out of court statements.

- As evidence of D's guilt in killing V with a baseball bat, that the victim, V, said sometime before the assault, "D is going to kill me soon."

    ___1. Hearsay?

    ___2. Admissible?

- Slip-and-fall case. To prove knowledge, the plaintiff testifies that right after he fell he heard a witness say in a calm voice, "That's the slippery spot I warned the owners about."

  ___3.   Hearsay?

  ___4.   Admissible?

- To prove that defendant in a first-degree murder case acted with premeditation, the State will offer the testimony of X. X will say that shortly before defendant shot the victim, X asked defendant if he was "out to get" the victim, and the defendant took a pistol from his pocket, showed it to X, and "snarled."

  ___5.   Hearsay?

  ___6.   Admissible?

- Will contest. To show the testator's feelings toward the defendant, the sole legatee, plaintiff offers to testify that the testator had defendant arrested for forgery.

  ___7.   Hearsay?

  ___8.   Admissible?

- As P was walking on D's lawn, P said to a neighbor, "D has a vicious dog." On the issue of P's assumption of the risk, the neighbor will testify to this statement when called by the defendant.

  ___9.   Hearsay?

  ___10.   Admissible?

- On the issue of whether D loved or hated Y, the statement by Y, "D hates me."

  ___11.   Hearsay?

  ___12.   Admissible?

- To prove that defendant was the driver, of the two possible drivers, who ran through a red light (colliding with the other car in the intersection), that his insurance company settled with the other driver. Assume insurance law requires your own carrier to pay when you were the one at fault.

  ___13.   Hearsay?

  ___14.   Admissible?

- To prove that X did not repay a loan to mobster, M, of over $90,000, that M put out a contract ($5,000 fee) on X's life. A fink will testify that if M says he will pay $5,000 for a contract, this always means the loan was over $90,000.

  ___15.   Hearsay?

  ___16.   Admissible?

- To prove that the victim was under a sense of immediate impending death as relevant in assessing weight to be given to a dying declaration, evidence that the victim said, "Call a priest."

    ___17.   Hearsay?

    ___18.   Admissible?

- To prove damage in a personal injury case, the plaintiff calls hospital attendants who testify that the plaintiff was screaming, "My God! My leg hurts!"

    ___19.   Hearsay?

    ___20.   Admissible?

- To prove bad health when an insured signed an insurance application form, evidence that the insured's doctor had her under three different high blood pressure pills at the time.

    ___21.   Hearsay?

    ___22.   Admissible?

- Sale of cocaine; defense of entrapment. The defendant testifies that the police informant told him that he needed the drug for the treatment of psoriasis.

    ___23.   Hearsay?

    ___24.   Admissible?

- Sale of cocaine; defense of entrapment. The prosecution calls a narcotics officer in charge of the investigation to testify that numerous addicts told him that the defendant was dealing in cocaine.

    ___25.   Hearsay?

    ___26.   Admissible?

- To prove that D had motive to kill Z, that W told D that Z had forced his daughter into prostitution.

    ___27.   Hearsay?

    ___28.   Admissible?

- To prove negligence in driving a bus out of the bus company's station, that a bus mechanic said to the driver, "The front axle is so weak, it could break at any time." Assume it did break later that morning and that three people died in the accident.

    ___29.   Hearsay?

    ___30.   Admissible?

- To identify the defendant as the person who assaulted an F.B.I. agent, a witness in a neighboring office testifies that he heard the victim shout, "No . . . Mike . . . don't shoot."

  ___31.   Hearsay?

  ___32.   Admissible?

- Action for libel. To prove damages, the plaintiff testifies that one of his colleagues said: "What's this I hear that John (the defendant) is saying you stole all of your footnotes from his article?"

  ___33.   Hearsay?

  ___34.   Admissible?

- To prove that the Veterans Administration Hospital in Miami did not discriminate against women employees, that an internal auditor of the V.A., as authorized by statute, investigated the Hospital and came to the conclusion that no sexual discrimination existed at the Hospital. Assume that the Government desires to enter this in a class suit by the Hospital's female employees, which charges illegal sex bias against the V.A.

  ___35.   Hearsay?

  ___36.   Admissible?

- On the issue whether the plaintiff has poison ivy, evidence that the plaintiff scratches.

  ___37.   Hearsay?

  ___38.   Admissible?

- Personal injury action. The plaintiff offers in evidence a police report stating that the defendant said that the accident was his fault.

  ___39.   Hearsay?

  ___40.   Admissible?

- Suit to quiet title on a claim of adverse possession. The plaintiff offers in evidence his signs that were posted on the premises reading: "No trespassing. John Smith, Owner."

  ___41.   Hearsay?

  ___42.   Admissible?

- On the issue whether there was marijuana in the suitcase, evidence that a dog, trained to wag its tail at marijuana, wagged its tail when sniffing the suitcase.

  ___43.   Hearsay?

  ___44.   Admissible?

- On the issue of D's good faith in discharging X, an employee testifies that the Chief of Police told D that X had been caught stealing in his store.

  ___45. Hearsay?

  ___46. Admissible?

- Same facts as above, but testimony used in X's criminal trial to prove that he stole from the store.

  ___47. Hearsay?

  ___48. Admissible?

- On the issue whether D is the White Rock flasher, a photo taken by a bank surveillance camera of D flashing a bank teller.

  ___49. Hearsay?

  ___50. Admissible?

HEARSAY EXAMS
TRUE-FALSE EXAM III

Instructions

For each of the fact patterns that follow, the first question asks whether the evidence is hearsay as defined in Rules 801(a)–(d) of the Federal Rules of Evidence. To signify that the evidence is hearsay answer "T." To signify that the evidence does not fall within the definition of hearsay contained in Rules 801(a)–(d) of the Federal Rules of Evidence answer "F." Thus if a statement, for example, is relevant as a "verbal act," or for its "effect upon listener," the correct answer to whether the statement is "Hearsay" is "F." The correct answer for a statement that meets the requirements of either Rule 801(d)(1), prior statements by witness, or Rule 801(d)(2), admission by party-opponent, is also "F." The second question with respect to each of the one hundred sets of facts asks whether the evidence is admissible pursuant to a hearsay exception contained in either Rule 803, 804 or 807 or as multiple level hearsay pursuant to Rule 805 of the Federal Rules of Evidence. Of course, if the answer to the first question in the set is "F", i.e., not hearsay, then the answer to the second question is always "T", i.e., admissible. With respect to the residual exception, Rule 807, assume that notice has been provided. Rule 807(b), and that the requirement of Rule 807(a)(2) is satisfied, i.e., concentrate solely upon whether the statement "is supported by sufficient guarantees of trustworthiness", Rule 807(a)(1). Assume that all necessary foundations have been offered, that the evidence is relevant, that no privilege is applicable, etc. In short, focus *solely* upon the hearsay issue.

Appendix A contains a comprehensive textual explanation of the Federal Rules of Evidence approach to the definition of hearsay including the defining as not hearsay some but by no means all prior statements by declarants who testify at the trial or hearing, Rule 801(d)(1), and admissions of a party-opponent as set forth in Rule 801(d)(2). Appendix A is extremely useful reading for all students trying to distinguish hearsay from not hearsay out of court statements.

- Will contest. To prove that the testator did not like P, D calls W, who testifies that a week before he died the testator told W, "I hate P."

    ___1.   Hearsay?

    ___2.   Admissible?

- To prove humiliation, that plaintiff heard people discussing the libelous statement about her.

    ___3.   Hearsay?

    ___4.   Admissible?

- On the issue whether P thought the sky was falling, P offers to testify that he listened to a radio broadcast, purporting to be an on-the-scene news report, in which Orson Wells said, "The sky is falling."

  ___5.   Hearsay?

  ___6.   Admissible?

- On the issue of the speed of D's car, the police officer will testify that his speedometer read 75 m.p.h.

  ___7.   Hearsay?

  ___8.   Admissible?

- In a civil case involving a U.S. government charge that the captain of a U.S. flagship was careless in his approach to another ship in the Panama Canal, the U.S. notices the captain that a deposition will be taken (under oath and before a U.S. consul) in Tokyo, of a seaman on the vessel. This was done, and the captain's attorney, though present, did not cross the seaman. The seaman stated that "the captain was blind drunk" at the time. At the civil trial, the seaman testified for the captain that "he was sober at the time." The seaman died of a heart attack before he could be crossed. The U.S. offers the seaman's deposition statement, taken in Tokyo.

  ___9.   Hearsay?

  ___10.   Admissible?

- To prove that a certain event occurred in the early morning, W testifies that he was in bed at the time of the event and heard his roosters crowing.

  ___11.   Hearsay?

  ___12.   Admissible?

- To prove that D committed the crime charged, P offers D's confession made to police officers.

  ___13.   Hearsay?

  ___14.   Admissible?

- To prove the decedent believed his death was imminent, testimony that just prior to his death his doctor told him, "You have only a few minutes left."

  ___15.   Hearsay?

  ___16.   Admissible?

- To prove the decedent believed his death was imminent, his statement "I'm going fast."

  ___17.   Hearsay?

  ___18.   Admissible?

- To prove the value of a stolen automobile, P offers a receipt for the purchase price, $10,000, signed by the dealer from whom he bought the car.

  ___19. Hearsay?

  ___20. Admissible?

- Action to commit a certain law professor to a mental institution. To prove that he is not in fact insane, the professor offers a letter he received by a publishing company offering him a lucrative contract to write the definitive text on the hearsay rule.

  ___21. Hearsay?

  ___22. Admissible?

- To show P's entitlement to damages for pain and suffering, P calls a nurse who testifies that right after the accident P was admitted to the hospital while holding his head and repeating over and over, "my head."

  ___23. Hearsay?

  ___24. Admissible?

- Action for personal injuries by a passenger in a car against the driver. To prove defective brakes, plaintiff offers testimony that, one hour before the accident, a mechanic told the defendant and the plaintiff, "The brakes are shot."

  ___25. Hearsay?

  ___26. Admissible?

- Same case and same evidence, this time offered to prove assumption of the risk.

  ___27. Hearsay?

  ___28. Admissible?

- Personal injury action by P against D arising out of the breakdown of D's roller coaster. To prove that the roller coaster was in bad condition, P testifies that just before he got on the ride, he heard a patron exiting the roller coaster say to D's employee, "The tracks are shaking something awful today!"

  ___29. Hearsay?

  ___30. Admissible?

- Action for breach of warranty. To prove the warranty, the plaintiff testifies that he asked the defendant's salesperson, "If I buy this deodorant, will it help me win the love of my life?" The salesperson nodded affirmatively.

  ___31. Hearsay?

  ___32. Admissible?

- Negligence action by P, an injured pedestrian against D City for not placing a traffic signal at the intersection at which P was struck by a car. Following the accident D City conducted an investigation and determined that there was no need for a traffic signal at that corner. D City offers its investigators report in evidence.

___33. Hearsay?

___34. Admissible?

- Breach of contract action. To prove that a contract existed, P testifies that just after a meeting with D, she (P) told her secretary, "I just made a deal to sell D three hundred cases of Madonna albums!"

___35. Hearsay?

___36. Admissible?

- On the issue whether or not X predeceased Y, W offers to testify that shortly after Y was pronounced dead X said, "I think Y is dead."

___37. Hearsay?

___38. Admissible?

- On the same issue, Z offers to testify that at the relevant time the paramedics put a sheet over X's head and, leaving X at the scene of the accident, rushed Y to the hospital.

___39. Hearsay?

___40. Admissible?

- Prosecution of D for battery upon V. To prove that D acted in self-defense, W testifies that V had a reputation in the community as a violent person.

___41. Hearsay?

___42. Admissible?

- On the issue of whether the testator intended to give C property in his will (case involving probate of a lost will), the testator's statement, made after the execution of the will, that "I left C one-half of my estate in my will."

___43. Hearsay?

___44. Admissible?

- Same issue as above, but the statement is made just before the will is signed, and the statement is, "C has treated me shamefully."

___45. Hearsay?

___46. Admissible?

- To prove that a certain kind of computer was useful in a law practice, a party offers evidence that the partner in charge of purchases for the practice bought twenty of the machines.

    ___47.   Hearsay?

    ___48.   Admissible?

- To prove that D committed an assault, P (suing for civil damages) offers into evidence a certified copy of a prior judgment of a felony criminal conviction arising out of the same incident.

    ___49.   Hearsay?

    ___50.   Admissible?

HEARSAY EXAMS
TRUE-FALSE EXAM IV

Instructions

For each of the fact patterns that follow, the first question asks whether the evidence is hearsay as defined in Rules 801(a)–(d) of the Federal Rules of Evidence. To signify that the evidence is hearsay answer "T." To signify that the evidence does not fall within the definition of hearsay contained in Rules 801(a)–(d) of the Federal Rules of Evidence answer "F." Thus if a statement, for example, is relevant as a "verbal act," or for its "effect upon listener," the correct answer to whether the statement is "Hearsay" is "F." The correct answer for a statement that meets the requirements of either Rule 801(d)(1), prior statements by witness, or Rule 801(d)(2), admission by party-opponent, is also "F." The second question with respect to each of the one hundred sets of facts asks whether the evidence is admissible pursuant to a hearsay exception contained in either Rule 803, 804 or 807 or as multiple level hearsay pursuant to Rule 805 of the Federal Rules of Evidence. Of course, if the answer to the first question in the set is "F", i.e., not hearsay, then the answer to the second question is always "T", i.e., admissible. With respect to the residual exception, Rule 807, assume that notice has been provided, Rule 807(b), and that the requirement of Rule 807(a)(2) is satisfied, i.e., concentrate solely upon whether the statement "is supported by sufficient guarantees of trustworthiness," Rule 807(a)(1). Assume that all necessary foundations have been offered, that the evidence is relevant, that no privilege is applicable, etc. In short, focus *solely* upon the hearsay issue.

Appendix A contains a comprehensive textual explanation of the Federal Rules of Evidence approach to the definition of hearsay including the defining as not hearsay some but by no means all prior statements by declarants who testify at the trial or hearing, Rule 801(d)(1), and admissions of a party-opponent as set forth in Rule 801(d)(2). Appendix A is extremely useful reading for all students trying to distinguish hearsay from not hearsay out of court statements.

- Personal injury action. Plaintiff calls W, who testifies that plaintiff had the green light. To impeach W's credibility, defendant offers a portion of the transcript of W's deposition in which W stated that defendant had the green light.

    ___1.   Hearsay?

    ___2.   Admissible?

- To prove that a testator was competent to make a will, a party offers evidence that a week before the testator died, her psychiatrist wrote her a letter in which he stated, "You've made marvelous progress on your emotional problems. You won't be needing my services anymore."

  ___3.   Hearsay?

  ___4.   Admissible?

- Medical malpractice action. To prove that he required additional surgery to correct defendant's surgical errors, plaintiff offers evidence that the day after defendant operated, another surgeon operated on him again.

  ___5.   Hearsay?

  ___6.   Admissible?

- Civil action by P against D Police Department for police brutality following an officer's shooting of X in an alley. Plaintiff claims that X was just standing around when the officer suddenly entered the alley, called out X's name, and when X turned around, shot X. To prove that the officer acted in good faith, the officer testifies that before he entered the alley, another person told him that X had a gun.

  ___7.   Hearsay?

  ___8.   Admissible?

- Personal injury action by P against D arising out of a slip-and-fall in D's pet shop. To prove that he notified P of the hazard on the floor, D testifies that as P entered the store, D said to him, "Watch the slippery floor. We've got a bunch of guinea pigs with intestinal problems."

  ___9.   Hearsay?

  ___10. Admissible?

- Breach of contract action by P against D. To prove that she offered to sell D 200 crates of kiwi fruit, P testifies that she said to D, "I offer to sell you 200 crates of kiwi fruit for $2.50 a case."

  ___11. Hearsay?

  ___12. Admissible?

- To prove that she was in great pain after the accident for which she is now suing D, P calls her mother to testify that on the way to the hospital in the mother's car, P screamed, "Owwwwww!"

  ___13. Hearsay?

  ___14. Admissible?

- Defamation action by P against D. To prove that P suffered no damage to his reputation from the story in D's newspaper asserting that P was a "womanizer," D calls W who testifies that before the story was printed, P had a reputation in the community as a womanizer.

  ___15. Hearsay?

  ___16. Admissible?

- To prove that the traffic light at an intersection was red for cars going in a certain direction, a party offers evidence that all drivers going in that direction stopped their cars when they reached the intersection.

  ___17. Hearsay?

  ___18. Admissible?

- To prove which of two persons—husband or wife—survived an accident, testimony that right after the crash, the husband sobbed, "That bastard in the red car ran the red light."

  ___19. Hearsay?

  ___20. Admissible?

- The same statement as above to prove that the driver in the red car did run the red light.

  ___21. Hearsay?

  ___22. Admissible?

- Personal injury action. Plaintiff claims that he was treated by Dr. X. D calls Dr. X who testifies that his records contain no mention of plaintiff.

  ___23. Hearsay?

  ___24. Admissible?

- Prosecution of D for battery upon V. To prove that V struck the first blow, D testifies that the day before the fight, X told D that V had killed six people in the past year.

  ___25. Hearsay?

  ___26. Admissible?

- To show that X was ill on a certain date, W offers to testify that on that date X twice doubled over and groaned.

  ___27. Hearsay?

  ___28. Admissible?

- Action by P to commit a certain law professor to a mental institution. To prove that the law professor was insane, P calls W who testifies that while the professor was in the middle of an evidence class, two white-coated gentlemen entered the classroom, gently laid their hands on the professor, and led him away.

  ___29.   Hearsay?

  ___30.   Admissible?

- Defamation action by P against D. To prove that D uttered the defamatory remarks, P calls W who testifies that she was at a PTA meeting when D stood up and called P a "gigolo."

  ___31.   Hearsay?

  ___32.   Admissible?

- Negligence action by the owner of a ship against the operators of a lighthouse after the ship was destroyed on the rocks in a dense fog. Plaintiff claims that as the ship approached the rocks, defendant neither flashed the light nor sounded the foghorn. To prove that she was not negligent, defendant testifies that as the ship approached, she blew the foghorn.

  ___33.   Hearsay?

  ___34.   Admissible?

- To show that D was home and thus could have killed W, his wife, P calls W's paramour who testifies that when D was away and the coast was clear, W always pulled the bedroom shade down, but that she left it up when he was home. Then P calls Z, D & W's next door neighbor, who testifies that on the murder night the shade was open. With respect to the paramour's testimony—

  ___35.   Hearsay?

  ___36.   Admissible?

- Same as above. With respect to Z's testimony—

  ___37.   Hearsay?

  ___38.   Admissible?

- Will contest. To prove that the testator did not like P, D calls W, who testifies that a week before he died the testator told W, "P is a no-good slob."

  ___39.   Hearsay?

  ___40.   Admissible?

- Action by P against D to recover unpaid rent based on a month-to-month tenancy. D claims that she told P a month in advance that she was terminating the tenancy. To prove that D did not give notice, P testifies that though he saw D twice around the time D claims to have given notice, D never mentioned anything about terminating the tenancy.

  ___41. Hearsay?

  ___42. Admissible?

- To prove that X and Y were really married, X calls a witness who testifies that he was in a courtroom on the day X and Y claim to be married, and that he heard the judge say to X and Y, "I now pronounce you husband and wife."

  ___43. Hearsay?

  ___44. Admissible?

- Civil action by P against Police Officer D for false arrest at a baseball game. D's defense is good faith. To prove that he acted in good faith in arresting P, Officer D testifies that one of P's friends told him that P was carrying a concealed bomb under his coat.

  ___45. Hearsay?

  ___46. Admissible?

- To prove the value of a stolen automobile, P offers to testify that he accepted the dealer's offer to sell the car and that he paid $10,000 for it.

  ___47. Hearsay?

  ___48. Admissible?

- Negligence action by the owner of a small plane attempting to land against the owner of another plane that was sitting on the runway. The two planes collided, causing extensive damage and personal injuries. To prove that defendant knew another was going to attempt to land, plaintiff calls W, the air traffic controller on duty at the time of the crash. W testifies that about a minute before the crash, he told the owner of the plane sitting on the ground that another plane had been cleared to land.

  ___49. Hearsay?

  ___50. Admissible?

HEARSAY EXAMS
MULTIPLE CHOICE EXAM I

1. Negligence action by P against D following a slip-and-fall. The incident occurred in a shopping mall near the doorway of D's store. P claims that the floor was extremely wet and that this condition caused the fall. D claims that the mall owners were legally responsible for keeping the area outside the store free of water. P calls the store manager to testify that ten minutes before the accident, he observed a clerk mopping up some spilled water. This evidence is:

    (a) admissible hearsay since the manager is authorized to speak for the corporation on these matters.

    (b) inadmissible hearsay.

    (c) admissible to impeach the credibility of D.

    (d) admissible non hearsay to prove that D controlled the area outside the store entrance.

2. Prosecution of Miss Hood for poisoning her grandmother. Immediately before the elderly lady expired, her doctor told her that she had gingerbread poisoning and would not live out the night. He asked where she got the gingerbread, and she said, "Miss Hood gave it to me." The doctor is called by the prosecution to testify to the above for the purpose of proving Miss Hood supplied the poisoned gingerbread.

    (a) This statement comes within the present sense impression exception.

    (b) This statement comes within the then existing state of mind exception.

    (c) The statement cannot come within the excited utterance exception because grandmother is unavailable.

    (d) This is admissible hearsay for none of the reasons stated above.

3. Winter sued Hyland for $100,000 for injuries received in a traffic accident. Hyland charges Winter with contributory negligence and alleges that Winter failed to have his lights on at a time when it was dark enough to require them. Hyland calls Bystander to testify that Passenger, who was riding in Winter's automobile and who also was injured, confided to him at the scene of the accident that "we should have had our lights on." Bystander's testimony is:

    (a)   admissible as an admission of a party opponent.

    (b)   admissible as a declaration against interest.

    (c)   inadmissible because it is hearsay not within any exception.

    (d)   inadmissible because it is opinion.

4. Same facts as above. Hyland offers to have Bystander testify that he was talking to Witness when he heard the crash and heard Witness, now deceased, exclaim, "That car doesn't have any lights on." Bystander's testimony is:

    (a)   admissible as a statement of present sense impression.

    (b)   inadmissible because Witness is not available to testify.

    (c)   inadmissible as hearsay not within any exception.

    (d)   inadmissible because of the Dead Man's Statute.

5. In a criminal case the defendant pleads insanity. He calls the nurse of a psychiatrist he had consulted for treatment ten years prior to the alleged crime. The nurse is the custodian of the records for the psychiatrist and will testify that she was present when the defendant was examined and, immediately after the examination, the psychiatrist dictated a summary of the examination to her including the following passage concerning the defendant: "The patient suffers from acute, chronic, dual ding-bat paraphernalia syndrome—conversion type." Moreover, she will testify that these records were created and kept as part of the standard routine of running the psychiatrists' office. Which is the court's best response to the offer of the report?

    (a)   The nurse could testify to the contents of this record as past recollection recorded.

    (b)   The court should accept this record as a business record.

    (c)   The court should accept the report as double hearsay fitting within (1) either the past recollection recorded exception or the business records exception and (2) the present sense impression.

       (d)   The report should be rejected, but the nurse should be permitted to testify from her own memory (assuming that she has one) to what the doctor said.

6.   At Lyon's trial for criminal tax fraud the prosecution seeks to establish criminal intent by introducing (through the appropriate custodian of IRS records) a portion of a report of an investigation conducted by Ludtke, an IRS special enforcement agent. The portion of the report that the prosecution is seeking to introduce is a statement ("I understated my loansharking income because I wanted to screw the government out of some money") that Lyons made during the course of an interview he had with Ludtke while he was conducting his investigation. The portion of the report containing Lyons' statement:

       (a)   is hearsay and is not admissible under any exception to the hearsay rule.

       (b)   comes within the definition of hearsay at common law but is an admission by a party opponent defined as not hearsay by Rule 801(d)(2).

       (c)   is hearsay but is admissible double hearsay as a public record exception, Rule 803(8), and an admission by a party opponent defined as not hearsay by Rule 801(d)(2).

       (d)   is double hearsay but is admissible as a public record and a statement of then existing state of mind.

7.   Prosecution of D for robbery of an ice cream parlor. The robbery occurred at 10:30 p.m. on a certain date. D's defense is that she was home in bed at the time the crime was committed. D takes the stand to testify that at 9:00 on the evening of the robbery, she said to her husband, "Honey, I'm feeling really tired, so I think I'll go to sleep now." This evidence is:

       (a)   hearsay but admissible to prove that D was in fact tired and planned to go to bed, which tends to show that she indeed went to sleep.

       (b)   hearsay but admissible because the Constitution requires that exculpatory statements by criminal defendants be admitted.

       (c)   inadmissible hearsay because the statement involves another person (the husband) in addition to D.

       (d)   inadmissible because there is no evidence that D in fact went to sleep, and without such evidence, the statement is irrelevant.

8.   In a prosecution of Perlman for aggravated assault in the shooting of Gradwohl, Perlman pleads self-defense. On the issue of Perlman's fear of Gradwohl, Potuto testifies she heard Duncan say to Perlman, "Gradwohl has slashed three people this year with his switchblade."

      (a)   The item is hearsay and is not admissible under any exception to the hearsay rule.

      (b)   The item comes within the definition of hearsay at common law, but is an admission by a party opponent defined as not hearsay by Rule 801(d)(2).

      (c)   The item is hearsay but is admissible under the then existing state of mind exception to the hearsay rule.

      (d)   The item is not hearsay under the definition in Rule 801(a)–(d).

9.   On the issue of Perlman's sanity, Shaneyfelt, Perlman's closest friend, testifies that Perlman was confined to the Snowden Center for the Criminally Insane.

      (a)   The item is hearsay and is not admissible under any exception to the hearsay rule.

      (b)   The item is hearsay but is admissible as a statement made for purposes of medical diagnosis or treatment.

      (c)   The item is hearsay but is admissible under the business records exception to the hearsay rule.

      (d)   The item is not hearsay under the definition in Rule 801(a)–(d).

10.   Driver ran into and injured Walker, a pedestrian. With Driver in his car were Paul and Ralph Passenger. Passerby saw the accident and called the police department, which sent Sheriff to investigate. All of these people are available as potential witnesses in the case of *Walker v. Driver*. Walker alleges that Driver, while drunk, struck Walker, who was in a duly marked crosswalk. Counsel for Walker calls Paul Passenger to testify that just before the accident, Ralph exclaimed, "Watch out! We're going to hit that man in the crosswalk!" The trial judge should rule this testimony:

      (a)   admissible as a spontaneous utterance reflecting Ralph Passenger's impression at the time his statement was made.

      (b)   admissible since it constitutes a declaration against interest as to the declarant, Ralph Passenger.

      (c)   inadmissible because Ralph Passenger is available as a witness.

   (d) inadmissible because the statement preceded the accident and therefore could not have been part of the *res gestae*.

11. Same facts as above. Walker's counsel calls Sheriff to testify that in Driver's presence Paul said, "We hit him while he was in the crosswalk," and that Driver remained silent. The trial judge should rule this testimony:

   (a) admissible because Driver, by his silence, has made Paul his agent and would thereby be bound by any admission Paul made.

   (b) admissible because Driver's silence constitutes an admission of a party.

   (c) inadmissible as "double hearsay" in that Driver's silence is being used to prove the truth of what Sheriff said Paul said.

   (d) inadmissible unless Driver is first called and asked to admit or deny the incident.

12. Same facts as above. Walker's counsel seeks to introduce testimony concerning Walker's statement three days after the accident that, "My ankle must be broken because it hurts so much." The trial judge should rule this testimony:

   (a) admissible as a statement of the declarant's physical suffering.

   (b) admissible to prove that Walker's ankle was broken.

   (c) inadmissible as a self-serving hearsay declaration.

   (d) inadmissible because Walker's medical condition is a subject for expert testimony, not subject to proof by lay opinion evidence.

13. Same facts as above. Walker's counsel wants to introduce testimony from Sheriff concerning a discussion between Sheriff and Passerby at the police station after the accident when Passerby excitedly exclaimed, "Walker ran out in the street and was not in the crosswalk!" Sheriff duly recorded the statement in an official police report. The trial judge should rule Sheriff's oral testimony:

   (a) admissible as a spontaneous utterance.

   (b) admissible as based on past recollection recorded.

   (c) inadmissible because Passerby has not been shown unavailable as a witness.

    (d)   inadmissible under the excited utterance exception because it can be a product of reflection and deliberation.

14.   Same facts as above. Walker's counsel wants to introduce testimony of Sheriff that at the police station Driver told Sheriff, 'I think this was probably my fault.' The trial judge should rule this testimony:

    (a)   admissible as part of the *res gestae*.

    (b)   admissible as an admission of a party-opponent.

    (c)   inadmissible because it includes a conclusion of law that the declarant was not qualified to make.

    (d)   inadmissible because it constitutes an opinion rather than an admission of specific facts.

15.   Frank is charged with the murder of Adams. To prove that Frank was with Adams at the time of the murder the prosecution offers the testimony of Works that Adams said as he was leaving the law school on the night of his murder: "I'm mooching another meal off Frank tonight."

    (a)   The item is hearsay and is not admissible under any exception to the hearsay rule.

    (b)   The item is hearsay but is admissible under the then existing state of mind exception to the hearsay rule.

    (c)   The item is hearsay but is admissible under the present sense impression exception to the hearsay rule.

    (d)   The item is not hearsay under the definition in Rule 801(a)–(d).

16.   Same facts as in the preceding question except that Works' testimony is offered to prove that Adams went to Frank's house that night.

    (a)   The item is hearsay and is not admissible under any exception to the hearsay rule.

    (b)   The item comes within the definition of hearsay at common law but is an admission by a party-opponent defined as not hearsay by Rule 801(d)(2).

    (c)   The item is hearsay but is admissible under the then existing state of mind exception to the hearsay rule.

    (d)   The item is not hearsay under the definition in Rule 801(a)–(d).

17.   Lake, a motorcycle policeperson, stopped Potuto for speeding. As Potuto handed Lake her driver's license, which had a $20 bill attached to it with a paper clip, she said, "Officer, close inspection of my driver's license will show I was not violating any law." In a prosecution of Potuto for attempted bribery, Works, a witness, is prepared to testify for the prosecution to Potuto's words and actions.

- (a)   The item is hearsay and is not admissible under any exception to the hearsay rule.

- (b)   The item comes within the definition of hearsay at common law but is an admission by a party opponent defined as not hearsay by Rule 801(d)(2).

- (c)   The item is hearsay but is admissible under the then existing state of mind exception to the hearsay rule.

- (d)   The item is not hearsay under the definition in Rule 801(a)–(d).

18.   Defendant and X were arrested for conspiracy to illegally export armadillo Frisbees (an endangered species) in violation of federal law. At defendant's trial alone, X claims the Fifth Amendment and refuses to testify. Defendant calls W to testify that after X's arrest, X told W, a friend of defendant, that only he, and not defendant, was responsible for the exportation. Which is the most appropriate response by the court to the prosecution's hearsay objection?

- (a)   X's statement to W is inadmissible hearsay because it is not corroborated.

- (b)   X's statement to W qualified as a statement against interest.

- (c)   X's statement to W qualifies as an ordinary admission of a party-opponent.

- (d)   X's statement to W qualifies as an admission of a co-conspirator.

19.   Harnsberger is charged with killing Lenich. On the issue of Harnsberger's guilt, the State offers Duncan's testimony that Harnsberger told Duncan that he (Harnsberger) fled the Faculty Lounge, the scene of the crime, immediately after Lenich's murder.

- (a)   The item comes within the definition of hearsay at common law but is an admission by a party opponent defined as not hearsay because of Rule 801(d)(2).

- (b)   The item comes within the definition of hearsay at common law but is a prior statement by a witness defined as not hearsay by Rule 801(d)(1).

(c)   The item is hearsay but is admissible as a statement against interest.

(d)   The item is not hearsay under the definition in Rule 801(a)–(d).

20.   In an action by Duncan against Harnsberger for malpractice in letting the statute of limitations run before filing a potential action, Perlman will testify that Shaneyfelt (Harnsberger's partner) told Harnsberger on the day he got the case, "The statute of limitations in this action is one year from the time of the accident and will not run out for another month." Perlman's testimony is offered by Duncan to rebut Harnsberger's testimony that he was not aware that the statute of limitations was one year instead of two.

(a)   The item is hearsay and is not admissible under any exception to the hearsay rule.

(b)   The item comes within the definition of hearsay at common law but is an admission by a party opponent defined as not hearsay by Rule 801(d)(2).

(c)   The item is hearsay but is admissible under the then existing state of mind exception to the hearsay rule.

(d)   The item is not hearsay under the definition in Rule 801(a)–(d).

21.   Same facts as in the preceding question. Perlman also will testify that he heard Harnsberger reply to Shaneyfelt, "I know that; you don't have to lecture me on the basics." Perlman's testimony is offered to rebut Harnsberger's testimony that he was not aware that the statute was one year instead of two.

(a)   The item is hearsay and is not admissible under any exception to the hearsay rule.

(b)   The item comes within the definition of hearsay at common law but is an admission by a party opponent defined as not hearsay by Rule 801(d)(2).

(c)   The item is hearsay but is admissible under the present sense impression exception to the hearsay rule.

(d)   The item is not hearsay under the definition in Rule 801(a)–(d).

22.   Prosecution of D for murder. D claims that he stabbed the victim in self-defense. Before the victim's body was moved, Q, a police pathologist, visited the scene and examined the body. Shortly thereafter, Q made a report in which he concluded that from the condition of the body, the victim must have been knifed in the back. At D's trial the prosecution calls Q, who identifies a document as his report. The prosecutor then moves the admission of the report into evidence. The report is:

   (a)   admissible because it has been properly authenticated.

   (b)   hearsay but admissible under the past recollection recorded exception.

   (c)   hearsay but admissible under the public records exception.

   (d)   inadmissible.

23.   Rider, a bus passenger, sued Transit Company for injuries to his back from an accident caused by Transit's negligence. Transit denies that Rider received any injury in the accident. Rider's counsel seeks to introduce an affidavit he obtained in preparation for trial from Dr. Bond, who has since died. The affidavit avers that Dr. Bond examined Rider two days after the Transit Company accident and found him suffering from a recently incurred back injury. The judge should rule the affidavit:

   (a)   admissible as a statement of present bodily condition made to a physician.

   (b)   admissible as prior recorded testimony.

   (c)   admissible as a business record.

   (d)   inadmissible because it is hearsay not within any exception.

24.   Under questioning at the police station, and after being Mirandized, X says to the police, "Blinky and I robbed the liquor store."

   (a)   This statement would be admissible against Blinky under the co-conspirator exception.

   (b)   This statement would be admissible against Blinky as an admission.

   (c)   If X takes the Fifth Amendment, this statement would be admissible against Blinky as a statement against interest.

   (d)   None of the above.

25. Action by P against D for breach of an oral contract. To prove that a contract was formed, P calls W to testify that she watched P and D negotiating the contract, and that a moment after negotiations were concluded, W said, to nobody in particular, "They've shaken hands. At last the deal is struck." Testimony concerning W's statement is:

    (a)   admissible as a non hearsay "verbal act."

    (b)   hearsay but admissible as a present sense impression.

    (c)   hearsay and not admissible as a present sense impression because the event of forming the contract is not a startling event or condition.

    (d)   inadmissible because the statement is not the best evidence of the formation of the contract.

HEARSAY EXAMS
MULTIPLE CHOICE EXAM II

1. Smith testifies on behalf of Jones in Jones' action against Swartz. On cross-examination Smith denies bias against Swartz. Swartz later calls Brown who testifies that he saw Smith write "Swartz is a Fool" with spray paint on Swartz's office door. Brown's testimony is offered to show Smith's bias.

    (a)   The item is hearsay and is not admissible under any exception to the hearsay rule.

    (b)   The item is hearsay but is admissible under the then existing state of mind exception to the hearsay rule.

    (c)   The item is hearsay but is admissible under the present sense impression exception to the hearsay rule.

    (d)   The item is not hearsay under the definition of Rule 801(a)–(d).

2. Same fact situation above except that Brown testifies that two days before the trial Smith said, "I hate Swartz." Brown's testimony is offered to show Smith's bias.

    (a)   The item is hearsay and is not admissible under any exception to the hearsay rule.

    (b)   The item is hearsay but is admissible under the then existing state of mind exception to the hearsay rule.

    (c)   The item is hearsay but is admissible under the present sense impression exception to the hearsay rule.

    (d)   The item is not hearsay under the definition in Rule 801(a)–(d).

3. Suit on a contract to sell a horse. In order to establish the contract, W testifies that X said he overheard defendant promise plaintiff to sell his horse, Gray Capulet, for fifty dollars.

    (a)   This is not hearsay.

    (b)   This is hearsay and comes within no exception.

    (c)   This is hearsay but comes within the statement against interest exception.

    (d)   This is not hearsay because it comes within the statement of a party-opponent definition.

4.   Personal injury action by P against D arising out of the crash of P's bicycle and D's motorcycle at an intersection. P offers into evidence a police report written by X, a police officer who went to the scene less than a minute after the accident. The report contains the following statement: "I immediately interviewed Y, who was sobbing uncontrollably. She said she saw the accident, and that D ran a red light on his motorcycle and struck P who had the green." The portion of the report containing this statement is:

   (a)   inadmissible because police reports do not satisfy the public records exception.

   (b)   inadmissible because X, the officer, did not have personal knowledge of the facts reported by Y.

   (c)   admissible because both the public records and excited utterance exceptions are satisfied.

   (d)   admissible because the officer was under a duty to report honestly, and Y's statement is not offered to prove the truth, but to prove Y's state of mind in observing a startling event.

5.   Works sues Lenich for negligence. In a deposition, Kirst, a witness to an automobile accident, testifies under oath that he saw Lenich's car smash into Works' car, which was stopped at a red light. On cross-examination, Kirst admits he is near-sighted and was not wearing his glasses at the time. At the time of trial, Kirst no longer lives in the jurisdiction, he is not subject to subpoena, and he will not voluntarily attend. Works reasonably did try to secure Kirst's attendance. Works seeks to introduce the portion of the deposition where Kirst testified that Lenich crashed into Works' stopped car. The deposition:

   (a)   is inadmissible because it is not offered in response to a prior inconsistent statement.

   (b)   is admissible because Kirst is unavailable.

   (c)   is not admissible unless Works tried to prevent Kirst from leaving the jurisdiction.

   (d)   can only be admissible if Kirst were available and subject to cross-examination.

6. Patent infringement action by ABM, a giant computer manufacturer, against Condor, a small company, alleging that Condor copied the design of the ABM personal computer. To prove that the public was fooled into thinking that the Condor machine was made by ABM, ABM calls W to testify that he was sitting at his Condor one day working on a novel when X a friend, walked up and said, "Hey, nice ABM you got there." This evidence is:

    (a) inadmissible hearsay.

    (b) inadmissible because ABM has not shown that this incident represents a true indication of consumer opinion, and is therefore irrelevant.

    (c) admissible as circumstantial evidence of X's state of mind, and is relevant to show that the public was fooled into thinking the Condor was an ABM.

    (d) hearsay but admissible under the state of mind exception, and is relevant to show that the public was fooled into thinking the Condor was an ABM.

7. Driver ran into and injured Walker, a pedestrian. Walker alleges Driver was drunk. Walker's counsel wants to have Sheriff testify to the following statement made to him by Ralph Passenger, out of the presence of Driver: "We were returning from a party at which we had all been drinking." The trial judge should rule this testimony:

    (a) admissible as an admission of a party.

    (b) admissible as a declaration against interest.

    (c) inadmissible as hearsay.

    (d) inadmissible because it would lead the court into nonessential side issues.

8. Same facts as above. On the evening of the day of the accident, Ralph Passenger wrote a letter to his sister in which he described the accident. When Ralph says he cannot remember some details of the accident, Walker's counsel seeks to show him the letter to assist him in his testimony on direct examination. The trial judge should rule this:

    (a) permissible under the doctrine of present recollection refreshed.

    (b) permissible under the doctrine of past recollection recorded.

    (c) objectionable because the letter was not a spontaneous utterance.

    (d)   objectionable because the letter is a self-serving declaration in so far as the witness, Ralph, is concerned.

9.   Prosecution of D for robbery of a record store. After the robbery, Officer X, a fingerprinting expert, visited the store and dusted for fingerprints. He then went back to the station, performed some tests, and concluded that the fingerprints he had lifted from the store safe were those of Y, a local thief. Officer X then recorded all of the above information in a report. At D's trial, D calls Officer X to testify. D first shows him the report he filed, and X identifies it as his report. D then moves the admission of the report into evidence in order to prove that D did not commit the crime. The report is:

    (a)   admissible non hearsay.

    (b)   hearsay but admissible under the business records exception.

    (c)   hearsay but admissible under the public records exception.

    (d)   inadmissible.

10.   Rider, a bus passenger, sued Transit Company for injuries to his back from an accident caused by Transit's negligence. Transit denied that Rider received any injury in the accident. Transit Company calls Observer to testify that right after the accident, Rider told him that he had recently suffered a recurrence of an old back injury. The judge should rule Observer's testimony:

    (a)   admissible as an admission of a party-opponent.

    (b)   admissible as a spontaneous declaration.

    (c)   inadmissible because it is irrelevant.

    (d)   inadmissible because it is hearsay not within any exception.

11.   In a civil trial, hearsay evidence subject to an exception (and not objectionable on other evidentiary grounds) is:

    (a)   always inadmissible because of the confrontation clause.

    (b)   always admissible despite the confrontation clause.

    (c)   generally inadmissible because of the confrontation clause.

    (d)   generally admissible despite the confrontation clause.

12. Patty sues Mart Department Store for personal injuries, alleging that while shopping she was knocked to the floor by a merchandise cart being pushed by Handy, a stock clerk, and that as a consequence her back was injured. Handy testified that Patty fell near the cart but was not struck by it. Thirty minutes after Patty's fall, Handy, in accordance with regular practice at Mart, had filled out a printed form, "Employee's Report of Accident—Mart Department Store," in which he stated that Patty had been leaning over to spank her young child and in so doing had fallen near his cart. Counsel for Mart offers in evidence the report, which had been given him by Handy's supervisor. The judge should rule the report offered by Mart:

   (a) admissible as *res gestae*.

   (b) admissible as a business record.

   (c) inadmissible because it is hearsay not within any exception.

   (d) inadmissible because Handy is available as a witness.

13. Personal injury action by P, who was struck by D's car while crossing a street. D admits that he struck P, but denied that he was negligent. P takes the stand and testifies that in the hospital two hours after the accident, P said to a nurse, "D ran right through that red light!" This evidence is:

   (a) admissible as a party admission.

   (b) hearsay but admissible as a statement made for purposes of medical diagnosis or treatment.

   (c) inadmissible if offered to prove the truth of the matter asserted, but admissible to show P's belief about the past event.

   (d) inadmissible.

14. The most important criterion that will be applied in determining whether to adopt a hearsay exception for a particular kind of hearsay statement is:

   (a) whether the information is needed for a full determination of the issues in the case.

   (b) whether the declarant will generally be available for cross-examination concerning the substance of the statement.

   (c) whether this kind of statement is typically accompanied by circumstantial guarantees of trustworthiness.

(d)   whether the party against whom the evidence is offered will generally be able to offer evidence to contradict the hearsay statement.

15.   Negligence action by P against D after D's unattended car rolled down a hill and struck P's car. D had left his car for a few minutes while he went into a store. D denies negligence. At trial, P offers a police report that contains D's statement, taken at the scene, in which D told the investigating officer that the car must have slipped out of park. The statement in the report is:

(a)   inadmissible as an admission because it is more against the interest of the car manufacturer than against D's interests.

(b)   inadmissible as an admission because of lack of personal knowledge.

(c)   inadmissible because D was not under a duty to report accurately.

(d)   admissible.

16.   Prosecution of Wolf for murdering Miss Hood. Although no trace of Miss Hood has been found, it is the prosecution's theory that she was eaten by Wolf at Miss Hood's grandmother's house. In order to prove that Miss Hood went to her grandmother's house that evening, the prosecution calls W who testifies, "Miss Hood told me that in the evening she is going to go over-the-river-and-through-the-woods to her grandmother's house."

(a)   This is hearsay and comes within no exception.

(b)   This is an operative fact, therefore not hearsay.

(c)   This is considered hearsay, but would fall within an exception.

(d)   None of the above.

17.   In Polk's negligence action against Dell arising out of a multiple-car collision, Witt testified for Polk that Dell went through a red light. On cross-examination, Dell seeks to question Witt about her statement that the light was yellow, made in a deposition that Witt gave in a separate action between Adams and Baker. The transcript of the deposition is self-authenticating. On proper objection, the court should rule the inquiry.

(a)   admissible for impeachment only.

(b)   admissible as substantive evidence only.

(c)   admissible for impeachment and as substantive evidence.

        (d)   inadmissible because it is hearsay not within any exception.

18.   In order to show motive for committing suicide, W testifies that a week before A's death Dr. Jerry A. Trick told W that he had just told A that A had a loathsome, incurable disease.

        (a)   This is not hearsay because the declarant is an expert.

        (b)   This is not hearsay if Dr. Trick is present and can be cross-examined.

        (c)   This is hearsay, but is admissible under the then existing state of mind exception.

        (d)   None of the above.

19.   Lyons was on trial for the murder of his wife. The prosecution claimed that Lyons committed the murder by poisoning his wife with bichloride of mercury. Lyons' defense was that his wife committed suicide. Friend was called by the prosecution to testify that Lyons told him that he poisoned his wife. The trial judge should rule Friend's testimony:

        (a)   admissible because it was an admission of a party-opponent.

        (b)   inadmissible unless Lyons actually testifies.

        (c)   inadmissible because it was hearsay.

        (d)   inadmissible because it was a prior inconsistent statement, which can only be used for impeachment purposes.

20.   In a suit attacking the validity of a deed executed fifteen years ago, Plaintiff alleges mental incompetency of Joe, the grantor, and offers in evidence a properly authenticated affidavit of Harry, Joe's brother. The affidavit, which was executed shortly after the deed, stated that Harry had observed Joe closely over a period of weeks, that Joe had engaged in instances of unusual behavior (which were described), and that Joe's appearance had changed from one of neatness and alertness to one of disorder and absentmindedness. The judge should rule Harry's affidavit:

        (a)   inadmissible as opinion.

        (b)   inadmissible as hearsay not within any exception.

        (c)   admissible as an official document.

        (d)   admissible as an ancient document.

21.   Lyons is charged with armed robbery. Thorson will testify for the prosecution that he was asked by Lyons to lend him a gun "to commit a robbery."

    (a)   Thorson's testimony is inadmissible unless the prosecution first proves to the jury that there is a conspiracy between Lyons and Thorson.

    (b)   Thorson's testimony is inadmissible unless the prosecution first proves to the judge that there was a conspiracy between Thorson and Lyons.

    (c)   Thorson's testimony is not admissible unless Lyons is charged with conspiring with Thorson.

    (d)   Thorson's testimony is admissible against Lyons for the truth of the matter asserted as an admission of a party-opponent, Rule 801(d)(2).

22.   Criminal prosecution of D for petty theft and being a habitual criminal. Assume that in order to prevail on the habitual criminal charge, the State must prove that D was previously convicted of three crimes. To prove that D was once before convicted of petty theft, which carried a maximum six-month sentence, the prosecution offers in evidence the written judgment of conviction for that crime, bearing the signature of the clerk and the seal of the court, together with the clerk's statement that she had the capacity to prepare the document. This document is:

    (a)   admissible under the hearsay exception for judgments of previous conviction.

    (b)   admissible under the hearsay exception for public records.

    (c)   inadmissible because not properly authenticated.

    (d)   inadmissible because although authenticated, it does not satisfy the hearsay exception for judgments of previous conviction, which is the exception most applicable to the case.

23.   To prove the license number of a getaway car used in a bank robbery, the prosecution offers a crumpled sheet of paper on which appears the number "ABC 666" and the testimony of Denicola, a bystander at the time of the getaway, that though he cannot now recall the number of the car, he did, while the number was fresh in his mind, write the number down on the piece of paper offered in evidence.

    (a)   The item is hearsay and is not admissible under any exception to the hearsay rule.

(b) The item is hearsay but is admissible as past recollection recorded.

(c) The item is hearsay but is admissible as present recollection revived.

(d) The item is not hearsay under the definition in Rule 801(a)–(d).

24. To prove the license number of a getaway car used in a bank robbery, the prosecution offers a photograph of a retreating automobile bearing the license number "ABC 666" and the testimony of Denicola. Denicola testifies that, though he cannot now recall the license number of the car, he did know it at the time of the bank robbery and that he took the photograph offered in evidence, and the photograph is a fair and accurate representation of the getaway car as it left the scene.

(a) The item is hearsay and is not admissible under any exception to the hearsay rule.

(b) The item is hearsay but is admissible as past recollection recorded.

(c) The item is hearsay but is admissible as present recollection revived.

(d) The item is not hearsay under the definition in Rule 801(a)–(d).

25. Wrongful death action brought by P against D. P alleges that D shot and killed P's wife in the course of a burglary of the deceased's ice cream store. To prove that D committed the act, P wishes to offer evidence that D pleaded *nolo contendere* to felony murder in connection with the same event. This evidence is:

(a) inadmissible hearsay.

(b) inadmissible even though it is non hearsay.

(c) admissible as an admission of D.

(d) admissible as an admission of D only if the court carefully instructs the jury that it may not find for P because it believes that D is a bad person.

COMPREHENSIVE EXAMS

COMPREHENSIVE EXAMS
TRUE-FALSE EXAM I

___1.   Defendant in a criminal prosecution is charged with assault on a police officer. Defendant contends that the police officer assaulted him, and he merely used reasonable force to defend himself. The prosecution, as part of its case in chief, may call a witness to testify that, on numerous occasions, the witness has seen the defendant start fights with people.

___2.   Same case. The prosecution, as part of its case in chief, may call a witness to testify that the defendant has a reputation in the community for being quick to start fights.

___3.   Same case. As part of the defendant's case in chief, the defendant may call a witness to testify that, one year prior to assaulting the defendant, the officer also assaulted the witness.

___4.   Same case. Defendant may call the officer's former supervisor (the officer has since been fired) to testify that in his opinion the officer had a character trait for violence.

___5.   Same case. If the defendant testifies that he did not assault the officer, then the prosecution may show by cross-examination that the defendant often beats up his wife.

___6.   Same case. If the defendant testifies that he did not assault the officer, then the prosecution may show during examination of the defendant that he was convicted two years ago for filing a false income tax return, a misdemeanor.

___7.   Same case. Defendant calls W, who testifies that he saw the altercation, and the police officer started the fight. The prosecution may attack the credibility of W by calling a witness to testify that W has a poor reputation for truth and veracity in the community.

___8.   Same case. W gives the same testimony as in the immediately preceding question. The prosecution may call X, who will testify that on numerous occasions he saw W slash the tires of police cars.

___9.   Testimony by a lay witness that a person lacked testamentary capacity is admissible provided the elements comprising the concept of testamentary capacity are first explored.

___10.   Parents sue Excavation Co. for injuries to their child who fell into defendant's pit. At trial, plaintiff's call to the stand during their case in chief Company's site foreman. On direct examination, plaintiff's attorney asks the foreman, "Isn't it a fact that your company, the defendant here, dug the pit that plaintiff's child fell into?" The question is objectionable as leading.

___11.   Same case. On cross-examination, the foreman testifies that the pit is surrounded by a six-foot chain link fence. On redirect, plaintiff seeks to establish through the foreman that the fence was in fact installed by the company after the child fell into the pit. The questions on this subject are excludable because, if true, they establish a subsequent remedial measure.

___12.   Same case. On cross-examination of an Excavation Co. official, plaintiff's attorney seeks to establish, as circumstantial evidence, that the defendant had foreseen accidents such as this one, and that it had taken out liability insurance which specifically covered injuries to trespassing minors. This line of question is properly excludable upon proper objection by defendant.

___13.   Prosecution of Phineas T. Bluster for the murder of Howdy Doody. On the issue of Bluster's defense, suicide, Bluster calls Doody's accountant who testifies that he told Doody immediately prior to his death that Doody's business was in financial ruin and he would have to go into bankruptcy. Objection sustained; this testimony is privileged.

___14. The testimony above is inadmissible hearsay.

___15. The testimony above is admissible as expert testimony.

___16. The out-of-court statement "I intend to go to the movies with Joe" is admissible to prove Joe went to the movies.

___17. Same case. The same statement is admissible to prove the declarant went to the movies.

___18. A stipulation agreed to by the parties may be used at trial in place of live testimony as to a matter even if the stipulation goes to an essential element of a claim or defense.

___19. On the issue of whether or not W, who is not a party and is unavailable, was in Crooked Creek on July 24, a witness wishes to testify that on July 25 W said to him, "Yesterday I was in Crooked Creek." This would fall within an exception to the hearsay rule.

___20. On the same issue, the witness wishes to testify that on July 23 W (who is still not a party, but who is now available) said, "Tomorrow I will go to Crooked Creek." This would fall within an exception to the hearsay rule.

___21. A hearsay statement is always admissible provided the declarant also happens to be the witness testifying concerning the statement.

___22. Plaintiff in an intersection collision case calls W-1 who testified that the plaintiff ran through the red light. Plaintiff is obviously unhappy with this testimony. Plaintiff may not now call W-2 to testify that he saw the plaintiff wait until the light was green because this would violate the rule against extrinsic collateral contradiction.

___23.   Same case. Plaintiff may call W-3 to testify that W-1 has a poor
          reputation for truth and veracity in the community, even though
          W-1's testimony did not surprise plaintiff.

___24.   Prosecution of D for possession of cocaine. D's defense is that he
          did not know the substance he was carrying was cocaine. The
          prosecution may offer evidence that a year before the current
          arrest, D was arrested for trying to sell cocaine to an undercover
          agent.

___25.   An expert witness can define the law for the jury in the area of the
          witness's expertise.

___26.   P files a civil action against D for an assault in a bar. D may call
          W to testify to D's reputation in the community for being a docile,
          nonbelligerent individual.

___27.   Same case. D may call W to testify that in W's opinion, based on a
          long acquaintance with D, D is a docile, nonbelligerent person.

___28.   An expert witness may testify that another witness wasn't telling
          the truth.

___29.   A's expert doctor, on cross-examination, was asked, "Isn't it a fact
          that 'S on Y' is a recognized, authoritative work on the subject of
          Y?" The question is objectionable because it is leading.

___30.   Same case. Assuming the doctor answered "Yes" to the question,
          the doctor could be cross-examined about statements in the book
          contrary to the opinion he expressed.

___31.   Same case. Statements from the book contrary to the doctor's
          opinion are admissible orally, but only to impeach him.

___32.   An expert witness must disclose the basis of her opinion prior to
          offering the opinion.

___33.   In a diversity action in a federal court, the federal court usually must apply the privilege law of the state where located.

___34.   The four testimonial dangers are perception, recollection and recordation, narration, and sincerity.

___35.   An offer of proof may be done by avowal of counsel or in question-and-answer form, in the discretion of the trial judge.

___36.   P sues for his back injuries. He said to a neighbor, W, "My back hurts like hell. It hurt like hell yesterday, too." Over a hearsay objection W may testify to the statement "My back hurts like hell."

___37.   Same case. Over a hearsay objection, W may testify to the statement "It hurt like hell yesterday, too."

___38.   Evidence of a person's prior conduct, when offered to prove her conduct on a particular occasion, is not subject to a simple relevancy objection because the evidence satisfies the definition of relevance.

___39.   An opinion that Bob was negligent is inadmissible.

___40.   The primary reason behind the reluctance of some common law courts to permit lay witnesses to testify to their opinions is that the fact-finder is thought to be just as capable of forming its own conclusions.

___41.   If a party wishes to call to the stand one of the jurors sitting on that case, the juror may testify, but subject to the same degree of cross-examination to which any other witness could be subjected.

___42.   Pleas of *nolo contendere* are admissible in a subsequent civil action against the person as a prior conviction to impeach.

___43.   An objection is timely if made when the grounds for the objection first become apparent, even though the evidence has already been admitted. The objection may be coupled with a motion to strike.

___44.   "Authentication" means proving that an item of evidence is what its proponent claims it to be.

___45.   Will contest. Plaintiff asserts the will is a fake. Defendant will be unable to introduce a duplicate copy of the alleged original will if the alleged original will is available.

___46.   Doody's accountant tells Doody he is broke. To prove that Doody did not commit suicide but was murdered, the prosecution calls Tusinelda, his sister, and offers to prove that after Doody's accountant left, he said to Tusinelda, "I can always begin again. You can't keep a wood man down." This is a hearsay statement that is inadmissible.

___47.   To be admissible as a statement for purposes of medical diagnosis or treatment, the statement must be made to a person from whom such diagnosis or treatment is sought.

___48.   A court cannot take judicial notice of matters such as that racially segregated schools can never be truly equal.

___49.   The trial judge may call and examine a witness.

___50.   If the trial judge is uncertain whether proffered evidence is relevant, she should admit it and instruct the jury that it should disregard the evidence if it finds it to be irrelevant.

COMPREHENSIVE EXAMS
TRUE-FALSE EXAM II

___1.   A party who knows that a witness will testify unfavorably to him cannot impeach the witness unless the testimony is damaging to his case.

___2.   A witness can be asked on cross-examination about specific instances of prior lying by him.

___3.   Most lay witnesses can testify that the car was going well over 40 m.p.h.

___4.   Most lay witnesses can testify that the gunshot she heard came from a .45 caliber pistol.

___5.   A lay witness may not testify about facts unless it has first been shown that the witness has personal knowledge.

___6.   Defendant is prosecuted for possession of marijuana. On direct examination he denies that he knew that the material was marijuana, and he denies knowing what marijuana looks like. The district attorney may call W to testify that prior to D's arrest he (W) often smoked marijuana with D.

___7.   On the issue whether or not the store knew or should have known that a piece of lettuce which caused the accident was on the floor, the stock boy can testify that it was his invariable routine to sweep the floor of the produce section every fifteen minutes.

___8.   A reference to insurance that is an integral part of an admission of liability is admissible.

___9.   Evidence that is otherwise inadmissible may be admitted if the "door is opened."

___10.   If a party makes a specific objection to an item of proof and it is overruled, he can raise a different specific objection to the same evidence on appeal.

___11.   The common law rule requiring that a witness be shown a document before she can be examined regarding its contents was known as "the rule of the Queen's case."

___12.   An atheist is not a competent witness in federal court because he cannot take the oath.

___13.   Under Rule 403, "surprise" is not a ground for discretionary exclusion of evidence.

___14.   When a witness testifies in an action in which his church has a financial interest, the religion of the witness cannot be proved.

___15.   The character of a murder victim may be proved by the prosecution if the defendant has attacked his character.

___16.   A lay witness may testify that Harry assaulted John.

___17.   A lay witness can testify that another person was losing their mental faculties.

___18.   A tile layer can be by virtue of experience alone qualified as an expert.

___19.   The law gives preference to experts who qualify based upon education and training over those qualifying based upon experience.

___20. Testimony by a qualified expert that the explanative theory he employed is the product of reliable principles and methods satisfies Rule 702.

___21. An appellate court can reverse a trial court on the basis of an error not raised by counsel at trial.

___22. A prior conviction of a witness may be offered to impeach her credibility even if the conviction is currently under appeal.

___23. Evidence that a person has previously made a statement consistent with her trial testimony is generally admissible to corroborate her trial testimony.

___24. It is impermissible for a trial judge to allow jurors to take exhibits with them into the jury room during deliberations.

___25. An opinion by an expert that the defendant possessed the drugs with the intent and purpose of distribution is prohibited by Rule 704(b).

___26. An opinion that the defendant lacked the ability to tell right from wrong is prohibited by Rule 704(b).

___27. An opinion that the defendant suffered from a particular mental disease which affected him in a certain way is not prohibited by Rule 704(b).

___28. Prosecution for drunken driving. The arresting officer testifies that the defendant told him that he was driving. The defendant objects and calls his twin brother who testifies that he was the one who made the statement. If the judge believes the twin brother he can exclude the statement.

___29. The trial judge has discretion to alter the order of proof and permit a party to ask questions beyond the scope of the direct examination.

___30.   The plaintiff offers oral testimony as to the content of a document. The defendant objects that the evidence is "incompetent, irrelevant, and immaterial." The judge overrules the objection. On appeal, the defendant can raise a hearsay objection.

___31.   If a young child being examined for competency as a witness states her belief that if she lies she will never, ever be allowed to visit Disneyland, the child can be found competent to testify.

___32.   Under Rule 403, a trial court may refuse to permit a party to call witnesses whose testimony will simply repeat the testimony of other witnesses.

___33.   Rule 704(b) prevents a defendant in a murder case from calling a psychiatrist to testify that the defendant is psychotic.

___34.   A trial judge may not allow a criminal case to go to the jury if it is based solely on circumstantial evidence.

___35.   Reasonable reliance under Rule 703 implies a notion of sufficiently trustworthy to be relied upon.

___36.   In order for an out-of-court statement to be admissible as a statement against interest under Rule 804(b)(3), the declarant must be unavailable.

___37.   Polygraph evidence is infrequently admitted in criminal trials anywhere in the United States.

___38.   When a party introduces into evidence one part of an oral conversation, an adverse party may require him to introduce any other part of that conversation which in fairness ought to be considered contemporaneously with it.

___39.   D is arrested and read his rights. While he is under arrest the victim of the crime is brought to the police station. Within D's hearing, the victim points at D and says, "That is the man that robbed me." D remained silent. D's silence in the face of this accusation could not be used as an adoptive admission.

___40.   A letter that qualifies as past recollection recorded may be read to the jury, but the writing itself may not be introduced into evidence for the jury to read by either party so as to not give undue emphasis to any one witness's testimony.

___41.   S v. D. If W testifies for D and denies on cross-examination that he (W) regularly dates D's sister, the State may introduce, over objection, testimony by Y, W's roommate, that W does in fact regularly date D's sister.

___42.   If more than ten years have elapsed since a witness's conviction of a crime or his release from confinement for that conviction, whichever is later, the conviction may not be used to impeach the witness's credibility.

___43.   P v. D for failure to deliver merchandise at the time specified in a written contract. P may introduce in evidence, over objection, testimony of W, who has seen D write his signature in the past, to identify D's signature on the contract, even if W is not a handwriting expert.

___44.   Rule 408 pertaining to compromises and offers to compromise provides less protection than the common law to statements made in the course of compromise negotiations.

___45.   P sues the driver of a car for negligence and recovers a judgment for $20,000. It is not paid. P then discovers that the car was driven within the scope of the driver's employment, so P sues the employer on a theory of *respondeat superior*. Over objection, the properly authenticated final judgment in the P v. Driver suit is admissible to show driver's negligent driving in the P v. Employer suit.

___46.   In a *habeas corpus* proceeding where defendant has alleged ineffective assistance of counsel, the defendant contends that he was advised by his attorney to plead guilty to first degree murder because the maximum sentence was only twenty years, when in fact it is life without parole. The client may invoke the attorney-client privilege when the attorney is called by the district attorney and asked whether such advice was ever given.

___47. If the defendant in a slip-and-fall case testifies that he did everything possible to make the stairs safe, the plaintiff can introduce evidence that after the accident the defendant installed non-skid treads on the stairs.

___48. It is not necessary to object immediately to questions asked by the judge.

___49. Whether an expert has applied an explanative theory reliably to the facts of the case always goes to weight and not admissibility.

___50. The trial court must determine, Rule 104(a), whether an explanative theory being employed by an expert is the product of reliable principles and methods.

COMPREHENSIVE EXAMS
TRUE-FALSE EXAM III

___1. The "gatekeeping" requirement inspired by *Daubert* as an aspect of due process is applicable to the states.

___2. The judge may allow someone other than the photographer to lay a foundation for introduction of the photographs.

___3. Plaintiff in a land fraud case offers the testimony of W who will testify that she heard a non-party real estate man say that the land in question was under water each spring. In response to plaintiffs' attorney's question to W, "What did the realtor say?" defendants' attorney rises and says, "I object, your honor, the question calls for an inadmissible, incompetent, and prejudicial response." The objection is overruled. On appeal the defendant will be allowed to argue that the trial court erroneously admitted hearsay testimony.

___4. In order to qualify a document as a business record, the person who made the record (the entrant) must testify, and he must testify, among other things, that the records were a kind regularly kept by the business.

___5. Plaintiff sues the Rough & Rocky Railroad ("R.R.") for injuries sustained when defendant's train struck plaintiff's car at a crossing. Plaintiff alleges that the crossing is unreasonably dangerous to crossing traffic and seeks to prove that there were three similar crossing accidents and two near-misses that R.R. employees reported at that crossing within two years prior to plaintiff's accident. Defendant objects. The five prior incidents are admissible.

___6. P sues D claiming that D negligently entrusted a tractor to X. D may offer evidence that X had a reputation in the community as an extremely careful and prudent person.

___7.   Evidence of a previous felony conviction may be used to impeach only if the felony is a crime of dishonesty.

___8.   P v. D for personal injuries sustained when D allegedly ran a stop light. To prove improper brake maintenance, P may introduce, over objection, testimony of a mechanic that the week after the accident he installed new brake linings in D's automobile.

___9.   Argumentative questions are permissible during cross-examination.

___10.   Cross-examination should be limited to the scope of the direct examination and matters of credibility.

___11.   In order to qualify for the attorney-client privilege, the attorney involved in the communication must be a member of the bar in the state in which the communication takes place.

___12.   A trial judge may appoint her own experts to testify in the trial.

___13.   Prosecution of D for battery. To prove that the victim was the aggressor in the fight, D may call W to testify that she has known the victim for ten years, and that in her opinion, the victim is a violent person.

___14.   The attorney-client privilege is inapplicable when the client is not a party to the action.

___15.   An expert may be cross-examined concerning the facts, data, or opinions relied upon by the expert in forming an opinion.

___16.   In a murder trial in which a jury is sitting as fact-finder, the court should usually refuse to admit bloody photos of the victim because of the enormous potential for unfair prejudice against the defendant and the fact that they can't have any real probative value.

___17. An admission may be introduced against the party who made it even though the admission was not based on the firsthand knowledge of the declarant.

___18. When D was arrested for robbery, he tried to escape. D's attempt to escape would be inadmissible because it is conduct that would be considered hearsay.

___19. W told a police officer that D gave him the dope. When confronted at trial with the prior inconsistent statement, W denies making it. The Confrontation Clause in the U.S. Constitution would prevent the police officer from testifying to W's former statement.

___20. Doctors are a good illustration of a type of expert that may reasonably rely upon facts, data, or opinions that have not been admitted into evidence.

___21. Facts, data, or opinions reasonably relied upon may be disclosed as of right by the testifying expert in giving his expert witness testimony.

___22. Opinion evidence is admissible to prove character to the same extent as reputation evidence.

___23. An out-of-court declarant is unavailable if she is called to testify but claims not to remember making the statement inquired about.

___24. It is ordinarily permissible to lead a witness on direct in order to refresh the witness's recollection.

___25. With certain exceptions, a party may request the trial court to exclude witnesses from the courtroom so that they cannot hear the testimony of other witnesses.

___26. Testimony that a car went through a red light is barred by the opinion on an ultimate issue rule.

___27.   It is improper to inquire whether an expert witness has testified before for a client of the attorney who hired him.

___28.   A lay witness can testify that someone was drunk.

___29.   A lay witness can testify that a friend of hers was nervous and afraid when she got into the car to drive in an ice storm.

___30.   The present sense impression exception is limited to statements made spontaneously by the declarant at a time when he was under the stress of excitement caused by the event being described in the declaration.

___31.   For a statement by a party to qualify as an admission, the statement must have been against the declarant's interest at the time the statement was made.

___32.   A owned real property and conveyed it to B. B boasted to W that he had fraudulently convinced A to convey the property. B then conveyed the property to C. A sued C to recover the property. Over a hearsay objection, W may testify to B's statement on behalf of A. (B is nowhere to be found.)

___33.   P-1, the driver, and P-2, the passenger, were both injured in a collision with D. Several months later, D offered to settle P-l's $200,000 claim asserted in a lawsuit for $100,000. P-1 refused. Over objection, P-2 may not prove this offer to settle as evidence of D's admission of liability for the collision.

___34.   Plaintiff was injured by a metal sliver while eating from a can of Dower Beige Dwarf peas. The can with the label attached may not be introduced into evidence through the testimony of the plaintiff alone in a suit against the Dower Beige Dwarf Company to prove the source of the can because the writing on the label must be authenticated by the testimony of someone with firsthand knowledge of its authorship and the writing indicating the can is a product of the defendant is inadmissible hearsay.

___35.   The trade secret privilege is an absolute bar to disclosure of the trade secret, regardless of its importance to the litigation.

___36.   Evidence is relevant only if directed to matters in dispute.

___37.   All relevant evidence is admissible.

___38.   Prosecution for child molestation. Defendant may not introduce evidence that he has a reputation for paying his bills on time.

___39.   An expert witness not prepared to render an opinion applying an explanative theory to the facts of the case may not testify.

___40.   Expert witness testimony is subject to Rule 403.

___41.   A landowner may testify as to the value of his property.

___42.   An opinion that an event "could" have been caused by X is inadmissible.

___43.   The issue of whether particular evidence is relevant is ultimately one for the jury to decide.

___44.   A trial judge may admit hearsay evidence if she believes the evidence is crucial to an ultimate issue in the case.

___45.   In actions tried in federal court with respect to a claim or defense on which federal law supplies the rule of decision, there is no attorney-client privilege.

___46.   A trial court may take judicial notice of a fact even after both sides have rested.

___47.   Prosecution of D for the murder of V. D's defense is that she was
          not the one who killed V. The prosecution may offer evidence that
          a week before the killing, D had tried to run over V with her car
          after catching V kissing D's husband.

___48.   D seeks to testify that he received a telephone call from R, D must
          establish that he recognized R's voice or the testimony is
          inadmissible.

___49.   Even where the terms of the writing are in issue, the original need
          not be produced if the court concludes that the evidence is not
          closely related to a controlling issue.

___50.   Rule 706 provides that the fact an expert witness is court
          appointed must be disclosed to the jury.

COMPREHENSIVE EXAMS
TRUE-FALSE EXAM IV

___1.   Facts, data, and opinions customarily relied upon by experts in their particular field can form part of an expert's basis.

___2.   If ordinarily accidentologists rely upon statements from bystanders that have not been admitted in evidence, then it is reasonable for the testifying accidentologist to rely on such a statement in forming his opinion.

___3.   In a will contest, because neither the intestate takers nor those who take under the will may waive the deceased's attorney-client privilege, the deceased's attorney may not testify to confidential communications between himself and the deceased that demonstrate the lucidity of the deceased's mind when the will was drafted and signed.

___4.   If an attorney discloses privileged material without the client's consent, the privilege disappears since the matter is no longer confidential.

___5.   An eavesdropper may be prevented from testifying as to overheard confidential communications between an attorney and his client.

___6.   W received a letter from the defendant in which the defendant made certain incriminating statements. Assuming W is intimately familiar with D's handwriting, W may testify as to what the letter said over defendant's objection although W failed to bring the letter to court.

___7.   Suit on a life insurance policy. To show that the insured committed suicide, the defense introduces evidence that he purchased a large amount of life insurance shortly before his death. This evidence is admissible over objection under Rule 411.

___8.   When evidence of character in the form of reputation testimony is offered to prove conduct, reputation witnesses may only testify to the reputation of the person in the community in which the conduct took place.

___9.   To qualify as an expert witness one must at least have one advanced academic degree in the subject area of expertise.

___10.   An expert can be asked about the percentage of his income that comes from court related matters.

___11.   Rule 702 imposes a gatekeeping requirement on scientific evidence only.

___12.   The Federal Rules of Evidence incorporated the *Frye* test for determining the reliability of expert witness testimony.

___13.   Several days after an accident, W went to the scene of the accident and took some photographs of the intersection. Under the Original Writing Rule, W could not testify to what he saw because the photographs would show it better.

___14.   W and D are charged with a crime. Before trial, W agrees to assist the prosecution and is allowed to plead guilty to a lesser offense. At trial, after W testifies for the State, and after D attacks W's testimony by implying that W fabricated the evidence to receive the favorable plea bargain, the prosecutor will be allowed to introduce a prior consistent statement made by W shortly after he began cooperating. This statement is admissible both on the merits and to rehabilitate W's credibility.

___15.   In a rape case where the defense is that the defendant picked up the complainant in a bar and that she consented to have intercourse with him, the complainant's character is properly "in issue."

___16.   The spirit of the Sixth Amendment right to a jury trial does not preclude the trial judge in a criminal case from judicially noticing a fact that is an element of the offense charged.

___17.	The common law Best Evidence Rule was designed to require counsel to offer the best evidence available whenever possible.

___18.	Evidence must be excluded if it raises any impermissible inferences.

___19.	In criminal prosecution for robbery, W testifies that the robber he saw "had a very high voice and seemed scared." The testimony is inadmissible as being a conclusion.

___20.	Expert eyewitness identification testimony is frequently denied admissibility on the ground of being within the common knowledge of the jury.

___21.	Use of court appointed experts is extremely common in the federal court today.

___22.	Criminal prosecution of D for assault. D calls W, who testifies that she had known D for many years, and that D is a nonviolent person. On cross-examination, the prosecutor may ask W, "Did you know that on May 2, 2015, D was arrested for murdering a law professor?"

___23.	The rules of evidence are as applicable during depositions as they would be at trial.

___24.	So long as an out-of-court statement was made under oath, subject to cross-examination, and the declarant is unavailable, the statement will come into evidence under the prior testimony exception to the hearsay rule.

___25.	S v. D. If D's ex-spouse testifies on direct examination by D's attorney that she told her attorney that she had not seen a shoe box full of money in her broom closet, S may introduce, over her assertion of a privilege, testimony by her attorney that she said the contrary.

___26.   W, who was expecting to testify at trial, wrote some notes down about the event to which he expected to testify. Prior to testifying, W refreshed his recollection with these notes. If these notes are available, then after W testifies on direct an adverse party has the absolute right to inspect them or to ask that W's testimony be stricken in the event inspection is not permitted by the proponent of the witness.

___27.   A husband can prevent his wife from testifying against him in a criminal case even though she is willing to testify.

___28.   A statement of medical history made by a patient-litigant to a doctor for the purpose of securing the doctor as an expert for trial purposes qualifies as an exception to the hearsay rule.

___29.   The Confrontation Clause prohibits the introduction into evidence at defendant's trial of testimony of a witness given at a prior hearing at which defendant had the opportunity to cross-examine if the prosecution fails to make a reasonable effort to produce the witness at the trial.

___30.   A lay witness can testify that given the wintry conditions that May was driving unsafely by driving at the speed limit.

___31.   The issue of whether an out-of-court statement qualifies as a dying declaration is for the jury to decide.

___32.   A police officer can testify as an expert witness as to the initiation process of street gangs.

___33.   As a result of *Daubert/Kumho*/Rule 702, it is now more difficult for plaintiff's to prevail in product liability cases.

___34.   The attorney-client privilege bars disclosure of the confidential communication, regardless of its importance to the litigation.

___35.   The former testimony exception is limited to the situation in which the testimony is offered against a person (or against the successor in interest of such person) who offered it in evidence in his own behalf on the former occasion.

___36.   Most lay witnesses can testify that something looked like blood.

___37.   A was riding with a passenger in a car when they were passed by X. X was then involved in a wreck that A saw. Later that evening A said to W, "When X passed me I turned to my passenger and said that they must have been drunk, that we would find them somewhere on the road wrecked if they kept that rate of speed up." W would be permitted to testify to A's statement over a hearsay objection.

___38.   A dying declaration is not admissible if the declarant lacked personal knowledge of the matter asserted.

___39.   The Federal Court must apply the five *Daubert* factors in exercising their role as gatekeeper of expert witness testimony.

___40.   A prior inconsistent statement of a witness may be introduced even if the witness has not first been given an opportunity to explain or deny.

___41.   DNA testimony is admissible under Rule 702 but not *Daubert*.

___42.   In applying Rule 403, the court can take into consideration the opponent's willingness to stipulate to the fact that the evidence is offered to prove.

___43.   Hearsay may be admitted if there is no objection.

___44.   Murder prosecution. The sole eyewitness refuses to testify at trial because he has been threatened with death by members of the defendant's family. His testimony at the preliminary hearing is not admissible because he is not "unavailable as a witness."

___45.   Prosecution of D for battery that allegedly occurred in 2008. D calls W, who testifies that he is familiar with D's community reputation for peacefulness at that time. W testifies that D's reputation was that he was a nonviolent person. Assume that the prosecutor has learned that a rumor was circulating in the community in early 2008 that D had been arrested for assault, though the rumor was untrue. On cross-examination, the prosecutor may not ask W whether he had ever heard that in early 2008 D was arrested for assault.

___46.   An expert witness may be asked to consider contrary versions of facts supported by the evidence and asked whether, if the contrary version was correct, her opinion would remain the same.

___47.   P seeks to establish Dr. W as an expert. D may require that the foundational facts to qualify Dr. W as an expert be established outside the presence of the jury, since the question of whether Dr. W is qualified as an expert is one for the court to determine.

___48.   At common law, a party could introduce a prior inconsistent statement that contradicted material testimony of his own witness only if the party could show surprise, or that the witness is hostile or an adverse party.

___49.   When a trial judge erroneously admits hearsay testimony over the objection of the party against whom that testimony is offered, the appellate court must reverse.

___50.   P sues D for negligence arising out of an auto accident. D offers the testimony of X, an insurance investigator who interviewed P after the accident. After X's testimony, P asks X if he is employed by D's insurance company. If X says "no," P may introduce extrinsic evidence of X's employment by D's insurance company.

COMPREHENSIVE EXAMS
TRUE-FALSE EXAM V

___1.   P v. D. Automobile accident case. W testifies for P. D impeaches her testimony by introducing evidence that W is having a love affair with P and was having one at the time of the accident. In rebuttal, P may introduce evidence of W's prior consistent statements about the accident.

___2.   A lay witness cannot testify that he thinks but is not positive that it was Harry who robbed the store.

___3.   A "verbal act" is another term for hearsay.

___4.   A court may take judicial notice only of adjudicative, not legislative, facts.

___5.   The attorney-client privilege protects both communications from the client to the attorney and communications from the attorney to the client that would reveal confidential client communications.

___6.   In civil actions and proceedings, with respect to an element of a claim or defense as to which state law supplies the rule of decision, the Federal Rules of Evidence defer to the physician-patient privilege recognized by applicable state law.

___7.   A court may take judicial notice of a fact without first giving the parties an opportunity to be heard.

___8.   Circumstantial evidence of hearsay is not subject to the hearsay rule.

___9.   A statement made by a witness in a deposition is not hearsay when offered in the action for which the deposition was taken.

___10.   W made a declaration against penal interest. When offered
         against the defendant by the prosecution, it may be admissible
         even if W is available as a witness.

___11.   Where a witness has been impeached by the introduction of a prior
         conviction, the witness may always be rehabilitated by the
         introduction of a prior consistent statement.

___12.   State v. D for armed robbery. W testifies for D. The trial judge has
         discretion to allow the State to elicit from W testimony that W was
         recently suspended from college for falsifying a financial aid form.

___13.   A lay witness can testify that the bank robber was about 160
         pounds and 5 ft. 6 ins. tall.

___14.   A police report cannot qualify as a public record.

___15.   In determining whether a hearsay declarant is unavailable as a
         witness, a judge can rely on inadmissible hearsay.

___16.   A learned treatise may be employed on cross-examination of an
         expert witness.

___17.   A judge can take judicial notice of any adjudicative fact that he
         knows to be true.

___18.   P v. D. Civil action for battery. In his defense, D may introduce
         testimony of his neighbors about his reputation for peacefulness.

___19.   State v. D for embezzlement. After D's arrest, D and his spouse
         are divorced. After D's arrest, D's spouse consulted an attorney, E,
         about her possible criminal liability and told her attorney that
         before the arrest she saw a shoe box full of money in her broom
         closet. May the State call D's ex-spouse to the stand over D's
         objection.

___20.   It is always proper to use leading questions on cross-examination.

___21.   A party cannot make previously existing documents privileged by delivering them to his attorney.

___22.   A spontaneous statement that a declarant saw an exciting occurrence is admissible without any other proof that the declarant had personal knowledge.

___23.   Courts are especially strict about enforcing the prohibition against leading questions when suggestible witnesses such as the young, the mentally retarded, or those with poor memories are testifying on direct examination.

___24.   Rule 607, which provides that the credibility of a witness may be attacked by any party, including the party calling him, is basically a codification of the traditional common law.

___25.   Whether an expert has developed her opinion solely in order to be able to testify affects the likelihood of the opinion being admitted into evidence.

___26.   Admissions of a party-opponent may be used against the party-opponent only when the party-opponent is testifying.

___27.   A business record may be admissible even though the person who wrote it did not have personal knowledge of the matter stated.

___28.   P v. D. P introduces evidence that he received a letter on what on its face appears to be D's stationery that contained a signature purporting to be that of D. The letter is self-authenticating.

___29.   The plea of *nolo contendere* may be admitted as an admission in a subsequent civil case, but not in a subsequent criminal case.

___30.   Only the holder of a privilege may waive or assert it.

___31.   To refresh a witness's recollection, a party may show a witness a photograph of Princess Leia kissing Han Solo.

___32.   If a party fails to object to the calling of the judge as a witness, that party may not raise the propriety of the judge's testimony on appeal.

___33.   Because "recorded recollection" is an exception to the hearsay rule, the document will be admissible to prove the truth of the matters it asserts if a proper foundation has been laid for the application of the doctrine.

___34.   State v. D for armed robbery. W testifies for D. If W denies on cross-examination by the State he was ever suspended from college for cheating, the State may introduce, over objection, properly authenticated records of the college showing such suspension.

___35.   The plaintiff admits at trial an excited utterance made by an unavailable declarant that the light was red for the truck driven by the defendant. The defendant may introduce a certified copy of a two year old prior conviction of the witness for perjury.

___36.   A lay witness can testify in a design defect case that the product was defective and unreasonably dangerous.

___37.   A hypothetical question is used in the vast majority of examinations of expert witness in the federal court today.

___38.   A hospital record containing opinions of physicians is not admissible.

___39.   A witness may be both a lay and expert witness in the same case.

___40.   Under Rule 609, a witness may not be impeached by a prior conviction if the conviction was for a crime not punishable by death or more than a year in prison.

___41.   The declaration against interest exception to the hearsay rule applies only if the statement is against the declarant's interest at the time it is introduced at trial.

___42.   All preliminary questions of fact in connection with the application of the Original Writing Rule are for the judge alone to determine, Rule 104(a).

___43.   W is P's key witness in a case that turns on credibility. To impeach W, D offers evidence of W's felony convictions for robbery and burglary. P may then offer evidence of W's reputation for truth and veracity.

___44.   An expert witness must have firsthand knowledge of relevant facts in order to give his opinion.

___45.   State v. D for bribery. State may ask D's reputation witness, W, over objection, whether W had heard that two years ago D had been arrested for extortion.

___46.   Evidence of subsequent remedial measures taken after an event are always admissible as long as they are not offered to prove negligence or culpable conduct in connection with the event.

___47.   P v. D for injuries sustained as a result of D's allegedly negligent operation of an automobile. D may introduce, over objection, as part of his case in chief, evidence that he was never before involved in an automobile accident.

___48.   If a witness for P denies a felony conviction, D must prove its existence by extrinsic evidence on his case in chief.

___49.   P v. D for breach of contract. If the original of the contract is available, P may not introduce, over objection, testimony of W describing terms of the contract.

___50.   Normally, the prior inconsistent statement of a witness is not admissible unless the witness is given a chance at some time to explain the statement.

COMPREHENSIVE EXAMS
MULTIPLE CHOICE EXAM I

1. Dann, who was charged with the crime of assaulting Smith, admitted striking Smith but claimed to have acted in self-defense when he was attacked by Smith, who was drunk and belligerent after a football game. As part of the prosecution's case in chief, the state's attorney sought to introduce testimony of Watt that he knew Dann's reputation among those with whom he lived and worked, and that Dann had a reputation for provoking fights and rowdiness. The trial judge should rule this testimony:

    (a) admissible, if it is shown that Smith knew of that reputation.

    (b) admissible because it does not refer to specific acts or other offenses and proves motive and intent.

    (c) not admissible because an attack on Dann's character for peacefulness is improper during the prosecution's case in chief.

    (d) not admissible because Dann's reputation can only be proven by opinion evidence after a proper foundation therefor is laid.

2. Same facts as above. Dann offered testimony of Employer, that he had known and employed Dann for twelve years and knew Dann's reputation among the people with whom he lived and worked to be that of a peaceful, law-abiding, nonviolent person. The trial judge should rule this testimony:

    (a) admissible because relevant to show the improbability of Dann's having committed an unprovoked assault.

    (b) admissible because relevant to a determination of the extent of punishment if Dann is convicted.

    (c) not admissible because whether Dann is normally a person of good character is irrelevant to the specific charge.

    (d) not admissible because irrelevant without a showing that Employer was one of the persons among whom Dann lived and worked.

3.   Same facts as above. On cross-examination Dann's Employer, the state's attorney asked Employer if he had heard that Dann often engaged in fights and brawls. The trial judge should rule the question:

    (a)   objectionable because it seeks to put into evidence separate, unrelated offenses.

    (b)   objectionable because no specific time or incidents are specified and inquired about.

    (c)   not objectionable because evidence of Dann's previous fights and brawls may be used to prove his guilt.

    (d)   not objectionable because it tests Employer's knowledge of Dann's reputation.

4.   Same facts as above. Dann's friend, Frank, was called to testify that Smith had a reputation among the people with whom he lived and worked for frequently engaging in brawls. The trial judge should rule the testimony:

    (a)   admissible to support Dann's theory of self-defense, touching on whether Dann or Smith was the aggressor.

    (b)   admissible if Frank testifies further as to specific acts of misconduct on Smith's part of which Frank has personal knowledge.

    (c)   inadmissible on the question of Dann's guilt because Dann, not Smith, is on trial.

    (d)   inadmissible because Frank failed to lay a proper foundation.

5.   Same facts as above. As a part of the prosecution's case in chief, the state's attorney sought to introduce testimony that, thirty minutes prior to the altercation with Smith, Dann had ordered a hot dog at a concession stand and had run into the crowd without paying for it. The trial judge should rule this testimony:

    (a)   admissible because it tends to show Dann's propensity to commit unlawful acts.

    (b)   admissible because the prior incident was so close in time and place to the act for which Dann was charged as to be relevant to Dann's motive and intent in striking Smith.

    (c)   inadmissible because irrelevant unless there was a showing that Dann had been charged with a crime arising out of the prior incident.

    (d)   inadmissible because proof of such unlawful act is not allowed on the issue of Dann's guilt of the assault charged.

6.   Kalish sued Berger for $1,000 seeking damages for pain and suffering and medical expenses arising from a dog bite. Berger responded to Kalish's complaint by denying that Kalish was ever bit; and alleged that if Kalish was bit, it was not by a dog; that if Kalish was bit by a dog, it was not Berger's dog, Mutt; and that if Kalish was bit by Mutt, Mutt acted in self-defense. At trial Kalish calls Berger adversely and asks, "How much did Mutt cost you?" The trial judge should rule the question objectionable because it:

    (a)   lacks a proper foundation showing that Berger has personal knowledge of Mutt's cost.

    (b)   is irrelevant.

    (c)   is leading.

    (d)   calls for a conclusion.

7.   Same facts as above. Berger offers to testify that, whenever he leaves his home, he invariably and automatically latches the gate to Mutt's kennel. The trial judge should rule that Berger's offered testimony is:

    (a)   objectionable because specific instances of conduct may not be used to show character.

    (b)   objectionable because Berger's conduct may not be proved by introducing character evidence.

    (c)   objectionable because Berger's character may not be proved by introducing character evidence.

    (d)   unobjectionable as calling for evidence of habit.

8.   Same facts as above. Berger's own attorney asks him, "Did Kalish tell you that the dog that bit him was bigger than your dog?" The trial judge should rule the question objectionable because the question:

    (a)   is irrelevant.

    (b)   lacks a proper foundation.

    (c)   is leading.

    (d)   calls for an opinion of the witness.

9.   Brown is tried for armed robbery of the First National Bank. The
      prosecution, in its case in chief, offers evidence that when Brown
      was arrested one day after the crime, he had a quantity of heroin
      and a hypodermic needle in his possession. This evidence should be:

      (a)   admitted to prove Brown's motive to commit the crime.

      (b)   admitted to prove Brown's propensity to commit crimes.

      (c)   excluded because its probative value is substantially
            outweighed by the danger of unfair prejudice.

      (d)   excluded because such evidence may be offered only to
            rebut evidence of good character offered by defendant.

10.   Same facts as above. The prosecutor offers the testimony of a
      bartender that when he saw the money in Brown's wallet, he said,
      "You must have robbed a bank," to which Brown made no reply. This
      evidence is:

      (a)   admissible to prove that Brown's conduct caused the
            bartender to believe that Brown robbed the bank.

      (b)   admissible as a statement made in the presence of the
            defendant.

      (c)   inadmissible because it would violate Brown's privilege
            against self-incrimination.

      (d)   inadmissible because Brown had no reason to respond
            to the bartender's statement.

11.   Mrs. Works sued Fidelity Insurance Co. in the federal court for the
      District of Nebraska to collect death benefits on her husband's
      insurance policy. Mr. Works mysteriously disappeared more than
      five years ago while working on a construction project in the Middle
      East. Fidelity refuses to pay, claiming Mr. Works may still be alive.
      Assume that under Neb. Rev. Stat. § 30–2207 (1979) a person not
      heard from for five years is presumed dead. The presumption has
      been interpreted to be of the Morgan variety. Mrs. Works presents
      evidence that neither she, nor her husband's employer, nor any of
      her husband's friends have heard from her husband in five years.
      She asks the court to instruct the jury as to the effect of the
      presumption. Fidelity offers no evidence other than a rigorous cross-
      examination of the plaintiff's witnesses. The court should instruct
      the jury that:

      (a)   it must presume Mr. Works is dead.

      (b)   if it finds Mr. Works has not been heard from for five
            years, it may infer that Mr. Works is dead.

    (c)   if it finds Mr. Works has not been heard from for five years, it must find he is dead.

    (d)   it must find Mr. Works has not been heard from in five years unless Fidelity proves it is more likely than not that he has been heard from.

12.   Same facts and law as in the preceding question, except that Fidelity presents a witness, Thorson, who says he talked to Mr. Works in Egypt two years ago. Instead of giving the instruction in the preceding question, the court should:

    (a)   refuse to instruct the jury on the effect of the presumption because the basic fact has been controverted.

    (b)   refuse to instruct the jury on the effect of the presumption because the presumed fact has been controverted.

    (c)   instruct the jury to find Mr. Works is alive if they believe Thorson.

    (d)   instruct the jury that if they find that Mr. Works has not been heard from for five years to find that Mr. Works is dead unless Fidelity convinces them it is more likely than not that he is alive today.

13.   Kirst was hit at a street crossing by an automobile driven by Gardner. At the trial Kirst called Lyons, Gardner's mechanic, to testify that one day after the accident he installed new brake linings on Gardner's car. The trial judge should rule Lyons' testimony:

    (a)   admissible because it tends to prove negligence on the part of Gardner.

    (b)   admissible because it is an admission by a party-opponent defined as not hearsay by Rule 801(d)(2).

    (c)   inadmissible under Rule 407 because it is a subsequent remedial measure.

    (d)   inadmissible because it is hearsay not within any exception.

14.   Same facts as in the preceding question. Frank is called to testify that Gardner enjoyed a reputation for being a safe and prudent driver. The trial judge should rule Frank's testimony:

    (a)   admissible because where there are no unbiased eyewitnesses to an accident, his reputation as a safe driver may be used to prove that Gardner acted in conformity with his reputation at the time in question.

    (b)   admissible if Frank first testifies that he has personal knowledge of Gardner's driving habits.

    (c)   inadmissible because evidence of his reputation as a safe and prudent driver cannot be used to prove that Gardner acted in conformity with that reputation at the time in question.

    (d)   admissible because Mrs. Kirst opened the door to receipt of this testimony by filing her action.

15. At the request of police, the teller who was robbed prepared a sketch bearing a strong likeness to Brown, but the teller died in an automobile accident before Brown was arrested. At trial the prosecution offers the sketch. The sketch is:

    (a)   admissible as an identification of a person after perceiving him.

    (b)   admissible as past recollection recorded.

    (c)   inadmissible as hearsay not within any exception.

    (d)   inadmissible as an opinion of the teller.

16. Same facts as above. Brown testified on direct examination that he had never been in the First National Bank. His counsel asks, "What, if anything, did you tell the police when you were arrested?" If his answer would be, "I told them I had never been in the bank," this answer would be:

    (a)   admissible to prove Brown had never been in the bank.

    (b)   admissible as a prior inconsistent statement.

    (c)   inadmissible as hearsay not within any exception.

    (d)   inadmissible because it was a self-serving statement by a person with a substantial motive to fabricate.

17. Same facts as above. On cross-examination of Brown, the prosecutor asks Brown whether he was convicted the previous year of tax fraud. This question is:

    (a)   proper to show that Brown is inclined to lie.

    (b)   proper to show that Brown is inclined to steal money.

    (c)   improper because the conviction has insufficient similarity to the crime charged.

    (d)   improper because the probative value of the evidence is outweighed by the danger of unfair prejudice.

18.   Claude sued Bernie for injuries Claude received in an automobile accident. Claude claimed Bernie was negligent in (a) exceeding the posted speed limit of 35 m.p.h., (b) failing to keep a lookout, and (c) crossing the center line. Bystander, Claude's eyewitness, testified on cross-examination that Bernie was wearing a green sweater at the time of the accident. Bernie's counsel calls Donna to testify that Bernie's sweater was blue. Donna's testimony is:

   (a)   admissible as substantive evidence of a material fact.

   (b)   admissible as bearing on Bystander's truthfulness and veracity.

   (c)   inadmissible because it has no bearing on the capacity of Bystander to observe.

   (d)   inadmissible because it is extrinsic evidence of a collateral matter.

19.   Same facts as above. Bernie testified on his own behalf that he was going 30 m.p.h. On cross-examination, Claude's counsel did not question Bernie with regard to his speed. Subsequently, Claude's counsel calls Officer to testify that, in his investigation following the accident, Bernie told him he was driving 40 m.p.h. Officer's testimony is:

   (a)   admissible as a prior inconsistent statement.

   (b)   admissible as an admission of a party-opponent.

   (c)   inadmissible because it lacks a foundation.

   (d)   inadmissible because it is hearsay not within any exception.

20.   Personal injury action by P, an auto mechanic, against D, a tire manufacturer, after P was injured trying to mount a two-piece rim wheel assembly on a trailer axle. P alleges that the rim assembly was negligently designed. To prove that P negligently handled the rim assembly, D wishes to offer evidence that over a six-year period, P often appeared at work drunk, that he carried a cooler of beer in his truck, and that he often drank on the job. This evidence is:

   (a)   impermissible use of opinion evidence.

   (b)   impermissible use of character evidence under Rule 404(a).

   (c)   admissible to prove a common scheme or plan under Rule 404(b).

   (d)   admissible habit evidence under Rule 406.

21. To prove that X is dead, a party calls W, who testifies that she recently went to a cemetery where she saw a tombstone that read, "X. 4/10/25–5/2/95." This testimony is:

    (a)   inadmissible because it violates the Original Writing Rule.

    (b)   inadmissible because a tombstone can be easily faked or misread and is therefore unreliable.

    (c)   inadmissible because it is hearsay for which no exception applies.

    (d)   admissible.

22. P consulted his attorney about his personal injury case. The attorney referred P to Doctor X for the purpose of examination and preparation of a report for the attorney's assistance in preparing the trial. X did not treat P. X will not testify at trial. Defendant wishes to depose X about what P said to X. P objects. The court's *best* response would be:

    (a)   this comes within the attorney-client privilege.

    (b)   this comes within the physician-patient privilege.

    (c)   since the doctor did not treat and is not a member of the bar, it cannot fall within either privilege.

    (d)   the statements are subject to discovery, even if not admissible against P at trial.

23. Gradwohl is on trial for the murder of his wife. The prosecution claims that Gradwohl committed the murder by poisoning his wife with bichloride of mercury. Gradwohl's defense is that his wife committed suicide. Gradwohl is called to testify on his own behalf concerning matters surrounding the death of his wife. On cross-examination he is asked, "Isn't it true you were convicted of perjury three years ago?" The trial judge should rule the question:

    (a)   improper unless the crime was punishable by at least one year in prison.

    (b)   proper because on cross-examination counsel may inquire into such a matter as bearing directly upon the credibility of the witness.

    (c)   improper because the prosecution may not introduce evidence of Gradwohl's bad character until Gradwohl has opened the door by introducing evidence of his good character.

    (d)   improper because cross-examination is limited to matters testified to on direct examination.

24. Same facts as in the preceding question. Assume that Gradwohl denies that he has ever been convicted of perjury. If the prosecution offers in evidence a certified copy of the official court record of his conviction, the trial judge should rule the record:

    (a) admissible because counsel is not bound by Gradwohl's denial of the conviction but must prove it by extrinsic evidence.

    (b) admissible because the perjury conviction is relevant to the issue of Gradwohl's guilt.

    (c) inadmissible because the Original Writing Rule requires the original court record of Gradwohl's conviction to be produced.

    (d) inadmissible because specific instances of bad conduct of the accused may not be proved through the use of extrinsic evidence.

25. P has the burden of proving that D received a particular letter. There is a Thayer type presumption that a properly addressed and mailed letter was received. P testifies that he properly addressed and mailed it. D testifies about his routine office procedures designed to insure his prompt receipt of all incoming mail, and that he did not receive the letter. Which of the following is the most appropriate instruction: "Ladies and gentlemen of the jury, I charge you that

    (a) in order to find for P you must find that D received the letter by a preponderance of the evidence, and you may consider the fact that P testified that he mailed it and the fact that D denied receiving it in arriving at your decision."

    (b) if you find that the letter was properly addressed and mailed, then D must convince you by a preponderance of the evidence that he did not receive it."

    (c) if you find that it is more likely than not that the letter was mailed, then you must find that it was received unless you find that it is more likely than not that it was not received."

    (d) the evidence whether the letter was received is conflicting. You may consider that the law presumes that a letter properly addressed and posted has been received, along with the other evidence in the case in deciding whether P has discharged his burden of proof."

COMPREHENSIVE EXAMS
MULTIPLE CHOICE EXAM II

1. Driver ran into and injured Walker, a pedestrian. Walker's counsel wishes to prove that two months after the accident Driver went to Walker and offered $1,000 to settle Walker's $5,000 claim. The trial judge should rule this evidence:

   (a) admissible as an admission of a party-opponent.

   (b) admissible as an admission to show Driver's liability, provided the court gives a cautionary instruction that the statement should not be considered as bearing on the issue of damages.

   (c) inadmissible since it is not relevant either to the question of liability or the question of damages.

   (d) inadmissible because even though relevant and an admission, the policy of the law is to encourage settlement negotiations.

2. Defendant was accused of stealing money from the poor box of the church. On cross-examination, he was asked by the prosecutor whether he had ever sworn falsely in his life. He answered, "No, never in my life." The prosecution now wishes to ask about the fact that the defendant lied about his law school class rank on a signed and notarized employment application, which has not been the subject of conviction.

   (a) The prosecution would be allowed to ask about the prior falsehood because it is relevant as tending to show the defendant's disposition to dishonest acts, like theft.

   (b) The prosecution would not be allowed to ask about the prior falsehood because, even if relevant to show character or disposition to commit thefts, it was not the subject of criminal conviction.

   (c) The prosecution would be allowed to question the defendant about the falsehood on cross-examination on his credibility alone.

   (d) The prosecutor would not only be able to cross-examine about the application, but also to introduce it through other witnesses if the defendant denies the allegation on cross.

3. The State charged Rose with receiving stolen property. At trial, before testifying himself, Rose called White, who testified that Rose is a man whose reputation in the community for being honest and law-abiding is excellent. On cross-examination the prosecutor asked White whether Rose had been convicted five years ago of offering a bribe to a public official. The trial judge should rule the question:

    (a)   proper as bearing on the probability of Rose's guilt.

    (b)   improper because not the best evidence of the conviction.

    (c)   improper because it calls for hearsay.

    (d)   improper in form.

4. Which one of the following is not considered acceptable evidence to authenticate a document:

    (a)   evidence that the document was received in reply to a letter written by the proponent to the purported author.

    (b)   comparison, unaided by expert testimony, by the jury of the signature with a properly authenticated exemplar.

    (c)   a comparison opinion by a lay witness that the questioned signature is the same as that contained in a properly authenticated and properly introduced exemplar.

    (d)   all of the above are acceptable (none is unacceptable).

5. Mary Potts and her parents sued Dixon for $1,000 compensatory damages, claiming pain and suffering and medical expenses in that amount arising from a dog bite. The identity of the dog that bit Mary and the amount of damages done were the only issues in the case. Plaintiffs' counsel called Dixon adversely and asked, "How much did your dog cost you?" The trial judge should rule the question objectionable because it:

    (a)   calls for an opinion of the witness.

    (b)   has no bearing on any issue in the suit.

    (c)   is leading.

    (d)   is not the best evidence of cost.

6. Same facts as above. Plaintiffs' counsel asked Dixon, "Has your dog bitten anyone in the past?" The trial judge should rule the question:

    (a)   objectionable because an animal's acts may not be proved by showing its propensity to act in a particular way.

     (b)   objectionable because the question is not qualified by asking, "To your personal knowledge, has your dog bitten anyone in the past?"

     (c)   objectionable because it calls for a conclusion of the witness.

     (d)   unobjectionable because propensity of an animal may be proved by specific instances.

7.   Same facts as above. Dixon offered to testify that, whenever he leaves his home, he invariably and automatically locks the dog in the basement. The trial judge should find the offer:

     (a)   objectionable because propensity may not be proven by specific instances.

     (b)   objectionable as calling for a self-serving declaration.

     (c)   objectionable as calling for the conclusion of the witness.

     (d)   unobjectionable as calling for evidence of habit.

8.   Same facts as above. Dixon's own attorney asked him, "Could Mary have easily mistaken another dog for yours?" The trial judge should rule the question objectionable:

     (a)   because the answer would not be the best evidence.

     (b)   as calling for an unhelpful opinion of the witness.

     (c)   as asking for a hearsay answer.

     (d)   as irrelevant to the issues of the case.

9.   Same facts as above. Dixon's own attorney asked him, "Did Mary's mother tell you that the dog that bit Mary was slightly bigger than your dog?" The trial judge should rule the question objectionable as:

     (a)   lacking proper foundation.

     (b)   asking for a conclusion of the witness.

     (c)   leading the witness.

     (d)   irrelevant.

10.   Steve brought an action against Jeremy for injuries received in an automobile accident, alleging negligence in that Jeremy was speeding and inattentive. Steve calls Terry to testify that Jeremy had a reputation in the community of being a reckless driver and was known as "dare-devil Jeremy." Terry's testimony is:

     (a)   admissible as habit evidence.

    (b)   admissible because it tends to prove that Jeremy was negligent at the time of this collision.

    (c)   inadmissible because Jeremy has not offered testimony of his own good character.

    (d)   inadmissible to show negligence.

11.   Jones was tried for the July 21, 2020, murder of David. In his case in chief, Jones called as his first witness Mary to testify to Jones's reputation in his community during the summer of 2020 as "a peaceable man." The testimony is:

    (a)   admissible as tending to prove Jones is believable.

    (b)   admissible as tending to prove Jones is innocent.

    (c)   inadmissible because Jones has not testified.

    (d)   inadmissible because reputation is not a proper way to prove character.

12.   Same facts as above. Jones called Harry to testify to alibi. On cross-examination of Harry, the prosecutor asked, "Isn't it a fact that you are Jones's first cousin?" The question is:

    (a)   proper because it goes to bias.

    (b)   proper because a relative is not competent to give reputation testimony.

    (c)   improper because the question goes beyond the scope of direct examination.

    (d)   improper because the evidence being sought is irrelevant.

13.   Owner and his employee, Driver, consult Attorney about a motor vehicle collision resulting in a suit by Litigant against Owner and Driver as joint defendants. Attorney calls Irving, his investigator, into the conference to make notes of what is said, and those present discuss the facts of the collision and Owner's insurance. Owner thereafter files a cross-claim against Driver for indemnity for any damages obtained by Litigant. Litigant calls Driver to testify in Litigant's case in chief to admissions made by Owner in the conference. On objection by Owner, the court should rule that Driver's testimony is:

    (a)   admissible because of the presence of persons in the conference other than Attorney and Owner.

    (b)   admissible because Driver is an adverse party in the lawsuit.

    (c)   inadmissible because of the attorney-client privilege.

      (d)   inadmissible because the best evidence is Irving's notes of the conference.

14.   Same facts as above. Driver calls Irving in his defense against the cross-claim. He seeks to have Irving testify to admissions made by Owner. The court should rule Irving's testimony-

      (a)   admissible because the attorney-client privilege does not apply, in suits between those conferring with him, to joint consultations with an attorney.

      (b)   admissible because the attorney-client privilege does not apply to testimony by one who does not stand in a confidential relationship with the person against whom the evidence is offered.

      (c)   admissible because the conference was not intended to be confidential since it concerned anticipated testimony in open court.

      (d)   inadmissible because Owner has not waived the attorney-client privilege.

15.   Breach of contract action by P against D. After the jury renders a verdict in favor of D, P wishes to call Juror Y to testify that Juror X brought a copy of *Black's Law Dictionary* into the jury room and read aloud the definition of "consideration" to the other jurors. The judge should:

      (a)   grant P's request.

      (b)   deny P's request because Juror Y is incompetent to testify as to this matter.

      (c)   deny P's request because Juror Y's testimony would be inadmissible hearsay.

      (d)   deny P's request because even if Juror X did read the definition of "consideration" to the other jurors, this act did not contaminate the decision-making process.

16.   Prosecution of D for burglary. D claims that she was on vacation with her boyfriend in Peru at the time the burglary took place. At trial, D calls two people who grew up in the same small town as D. Both testify that D has an excellent reputation in the community for honesty. On cross-examination, the prosecution asks both witnesses, "Have you heard that just last year, D was arrested for committing fraud?" This cross-examination is:

      (a)   proper.

      (b)   improper because the prosecution will be limited to character testimony as to the bad reputation of D for honesty.

(c)   improper because it is unfairly prejudicial to D.

(d)   improper because it is beyond the scope of the direct examination.

17.   Alan is charged with the murder of Jackson. The prosecutor introduced testimony of a police officer that Jackson told a priest administering the last rites, "I was stabbed by Alan. Since I am dying, tell him I forgive him." Thereafter, Alan's attorney offers the testimony of Keith that the day before, when Jackson believed he would live, he stated that he had been stabbed by Jack, an old enemy. The testimony of Keith is:

(a)   admissible under an exception to the hearsay rule.

(b)   admissible to impeach the dead declarant.

(c)   inadmissible because it goes to the ultimate issue in the case.

(d)   inadmissible because irrelevant to any substantive issue in the case.

18.   In a federal bank robbery trial the prosecution wants to ask the defendant (who has taken the stand) whether he filed false income tax returns the previous year. There has been no trial, conviction, or arrest for the tax offense. The prosecutor tells the court that the question is prompted by a "hunch" that the defendant is a tax evader. The defendant's best objection would be:

(a)   prior specific instances of misconduct that have not at least been the subject of an arrest may not be inquired into on cross-examination.

(b)   the prosecution's question must be asked in good faith, and a hunch does not qualify.

(c)   prior bad acts cannot be proven out of the mouth of the witness, but must be proven by calling character witnesses.

(d)   the defendant's character for truth and veracity may be attacked only with the evidence of reputation or opinion.

19.   Prosecution of D for burglary of a home at night. The prosecution calls W, who testifies that he saw the break-in and that the perpetrator was D. On cross-examination, D asks W if it isn't true that the break-in occurred on a dark street. W answers that this is true. D next asks W if it isn't true that W was in fact standing about twenty feet from the house at the time of the break-in. W confirms this. D moves to strike all of W's testimony about the break-in. The court should:

    (a)   grant the motion.

    (b)   deny the motion if it believes that the prosecution has introduced sufficient evidence from which the jury could find that W had personal knowledge.

    (c)   cite W for contempt.

    (d)   direct a verdict for D.

20. Katie and John were arrested for holding up a gas station. They were taken to police headquarters and placed in a room for interrogation. As a police officer addressing both started to give them Miranda warnings prior to the questioning, Katie said, "Look, John planned the damned thing and I was dumb enough to go along with it. We robbed the place. What else is there to say?" John said nothing. John was escorted into another room and a full written confession was then obtained from Katie. If John is brought to trial on an indictment charging him with robbery, the fact that John failed to object to Katie's statement and remained silent after Katie had implicated him in the crime should be ruled:

    (a)   admissible because his silence was an implied admission by John that he had participated in the crime.

    (b)   admissible because a statement of a participant in a crime is admissible against another participant.

    (c)   inadmissible because, under the circumstances, there was no duty or responsibility on John's part to respond.

    (d)   inadmissible because whatever Katie may have said has no probative value in a trial against John.

21. Cars driven by Pugh and Davidson collided, and Davidson was charged with driving while intoxicated in connection with the accident. She pleaded guilty and was merely fined, although under the statute the court could have sentenced her to two years in prison. Thereafter, Pugh, alleging that Davidson's intoxication had caused the collision, sued Davidson for damages. At trial, Pugh offers the properly authenticated record of Davidson's conviction. The record should be:

    (a)   admitted as proof of Davidson's character.

    (b)   admitted as proof of Davidson's intoxication.

    (c)   excluded because the conviction was not the result of a trial.

    (d)   excluded because it is hearsay not within any exception.

22.   Action by P against D to recover the value of the contents of a box that P entrusted to D to deliver to him. D claims that he carefully handled the box, never dropping or hurting it in any way. To prove that the box was damaged, P testifies that the day after the box was delivered, he had his daughter take a photo of the box. The photograph, which P produces, shows a badly mangled box, torn and crushed in many places. P claims that the photograph accurately depicts the condition of the box at the time of the delivery and moves the admission of the photograph. D objects. The court should:

     (a)   refuse to admit the photograph because the person who took it (P's daughter) has not authenticated it.

     (b)   refuse to admit the photograph because it is hearsay for which no exception applies.

     (c)   refuse to admit the photograph on grounds that the Original Writing Rule requires that the actual box be produced.

     (d)   admit the photograph.

23.   W, H's wife, has consented to testify against H at his arson trial. W proposes to testify that while alone in bed together one night H said, "I will not be home for a few days because Blinky and I are going to burn down the Opera House." H objects.

     (a)   W's testimony is inadmissible because of the husband-wife confidential communication privilege.

     (b)   The statement is admissible because the husband-wife confidential communication privilege does not apply in that the statement relates to the commission of a future crime.

     (c)   The statement would be admissible because the husband-wife confidential communication privilege does not apply if the witness' spouse has consented to testify.

     (d)   The husband-wife confidential communication privilege does not apply because of the reason in either (b) or (c), but the statement would still be inadmissible because it is hearsay.

24.   Prosecution of D for a murder that occurred in Indianapolis. D's defense is that at the time of the murder, she was in New York with W. D calls W, who testifies that he was indeed with D in New York at the time of the murder. On cross-examination, W denies ever making a statement inconsistent with his trial testimony to the grand jury as to where D was at the time of the murder. The prosecutor then shows W a certified transcript of his testimony

before the grand jury on this matter, in which W testified that at the time of the murder, he was with D in *Indianapolis*. The procedure with the transcript is:

  (a)   admissible both to impeach W's credibility and to prove that D was in Indianapolis at the time of the murder.

  (b)   admissible to impeach W's credibility but inadmissible to prove that D was in Indianapolis at the time of the murder.

  (c)   inadmissible to impeach W but admissible to prove that D was in Indianapolis at the time of the murder.

  (d)   inadmissible either to impeach W or to prove that D was in Indianapolis at the time of the murder.

25.   Prosecution of D for assault with a deadly weapon. D shot and seriously wounded V with a medieval crossbow. D claims that the crossbow went off accidentally while he was demonstrating the device to V. The prosecution calls W to testify that a week before the incident, D shot at V with a shotgun after lying in wait outside V's home, narrowly missing her. This evidence is:

  (a)   inadmissible use of character evidence by the prosecution because D has not first offered evidence of his good character.

  (b)   inadmissible to prove intent because the earlier act is too different from the act for which D is on trial.

  (c)   admissible character evidence.

  (d)   admissible to prove intent.

COMPREHENSIVE EXAMS
MULTIPLE CHOICE EXAM III

1. Murder prosecution. The prosecution calls a witness who unexpectantly testifies that the victim died of natural causes. The prosecutor now introduces a tape of the witness's earlier statement to police that the defendant was the killer. The prior statement is:

    (a) admissible.

    (b) inadmissible because the prosecutor failed to lay foundation.

    (c) admissible but only to impeach the witness.

    (d) inadmissible because it constitutes impeachment of the prosecutor's own witness.

2. David is being tried in federal court for criminal conspiracy with John to violate federal narcotics law. At trial, the prosecutor calls David's new wife, Wanda, and asks her to testify about a meeting between David and John that she observed before she married David. Which of the following is the most accurate statement of the applicable rule concerning whether Wanda may testify?

    (a) The choice is Wanda's.

    (b) The choice is David's.

    (c) Wanda is permitted to testify only if both Wanda and David agree.

    (d) Wanda is compelled to testify even if both Wanda and David object.

3. Murder prosecution. A witness called by the prosecution testifies that the victim died of natural causes. The prosecutor then asks whether the witness did not make a statement to police shortly after the crime that the defendant was the killer. The question:

    (a) violates the Original Writing Rule.

    (b) is inadmissible because the prosecutor failed to lay a foundation.

    (c) is admissible but only to impeach the witness.

    (d) is inadmissible impeachment of the prosecutor's own witness.

4.   Personal injury action by P against D arising out of a hit-and-run accident in which P was struck by a speeding car while he crossed the street. D claims that he was in another state at the time of the accident and that therefore P sued the wrong person. P says that he got a quick look at the driver of the car just before he was struck. To prove the identity of the perpetrator, P claims that a week after the accident he picked D out of a line-up at the police station. This evidence is:

    (a)   admissible as a prior identification of a person made after perceiving him.

    (b)   admissible to prove that shortly after the accident, P believed that D was the driver of the car which struck him.

    (c)   inadmissible because P could not have seen the driver of the car that hit him, and therefore his identification of D at the police station was not supported by personal knowledge.

    (d)   inadmissible because a week after such a traumatic event, P's memory of the appearance of the driver could not have been fresh and accurate.

5.   Prosecution of D for robbing a liquor store. D's defense is that he was at a Colts game with his law fraternity at the time of the holdup. D calls three fraternity members, each of whom testifies that he or she was with D at the Colts game and that D never left his seat. D calls X, a fourth fraternity member, to testify to the same information, but the prosecution objects, saying, "Your honor, this is becoming cumulative." The court sustains the objection. D is convicted and appeals this ruling. The appellate court should:

    (a)   affirm on the basis that the trial court was within its discretion under Rule 403.

    (b)   affirm because X's proposed testimony would be irrelevant.

    (c)   reverse because X's proposed testimony makes D's defense stronger, and D has a right to put X's testimony before the jury.

    (d)   reverse because in a criminal case the court has no discretion to apply Rule 403 to relevant testimony defendant wishes to offer.

6. To prove that he had been legitimated, John, now forty-five years of age, offered in evidence a marriage certificate, apparently regular on its face and obviously an old document, which purported to reflect the marriage of John's mother to his father some three months after John's birth. John testified that he found the certificate in a trunk in the attic of his family home after the death of both of his parents. The trial judge should rule the certificate:

   (a) admissible as both properly authenticated and within the ancient documents exception to the hearsay rule.

   (b) admissible as both properly authenticated and within the records of vital statistics exception to the hearsay rule.

   (c) not admissible because not properly authenticated.

   (d) not admissible even though adequately authenticated because within no exception to the hearsay rule.

7. Prosecution of D for being a habitual criminal. Assume that in order to prove its case, the prosecution must demonstrate that D had been convicted of three felonies in the last fifteen years. At trial, the prosecution calls W, who testifies that she is a newspaper reporter whose beat has been the courthouse for twenty years. W then testifies that she has personally observed three trials in which D was found guilty of felonies. The testimony concerning W's observations is:

   (a) inadmissible because it violates the Original Writing Rule.

   (b) inadmissible because it is hearsay for which no exception applies.

   (c) inadmissible because W lacks personal knowledge.

   (d) admissible.

8. Negligence action by P against Ace Department Store following a slip and fall in Ace's toy department. To prove negligence, P wishes to testify that ten minutes after he fell, X, the toy department manager, said to him, "Kids come in and pull the toys off the shelf all the time. I should have my people clean the aisles more often. Sorry." X was fired the day after the accident. P's testimony is:

   (a) inadmissible unless Ace authorized X to speak for it.

   (b) inadmissible because X is not a party.

   (c) inadmissible because X no longer works for Ace.

   (d) admissible as an admission of an employee.

9.   Personal injury action by P against D arising out of an automobile accident. At trial, D testifies that he was driving carefully at the time of the accident. On cross-examination, P's counsel asks D if it isn't true that D has liability insurance covering him up to $1 million per accident. Under the facts as just related, this question is:

   (a)   proper because at least a weak inference of negligence may be drawn from D's having extensive liability coverage.

   (b)   proper because relevant to D's ability to satisfy any judgment against him.

   (c)   improper because irrelevant.

   (d)   improper because introduction of such evidence might cause the jury to decide the case on an improper basis.

10.   Pitt sued Dow for damages for injuries that Pitt incurred when a badly rotted limb fell from a curbside tree in front of Dow's home and hit Pitt. Dow claimed that the tree was on city property and thus was the responsibility of the city. At trial, Pitt offered testimony that a week after the accident, Dow had cut down the tree with a chain saw. The offered evidence is:

   (a)   inadmissible because there is a policy to encourage safety precautions.

   (b)   inadmissible because it is irrelevant to the condition of the tree at the time of the accident.

   (c)   admissible to show the tree was on Dow's property.

   (d)   admissible to show the tree was in a rotted condition.

11.   The Rule in Queen Caroline's Case:

   (a)   provides that a party may not impeach his own witness.

   (b)   deals only with impeachment of the very, very rich.

   (c)   has been abolished by the Federal Rules.

   (d)   is only in effect in the Principality of Monaco.

12.   Pratt sued Danvers for injuries suffered by Pratt when their automobiles collided. At trial, Pratt offers into evidence a properly authenticated letter from Danvers that says, "Your claim seems too high, but, because I might have been a little negligent, I'm prepared to offer you half of what you ask." The letter is:

   (a)   admissible as an admission by a party-opponent.

   (b)   admissible as a statement against pecuniary interest.

(c)   inadmissible because Danver's statement is a lay opinion on a legal issue.

(d)   inadmissible because Danver's statement was made in an effort to settle the claim.

13.   Legal malpractice action by P against D, P's former attorney. D represented P in a personal injury action, but P lost the case. P claims that D acted negligently in representing him because he did not relay to P a settlement offer made by the defendant in that action. D's defense in the malpractice action is that he did discuss the offer with P in great detail and that P had decided to decline it, hoping that a better offer would be forthcoming after a while. At the trial of the malpractice action, D wishes to testify that he told P about the settlement offer. This testimony is:

(a)   inadmissible hearsay.

(b)   inadmissible because of the attorney-client privilege.

(c)   hearsay but admissible under the admissions exception.

(d)   admissible non hearsay.

14.   Negligence action arising out of an auto accident. To prove damages, plaintiff's attorney pulls a document out of his briefcase, calls plaintiff to the stand, shows him the document (which appears to be a hospital bill), and asks plaintiff to identify the document. Plaintiff says he does not recognize it. Plaintiff's attorney asks the court to admit the document into evidence. Defendant says "I object! This is crazy!" The court sustains the objection. Plaintiff's attorney puts the document back in his briefcase and moves to another point. If plaintiff loses the trial and bases his appeal on the ground that the document should have been admitted, the appellate court should:

(a)   reverse on the ground that the trial court wrongly deprived plaintiff of the opportunity to prove an element of his prima facie case.

(b)   reverse on the ground that defendant did not state the grounds of his objection.

(c)   affirm on the ground that the document constituted inadmissible hearsay.

(d)   affirm on the ground that plaintiff has not preserved the point for appeal.

15. Criminal prosecution. Defense requests that all prosecution witnesses not essential to the presentation of the D.A.'s case be excluded from the courtroom. The judge denies the motion. This ruling:

    (a)   is a denial of the right of confrontation.

    (b)   is error under the Federal Rules of Evidence.

    (c)   is within the court's discretion.

    (d)   is not covered by the Federal Rules of Evidence.

16. Prosecution of D for assault with a deadly weapon on V. The assault occurred in a crowded stadium. D's defense is that he wasn't the attacker. At trial, the prosecution calls W to testify that during the attack, an unidentified bystander screamed, "The man with the punk haircut is killing that Purdue fan!" D concedes that at that time, he had a punk haircut. Evidence of this statement is:

    (a)   hearsay and inadmissible under the excited utterance exception because the bystander has not been identified.

    (b)   inadmissible because the evidence tends to impeach D by virtue of his appearance, which is impermissible.

    (c)   hearsay but admissible under the excited utterance exception.

    (d)   admissible as non hearsay to show the bystander's belief about the identity of the attacker.

17. Prosecution of D for burglary of an auto supply store. The prosecution calls W, the store owner. When asked what was stolen from the store, W lists a few items and then stops. The prosecutor is certain that other items were stolen, and in order to refresh W's recollection, she shows W a summary of items stolen, which W prepared shortly after the burglary. After giving W a chance to review the document, the prosecutor takes back the document and asks W if his memory has been refreshed. W says that it has been. The prosecutor then asks W if any other items were stolen, and W names fifteen more items. W's testimony concerning the additional items is:

    (a)   admissible.

    (b)   inadmissible because W has not testified that the document is an accurate listing of the stolen items.

    (c)   inadmissible because to refresh a witness's recollection, a party is not permitted to use a document that recites the very information the witness could not remember before looking at the document.

(d) inadmissible because the judge should rule as a matter of law that W's memory has not been refreshed.

18. Prosecution of D for murder. D's defense is an alibi. D calls W, who testifies that she was with D in Maui when the murder was occurring in Indiana. On cross-examination, the prosecutor asks W if it isn't true that just before she testified, D threatened to kill W's children if W didn't testify favorably to him. W denies this, repeating that she and D were in Maui at the time of the murder. The prosecutor then calls W2, who testifies that he was in the courtroom and overheard a conversation between D and W just before W took the stand. W2 says that D told W that if she didn't back up his story, he'd kill her kids. The evidence given by W2 is:

(a) inadmissible because it is impeachment by contradiction of W on a collateral matter.

(b) inadmissible because the prosecutor is stuck with W's answers during cross-examination.

(c) admissible to impeach D by showing that he has a propensity to lie.

(d) admissible to impeach W's testimony by showing that her testimony was influenced by improper outside pressure.

19. Civil action by P, the owner of a private day care center, against D, a newspaper publisher, for libel. P claims that an article in D's newspaper which called P a "child molester" was libelous and caused great harm to P's community standing. At trial, D calls W, a child who had attended P's day care center. W testifies that one day, P attacked him. This evidence should be:

(a) excluded because character evidence is inadmissible in civil cases.

(b) excluded because the witness's testimony must be limited to opinion or reputation.

(c) excluded because it is hearsay.

(d) admitted.

20. Personal injury action by P against D arising out of the collision of P's car with D's church bus. At trial, P calls W, who testifies that she saw D's bus swerve out of its lane and strike P's car. On cross-examination, D's counsel asks W if it isn't true that she is the vocal leader of an atheist group. The question is:

(a) proper because if true, it would show that W is incompetent to testify since she could not truthfully take the oath of a witness.

(b)   proper because if true, it might tend to impeach W by showing that her beliefs make her biased against D.

(c)   improper because it calls for an opinion as to what is meant by "vocal."

(d)   improper because a witness's religious beliefs may not be the subject of testimony at a trial.

21.   To prove that his father was married to his mother, plaintiff offers into evidence the photograph of a tombstone in his father and mother's hometown cemetery in Ireland. The photograph was taken by the plaintiff. The inscription on the tombstone reads: "Patrick O'Plaintiff (1900–1935) And His Beloved Wife Molly O'Dea O'Plaintiff (1905–1980)." The court, on objection, should rule:

(a)   the photograph is inadmissible hearsay and meets no exceptions.

(b)   the photograph is not hearsay and is admissible.

(c)   the photograph is admissible hearsay but the photograph violates the Original Writing Rule.

(d)   the photograph is admissible hearsay and does not violate the Original Writing Rule.

22.   Product liability suit. Plaintiff testifies that upon opening a can of Grue Giant sweet-and-sour peas he was shocked to see a partly decomposed mouse packed in the peas, and contracted syphilis from the shock. Plaintiff proposes to call a certain chiropractor as an expert witness to corroborate that severe shocks can cause syphilis. Such expert testimony would be:

(a)   an improper usurpation of the jury's function.

(b)   binding on the jury if the judge accepts the witness's credentials as an expert.

(c)   admissible provided only that the judge accepts the witness' credentials as an expert.

(d)   admissible if the judge accepts the witness' credentials as an expert and finds in addition that the expert's testimony is the product of reliable principles and methods, properly applied to sufficient facts, data, or opinions.

23.   Attorney Berger received a telephone call from Duncan, an acquaintance of Berger. Duncan asked Berger to arrange the return of a valuable Western art painting that had been taken from the Sheldon Art Gallery. Although he was not paid anything for his efforts, Berger returned the painting to the Sheldon Art Gallery. In a subsequent prosecution of Duncan for burglary, the prosecution called Berger to testify as to the identity of the person who asked him to return the painting. Berger asserted that the attorney-client privilege prevented him from testifying. The trial court should:

(a)   overrule Berger's privilege claim because the attorney-client privilege extends only to confidential communications, and it can never protect the identity of a client.

(b)   overrule Berger's privilege claim because Berger was not paid for his services.

(c)   overrule Berger's privilege claim if it is determined that Berger was not acting in his professional capacity in returning the painting.

(d)   overrule Berger's privilege claim, unless it is shown that he was authorized to claim the privilege on behalf of Duncan.

24.   Civil action for assault by P against D. P alleges that at a basketball game between I.U. and U.C.L.A., D threw a chair at him, narrowly missing him. At trial, D testifies that he was mad about something that happened on the court and threw the chair in a certain direction thinking there was nobody sitting in that area. On cross-examination, to impeach D's credibility, P's counsel offers a certified copy of a public record dated five years previously that adjudges D guilty of the crime of forgery. D's attorney objects to the question. The trial court should:

(a)   overrule the objection if it finds that the probative value of the evidence outweighs its prejudicial effect.

(b)   overrule the objection regardless of the balance of probative value and prejudicial effect.

(c)   sustain the objection because impeachment by prior conviction is not permissible in civil actions.

(d)   sustain the objection because the public record constitutes improper use of extrinsic evidence to impeach D.

25.   Racial discrimination action by P, a landlord, against a City Housing
       Authority (CHA). P, a black person, participated in a federal
       subsidized program that provided rent assistance to low-income
       persons. CHA's job was to determine the maximum rent that P could
       charge, based on the market rate in the area for similar units. P
       claims that CHA permitted white owners to charge more than he was
       allowed to charge for substantially similar units. To prove that it did
       not discriminate, CHA offered in evidence a chart that summarized
       a study it conducted after P filed the action. The chart summarized
       agreements that had been signed with other landlords, notes of
       inspectors, conversations with landlords, and other information
       which tended to demonstrate that P was permitted to charge the
       same rents as others. This chart is:

       (a)   inadmissible because the full study, and not a summary
              of it, must be offered.

       (b)   inadmissible because it contains hearsay statements to
              which no exception applies.

       (c)   hearsay but admissible because the chart is a public
              record.

       (d)   inadmissible because the study, conducted after the suit
              was filed, was irrelevant.

COMPREHENSIVE EXAMS
MULTIPLE CHOICE EXAM IV

1. Civil rights action by P, a prison inmate, against D, the state in which the prison is located. The action arises out of an alleged beating that the inmate suffered at the hands of prison guards. D claims that P attacked the guards and that their actions were therefore in self-defense and for the purpose of preventing his escape. At trial, P testifies that the guards attacked him without provocation. D then offers evidence that on eight occasions prior to the incident in question, P had attacked prison authorities. This evidence is:

   (a) admissible only to prove that P was the aggressor in the fight.

   (b) admissible only to prove that P had a character trait to be violent.

   (c) admissible only to attack P's credibility.

   (d) inadmissible.

2. A "conclusive presumption":

   (a) may be rebutted only by clear and convincing evidence.

   (b) shifts the burden of persuasion to the party against whom it operates.

   (c) will be declared invalid unless there is a rational connection between the basic (foundation) facts and the presumed facts.

   (d) cannot be rebutted even if a party possesses positive proof that it would lead to factual inaccuracy in the particular case.

3. Personal injury action by P against D arising out of an auto accident between a car driven by P and one driven by X. P claims that D lent his car to X knowing that X was a reckless driver. D admits that X drove recklessly but denies that he was aware of X's reckless driving record. P calls W to testify that X had been arrested for reckless driving four times in the year prior to P's lending him his car. This evidence is:

   (a) inadmissible use of character to prove conduct on a specific occasion.

(b)   inadmissible because only reputation or opinion may be used in this situation.

(c)   inadmissible because only convictions, not arrests, may be used.

(d)   admissible because character is in issue.

4.   Personal injury action by P against D arising out of an automobile accident. At trial, P calls W, who testifies that he is in the business of reconstructing automobiles following accidents in order to determine the precise chain of events and that he has been doing so for approximately seven years. P then begins to ask W whether he examined the automobiles involved in the accident at issue, but D objects to such testimony. At this point, the trial court should:

(a)   rule that W is not competent as an expert because the jury does not need an expert in order to draw its conclusions about the cause of the accident.

(b)   rule that W is not competent to testify because P has produced insufficient evidence as to W's expertise.

(c)   permit D to ask W questions at that point to determine whether he is qualified as an expert, even though P has not yet finished his direct examination of W.

(d)   rule that D must wait until P has completed his direct examination of W and then permit D to ask W questions in order to determine whether he is qualified as an expert.

5.   Personal injury action. To prove that defendant's red car ran a red light, plaintiff offers the testimony of X, who was standing alone on a street corner near the accident scene. X will testify that an hour after the accident, while sitting at home alone thinking about what happened, he muttered to himself, "I wonder why that red car went through the red light." X's testimony as to his muttered statement is:

(a)   inadmissible hearsay.

(b)   admissible because there was no assertion made to anyone, and therefore, the statement isn't hearsay.

(c)   inadmissible because speculation.

(d)   admissible as a contemporaneous utterance.

6.   In a personal injury action, plaintiff requests the court to take judicial notice of a 1910 city ordinance prohibiting the riding of bicycles in the park after dark. Defendant, while riding his bicycle, hit plaintiff at 11 p.m.

       (a)   This is a legislative fact not covered by the Federal Rules of Evidence.

       (b)   This is an adjudicative fact but is not judicially noticeable.

       (c)   This is an adjudicative fact not noticeable because it is not a commonly known fact.

       (d)   This law may be judicially noticed even if it is not commonly known.

7.   P v. D for breach of an oral contract. As part of her case in chief, P's attorney calls D to the stand and asks, "Isn't it true that you agreed to purchase five tons of manure per month from P?" This procedure is:

       (a)   improper because one party may not call the other party as part of her case in chief.

       (b)   improper because it is impermissible to lead a witness on direct examination except with regard to uncontroverted or preliminary matters.

       (c)   proper because the subject of the question constitutes an act of independent legal significance.

       (d)   proper because a party may call the adverse party and examine him as though on cross-examination.

8.   After a slip and fall on icy steps leading to D's jewelry store, P filed a negligence action seeking compensatory damages. D denies negligence. To prove D's net worth, P calls D's accountant, shows her a document, and asks the accountant to identify it. The accountant says that it is a financial statement she prepared for D. P moves the admission of the document. The evidence is:

       (a)   inadmissible because of privilege.

       (b)   inadmissible because it is irrelevant.

       (c)   inadmissible because the document has not been properly authenticated.

       (d)   admissible.

9.   Civil action for battery brought by P against D arising out of a fight
        at a Colts game. P was knocked unconscious and was carried out of
        the stadium on a stretcher and rushed to the hospital. He did not
        regain consciousness for three days. When he did regain
        consciousness, he saw D and a nurse standing over him. An angry
        look immediately came over P's face, and P exclaimed, "You bastard!
        You attacked me from behind when all I was doing was watching the
        game!" This statement is:

        (a)   admissible to show P's state of mind but not to prove the
               truth of the matter asserted.

        (b)   admissible to prove that D attacked P if the judge finds
               that a reasonable jury could believe that P was still
               under the influence of the event and did not have time
               to reflect.

        (c)   admissible to prove that D attacked P if the judge finds
               that P was still under the influence of the event and did
               not have time to reflect.

        (d)   admissible as an admission of a party-opponent
               regardless of whether P was acting under the influence
               of the exciting event.

10.   Action for an accounting. Defendant's lawyer receives his client's
        books from the client and turns them over to an accountant who
        renders a report to the lawyer stating that the defendant owes
        plaintiff $250,000. At the trial, which of the following is admissible
        over a privilege objection:

        (a)   the accountant's subsequent discussion with the
               attorney concerning the report.

        (b)   the accountant's report.

        (c)   the books.

        (d)   all of the above.

11.   Frank sues Lenich for personal injuries arising out of an automobile
        accident. To prove damages Frank calls Doctor Tremper, a specialist
        in radiology, who is willing to testify as to his opinion of the extent of
        Frank's injuries based on his analysis of certain X-rays that were
        taken of Frank after the accident. The x-rays themselves have not
        been admitted into evidence. The court should rule that Doctor
        Tremper's testimony is:

        (a)   inadmissible since the contents of the X-rays cannot be
               proved through secondary evidence, such as Doctor
               Tremper's testimony.

(b) admissible because the Original Writing Rule does not apply to X-rays.

(c) admissible if experts in radiology reasonably rely on X-rays to form opinions as to the extent of a person's injuries.

(d) admissible because the Original Writing Rule applies to writings only and not to oral testimony, such as Doctor Tremper's.

12. Prosecution of D for the murder of two gang members on a subway. The prosecution alleges that D dressed in a bright blue spandex outfit with the words "Subway Protector" printed on the front, that he got on the train, walked from car to car brandishing a handgun, saw the gang members, screamed "Scum!" and shot them. D claims that he was at home baking a quiche when the crimes occurred. In his defense, D calls three witnesses who each testify that in their opinion, D is a nonviolent person. The prosecution calls W to testify that a week after the shooting, D was convicted of another subway shooting in which he was found to have worn a similarly described outfit and yelled "Scum!" before firing the fatal shots. Evidence of D's conviction for the other crime is:

(a) inadmissible use of a specific instance of conduct to prove D's character.

(b) inadmissible because the probative value of the evidence is greatly outweighed by its prejudicial impact.

(c) admissible to prove *modus operandi,* which is in turn relevant to prove identity.

(d) admissible use of bad character evidence to rebut D's good character evidence.

13. Defamation action by P against D arising out of an article in D's newspaper that referred to P, an accountant, as a "mild-mannered accountant by day but an obnoxious barfly by night." P alleges that as a result of the article, he has suffered severe mental distress. Prior to trial, D takes the deposition of Y, P's psychiatrist. At the deposition, which P does not personally attend, D asks X what information he learned in the course of the psychotherapeutic relationship. X refuses to answer on ground of the psychotherapist-patient privilege. D seeks a court order requiring X to answer the questions. The court should:

(a) grant the order because even though X will not be required to testify at trial about these matters, he must answer questions asked in the course of discovery as long as the questions are reasonably calculated to lead to the discovery of admissible evidence.

    (b)   grant the order because P, the holder of the privilege, has failed to claim it.

    (c)   grant the order because by seeking damages for emotional distress, P has waived the privilege with regard to that subject.

    (d)   deny the order.

14. P sues D to rescind a land sale contract. P alleges D fraudulently misrepresented that the land was not in a flood plain. The trial is in 2010. After D testifies on direct, P seeks to impeach D with the following certified court documents. Which of the following has the best chance of being admitted:

    (a)   a misdemeanor stock fraud conviction in 2005.

    (b)   a civil judgment against D for stock fraud in 2009.

    (c)   a felony assault conviction in 1998.

    (d)   a misdemeanor forgery and uttering of a check conviction in 1995.

15. Breach of contract action by P against D, an automobile manufacturer, for failure to deliver five specified cars to P's dealership by August 1, 2020. D claims that it delivered all of the cars by the agreed date. At trial, the judge takes the stand and testifies that he was driving by P's dealership on July 25, 2020, and that he saw these five cars on the lot. P makes no objection. D offers no further evidence on the question of the date of delivery of the cars. The jury renders a verdict for D and P appeals. The appellate court should:

    (a)   affirm because P did not object to the judge's testifying.

    (b)   affirm because the error was not prejudicial.

    (c)   reverse because the judge has not stated how he knew that the five cars he saw while driving past the dealership were the ones over which the suit was brought.

    (d)   reverse even in the absence of an objection.

16. Personal injury action by P against D arising out of a slip and fall on D's front porch in which P is seeking $10,000. At trial, P wishes to testify that immediately following the accident D offered to pay P $150 "to end this matter here and now." This evidence is:

    (a)   inadmissible hearsay.

    (b)   inadmissible as an offer to compromise.

    (c)   admissible as an admission of D.

    (d)   admissible if the trial court believes that the probative value of the evidence substantially outweighs its prejudicial impact.

17.   Action by P against D to recover an emerald ring that P claims X, now deceased, gave him many years ago. D, X's beneficiary, claims he's entitled to the ring. To prove that the ring was given to him, P offers a page from X's 1945 diary. On that page, X wrote, "I'm glad I gave P that emerald ring last week to show my gratitude for all that P has done for me." The diary was found in X's night stand, next to his bed. The page of the diary is:

    (a)   inadmissible hearsay.

    (b)   inadmissible because of the Dead Man's Statute.

    (c)   inadmissible because it has not been properly authenticated.

    (d)   hearsay but admissible as an ancient document.

18.   Leading questions are proper:

    (a)   on cross-examination.

    (b)   to refresh recollection.

    (c)   on direct examination of the opposing party on matters crucial to the case.

    (d)   all of the above.

19.   After the death of his rich aunt, Wilma, Lenich was left with her entire estate and named as its executor under her will. At the probate hearing his cousin, Horatio, contested the will on the ground that Lenich had exercised undue influence over Wilma. During the probate hearing Horatio called Attorney Hoffman and asked him to testify as to the reasons Wilma expressed for changing her will during the previous year. Lenich promptly asserted a claim to the attorney-client privilege on behalf of his aunt's estate. The claim by Lenich of the attorney-client privilege should be:

    (a)   overruled because its holder, Wilma, is not available to claim the privilege.

    (b)   sustained because, as Wilma's executor, Lenich can claim the privilege on her behalf.

    (c)   overruled because as Wilma's attorney, Hoffman, rather than Lenich, should claim it on her behalf.

    (d)   overruled because Lenich and Horatio both claim a right to Wilma's estate, and the communication is relevant to the validity of their claims.

20. Civil action for personal injuries arising out of an auto accident. Plaintiff calls a witness, establishes that the witness saw the accident, and then says, "Now tell us exactly what you saw." This question:

   (a) is objectionable as ambiguous.

   (b) calls for a narrative, but even after proper objection the trial judge may permit it in her discretion.

   (c) calls for a narrative, and the trial judge must sustain a proper objection.

   (d) is proper.

21. Will contest. To prove that the will was properly executed, one party calls the lawyer who prepared the will to testify that though he does not specifically remember the execution of this will, he has written hundreds of wills and always has them executed according to statutory requirements. This evidence is:

   (a) inadmissible for lack of personal knowledge.

   (b) inadmissible because of attorney-client privilege.

   (c) admissible evidence of the lawyer's character for carefulness.

   (d) admissible evidence of habit to prove conduct on the occasion in question.

22. Personal injury suit arising out of the collision of cars driven by a rabbi and a Roman Catholic bishop. A witness testifies that both were at fault. On cross-examination, the witness is asked if he is a member of the Ku Klux Klan (which preaches dislike of Jews and Catholics). The question:

   (a) is improper innuendo upon the witness's character.

   (b) is proper impeachment if asked "in good faith."

   (c) is irrelevant.

   (d) violates the rule against impeaching a witness on the basis of his religious opinions.

23. Personal injury action by P against D arising out of the collision of two small airplanes. At trial, P calls W, an expert in the field of accident reconstruction. W testifies that following the collision, she examined the remains of the two aircraft, interviewed two occurrence witnesses to the accident, and read two articles in a technical journal called "Accident Reconstructionist." She also testifies that each of these sources is of a kind upon which accident reconstruction experts generally rely. Finally, she testifies that on the basis of the information learned from these sources, she believes that D's plane crashed into the side of P's plane. This testimony is:

    (a) inadmissible because it is based in part on hearsay.

    (b) inadmissible because it contains an opinion on the ultimate facts at issue in the action.

    (c) inadmissible because W's testimony alone will not suffice to establish that the sources of the information are the kind on which experts in the field reasonably rely.

    (d) admissible.

24. Wrongful death action in federal district court in Illinois. Plaintiff alleges that defendant drove recklessly and was responsible for his head-on collision with the deceased's car, as a result of which the deceased died. Defendant offers to testify that the deceased's car swerved into defendant's lane, thus causing the collision. Defendant's testimony is:

    (a) admissible.

    (b) incompetent.

    (c) an unhelpful lay opinion.

    (d) an attempt to usurp the function of the jury.

25. Prosecution of D for murder. D testifies that he did run over the victim with his snowblower, but did so accidentally. On cross-examination, for the purpose of impeachment, the prosecutor asks, "Isn't it true that five years ago you were convicted of grand larceny?" D's attorney objects to this question. Assume that grand larceny carries a sentence of two to ten years. The trial court should:

    (a) overrule the objection if it finds that the probative value of the evidence outweighs its prejudicial effect.

    (b) overrule the objection regardless of the balance of probative value and prejudicial effect.

    (c) sustain the objection because having committed grand larceny does not bear on D's credibility.

(d)   sustain the objection because the question assumes a
        fact not in evidence.

COMPREHENSIVE EXAMS
MULTIPLE CHOICE EXAM V

1.   Robbery prosecution. In the middle of his testimony, W, a key defense witness, is unable to remember his version of the facts. Defense counsel then shows W a document, after which W continues his testimony. If the prosecution claims that W's memory has not been refreshed and moves the admission of the document into evidence, the judge should:

   (a)   admit W's testimony if she believes that a reasonable jury could find that W's memory has been refreshed and grant the prosecution's motion to admit the document.

   (b)   admit W's testimony if she believes that a reasonable jury could find that W's memory has been refreshed but deny the prosecution's motion to admit the document.

   (c)   admit W's testimony if she believes that W's memory has been refreshed and grant the prosecution's motion to admit the document.

   (d)   admit W's testimony if she believes that W's memory has been refreshed but deny the prosecution's motion to admit the document.

2.   Burglary prosecution. A witness testifies that he saw the defendant with the loot the day after the crime. On cross-examination, the witness is asked if he was drunk at the time. This cross-examination:

   (a)   is proper to impeach.

   (b)   is improper because it is beyond the scope of the direct.

   (c)   is improper because it is not tailored to character for truth and sincerity.

   (d)   is improper because it is extrinsic.

3.   Criminal prosecution of D for burglary of an ice cream store. At trial, the prosecutor calls W to testify that after D had been taken into custody and advised of his Miranda rights, D told the prosecutor that he would plead guilty to a lesser charge. This evidence is:

   (a)   inadmissible hearsay.

   (b)   inadmissible as an offer to compromise.

   (c)   admissible hearsay.

(d)   admissible if the court finds that its probative value substantially outweighs its prejudicial impact.

4.   In a forgery trial the prosecution offers a two-year-old armed robbery (a felony) arrest to impeach the defendant who has testified. Which is the most appropriate ruling?

(a)   The prior arrest is admissible only if the court concludes that the probative value of the arrest outweighs its prejudicial impact.

(b)   Armed robbery involves dishonesty or false statement, therefore the court has no discretion to exclude the arrest.

(c)   The arrest should be excluded because the character for lack of truth and veracity of a defendant who testifies may not be attacked until the defendant offers evidence of his good character.

(d)   The arrest should be excluded.

5.   Prosecution of D for burglarizing the home of X at 1:00 in the morning on a certain day. D claims that he was home in bed at the time. To prove that he was home at 1:00 a.m., D testifies that he works the 2:00 a.m. to 11:00 a.m. shift at the local plant and that on the day in question, as always, he set his alarm clock to wake him up at 1:00. He then offers to testify that he woke up to a ringing sound, asked his wife what time it was, and that she answered, "1:00." His testimony relating to his wife's statement concerning the time is:

(a)   inadmissible hearsay.

(b)   hearsay but admissible under the present sense impression exception.

(c)   inadmissible evidence of habit or custom.

(d)   admissible.

6.   Burglary prosecution. On direct examination, the prosecutor hands the complaining witness a document and says, "After looking at this piece of paper, can you remember what items were missing from your house after the burglary?" The question is objectionable and the answer will be inadmissible:

(a)   as a lay opinion.

(b)   if the defense lawyer has not been shown the document before the trial.

(c)   if it has not been shown that the witness's recollection needs refreshing.

      (d)   if the paper does not list missing items.

7.   Personal injury action arising out of an intersection collision between a car driven by defendant and a bicycle ridden by plaintiff. To prove that he stopped at the stop sign in the intersection, defendant offers to testify that just after the accident he got out of his car, walked over to plaintiff, and said, "I stopped at that stop sign, just like I do three times a day every day." This statement:

      (a)   is inadmissible hearsay.

      (b)   is hearsay but admissible as evidence of habit or custom.

      (c)   is admissible as an admission.

      (d)   is hearsay but admissible as an excited utterance.

8.   Prosecution of D, a bank teller, for embezzling money from the bank. D claims that he never took any money from the bank. The prosecution calls W to testify that a year before D went to work for the bank, he stole $1,000 that W had given him to carry to W's aging grandmother. This evidence is:

      (a)   inadmissible character evidence.

      (b)   inadmissible because W should have testified that he'd heard that D had stolen the $1,000, not that D actually had done so.

      (c)   admissible to prove identity.

      (d)   admissible as an admission of D since his prior act was assertive conduct.

9.   Murder prosecution. Defendant admits killing the victim but claims self-defense. The prosecution calls an officer who saw the scene of the crime and shows her a photograph of the horribly mutilated victim lying in a pool of blood. The officer states that though she did not take the photograph herself, she knows that it accurately depicts the scene of the crime as it was when she arrived. The photograph is:

      (a)   inadmissible because it is irrelevant.

      (b)   inadmissible because, though relevant, its probative value is substantially outweighed by its prejudicial impact.

      (c)   inadmissible because it has not been properly authenticated.

      (d)   admissible.

10.   Criminal prosecution of D for the axe murder of V. D's defense is self-
       defense. At trial, D calls W, who testifies that he has known D for ten
       years and that in his opinion, D is totally nonviolent. On cross-
       examination of W, the prosecutor asks: "Isn't it true that two years
       ago, you participated in a riot at a rock concert?" On objection by D,
       the prosecutor argues that the question goes to W's credibility. Under
       the Federal Rules of Evidence, the trial court should:

   (a)   sustain D's objection because D did not attempt to
          establish that W was a credible witness, and the
          question is therefore beyond the scope of the direct
          examination.

   (b)   sustain D's objection because participation in a riot at a
          rock concert does not reflect on W's character for
          truthfulness or untruthfulness.

   (c)   overrule D's objection as long as it instructs the jury that
          it may not infer that because D was at a rock concert, he
          would lie on the witness stand.

   (d)   overrule D's objection even without the limiting instruction
          because W is not the defendant, so no undue prejudice can
          result from admission of the evidence.

11.   P sues for personal injuries and includes a claim for lost wages for
       2019. P's 2019 income tax returns were prepared by P. P supplied a
       copy of the return to his attorney to assist the attorney in evaluating
       the case. D notices P's deposition and sends to P a subpoena duces
       tecum for P's 2019 income tax return. P moves to quash the
       subpoena. The court would rule:

   (a)   the privilege for income tax returns applies.

   (b)   the Fifth Amendment privilege applies.

   (c)   the attorney-client privilege applies.

   (d)   plaintiff must produce his tax returns.

12.   Prosecution of D for conspiracy to import cocaine. The prosecution
       alleges that D was hired to pilot an airplane from Colombia to
       Louisiana containing cocaine and that D engaged in various steps in
       preparation for this trip, which was to take place next month. D's
       defense is that he is a minister who loves flying and that he had no
       involvement with drug traffic or knowledge of the cocaine business.
       To rebut this defense, the prosecution calls W who testifies that in
       2009 D had flown marijuana into the United States. This testimony
       is:

   (a)   inadmissible because irrelevant.

   (b)   inadmissible because it constitutes improper use of
          extrinsic evidence to impeach D's credibility.

(c) inadmissible use of character evidence to prove that D acted in conformity with his bad character on this occasion.

(d) admissible to show that P had knowledge of the drug trade.

13. In the Conference Report on enacted Rule 301 is found the following sentence: "If the adverse party offers no evidence contradicting the presumed fact, the court will instruct the jury that if it finds the basic fact [exists], it may presume the existence of the presumed fact." Based on your understanding of how presumptions work in civil cases under adopted Rule 301, choose the correct statement.

(a) The above-quoted statement is correct.

(b) The above-quoted statement should include a statement that the jury must find the presumed fact only if they believe the presumed fact logically follows from the basic fact.

(c) The statement above should read "the jury . . . must presume . . . the presumed fact."

(d) The statement should state that the jury must find the presumed fact because the party against whom the presumption runs has failed to meet its burden of persuasion.

14. Potts sued Dobbs on a product liability claim. Louis testified for Potts. On cross-examination, which of the following questions is the trial judge most likely to rule improper?

(a) "Isn't it a fact that you are Potts' close friend?"

(b) "Isn't it true that you are known in the community as 'Louie the Lush' because of your addiction to alcohol?"

(c) "Didn't you fail to report some income on your tax return last year?"

(d) "Weren't you convicted, seven years ago in this court, of obtaining money under false pretenses?"

15. In an intersection auto collision case, extrinsic evidence is most likely to be admissible to prove:

(a) that a witness has been convicted of simple assault (misdemeanor).

(b) that a witness is not employed where he testified he is employed.

(c)   that a witness was not standing where he testified he was standing when he observed the accident.

(d)   that a witness was not on his way to mail a letter, as he testified, when he saw the accident.

16.   Personal injury action by P against D Garbage Removal Co. P claims that as he was walking about thirty feet from D's truck, the mechanism at the back of the truck suddenly "threw" a loaded barrel at him, causing him injury. D calls W, who testifies that he has been working in garbage trucks similar to the one involved in this case for twenty years, and that the way the loading mechanism is designed, it is not possible for a barrel to be "thrown" a distance of twenty feet. W's opinion testimony is:

(a)   inadmissible because it goes to the ultimate issue.

(b)   inadmissible because W has not stated how he knows that the truck involved in this case is "similar" to the ones he has worked on for twenty years.

(c)   inadmissible because this is not a situation in which expert testimony is needed.

(d)   admissible.

17.   Action for breach of contract. Plaintiff offers in evidence a copy of a letter defendant wrote to his attorney admitting that he failed to perform. Plaintiff purloined the letter from the defense attorney's file cabinet, copied it, and returned the original.

(a)   The letter is admissible as an admission of a party-opponent.

(b)   The letter is inadmissible hearsay.

(c)   The letter is privileged.

(d)   The letter violates the Original Writing Rule.

18.   Redirect examination of a witness must be permitted in which of the following circumstances?

(a)   to reply to any matter raised in cross-examination.

(b)   only to reply to significant new matters raised in cross-examination.

(c)   only to reiterate the essential elements of the case.

(d)   only to supply significant information inadvertently omitted on direct examination.

19. Action by P against D for breach of a written contract. P alleged that he met with D in an effort to strike a bargain to sell D some Twisted Sister albums and that two days later he received a letter signed, "D," which said, in essence, "send me those great records." P claims that this was indeed D's signature and that he knows it is because he once watched D sign a credit card slip in a record store. D admits that he met with P but claims that he never sent P any letter. P moves for admission of the letter, and D objects. The court should:

    (a)   admit the letter if it finds that D wrote the letter.

    (b)   admit the letter if it believes that a reasonable jury could find that D wrote the letter.

    (c)   refuse to admit the letter because the identity of handwriting is a matter about which an expert must testify, and P has not qualified as an expert.

    (d)   refuse to admit the letter because it is inadmissible hearsay.

20. In a medical malpractice action, the defendant testifies that he does not know how many sponges he removed from the plaintiff's abdomen following surgery, that standard operating room procedure is that the nurses count all the sponges and alert the surgeon if fewer came out than went in, and that he was not alerted on this occasion. This testimony is:

    (a)   inadmissible for want of personal knowledge.

    (b)   inadmissible hearsay.

    (c)   irrelevant.

    (d)   admissible.

21. Marilyn was arrested on a murder charge. She was given Miranda warnings and refused to talk further with the police. At trial, she testified in her own defense. She recounted in some detail her whereabouts on the day of the crime and explained why she could not have committed the crime. On cross-examination and over defense objection, the prosecution emphasized the fact that she did not tell the police this story following her arrest. The prosecution thereby suggested that her testimony was false. The defendant was convicted. On appeal, she claims error in the prosecutor's cross-examination. Her conviction will most probably be:

    (a)   affirmed because defendant's silence at time of arrest is tantamount to a prior inconsistent statement, giving rise to an inference that the story was fabricated.

(b)   affirmed because defendant's silence was not used as direct evidence but only for impeachment, a purpose consistent with legitimate cross-examination.

(c)   reversed because post-arrest silence constituted defendant's exercise of her Miranda rights and use of that silence against her at trial violated due process.

(d)   reversed because to require the defense to acquaint the prosecution with defendant's testimony prior to trial would constitute unconstitutional pre-trial discovery.

22.   Powers sued Debbs for battery. At trial, Powers' witness Wilson testified that Debbs had made an unprovoked attack on Powers. On cross-examination, Debbs asks Wilson about a false claim that Wilson had once filed on an insurance policy. The question is:

(a)   proper because the conduct involved untruthfulness.

(b)   proper provided that the conduct resulted in conviction of Wilson.

(c)   improper because the impeachment involved a specific instance of misconduct.

(d)   improper because the claim form would be the best evidence.

23.   Murder prosecution. The prosecutor shows the police officer who investigated the murder a photo of the murder scene taken by a police photographer showing the victim lying in a pool of blood and asks: "Is that a fair and accurate representation of the scene as you found it when you arrived?" Answer: "Yes, it is." The photo:

(a)   is admissible.

(b)   is inadmissibly cumulative in view of the officer's availability to testify.

(c)   is not admissible unless the photographer is called to authenticate and chain of custody is established.

(d)   is a violation of the Original Writing Rule.

24.   Prosecution of D for a murder that took place in Chicago. At trial, D testifies that he was in Monaco visiting with a princess when the murder was committed. On cross-examination, to impeach D's credibility, the prosecution asks D whether it isn't true that when D's lawyer initially interviewed him at the police station following his arrest, D told the lawyer that he was in Chicago at the time of the crime. D's lawyer asserts the attorney-client privilege. The trial court should:

     (a)   overrule the objection because D, not the lawyer, must assert the privilege.

     (b)   overrule the objection because the prosecutor's question goes only to D's credibility, not to establish that D was in fact in Chicago.

     (c)   overrule the objection because the privilege protects only the communication, not the information.

     (d)   sustain the objection.

25.   Product liability suit. Plaintiff introduces a can with a printed label identifying the contents as Grue Giant sweet-and-sour peas. Plaintiff testifies that while enjoying these peas he discovered among them a partially decomposed mouse. He introduces the can as evidence that Grue Giant packed and distributed the item. The exhibit is:

     (a)   inadmissible without extrinsic authentication.

     (b)   inadmissible as not the best evidence.

     (c)   inadmissible extrinsic evidence.

     (d)   admissible without extrinsic authentication.

COMPREHENSIVE EXAMS
MULTIPLE CHOICE EXAM VI

1. Prosecution of D for drug smuggling. D's defense is that he had no involvement in the drug trade, and that he did not know that the plane he was flying from South America to Florida contained drugs. To rebut this defense, the prosecution offers to prove that on three prior occasions, D had flown planeloads of drugs from Central America to Texas. D's strongest argument for keeping out this evidence is:

   (a) that it is impermissible use of character evidence to prove that he had the propensity to commit this crime.

   (b) that even if the evidence is admissible to prove knowledge of the drug trade, the chance that the jury will consider the evidence to show D's propensity to commit the crime creates a possibility of unfair prejudice which greatly outweighs the probative value of the evidence.

   (c) that the prior acts are not sufficiently similar to the present one to be admissible on the issue of knowledge.

   (d) that the evidence is irrelevant to the question of whether he committed the crime for which he is on trial.

2. Prosecution of D for the murder of V with a sawed-off shotgun. At trial, the prosecutor calls W, D's wife, and asks her whether D came home with a sawed-off shotgun on the night of the murder. W refuses to answer, claiming privilege. The prosecution moves to compel her to answer the question. The court should:

   (a) not compel her to answer because of the privilege for confidential marital communications.

   (b) not compel her to answer because of the privilege not to testify against her husband.

   (c) compel her to answer because of the crime or fraud exception.

   (d) compel her to answer because D, not W, is the holder of the privilege.

3. Negligence action by P against D, a babysitter, for injuries suffered by P's one-year-old child X when X fell out of the door of D's moving car. P had given D permission to take X on a ride. P claims that X fell out the car door because D failed to lock the door and X managed to open it. To prove that he locked the door, D testifies that although he does not specifically remember locking the door on the occasion in question, he "always" locks all the car doors before starting the engine. This testimony is:

    (a)   inadmissible evidence of a character trait of carefulness.

    (b)   inadmissible because it is speculation.

    (c)   admissible evidence of habit.

    (d)   admissible evidence of a character trait of carefulness.

4. Breach of contract action by X against Y. X alleges that Y failed to deliver 1,000 ZZ Top albums to X's record store. Y, a record distributor, claims that he never agreed to deliver the albums. At trial, X calls W, Y's former wife, to testify that one day when they were still married, Y came home from the office and said to her, "Don't tell anyone, but I just closed one heck of a deal with X for some ZZ Top albums." Y objects to this testimony. W's testimony about Y's statement is:

    (a)   inadmissible because of the privilege for confidential marital communications.

    (b)   inadmissible hearsay.

    (c)   inadmissible because W lacks personal knowledge.

    (d)   admissible because the privilege for confidential marital communications no longer applies to Y and W.

5. Wrongful death action by P against D arising out of an automobile accident in which P's deceased, a child, was killed. At trial, P calls W, a clergyman, and asks W whether "confession" is a ritual of her religion. W answers that her religion makes no provision for a formal "confession." P then asks W whether D came to her office shortly after the accident and told W that he had just run a red light and struck a child. D makes no objection, but W refuses to answer. The court should:

    (a)   order W to answer because D has waived the privilege.

    (b)   order W to answer because no privilege is applicable.

    (c)   honor W's refusal to answer because the question calls for inadmissible hearsay.

    (d)   honor W's refusal to answer because of privilege.

6.   Personal injury action by P against D following an accident in which D's car struck P while P was in a crosswalk. P alleges that D ran through a red light and struck him. D's defense is that he was stopped at the light but was struck from behind by a car driven by W and propelled into P. At trial, D calls W, who testifies that he ran into D while D was stopped at the light. On cross-examination, P asks W if it isn't true that following the accident, D paid W $1,000 for damage done to W's car in the accident. This evidence is:

    (a)   admissible only to impeach W by showing that he has a reason to be biased in D's favor.

    (b)   admissible both to show bias and to prove that D was at fault in the accident.

    (c)   inadmissible for both purposes because the law forbids evidence of compromises for any purpose.

    (d)   inadmissible because the evidence is hearsay.

7.   Assume that in a particular civil action by P against D, it is necessary for P to prove that X was the secretary of state of the jurisdiction on July 28, 2017. At trial, P asks the court to take judicial notice of that fact and provides the judge with an official state publication listing the secretaries of state for the last one hundred years. X is listed as secretary of state from June 1, 2001, to March 15, 2018. D objects to the taking of judicial notice and asks to be permitted to call witnesses who will deny the fact. The court should:

    (a)   take judicial notice of the fact and not permit D to call his witnesses because the accuracy of the official state publication is not subject to reasonable dispute.

    (b)   take judicial notice of the fact but instruct the jury that it need not accept as conclusive that X was secretary of state on the date in question.

    (c)   refuse to take judicial notice because of D's objection.

    (d)   listen to D's witnesses and then determine the propriety of taking judicial notice.

8.   Prosecution of D for murder. The prosecution calls W to testify. Before being seated on the witness stand, the bailiff approaches W and says, "Hey! This trial is serious business. Do you affirm on your grandmother's grave that you won't lie up here?" W answers, "You bet. I swear on *both* my grandmother's *and* Old Boston's graves." D objects to W's testifying. The court should:

    (a)   refuse to allow W to testify because he has not taken a formal oath.

    (b)   refuse to allow W to testify because D's constitutional rights would be violated.

    (c)   refuse to allow W to testify if the court finds that no reasonable jury could believe W was taking his testimony seriously.

    (d)   allow D to testify.

9.   Personal injury action by P against D. At trial, P calls W, a physician. After qualifying W as an expert, P elicits testimony concerning the likely permanent nature of some of P's injuries. On cross-examination, D asks W if it isn't true that W will be paid by P following his testimony. This question is:

    (a)   improper because it is an attempt to elicit evidence of subsequent measures.

    (b)   improper because it is argumentative.

    (c)   improper because it is irrelevant.

    (d)   proper.

10.   Prosecution of D for murder of a convenience store clerk in the course of a robbery. The prosecution calls W to testify that two years ago she picked D out of a line-up following a bank robbery which she witnessed. This evidence is:

    (a)   inadmissible to prove that D acted in conformity with his past behavior but admissible to prove the identity of the perpetrator.

    (b)   inadmissible to prove either that D acted in conformity with his past behavior or to establish the identity of the perpetrator.

    (c)   admissible as a prior identification of D made after perceiving him.

    (d)   admissible to impeach D's credibility, but only if he takes the witness stand on his own behalf.

11. Personal injury action by P against D arising out of a skateboard collision. P alleges that he suffered severe head injuries in the accident. At trial, P calls W, a physician, who testifies that he was working at the hospital emergency room when P was brought in and that P was unconscious. W testifies that he asked the nurse to perform an electroencephalogram (EEG) test and that a few minutes later the nurse presented him with the test results, which consisted of a needle tracing on a long sheet of paper. P's counsel then asks W if he brought the paper with him, and W states that P's entire file (along with many others) was destroyed in a basement flood at the hospital during heavy rains. P's counsel then asks W about the results of the EEG test. D's counsel objects. The court should:

   (a) sustain the objection on the ground that the testimony would violate the Original Writing Rule.

   (b) sustain the objection on the ground that the question calls for inadmissible hearsay.

   (c) sustain the objection on the ground that W lacks personal knowledge.

   (d) overrule the objection.

12. Prosecution of D, a bank teller, for embezzling $1,000,000 from the bank over a period of years. D claims that he never took any money from the bank. To prove this, D calls three witnesses, all lifelong friends of D, who each testify that in their opinion, D is a nonviolent person. This evidence is:

   (a) inadmissible because the witnesses are obviously biased.

   (b) inadmissible character evidence because the crime for which D is charged is not a crime of violence.

   (c) admissible character evidence offered by an accused to prove lack of propensity to commit the crime.

   (d) admissible to prove lack of intent to commit the crime.

13. In the trial of a civil action, character evidence is:

   (a) never admissible.

   (b) admissible for any purpose if the trial court exercises careful discretion.

   (c) admissible only if character is in issue.

   (d) admissible if character is in issue and to impeach a witness.

14.   Prosecution of D for child abuse on X, a three-year-old. The prosecution calls X and after establishing her name, asks her what happened on the occasion that is the subject of the prosecution. X hesitates and answers in a very soft voice that she doesn't remember. The prosecutor then asks, "Weren't you with D that day?" X answers, "I guess so. I'm not sure." The prosecutor then asks, "Do you remember that D touched you a few times?" X answers, "Yes." If D moves to strike X's testimony, the court should:

    (a)   grant the motion because it is improper to lead a witness on direct examination.

    (b)   grant the motion because X has not been shown to be a competent witness.

    (c)   deny the motion if it believes that the prosecutor has reasonable grounds to state these facts to X.

    (d)   deny the motion if it believes that the prosecutor's questions are necessary to develop X's testimony.

15.   Personal injury action by P against D following an auto accident. P claims she suffered a back injury. To prove that she had sustained a back injury, P calls W, her husband, to testify that almost every day for six months after the accident, P said to him, "My back is killing me." This evidence is:

    (a)   hearsay but admissible under the exception for then existing physical sensation.

    (b)   admissible as a party admission.

    (c)   inadmissible because of the privilege protecting confidential communications between spouses.

    (d)   inadmissible because the statement was clearly self-serving and is therefore unreliable.

16.   Personal injury action by P, an apartment tenant, against D, the landlord. P fell on a dark set of stairs leading from her second floor apartment to the first floor. There was only minimal lighting on the stairs at the time of the accident. D claims that given the design of the stairwell, it was not possible to better illuminate the area. P takes the stand to testify that a month after the accident, D installed more lighting on the stairs. This evidence is:

    (a)   inadmissible evidence of subsequent remedial measures.

    (b)   inadmissible evidence of a specific instance of conduct to prove D's character.

    (c)   inadmissible to prove negligence but admissible to prove the feasibility of better lighting.

    (d)   inadmissible to prove negligence but admissible to prove that D controlled the stairwell area.

17.   Prosecution of D for driving while intoxicated and driving with an expired license. At trial, in order to prove D was driving with an expired license, the prosecution calls W, the arresting officer. W testifies that he asked to see D's license and that upon examining the license, he noted it had expired in 2015. This testimony is:

    (a)   inadmissible because it violates the Best Evidence Rule.

    (b)   inadmissible because it violates D's right to confrontation since it involves a document that the prosecution has not produced at trial.

    (c)   inadmissible because it is hearsay for which no exception applies.

    (d)   admissible because although W is testifying about the contents of a document, that document is in D's possession.

18.   Prosecution of D for assault with a deadly weapon. D shot and seriously wounded V with a shotgun. D's defense is that he did not intend to fire the gun but that it went off accidentally. The prosecution offers evidence that two days before the shooting, D caught V in bed with D's wife. This evidence is:

    (a)   inadmissible use of character evidence concerning the victim of a crime because D has not first attacked V's character.

    (b)   inadmissible because irrelevant.

    (c)   admissible to prove that D had a motive to shoot V.

    (d)   admissible to prove that D was the attacker.

19.   Prosecution of D for the unlawful possession of beer in a city park, in violation of a statute. At trial, the prosecution offers proof that D was arrested at a certain location and that she was holding a can of beer at the time. At the conclusion of the prosecution's case, D moves for a directed verdict on the ground that no evidence was offered that the particular location was within a city park. The prosecution asks the court to take judicial notice of that fact. Assume that it is well known in the city where the trial is taking place that the location is within the park. The court:

    (a)   may take judicial notice of the fact but must instruct the jury that it may, but is not required to, accept the fact as true.

    (b)   may take judicial notice of the fact and may instruct the jury that it must accept the fact as true.

    (c)   may not take judicial notice of the fact because this is a criminal case.

    (d)   may not take judicial notice of the fact because very little time would be absorbed in proving the matter with maps.

20.   Criminal prosecution of D, a prominent citizen, for paying prostitutes for sexual favors at Madame X's establishment, a house of prostitution. D claims that he never went to the establishment. The prosecution calls Madame X, who testifies that she kept meticulous contemporaneous records of the customers of her "business." The prosecution then offers in evidence a page out of Madame X's appointment book, which contains D's name, the date and time of day on which he "registered," the room he was assigned, and the amount he paid. The page out of Madame X's appointment book is:

    (a)   admissible as non hearsay to show that Madame X believed D was at her establishment.

    (b)   hearsay but admissible under the business records exception to prove the matters asserted in the appointment book.

    (c)   inadmissible to prove the matters asserted in the appointment book because Madame X's illegal establishment does not qualify as a "business."

    (d)   inadmissible use of character evidence to prove D's conduct on the occasion in question.

21.   Personal injury action arising out of an incident that occurred in D's drug store. At trial, P calls W, the admitting nurse from the hospital to which P was taken. P shows W a document, which W identifies as the form she filled out when admitting P. To prove how P was injured, P asks W to read from the form the line, "Patient reports that he was shopping in D's drug store when an employee ran him down with a broom." The line from the document is:

    (a)   inadmissible because W has not properly authenticated the document.

    (b)   inadmissible because P's statement is not reasonably related to diagnosis or treatment.

    (c)   inadmissible because the document does not fit within the business records exception.

    (d)   admissible.

22.   Wrongful death action by P against D arising out of an automobile accident in which X, P's wife, was killed. At trial, P testifies that just before she died, X said, "I know my time's up. D's car ran through the red light and smashed me up really badly." To impeach X's credibility, D calls W to testify that X had a reputation in the community as a compulsive liar. W's testimony is:

      (a)   admissible.

      (b)   inadmissible because evidence of the bad character of a witness may not be used to impeach the witness until good character evidence has first been offered to bolster her credibility.

      (c)   inadmissible because by admitting X's statement, the court has already determined that it is credible.

      (d)   inadmissible because X was not a witness.

23.   Prosecution of D for murder. The jury rendered a verdict of guilty. Following the trial, D receives information that during deliberations Juror X said that he was going to vote to convict because he was sure that D was lying when he testified and that he could tell by looking into D's eyes while he was speaking. D wishes to call Juror Y to testify to Juror X's comments in order to build a case for new trial on grounds of prejudice. The court should:

      (a)   grant D's request.

      (b)   reconvene the jury and ask all members whether this statement on the part of juror X affected their decision.

      (c)   refuse D's request.

      (d)   cite D's lawyer for contempt for speaking with the jurors after the trial was over.

24.   Action by P to recover on a life insurance policy written by D Co. on which P was the named beneficiary. To prove that P had been convicted of murdering the insured (which would prevent him from recovering the proceeds of the policy), D Co. calls W, a court clerk, to testify that she was the clerk at P's criminal trial and that she heard the judge pronounce a final judgment of conviction for murder. This evidence is:

      (a)   admissible non hearsay.

      (b)   admissible under the hearsay exception for judgments of previous conviction.

      (c)   inadmissible because the official court record is the best evidence of P's conviction.

(d)   inadmissible use of character evidence under Rule 404(a).

25.   Action by P against D for breach of an oral contract. P alleges that D promised to deliver six tons of cotton balls but never delivered any. D claims that there was no contract; that the parties negotiated for a while, but never reached agreement on the deal. At trial, P testifies that he and D negotiated, then said, "we have a deal," and shook hands. On cross-examination, P denies ever having told anyone that no deal was actually made. D then calls W, who testifies that two weeks after the alleged deal was made, P said to her, "I wish I could have nailed down that deal with D for the cotton balls. I could sure use them now." W's testimony is:

(a)   inadmissible either to impeach P or to prove that no contract existed.

(b)   inadmissible to impeach P but admissible to prove that no contract existed.

(c)   admissible to impeach P but inadmissible to prove that no contract existed.

(d)   admissible both to impeach P and to prove that no contract existed.

SPECIFIC SUBJECT MATTER
REVIEW ANSWER KEY

SPECIFIC SUBJECT MATTER
REVIEW ANSWER KEY
TRUE-FALSE QUESTIONS

1. **Relevance and the Exclusion of Relevant Evidence: Fed.R.Evid. 401–403**

False 1. Circumstantial evidence must only possess "any" tendency to establish a fact of consequence, i.e., more than zero, to be relevant.

False 2. Fact of consequence includes material proposition, i.e., an ultimate fact constituting an element of the claim for relief, charge, or affirmative defense as well as evidence of an intermediate fact which tends to establish an ultimate fact. In addition, fact of consequence includes facts bearing circumstantially upon the evaluation of the probative value to be given to other evidence in the case, including demonstrative evidence and the credibility of witnesses. Included in this latter category are personal knowledge, demeanor, impeachment, rehabilitation, and background information.

True 3. See above.

True 4. See answer to question 2 above.

True 5. The fact the evidence tends to establish may not itself be in the case, i.e., not an ultimate fact of consequence, referred to as a material proposition at common law. Such evidence is "irrelevant" under Rule 401. At common law such evidence would be inadmissible as "immaterial."

False 6. The risk of unfair prejudice must substantially outweigh the probative value of the evidence under Rule 403 to be excluded.

False   7.   Surprise is not balanced against probative value under Rule 403.

True   8.   The right of every litigant to prove its case "free from any [opponent's] option to stipulate the evidence away rests on good sense." Old Chief v. United States, 519 U.S. 172, 189, 117 S.Ct. 644, 136 L.Ed.2d 574 (1997).

True   9.   The risk of unfair prejudice includes not only an undue tendency to suggest decision on an improper emotional basis, the risk of unfair prejudice also encompasses the risk that the jury might employ evidence for a purpose for which it has not been admitted in spite of a limiting instruction not to do so.

True   10.   Such improper evaluation may occur, for example, because of the sheer weight of time devoted to a matter or because demonstrative evidence varies substantially from the fact of consequence sought to be illustrated.

2.   **Competency of Lay Witnesses: Fed.R.Evid. 601–606**

True   1.   Under Rule 601, since state law provides the rule of decision, state law providing for incompetence pursuant to a Dead Man's Act may declare the defendant incompetent.

False   2.   A young child, like any other witness, must possess minimum credibility and be shown able to take an oath or affirmation. Rarely can it be shown that a two year old understands the difference between the truth and a lie or fantasy and understands the duty to tell the truth.

True   3.   The Federal Rules of Evidence in Rule 601 state that every person is competent to be a witness except as otherwise provided in these rules. There is no Federal Rule of Evidence dealing with the competence of attorneys.

False   4.   Under Rule 605 a judge is only incompetent to testify in the trial over which the judge is presiding.

False   5.   Rule 602 provides that a witness may not testify to a matter unless evidence is introduced sufficient to support a finding that the witness has personal knowledge of the matter.

True   6.   Experimentation by a juror constitutes extraneous prejudicial information improperly brought to the jury's attention properly forming the basis of a challenge to the jury verdict under Rule 606(b)(2)(A).

False   7.   The fact that a juror is drunk is a matter occurring during the course of jury deliberation which, under Rule 606(b)(1), may not form the basis upon which to challenge the jury verdict rendered in that matter.

True   8.   The statement of the bailiff constitutes extraneous prejudicial information improperly brought to the jury's attention properly forming the basis of a challenge to the jury verdict under Rule 606(b)(2)(A).

False   9.   No rule of evidence speaks to whether an attorney is ever incompetent to testify. Thus pursuant to Rule 601 since no rule of evidence otherwise provides, an attorney is competent to testify. Pursuant to ABA Model Rules of Evidence the partner of the lawyer trying a case will be competent to testify absent a conflict of interest.

False   10.   The requirement of personal knowledge, Rule 602, is a specific application of the concept of conditional relevancy for both judge and jury as provided in Rule 104(b).

3.   **Direct Examination: Fed.R.Evid. 106, 611(c), 612, 615**

False   1.   Rule 611(c) provides that leading questions should not ordinarily be permitted on direct examination. Leading questions are permitted on direct examination only when necessary to develop the witness' testimony or the witness is hostile in law.

True   2.   The mother of the defendant is almost certainly to be declared a hostile in law witness under Rule 611(c)(2) as being a witness identified with an adverse party.

False   3.   A leading question is one that suggests the answer. The question "Was the traffic light red or was it otherwise?" is suggestive and thus leading although not subject to a "Yes" or "No" answer.

True   4.   A sustained objection to a leading question will usually be followed by a nonleading question directed toward the same subject matter. The witness, having just heard the suggestive leading question, will ordinarily now be able to provide the previously suggested answer in response to the nonleading question next presented. In any event, given that witnesses are properly heavily prepared prior to their testifying in the first place, reversals based upon the excessive employment of leading questions are rare.

True   5.   A child witness is more likely to be permitted to be lead as "necessary to develop the witness' testimony," Rule 611(c). A child is more likely to forget, become frightened, nervous or upset or have difficulty communicating to the jury.

False   6.   Whether a witness who testifies incorrectly to a fact may have his recollection refreshed is the subject of disagreement in reported decisions. It is sometimes stated that a party may seek to refresh the recollection of a witness only if the witness testifies that his recollection is exhausted and that he can't recall the matter forming the subject of the inquiry. Thus under such authority, if a witness replies in an absolute fashion, for example, that nothing else was said or nothing else happened, refreshment of recollection would not be permitted. However other decisions reach the sensible position that refreshing recollection is proper even if the witness gives a positive albeit unanticipated answer. As McCormick, Evidence § 9 at 37 (5th ed.1999) states, "The witness may believe that she remembers completely but on looking at the memorandum, she would recall additional facts."

Counsel can sometimes avoid having to face the issue by incorporating lack of recollection in the question asked, such as "Do you recall whether anything else was said?" Where such a question would be inconvenient as a matter of form or where counsel does not wish to suggest to the jury that the witness has memory problems, counsel must fall back on a general instruction to the witness to respond to questions such as "Was anyone else present?" with the answer, "I don't recall."

False   7.   A leading question may be used to refresh recollection, even if a document is available, if the subject matter as to which the witness is being refreshed is not critically significant to the trier of fact in deciding the matter before it.

True   8.   See answer to question 7 id.

True   9.   Anything may be shown to the witness if calculated to refresh the witness' recollection. It need not be a document prepared by the witness. Nor need the item ever have been observed by the witness before. Protection against counsel acting as suggested in the question is provided in Rule 612(b) which states that the adverse party is entitled to inspect the item, to cross-examine the witness thereon, and to introduce into evidence those portions which relate to the testimony of the witness for the purpose of evaluating credibility.

True   10.   See answer to question 9 id.

True   11.   Rule 106 provides that "[i]f the court admits evidence that is admissible against a party or for a purpose—but not against another party or for another purpose—the court, on timely request, must restrict the evidence to its proper scope and instruct the jury accordingly."

True   12.   Rule 106 quoted above does not relate to oral conversations, only to a writing or recorded statement.

True   13.   The government, not being a natural person, may under Rule 615(2) designate as its representative to remain in the courtroom throughout the trial an officer or employee of the government, including the lead law enforcement officer.

False   14.   Under Rule 615(c), a witness is not subject to the rule of exclusion if the presence of the person is shown by a party to be essential to the presentation of the party's claim or defense. An expert witness most certainly may fall within this category. It may certainly be essential to give counsel the benefit of his expert's assistance while an expert for the other party is testifying. Similarly assistance may be needed in connection with other technical matter as to which counsel lacks sufficient familiarity to try the case effectively on his own. A strong argument can be made for also permitting the presence of an expert witness who intends to give his opinion at trial based in part on evidence presented at trial, Rule 703.

False   15.   A witness who violates "The Rule" is likely to be precluded from testifying only if the witness remained in court with the consent, concurrence, procurement, or knowledge of the party seeking his testimony.

4.   Hearsay Definition: Fed.R.Evid. 801(a)–(d)

False   1.   The statements are relevant for the fact said—the law attaches independent legal significance to the making of the statements themselves—an operative act—application of objective theory of contract.

False   2.   Giving someone plants to care for is nonverbal conduct not intended as an assertion—no intent to communicate by act—thus no sincerity risk.

False   3.   Kissing a horse is nonverbal conduct not intended as an assertion—no intent to communicate by act—thus no security risk.

True   4.   The only way you know someone is your father is being told who your father is—obviously no personal knowledge—out-of-court statement admitted for its truth.

False   5.   The statement is not being offered to prove the contract but rather the act of payment. Although the statement, "Here is $5,000 in payment for the car," must be true—there was actually $5,000 handed over—the statement is also an admission of a party-opponent—Rule 801(d)(2)(B) adoptive admission by silence—and thus not hearsay.

True   6.   Statement is relevant to establish house of prostitution only if person making telephone call was relying upon previously acquired personal knowledge that the number did handle Candy's business interests and that Candy is available for hire. See Appendix A gambling illustration under *Character of establishment.*

False   7.   Losing money at poker is nonverbal conduct not intended as an assertion—no intent to communicate by act—thus no sincerity risk.

True   8.   The statement is relevant in establishing D's motive only if the statement is true—D owes V $10,000 from a poker game—statement is not relevant for fact said, effect on listener, because the statement was not made to D.

False   9.   Statement relevant only if believed by D to be true—that he was cheated—hearsay risks of sincerity and narration. Statement, however, is defined as a not hearsay admission of a party opponent by Rule 801(d)(2)(A).

False   10.   The statement is relevant for the fact said—effect on listener—on issue of self-defense—a reasonable person's apprehension of danger would be affected by having heard the content of the statement—if offered to prove Jake believed he was cheated for the inference that he was actually the first aggressor, the statement would be hearsay.

True   11.   The government report is an out-of-court writing offered in evidence to prove the truth of the matter asserted, i.e., that the tire was defective—all four hearsay risks are present.

False   12.   Fixing the brakes is nonverbal conduct not intended as an assertion—no intent to communicate by act—thus no sincerity risk.

False   13.   The children's conduct is nonverbal conduct not intended as an assertion—no intent to communicate by act—thus no sincerity risk.

False   14.   The yelled statements are relevant on the issue of the mother's unfitness, i.e., verbal abuse, because they were said, the content itself does not matter—the statement is not being offered to prove the children are spoiled brats, the matter asserted—verbal conduct not offered to prove either the truth of the matter asserted or the declarant's belief in the truth of the matter asserted—functionally equivalent for hearsay analysis purpose to the mother beating the children.

True   15.   The hospital record is an out-of-court writing offered in evidence to prove that the truth of the matter asserted, i.e., the extent of her injuries—all four hearsay risks are present.

True   16.   The death certificate is an out-of-court writing offered in evidence to prove the truth of the matter asserted, i.e., the fact of death—all four hearsay risks are present.

False   17.   The police officer's statement is a not hearsay prior statement of identification of a person made after perceiving the person again, Rule 801(d)(1)(C), which may be testified to by anyone with personal knowledge of its making, provided that the declarant, the bank teller, testifies at the trial and is subject to cross-examination concerning the statement—a requirement that is satisfied if a previous witness is still under subpoena.

True   18.   An out-of-court statement offered in evidence to prove the truth of the matter asserted, i.e., light green for plaintiff, in the form of testimony at a prior trial of the same matter is under Rules 801(a)–(c) hearsay. The prior testimony is a "statement, other than one made by the declarant while testifying at the [current] trial"—all four hearsay risks are present.

False   19.   Screaming and moaning is nonverbal conduct not intended as an assertion—no intent to communicate by act—thus no sincerity risk.

False   20.   Raising of a hand in this context is operative—the law attaches independent legal significance to the act itself.

False   21.   Leaving the key is nonverbal conduct not intended as an assertion—no intent to communicate by act—thus no sincerity risk.

True   22.   The statement is being offered for the inference that the declarant acquired his knowledge of the birthmark by personal observation—the statement is relevant only if truth—all four hearsay risks are present. See Appendix A Sharon Shunck illustration under *Personal knowledge of independently established facts*.

True   23.   The out-of-court assertion is being offered to prove the truth of the matter asserted, i.e., he had a pain in his chest—relevance thus rests upon the credibility of the out-of-court asserter.

False   24.   Statements forming a contract are relevant for the fact said under the objective theory of contract—the law attaches independent legal significance to content of the statement itself. What is of concern in the question is only however the secretary telling her mother of the contract. As an employee of the defendant, if her statement to her mother concerns a matter with the scope of her employment, which it most likely does, the statement is defined as a not hearsay admission of a party-opponent under Rule 801(d)(2)(D) even though all four hearsay risks are present.

False   25.   Hearsay requires that there be a statement by a person, Rule 801(b)—Hal is not a person.

True   26.   A receipt is a memorialization; it is not itself an operative act and thus does not have independent legal significance. When one checks out at the food store, the operative acts are the ringing up of the total and the handing over of money constituting payment. The receipt handed over with the change is not itself part of the contract but rather simply a memorialization of the transaction—a written statement offered in evidence to prove the truth of its contents—all four hearsay risks are present.

False   27.   There is no out-of-court statement thus no hearsay issue.

False   28.   The statement is relevant for the fact said for its effect on listener on the issue of motive or provocation of D for assaulting Y. A person is more likely to assault another once being told that the other person raped his wife. If offered to prove the rape occurred, the statement is hearsay—all four hearsay risks present—the statement is offered to prove the truth of the matter asserted, i.e., Y raped D's wife.

False   29.   An element of defamation is publication. Thus evidence that D said P is a "heavy drinker" is an operative act—the law attaches independent legal significance to the making of the statement itself.

False   30.   The note is not being offered to prove the truth of the matter asserted, i.e., the formula for plastic scissors, but solely to show that it was written by the defendant and is identical in content to the actual formula for plastic scissors which will be established through plaintiff's testimony. See Appendix A Red Fox Inn illustration in text under *Mechanical traces.*

False   31.   D's statement that the child is his son is an out-of-court statement offered in evidence to prove the truth of the matter asserted, Rules 801(a)–(c)—all four hearsay risks are present. However because the statement was made by the defendant and is offered by the plaintiff, under Rule 801(d)(1)(A) the statement is defined as a not hearsay admission of a party-opponent.

False   32.   The letter is an operative act relevant for the fact said. Under the objective theory of contract the law attaches independent legal significance to the fact the letter of acceptance was sent.

False   33.   V's conduct upon seeing D is nonverbal conduct not intended as an assertion—no intent to communicate by act—thus no sincerity risk.

True   34.   The out-of-court statement is one of intent of the declarant relevant if believed to be true by the declarant—two hearsay risks (sincerity and narrative) present—for the further inference that declarant acted consistently with the expressed intent, i.e., left jewelry at home.

False   35.   The "Yield Right of Way" sign is an operative or verbal act to which the law attaches independent legal significance. The sign is thus relevant for the fact said and not hearsay.

False   36.   The statement by W to X is relevant for the fact said in that it provides notice to X and thus is relevant in finding knowledge by X that the resolution was passed by the corporate board. If W's statement is offered to prove that the board actually passed the resolution, it is hearsay—all four hearsay risks are present—the statement is offered to prove the truth of the matter asserted, Rule 801(c)—the board passed the resolution. This is correct even though the passing of a resolution by the corporate board itself is not hearsay—voting is an operative act having independent legal significance. If W testifies on personal knowledge to the board passing the resolution, W's testimony is not hearsay. Here the testimony is of W telling X that the corporate board passed the resolution.

False   37.   Offering a bribe is an operative act relevant for the fact said. The law attaches independent legal significance to the statement, i.e., the crime itself is defined as offering a bribe.

False   38.   When the witness recalls the items stolen after refreshing his recollection with the document, the witness is testifying from personal knowledge, Rule 602, as to the items that were stolen—no out-of-court statement is being offered into evidence.

True   39.   This is a *Tatham* problem. See Appendix A Basis for Nonasserted Inference or "Implied Assertion." The declarant must have worked with the engineer before to form a basis for the implied assertion of the engineer's competency. Because this basis, whether or not expressed in the letter, in addition to the request to conduct a complex engineering survey, must be true for any inference desired to be relevant, the statement is hearsay—all four hearsay risks are present.

False   40.   The statement is relevant for the fact said for its effect on listener on the issue of self-defense. A reasonable person's apprehension of danger would be affected by them having heard the content of the statement—if offered to prove V intended to kill the defendant the statement would be hearsay.

False   41.   There is no statement by a person—a thermometer is not a person.

True   42.   The statement, "I feel hot and feverish," is being offered to prove the truth of the matter asserted, Rules 801(a)–(c),—the plaintiff feels hot and feverish for the inference the plaintiff had a temperature.

False   43.   Wrapping in a wet blanket is nonverbal conduct not intended as an assertion—no intent to communicate by act—thus no sincerity risk.

True   44.   The out-of-court statement is being offered into evidence to prove the truth of the matter asserted, Rules 801(a)–(c),—the plaintiff had a temperature.

False   45.   The witness is testifying on personal knowledge about a past event—how she felt—not as to an out-of-court statement.

True   46.   The nurse's out-of-court statement that the thermometer registered 105° is being offered in evidence to prove the truth of the matter stated, Rule 801(c)—the thermometer registered 105° for the inference that the plaintiff had a temperature.

False   47.   The witness' conduct in identifying the defendant as the attacker is nonverbal conduct intended as an assertion *made while testifying at the trial*—oath, demeanor and cross-examination are present as to a witness testifying upon personal knowledge.

False   48.   The statement is relevant for the fact said for its effect upon the listener, the plaintiff, as to his claim for humiliation and embarrassment. The statement is hearsay if offered to prove that plaintiff actually has a "Hose-Nose."

False   49.   Wearing short sleeve shirts and shorts is nonverbal conduct not intended as an assertion—no intent to communicate by act—thus no sincerity risk.

False   50.   The statement "You can take your contract and cram it," is relevant for the fact said as an operative having independent legal significance—the statement constitutes under the objective theory of contract an anticipatory breach.

5.   **Hearsay Definition and Exceptions: Fed.R.Evid. 801–807**

True   1.   The contents of the crumpled slip of paper—an out-of-court written assertion—is being offered in evidence to prove the truth of the matter asserted, Rules 801(a)–(c), i.e., that the license number of the hit and run car is EE2468—all four hearsay risks are present.

True   2.   The crumpled slip of paper bearing the license plate number EE2468 is admissible under Rule 803(5) as recorded recollection.

False   3.   There is no out-of-court statement by a person being offered into evidence but rather the in court testimony of a witness upon personal knowledge authenticating a photograph as fairly and accurately representing what it purports to represent. The non hearsay nature of the photograph is easily seen if what is depicted is an intersection. The picture of the license plate is not being offered as a written assertion for its truth. EE2468 on a license plate on its face is not even relevant. We can't read the words, in this case letters and numbers, and learn anything. The license plate EE2468 becomes relevant only when connected through the department of motor vehicles or other evidence tying the license plate to a particular person.

True   4.   As structured, if the answer to question 1 of a set is False, the answer to question 2 is True.

True   5.   Plaintiff's reenactment is nonverbal conduct intended as an assertion offered to prove the truth of the matter asserted, Rules 801(a)–(c). It is as much hearsay as if the plaintiff had explained out-of-court how the accident happened.

False   6.   No not hearsay definition, Rules 801(d)(1) and (2), and no hearsay exception, Rules 803, 804, and 807, is satisfied.

False   7.   Getting around is nonverbal not intended as an assertion—no intent to communicate by act—thus no sincerity risk.

True   8.   As structured, if the answer to question 1 of a set is False, the answer to question 2 is True.

True   9.   The statement is relevant only if T believed that she is Michael Jordan—two hearsay risks are present, i.e., sincerity and narration.

True   10.   The statement "I am Michael Jordan" is admissible under Rule 803(3) as a statement of the existing mental, emotional, or physical condition.

False   11.   Plaintiff's out-of-court statement that D is telling everyone that he owns Blackacre is being offered to prove the truth of the matter asserted, Rules 801(a)–(c). However, Rule 801(d)(1)(A) defines as not hearsay a party's own statement as an admission by party-opponent—D here is offering P's statement—the statement of a party-opponent. The same statement of D testified to in court by a witness who heard it would be not hearsay—relevant for fact said—act having independent legal significance.

True   12.   As structured, if the answer to question 1 of a set is False, the answer to question 2 is True.

False   13.   A's out-of-court statement that he is an agent of D is being offered to prove the truth of the matter asserted, Rules 801(a)–(c). However, Rule 801(d)(2)(C) defines as not hearsay a statement by a person authorized by a party to make a statement concerning the subject when offered by a party-opponent—here P offering a statement of D's agent—and that in determining whether A is in fact D's agent. Rule 801(d)(2) provides that the content of the statement itself may be considered but is not alone sufficient to establish the declarant's authority as agent.

True   14.   As structured, if the answer to question 1 of a set is False, the answer to question 2 is True.

True   15.   The testator says to the police "X is threatening to kill him." On the issue of whether the testator's will is a forgery, the relevancy of the statement requires that it be believed by the testator to be true (relevancy does not require it to be true) and thus two hearsay risks are present, i.e., sincerity and narration. A testator who *believes* that X is threatening him is less likely to make X the sole legatee of his will—the will is a forgery.

True   16.   The statement "[I believe that] X is threatening to kill me" is admissible under Rule 803(3) as a statement of their existing mental, emotional, or physical condition.

False   17.   The statement "D is in the city," is relevant for the fact said for its effect on listener in this case as proving notice or knowledge. A reasonable person is more likely to know that something exists after being told about it than without the statement being made.

True   18.   As structured, if the answer to question 1 of a set is False, then the answer to question 2 is True.

True   19.   When the statement is offered to prove D was in the city, it is an out-of-court statement offered in evidence to prove the truth of the matter asserted, Rules 801(a)–(c).

False   20.   The statement is not defined as not hearsay as an admission of a party-opponent under Rule 801(d)(2)(B) as an adoptive admission because as P responds by saying "No Way". The statement also fails to meet any other not hearsay definition in Rule 801(d) or an exception in Rules 803, 804, or 807.

False   21.   The out-of-court statement "I know that D is in the city" is offered to prove the truth of the matter asserted under Rules 801(a)–(c). However, D is offering P's statement—a statement of a party-opponent—which is defined as not hearsay by Rule 801(d)(2)(A).

True   22.   As structured, if the answer to question 1 of a set is False, the answer to question 2 is True.

False   23.   The statement is relevant for the fact said, effect on listener, on issue of self-defense—a reasonable person's apprehension of danger would be affected by having heard the content of the statement.

True   24.   As structured, if the answer to question 1 of a set is False, the answer to question 2 is True.

True   25.   When offered to prove that V is the aggressor, the statement "V has knifed three people in the last year" is relevant only if true—all four hearsay risks—an out-of-court statement offered in evidence to prove the truth of the matter asserted, Rules 801(a)–(c). The statement fails to satisfy any of the hearsay by definition provisions of Rule 801(d)(2).

False   26.   The statement fails to satisfy any of the not hearsay exceptions provided in Rules 803, 804, and 807.

False   27.   The statement by the employee to her boss "I just didn't see the light," is being offered in evidence to prove the truth of the matter asserted, Rules 801(a)–(c). However, Rule 801(d)(2)(D) provides that a statement is defined as not hearsay when the statement is offered against a party by the opposing party and the statement is a statement of the party's employee concerning a matter within the scope of employment made during the existence of the relationship. Rule 801(d)(2) provides further that in determining the employment relationship and the scope thereof, the content of the statement should be considered but is not alone sufficient.

True   28.   As structured, if the answer to question 1 of a set is False, the answer to question 2 is True.

True   29.   V pointing out the defendant as the assailant at a line-up is nonverbal conduct extended as an asserted, Rules 801(a)–(c),—all four hearsay risks are present. Y's testimony that V identified the defendant after perceiving him again at the line-up is not defined as not hearsay by Rule 801(d)(1)(c) because V is unavailable at trial—Rule 801(d) requires that the out-of-court declarant testify at the trial and be subject to cross-examination. The statement also fails to satisfy any of the other not hearsay by definition provisions of Rule 801(d).

False   30.   The statement fails to satisfy any of the hearsay exceptions provided in Rules 803, 804, and 807.

False   31.   The statement of D stating that "It's a deal," is relevant for the fact said—an operative act—the law attaches independent legal significance to the statement—application of the objective theory of contract. In addition, since P is offering D's statement, a statement of a party-opponent, the statement is an admission of a party-opponent defined as not hearsay by Rule 801(d)(2)(A).

True   32.   As structured, if the answer to question 1 of a set is False, the answer to question 2 is True.

False   33.   The statement is relevant for the fact said, effect on listener on issue of motive. A person is more likely to be the killer having been told that the person killed had raped his sister than if not so advised.

True   34.   As structured, if the answer to question 1 of a set is False, the answer to question 2 is True.

False   35.   The statement is relevant for the fact said. The sign "Slow, repairs ahead," is both operative—the law attaches independent legal significance to the statement (like a stop sign) as well as relevant for its effect upon listener in that the reasonableness of subsequent conduct of a person given notice of danger differs from that of a person who has not been so advised.

True   36.   As structured, if the answer to question 1 of a set is False, the answer to question 2 is True.

False   37.   The out-of-court statement of the in court declarant, W1, is relevant for the fact said when offered to impeach credibility. The weight to be given to the witness' testimony in court by the jury is affected by the fact that the witness earlier in time closer to the event had maintained a contradictory position—brings into question personal knowledge and/or sincerity of the witness.

True   38.   As structured, if the answer to question 1 of a set is False, the answer to question 2 if True.

True   39.   The out-of-court statement of the in court witness is being offered to prove the truth of the matter asserted, Rules 801(a)–(c),—all four hearsay risks are present. The statement is not defined as not hearsay under Rule 801(d)(1)(A) because although the declarant is in court testifying at the trial subject to cross-examination, the out-of-court statement was not made under oath subject to the penalty of perjury at a trial, hearing, other proceeding [grand jury], or deposition. The statement also fails to satisfy any of the other not hearsay by definition provisions of Rule 801(d).

False   40.   The statement fails to satisfy any of the hearsay exceptions provided by Rules 803, 804, and 807.

True   41.   The police accident report is an out-of-court statement being offered in evidence to prove that the witness W1 *said* "D was going slowly"—all four hearsay risks are present—and the out-of-court statement by W1 itself is being offered in evidence to prove the truth of the matter asserted, i.e., that "D was going slowly"—all four hearsay risks are present.

False   42.   What is involved is multiple level hearsay, Rule 805. While under Rule 803(8), the public records hearsay exception, the police report is admissible to prove that W1 made the statement, W1's statement, which is offered to prove the truth of the matter asserted, Rules 801(a)–(c), i.e., D was going slowly, fails to meet the requirements for being defined as not hearsay (see answer to question 39 above), nor does it meet the requirements of a hearsay exception in Rules 803, 804, or 807.

False   43.   Entering and leaving the establishment is nonverbal conduct not intended as an assertion—no intent to communicate by act—thus no risk of sincerity.

True   44.   As structured, if the answer to question 1 of a set is False, the answer to question 2 is True.

False   45.   The statement concerning the corporation mailing the literature is offered in evidence to prove the truth of the matter asserted, Rules 801(a)–(c)—all four hearsay risks. The statement is defined as a not hearsay admission of a party-opponent under Rule 801(d)(2)(C),—the plaintiff is offering the statement of the defendant corporation's president who is authorized to speak on behalf of the corporation.

True   46.   As structured, if the answer to question 1 of a set is False, the answer to question 2 is True.

False   47.   The statement "this is full payment for the piano," characterizes an independently relevant act and is for this purpose relevant for the fact said. The law attaches independent legal significant to payment accompanied by a statement that it is payment in full under the objective theory of contract.

True   48.   As structured, if the answer to question 1 of a set is False, the answer to question 2 is True.

True   49.   The statement is multiple level hearsay. The first statement is the appearance on the computer screen of the closing price of AOL and the second is the out-of-court statement by D to P offered by D to prove the truth of the matter asserted, i.e., AOL closed at 30.

False   50.   Rule 803(1), present sense impression, provides a hearsay exception for the reporting of the observation of the closing price of AOL on the computer. As to the truth of the matter asserted on the computer itself, one might argue that Rule 803(17) entitled "market reports, commercial publications" applies. However, Rule 803(17) in its text prior to restyling stated "or other published compilations" and observation of a computer screen is not a published, i.e., printed, compilation. In my opinion, Rule 803(17) requires the actual introduction in court of a hard copy "published compilation". It can be argued, I guess, that the computer display that AOL closed at 30 is not a statement of a person but rather the output of a machine. This is incorrect as the computer display is the result of someone entering into the computer what that person observed, a sale of AOL for 30. Query: What about true electronics trading where I believe the entire process is conducted by the computer including of course entry of the sales which become the price display? If no person was involved, then with a proper foundation, the statement can be argued to be admissible under Rule 803(1). However, not in my court. Since there are so many other more reliable ways to prove the closing price of AOL at 30 on a given day than the testimony of the defendant as to having observed same on a computer screen and his testimony that he now recalls telling such immediately to another, I wouldn't buy it. I would figure out a reason as applied to the facts at hand such as for example lack of authentication of the process or system, Rule 901(b)(9)—nor would one even expect the defendant to actually proceed to prove the closing price of AOL on that day at 30 in the foregoing fashion.

True   51.   The showing of the airline ticket is a statement of intent to go to Chicago on November 20, 2020, relevant only if believed by the declarant to be true—the hearsay risks of sincerity and narration are present.

True   52.   Rule 803(3) as interpreted provides a hearsay exception for statements of current intent to prove not only the declarant's current intent but also as evidence that the intent was actually carried forth, i.e., that X actually went to Chicago on November 20, 2020. The availability or unavailability of the declarant, as well as the actual testimony of the declarant if he testifies, is irrelevant in determining whether a hearsay statement is admissible pursuant to any Rule 803 exception.

True   53.   The expense voucher is being offered in evidence to prove the truth of the matter asserted, Rules 801(a)–(c), i.e., that X was in Chicago on November 20, 2020—all four hearsay risks are present.

True   54.   The expense voucher is admissible as a business record under Rule 803(6) upon introduction of a proper foundation which is assumed by the instructions.

True   55.   The statement "I plan to go to Chicago tomorrow," is a statement of intent to go to Chicago tomorrow, relevant only if believed by the declarant to be true—the hearsay risks of sincerity and narration are present.

True   56.   Rule 803(3) as interpreted provides a hearsay exception for statements of current state of mind to prove not only the declarant's current intent but also as evidence that the intent was actually carried forth, i.e., that X actually the next day went to Chicago.

True   57.   The statement "Yesterday I went to Chicago," is a statement asserting the existence of a past event offered in evidence to prove the past event—all four hearsay risks are present.

False   58.   The statement is not admissible under Rule 803(3) which specifically states that a statement of current state of mind—"[I know] yesterday I was in Chicago"—is not admissible as a statement of current state of mind "to prove the fact remembered or believed."

True   59.   The hospital report is multiple level hearsay. The first statement is by the plaintiff stating that he is 42 years old. The second statement is by a hospital employee entering this information in his medical records. Since the statement concerning age is being offered for its truth, i.e., that plaintiff was over 40 at the time made, the statement is hearsay—all four hearsay risks are present.

True 60. The statement is multiple level hearsay as to which there is a hearsay exception for each level, Rule 805. Since the statement is pertinent to medical diagnosis or treatment, Rule 803(6), business records, provides a hearsay exception to prove that the statement concerning age was made while Rule 803(4), statements for purposes of medical diagnosis or treatment, provides a hearsay exception for the truth of the statement, i.e., that plaintiff was 42 years old when the statement was made in 2010.

True 61. The statement "D's tire is about ready to blow," is being offered in evidence to prove the truth of the matter asserted, Rules 801(a)–(c),—tire about to blow, for the further inference that the defective tire caused the accident—all four hearsay risks are present. The statement fails to meet the requirements for being defined as not hearsay under Rules 801(d)(1) or (2).

False 62. The statement does not meet the requirements of any hearsay exception provided in Rules 803, 804, and 807.

False 63. The statement is relevant for the fact said—effect on listener. Whether D assumed the risk, i.e., voluntarily encountered a known risk or danger, is affected by what D's is aware of. The statement is relevant providing notice or knowledge to D and for this purpose is not hearsay.

True 64. As structured, if the answer to question 1 of a set is False, the answer to question 2 of the set is True.

True 65. The statement that the back tire has blown out is being offered to prove the truth of the matter asserted, Rules 801(a)–(c), i.e., that the back tire blew out—all four hearsay risks are present.

True   66.   The statement is admissible under Rule 803(2) as an excited utterance regardless of the fact that it is plaintiff's own statement which might indicate "bad faith" and regardless of the fact that plaintiff will testify on personal knowledge to the same fact at trial.

False   67.   D's barking like a dog is nonverbal conduct not intended as an assertion—no intent to communicate—thus no sincerity risk.

True   68.   As structured, if the answer to question 1 of a set is False, the answer to question 2 is True.

True   69.   The statement pointing out the gun is an out-of-court statement offered in evidence to prove the truth of the matter asserted, Rules 801(a)–(c), i.e., that D has a revolver sticking out of her pocket—all four hearsay risks are present.

True   70.   The statement is admissible under the hearsay exception provided in Rule 803(1) as a present sense impression.

True   71.   The statement "My leg hurts something awful," is an out-of-court statement offered in evidence to prove the truth of the matter asserted, Rules 801(a)–(c), i.e., P's leg hurts something awful. The statement is relevant only if true—all four hearsay risks are present.

True   72.   The statement is admissible under the hearsay exception provided in Rule 803(3) as a statement of then existing mental, emotional or physical condition.

False   73.   The statement "My leg hurts something awful," is relevant when offered to prove that the declarant was conscious merely because it is a coherent thought, i.e., relevant for the fact said. The statement is relevant to establish consciousness after the accident regardless of whether true or believed to be true by the declarant.

True   74.   As structured, if the answer to question 1 of a set is False, the answer to question 2 is True.

False   75.   Flight is nonverbal conduct not intended as an assertion—no intent to communicate—thus no risk of sincerity.

True   76.   As structured, if the answer to question 1 of a set is False, the answer to question 2 is True.

True   77.   For the statement "You stole money," to be relevant, the declarant must "believe" that D stole money, for the inference the declarant doesn't like people who steal and thus is "prejudiced" against D. Since the statement is relevant only if believed by the declarant to be true—"[I believe] D stole money"—the hearsay risks of sincerity and narration are present.

True   78.   The statement "[I believe] that D stole money," is admissible under the hearsay exception provided in Rule 803(3) for statements of then existing mental, emotional, or physical condition.

False   79.   The statement when made to D was not denied by the defendant—he remained silent. Thus although the statement "You stole money," is being offered to prove the truth of the matter asserted, Rules 801(a)–(c), i.e., D stole money, the statement when offered by P is defined as a not hearsay admission of a party-opponent of D under Rule 801(d)(2)(B), as an adopted admission by silence—it would naturally be expected that under the circumstances D would deny such an accusation if not true.

True   80.   As structured, if the answer to question 1 of a set is False, the answer to question 2 is True.

False   81.   The giving of x-ray treatment is nonverbal conduct not intended as an assertion—no intent to communicate—thus no risk of sincerity.

True   82.   As structured, if the answer to the first question of a set is False, the answer to question 2 is True.

True   83.   The statement of E, the doctor, to P that he has cancer is an out-of-court statement offered in evidence to prove the truth of the matter asserted, Rules 801(a)–(c), i.e., P has cancer—all four hearsay risks are present. The statement fails to meet the requirements for being defined as not hearsay under Rules 801(d)(1) or (2).

False   84.   The statement does not meet the requirements of any hearsay exception provided in Rules 803, 804, and 807. Rule 803(4) does not encompass statements by the doctor to the patient.

True   85.   The notation by the doctor of a malignant tumor in P in the hospital record is an out-of-court statement offered in evidence to prove the truth of the matter stated, Rules 801(a)–(c), i.e., P has a malignant tumor—all four hearsay risks are present.

True   86.   The doctor's notation is admissible as a business record under Rule 803(6) upon introduction of a proper foundation which is assumed by the instructions.

True   87.   The hospital record is multiple level hearsay. The first statement is by P that he has a cancerous tumor. The second statement is by the receiving physician entering this information in P's medical records. Since the statement concerning the cancerous tumor is being offered for its truth, i.e., P then had a cancerous tumor, the statement is hearsay—all four hearsay risks are present.

True   88.   The statement is multiple level hearsay as to which there is a hearsay exception for each level, Rule 805. Since the statement is pertinent to medical diagnosis or treatment, Rule 803(6), business records, provides a hearsay exception to prove that the statement about the cancerous tumor was made while Rule 803(4), statements for purposes of medical, diagnosis or treatment, provides a hearsay exception for the truth of the statement, i.e., P had a cancerous tumor.

True   89.   The statement by D, being offered in evidence by D, that he owns Blackacre is an out-of-court statement offered in evidence to prove the truth of the matter asserted, Rules 801(a)–(c),—all four hearsay risks are present. The statement fails to meet the requirements for being defined as not hearsay under Rules 801(d)(1) or (2).

False   90.   The statement does not meet the requirements of any hearsay exception provided in Rules 803, 804, and 807.

False   91.   The statement by P acknowledging that Blackacre belongs to D is an out-of-court statement offered in evidence to prove the truth of the matter asserted, Rules 801(a)–(c). When offered by P, a party-opponent, the statement is an admission of a party-opponent defined as not hearsay, Rule 801(d)(2)(A).

True   92.   As structured, if the answer to question 1 of a set is False, the answer to question 2 is True.

True   93.   X's statement that he subscribes to Credit Bureau is relevant to establish that he heard of the Credit Bureau only if the statement is believed by the declarant to be true—if the declarant lied about the subscription to impress Y the statement is not relevant. Since X must believe the statement to be true, the hearsay risks of sincerity and narration are present.

True   94.   The statement by X is admissible under the hearsay exception provided in Rule 803(3) for statements of the declarant's then existing state of mind, emotion, sensation or physical condition.

True   95.   The Credit Bureau report that Q is bankrupt is being offered in evidence to prove the truth of the matter asserted, Rules 801(a)–(c), i.e., that Q is bankrupt.

False   96.   While the Credit Bureau report may be argued to meet the requirements of the hearsay exception for market reports and commercial publications, Rule 801(17), it is suggested that the text of Rule 803(17) limits its scope to "published compilations" and thus excludes evaluative reports such as that of the Credit Bureau stating that Q was bankrupt.

False   97.   The Credit Bureau report that Q was having financial difficulties is relevant for the fact said for its effect on the listener. Whether a person acted in good faith depends in part upon what they know, have heard, are aware. The Credit Bureau report provides knowledge, notice, awareness of possible financial difficulty regardless of its truth.

True   98.   As structured, if the answer to question 1 of a set is False, the answer to question 2 is True.

True   99.   The annual financial report disclosing bankruptcy is being offered in evidence to prove the truth of the matter asserted, Rules 801(a)–(c), i.e., that Q is bankrupt.

True   100.   The annual financial report of Q is a business record admissible under the hearsay exception provided by Rule 803(6) upon introduction of a proper foundation which is assumed by the instructions.

6.   **Authentication and Identification: Fed.R.Evid. 901–903**

True   1.   The more authentication is genuinely in issue, the greater the need to negate the possibility of alteration substitution, or change in condition and the more likely the court will exclude the item of evidence if a gap in the chain of custody appears.

False   2.   Once a letter, e-mail, fax, telegram, or telephone call is shown to have been mailed, sent or made, a letter, e-mail, fax, telegram, or telephone call shown by its contents to be in reply is authenticated without more.

False   3.   Rule 901(b)(2) provides for authentication by nonexpert opinion as to the genuineness of handwriting based upon familiarity not acquired for purposes of litigation.

False   4.   When both parties produce properly authenticated transcripts of the same recorded conversation, both transcripts should be provided to the jury to assist them in listening to the tape recording.

False   5.   An actual break in the chain of custody will not result in exclusion of the evidence when the chain of custody established to have occurred viewed as a whole supports the improbability of alteration, substitution, or change of condition.

True   6.   Once a letter, e-mail, fax, telegram, or telephone call is shown to have been mailed, sent or made, a letter, e-mail, fax, telegram or telephone call shown by its contents to be in reply is authenticated without more.

False   7.   An item purporting to be a newspaper is self-authenticating, Rule 902(6). However, the story contained therein that Elm Street was widened in the spring of 2020 is hearsay as defined in Rules 801(a)–(d) falling within no hearsay exception.

False   8.   The sound recording constitutes the evidence of the conversation. The transcripts are admitted to assist the jury in listening to the sound recording.

True   9.   Rule 902(4) combined with Rule 803(10) may be employed to establish that a California driver's license was not issued to Notowana Sims.

False   10.   Rule 901(b)(5) provides that identification of a voice, whether heard firsthand or through mechanical or electronic transmission or recording, by opinion based upon hearing the voice at any time under circumstances connecting it with the alleged speaker is sufficient authentication.

7.   **The Original Writing (Best Evidence) Rule: Fed.R.Evid. 1001–1008**

True   1.   As provided in Rule 1008(b), which is a specific application of Rule 104(b), whether a particular writing, recording, or photograph produced at trial is in fact an original is an issue for the trier of fact to determine as in the case of other issues of fact.

False   2.   When the objection "The document speaks for itself," is interposed, opposing counsel is objecting to permitting the witness to read the document to the jury because of the possibility of undue influence arising from the way the document is read, in favor instead of another means to publish the document, such as a placard, individual copies given to the jury, etc.

True   3.   The lettering on the truck is a writing. The proponent is seeking to prove the content of that writing to show ownership of the truck, see Rule 902(7). Since the writing on the truck is itself not realistically obtainable by available judicial process or procedure as the truck won't fit in the elevator, etc., Rule 1004(b, secondary evidence becomes available, in this case a photograph.

True   4.   It is sometimes relevant which party drafted a particular part of a document and when was such addition or modification made. A xerox copy of an original will obscure the cut and paste nature of the original thus making it unfair under the circumstances to admit the duplicate in lieu of the original, Rule 1003.

False   5.   Rule 1006 does not make authorize presentation to the jury of evidence that is not otherwise admissible in evidence or could be reasonably relied upon by the expert and disclosed to the jury under Rule 703.

False   6.   Testimony which was given on another occasion is a proper subject for the testimony of any witness who heard it, despite the fact that it was taken down in shorthand or otherwise contemporaneously recorded, thereby affording a means of proof far more accurate than the recollection of the witness. The Original Writing Rule does not apply for it is the occurrence of the happening rather than the contents of the transcript which is sought to be proved.

True   7.   The Original Writing Rule, according to the Advisory Committee's Note, applies to photographs only when the contents of the photograph possess independent probative value rather than being merely illustrative of a witness' testimony as to matters observed.

False   8.   A notice to produce served on a party is without compulsive force. It is designed merely to account for nonproduction of the writing, recording, or photograph by the proponent, and thus enable him to use secondary evidence of the item's terms. If the original writing, recording, or photograph is essential at trial, a subpoena duces tecum rather than a notice to produce should be served on the opponent.

False   9.   Rule 1003 provides that a duplicate is admissible to the same extent as an original unless a genuine question is raised as to the authenticity of the original or in the circumstances it would be unfair to admit the duplicate in lieu of the original.

False   10.   An original is unavailable pursuant to Rule 1004(b) if it cannot be obtained by any available judicial process or procedure; judicial process or procedure is available to secure an original documents located outside the territorial jurisdiction of the trial court.

8.   Opinions and Expert Testimony: Fed.R.Evid. 701–706

False   1.   An opinion by either a lay or expert witness that one party or another should win is inadmissible because it is not helpful, Rule 702. Moreover, testimony that a witness was at fault is equivalent to a statement that X was negligent which is also unhelpful and inadmissible as encompassing unexplored legal criteria. In an accident case, more specific less conclusionary evidence from the police officer is clearly available.

False   2.   Rule 702 does not require that in order to be qualified as an expert in a litigation that the witness have prior experience working with the particular item, matter, or product involved in the litigation.

False   3.   Rule 704 permits an expert to testify as to an ultimate issue in a criminal case, if helpful, provided that in a criminal case a witness may not state an opinion that the defendant possessed the mental state constituting an element of the crime charged, Rule 704(b). Here the expert did not address the mental state of the person possessing the drugs but testified that the drugs were possessed to be distributed. This is permitted.

True   4.   As stated above, Rule 704(b) is violated by testimony that the accused "intended" to distribute drugs in her possession, i.e., it is an opinion that the accused possesses the mental state constituting an element of the offense.

False   5.   One can only testify that the room smelled like Limburger cheese if the witness has a sufficient experiential basis to make the comparison, i.e., smelled Limburger cheese before under circumstances that provided personal knowledge that the smell came from a cheese called Limburger.

False   6.   Civil plaintiffs were able prior to *Daubert/Kumho/*Rule 702 to present expert witness' testify provided solely that the explanative theory being presented was not so obviously unsupported (wrong) as to flunk the laugh test, referred to as conjectural or speculative. *Frye* was effectively applied for all practical purposes solely to prosecution evidence of forensic science in criminal cases. Now judicial gatekeeping is applied to explanative theories across the board resulting in a significant number of plaintiff expert witnesses being precluded from testifying.

True 7. An opinion by either a lay or expert witness that one party or another should win is inadmissible because it is not helpful, Rules 701 and 702.

False 8. Reasonably relied upon in Rule 703 refers to the notion that the facts, data, or opinions are sufficiently trustworthy to make reliance by the expert reasonable, i.e., possesses the trustworthiness associated with statements admissible pursuant to a hearsay exception. Regularly, customarily and ordinarily relied upon by an expert in the particular field is not enough.

True 9. Rule 702 provides that a witness may be qualified as an expert by knowledge, skill, *experience*, training, *or* education.

False 10. Although when one doctor relies upon the opinion of another doctor such reliance is reasonable, i.e., possesses the trustworthiness associated with statements admissible pursuant to a hearsay exception, Rule 703 provides that facts, data, or opinions that are otherwise inadmissible shall not be disclosed to the jury by the proponent of the opinion or inference unless the court determines that their probative value in assisting the jury to evaluate the expert's opinion substantially outweighs their prejudicial effect.

True 11. A lay witness may testify in the form of an opinion where it is helpful to the determination of a fact in issue, Rule 701. An opinion that it was bitter cold outside is rationally based upon the perception of the witness. While the witness could have been more detailed, for example by stating the approximate temperature, the witness' opinion that it was bitter cold that day is in fact more than simply the temperature and represents an instance where accounting of the details would not accurately convey the total impression received by the witness.

False   12.   Under Rule 702 the admissibility of expert testimony is to be determined solely on the basis of assisting the trier of fact. Thus even as to matters within the general common knowledge and experience of jurors, where helpful to comprehension or explanation, expert testimony is permitted.

False   13.   Absolute certainty on the part of the lay witness is not required; opinions expressed with qualifications such as "I believe" or "I can't be positive, but" may be admitted, as may opinions expressed in terms such as "could", or "most probably", or "is similar to". Helpful opinions rationally based upon the perception of the witness couched in terms of an estimate are also admissible.

True   14.   In determining whether an explanative theory has been shown to possess sufficient assurances of trustworthiness to be considered by the jury, i.e., is the product of reliable principles and methods, Rule 702(c), whether the explanative theory has received general acceptance is properly considered.

True   15.   A lay witness may present opinion testimony as to the condition of another person including such things as age, condition of health, etc., including that another person appeared nervous.

False   16.   Rule 704(b) states that *no expert witness* testifying with respect to the mental state or condition of a defendant in a criminal case may state an opinion or inference as to whether the defendant did or did not have the mental state or condition constituting an element of the crime charged or of a defense thereto.

False   17.   The closer the subject of the opinion approaches critical issues, the greater the likelihood the court will require more concrete expression from the witness either alone or prior to the offering of an opinion conveying the witness' overall impression. The court may insist that loaded words like "murdered," "stolen" or "assaulted" be avoided in a shorthand rendering.

True   18.   Gatekeeping as mandated by Rule 702 and illustrated by the discussion in *Kumho* is an as applied test.

True   19.   Rule 701 permits a lay witness opinion as helpful to a clear understanding of the witness' testimony or the determination of a fact in issue when accounting for the details alone would not as accurately convey the impression received by the witness.

False   20.   *Daubert* was decided pursuant to the supervisory power of the United States Supreme Court over the Federal Rules of Evidence; it is not in any way binding on state courts.

False   21.   Failure to publish a publishable explanative theory is a negative factor in the determination of sufficient assurances of trustworthiness required by *Daubert/Kumho*/Rule 702 but is not preclusive. It is, however, particularly telling if the explanative theory was developed for purposes of litigation and although publishable was not published.

True   22.   It is improper for an expert to be compensated on a contingent fee basis. In responding to arguments based upon right to access to courts, the prohibition has been upheld on the ground that the inducement placed upon the expert by a contingent fee to tailor his testimony is too great.

False   23.   Expert witnesses frequently express an opinion in response to a question such as "Do you have an opinion to a reasonable degree of [scientific, medical or other technical] certainty as to * * * ?" While the expert usually replies to follow up questions indicating his opinion in absolute terms such as "did" or "was caused", less than absolute certainty is permissible. Thus opinions expressed in terms such as "could", "most probably", or "is similar to" are properly received.

False   24.   Pursuant to Rule 702, an expert witness may not testify that any witness, including a child, is or is not telling the truth; such an opinion is not helpful. It is the trier of fact's role to evaluate the credibility of the witnesses.

False   25.   Rule 706(d) provides that in the exercise of discretion, the court may, not must, authorize disclosure to the jury of the fact that the court appointed the expert witness.

9.   **Character, Habit and Routine Practice: Fed.R.Evid. 404–406, 412–415**

True   1.   Where evidence of crimes, wrongs, or other acts is admitted under Rule 404(b)(2), the jury should be given a limiting instruction, Rule 105, to the effect that they are not to consider the evidence as going to the character of the accused in order to show action in conformity therewith but only as going to the particular other purpose for which offered such as motive, identity, etc. However, failure of the court to give such an instruction *sua sponte* is unlikely to be considered plain error, Rule 103(e).

False   2.   Evidence that a car used in a bank robbery had been stolen two weeks before is not "inextricably intertwined" in the sense that it is so linked together in point of time and circumstance with the crime charged that one cannot be fully shown without proving the other. Rather evidence of the earlier car theft is crimes, wrongs, or other acts evidence admissible under Rule 404(b)(2) for the purpose of establishing plan and preparation.

False   3.   Rule 404(b)(2) provides that while evidence of crimes, wrongs, or other acts is not admissible to prove the character of a person in order to show action in conformity therewith, it may, however, be admissible for other purposes, *such as* proof of motive, opportunity, intent, preparation, plan, knowledge, identity, absence of mistake, or lack of accident.

True   4.   Rule 405(b) provides:

When a person's character or character trait is an essential element of a charge, claim, or defense, the character or trait *may also be proved by relevant specific instances* of the person's conduct.

False   5.   The prosecution may offer character evidence in the form of reputation or opinion testimony as to a pertinent trait of character of the victim only to rebut character evidence in the form of reputation or opinion testimony as to the same pertinent trait of character of the victim offered by an accused, Rule 404(a)(2)(A).

True   6.   Rule 404(a)(2)(B)(ii) provides:

(2) Exceptions for a Defendant or Victim in a Criminal Case. The following exceptions apply in a criminal case:

* * *

(B) subject to the limitations in Rule 412, a defendant may offer evidence of an alleged victim's pertinent trait, and if the evidence is admitted, the prosecutor may:

* * * ; and

(ii) offer evidence of the defendant's same trait; and

* * *

Rule 405(a) provides:

(a) By Reputation or Opinion. When evidence of a person's character or character trait is admissible, it may be proved by testimony about the person's reputation or by testimony in the form of an opinion. On cross-examination of the character witness, the court may allow an inquiry into relevant specific instances of the person's conduct.

True   7.   Rule 404(a)(1) provides that evidence of a person's character or a trait of character is not admissible for the purpose of proving action in conformity therewith on a particular occasion in a civil case.

True   8.   Rule 406 provides:

Evidence of a person's habit or an organization's routine practice may be admitted to prove that on a particular occasion the person or organization acted in accordance with the habit or routine practice. The court may admit this evidence regardless of whether it is corroborated or whether there was an eyewitness.

False   9.   Absent extraordinary circumstances, the prosecution is entitled to present otherwise admissible evidence for the fair and legitimate weight introduction of the evidence could have on the trier of fact even though the defendant has offered to stipulate as to the matter for which the evidence is relevant. As stated by the United States Supreme Court in Old Chief v. United States, 519 U.S. 172, 189, 117 S.Ct. 644, 136 L.Ed.2d 574 (1997):

In sum, the accepted rule that the prosecution is entitled to prove its case free from any defendant's option to stipulate the evidence away rests on good sense. A syllogism is not a story, and a naked proposition in a courtroom may be no match for the robust evidence that would be used to prove it. People who hear a story interrupted by gaps of abstraction may be puzzled at the missing chapters, and jurors asked to rest a momentous decision on the story's truth can feel put upon at being asked to take responsibility knowing that more could be said than they have heard. A convincing tale can be told with economy, but when economy becomes a break in the natural sequence of narrative evidence, an assurance that the missing link is really there is never more than second best.

False   10.   Rule 404(a)(2)(A) and Rule 405(a) provide that the prosecution in rebuttal may offer evidence in the form of reputation or opinion testimony as to the character of the defendant for unpeacefulness but may not introduce evidence of specific instances of conduct to prove the accused's character for unpeacefulness.

True   11.   As stated in People v. Barbour, 106 Ill.App.3d 993, 999–1000, 62 Ill.Dec. 641, 436 N.E.2d 667 (1982):

The State (and, indeed, some of the authorities) have used "common design" and "*modus operandi*" interchangeably but the concepts are quite distinguishable. A common design refers to a larger criminal scheme of which the crime charged is only a portion. *Modus operandi* means, literally, "method of working," and refers to a pattern of criminal behavior so distinctive that separate crimes are recognizable as the handiwork of the same wrongdoer. See generally McCormick, Evidence sec. 190, at 448–49 (2d ed. 1972). A common design is frequently relevant to show the motive for the crime charged. *Modus operandi* is most useful in showing that the accused is the perpetrator of the crime charged.

False   12.   Rule 406 provides:

Evidence of a person's habit or an organization's routine practice may be admitted to prove that on a particular occasion the person or organization acted in accordance with the habit or routine practice. The court may admit this evidence regardless of whether it is corroborated or whether there was an eyewitness.

False   13.   For other crimes, wrongs, or acts evidence to be admitted, the proponent must introduce evidence sufficient when viewed most favorably by a reasonable jury to permit a finding that the existence of the other crime, wrong, or act is more probably true than not true, Rule 104(b); clear and convincing evidence is *not* required.

True   14.   Proposed rule 406(b), not enacted but reflective of the common law, provided:

Method of proof. Habit or routine practice may be proved by testimony in the form of an opinion or by specific instances of conduct sufficient in number to warrant a finding that the habit existed or that the practice was routine.

True   15.   Negligent hiring requires a finding that the person hired possesses a particular character trait, the possession of which makes it negligent to hire the individual for the particular job under consideration. Character is thus an essential element of a claim for negligent hiring. In cases in which character is an essential element of a claim, Rule 405(b) provides that proof may be in the form of specific instances of the person's conduct in addition to character evidence in the form of testimony as to reputation or testimony in the form of an opinion.

True   16.   Rule 405(a) provides:

(a) By Reputation or Opinion. When evidence of a person's character or character trait is admissible, it may be proved by testimony about the person's reputation or by testimony in the form of an opinion. On cross-examination of the character witness, the court may allow an inquiry into relevant specific instances of the person's conduct.

False   17.   With respect to reputation testimony, Rule 405(a) provides that in all cases in which evidence of character or a trait of character of a person is admissible, proof may be made by testimony as to reputation or by testimony in the form of an opinion. Rule 404(b)(1) provides, moreover, that evidence of crimes, wrongs, or other acts is *not* admissible to prove the character of a person in order to show action in conformity therewith.

False   18.   Evidence which comprises the crime for which the accused in on trial, whether or not the crime of conspiracy, is offered as direct evidence of the crime and thus not as "other" crimes, wrongs, or acts evidence governed by Rule 404(b). Accordingly, the notice requirement of Rule 404(b)(2)(A) and (B) would be inapplicable.

True   19.   Rule 404(b)(2), crimes, wrongs, or other acts, includes specific instances of conduct which are not criminal.

False   20.   The proper question to the reputation witness was, and still is, "Have you heard?"

True   21.   Rule 412(a)(2) provides that evidence offered to prove any alleged victim's sexual predisposition (character) is not admissible in any civil or criminal proceeding involving alleged sexual misconduct.

True   22.   Rule 412(b)(1)(A) provides that in criminal cases evidence of specific instances of sexual behavior by the alleged victim offered to prove that a person other than the accused was the source of semen, injury or other physical evidence is admissible.

False   23.   Rule 412(b)(2) provides that in a civil case, evidence offered to prove the sexual behavior or sexual predisposition of any alleged victim is admissible if it is otherwise admissible under the Federal Rules of Evidence and its probative value substantially outweighs the danger of harm to any victim and of unfair prejudice to any party. Evidence of an alleged victim's reputation is admissible only if it has been placed in controversy by the alleged victim.

True   24.   Rule 414(a) provides that in a criminal case in which the defendant is accused of an offense of child molestation, evidence of the defendant's commission of another offense or offenses of child molestation is admissible, and may be considered for its bearing on any matter to which it is relevant.

False   25.   Rule 403 governs the admissibility of evidence of the defendant's commission of another offense or offenses of sexual assault when offered in a criminal case in which the defendant is accused of an offense of sexual assault.

10.   **Real and Demonstrative Evidence, Experiments and Views**

False   1.   Most experiments are conducted out of court with the results of the experiment being presented in court.

True   2.   Anyone with personal knowledge that the photograph fairly and accurately represents what it purports to represent at the relevant time may authenticate the photograph; the photographer is not required.

False   3.   Courtroom demonstrations including those employing tangible items are permissible within the discretion of the trial court.

True   4.   A greater degree of accuracy is often required of models and computer animations than other types of demonstrative evidence because of their capacity to persuade.

False   5.   While a narcotic seized from the drug pusher is direct evidence, a jacket worn by a bank robber is circumstantial evidence.

True   6.   With respect to an experiment to determine how an event occurred, since the possibility of varying a condition to produce the desired result clearly exists, instances upon substantial similarity of conditions is usually strict.

True   7.   The Advisory Committee's Note to Rule 1002 states:

The usual course is for a witness on the stand to identify the photograph or motion picture as a correct representation of events which he saw or of a scene with which he is familiar. In fact he adopts the picture as his testimony, or, in common parlance, uses the picture to illustrate his testimony.

The artificiality and theoretical soundness of such position is certainly subject to criticism.

True   8.   Real evidence involves the production of an object which usually but not always (e.g., a bullet used as an exemplar for comparison purposes) had a direct or indirect part in the incident, such as a murder weapon, piece of exploding bottle, or article of clothing. It also includes the exhibition of injured parts of the body. Real evidence provides the trier of fact with an opportunity to draw a relevant first hand sense impression. Such evidence may be either direct, such as an exploding bottle, or circumstantial, such as an article of clothing worn at the time of arrest by the defendant in a robbery prosecution exhibited to the jury to show conformity with eyewitness description.

False   9.   Views are not limited to real property; a jury may be taken to view a subway car where a crime allegedly occurred or to any to other location deemed worthy.

False   10.   The passage of three months does not mean that the intersection has changed. Thus the photograph may still fairly and accurately reflect the intersection at the time of the accident even though taken three months later. If conditions have changed, the fact of changed conditions alone do not render any photograph inadmissible if after the changes are explained the trier of fact can understand the correct and helpful representation and thus will not be confused or misled by the photograph. However, since the nature of a photograph makes difficult any separation of illustration from assertion, a change of conditions may make the picture so confusing or misleading as to require exclusion, Rule 403.

False   11.   Admissibility of testimony at a view is governed by the common law; there is no Federal Rule of Evidence addressing the conduct of a view.

True   12.   Even the Advisory Committee's Note to Rule 1002 recognizes where a person is not available to testify that the photograph fairly and accurately represents what it purports to represent at the relevant time and the photograph is authenticated instead by means of process and system testimony combined with a chain of custody, the photograph is admitted as substantive evidence:

On occasion, however, situations arise in which contents are sought to be proved. Copyright, defamation, and invasion of privacy by photograph or motion picture falls in this category. Similarly as to situations in which the picture is offered as having independent probative value, e.g., automatic photograph of bank robber. See People v. Doggett, 83 Cal.App.2d 405, 188 P.2d 792 (1948), photograph of defendants engaged in indecent act; Mouser and Philbin, Photographic Evidence—Is There a Recognized Basis for Admissibility? 8 Hastings L.J. 310 (1957). The most commonly encountered of this latter group is of course, the X-ray, with substantial authority calling for production of the original.

False   13.   As stated in Old Chief v. United States, 519 U.S. 172, 189, 117 S.Ct. 644, 136 L.Ed.2d 574 (1997), the accepted rule that a litigant is entitled to prove its case free from any other litigant's option to stipulate the evidence away rests on good sense:

> In sum, the accepted rule that the prosecution is entitled to prove its case free from any defendant's option to stipulate the evidence away rests on good sense. A syllogism is not a story, and a naked proposition in a courtroom may be no match for the robust evidence that would be used to prove it. People who hear a story interrupted by gaps of abstraction may be puzzled at the missing chapters, and jurors asked to rest a momentous decision on the story's truth can feel put upon at being asked to take responsibility knowing that more could be said than they have heard. A convincing tale can be told with economy, but when economy becomes a break in the natural sequence of narrative evidence, an assurance that the missing link is really there is never more than second best.

True   14.   Since taking a jury on a view closely resembles taking a third grade class to a firehouse, the alternative of reliance upon demonstrative aids such as diagrams, photographs, or computer animations should not be overlooked.

False   15.   Despite their gruesomeness and thus arguably prejudicial effect on the jury, relevant photographs will ordinarily be admitted in the court's discretion where they tend to prove such things as the existence of a crime, the cause of death, the number and location of the wounds, the manner in which they were inflicted, the amount of force used, the willfulness of the act in question, a person's identity, or to corroborate evidence concerning an unusual cause of death. By its very nature, the more gruesome the crime, the more gruesome the photographs which will be admitted.

11.   Cross-Examination

A.   Leading Questions; Scope and Extent: Fed.R.Evid. 611(b) and (c)

False   1.   Rule 611(c)(1) provides that *ordinarily* leading questions should be permitted on cross-examination. Where a party exceeds the scope of direct examination or is cross-examining a witness called by an opposing party determined by the trial court to be a "hostile witness, an adverse party, or a witness identified with an adverse party," 611(c)(2), cross-examination should ordinarily be conducted *without* the use of leading questions.

False   2.   If the witness has testified to purely technical matters or does not harm the cross-examiner's case, an attack on credibility, even if possible, will most often be ill advised. For example, if a records custodian is authenticating medical records from a hospital admission, establishing that the records custodian three years ago has an armed robbery conviction is very likely to repel the jury who most likely would find such a personal attack unwarranted under the circumstances.

True   3.   Rule 611(c)(2) provides that when a party calls a hostile witness, an adverse party, or a witness identified with an adverse party, interrogation may be by leading questions.

False   4.   If the witness is called as a hostile witness, the cross-examining attorney may not employ leading questions as a matter of course because the witness is presumably friendly to him, Rule 611(c)(1), i.e., not ordinary, but may employ leading questions to the extent necessary to develop the witness' testimony as if the witness was on direct examination, Rule 611(c).

False   5.   Rule 611(b) provides that the scope of cross-examination should be limited to the subject matter of the *direct examination* and matters affecting the credibility of the witness.

True   6.   Counsel on cross-examination may (1) attempt to elicit disputed facts from the witness favorable to his case, (2) have the witness repeat those facts testified to on direct favorable to the cross-examiner, (3) have the witness testify to nondisputed facts essential to presentation of his theory of the case, (4) attempt to have the witness qualify, modify, or otherwise shed light upon his testimony with respect to unfavorable versions of disputed facts given on direct examination, (5) establish that the witness' testimony is not harmful to the advocate's case on the critical points under dispute and/or (6) ask questions to the witness designed primarily to keep the cross-examiner's theory of the case before the trier of fact.

False   7.   The purpose of prohibiting the use of leading questions on direct examination except to the extent necessary to develop the witness' testimony is that on direct examination the ordinary witness will be responsive to the suggestions of counsel; it is the witness' testimony and not counsel's which is being sought. Responsiveness by the witness to suggestive questions by counsel is ordinarily not a risk present on cross-examination.

False   8.   Rule 611(b) provides that the trial court *may*, in the exercise of discretion, permit inquiry into additional matters as if on direct examination.

False   9.   Rule 611 does not purport to determine the extent to which an accused waives his privilege against self-incrimination by testifying.

True   10.   Yes, according to Wigmore, but the "greatest legal engine ever invented for the discovery of truth" often has real problems making it over the hill.

True   11.   The criminal defendant under the confrontation clause must be given wide latitude with respect to cross-examination for the purpose of establishing untrustworthy partiality or otherwise challenge the credibility of the witness and to present a theory of defense. Curtailment of cross-examination becomes discretionary only after the right of the defendant to confront witnesses against him has been substantially and thoroughly exercised. Of course, even the criminal defendant's right to cross-examine is not without its limits.

False   12.   The criminal defendant's confrontation clause rights are implicated by the extent of cross-examination permitted the accused by the trial judge.

True   13.   Avoidance of the witness having to be recalled at a later time in the trial is a significant reason why a trial court may permit cross-examination beyond the scope of direct examination.

False   14.   Rule 104(d) provides that the accused does not, by testifying upon a preliminary matter, become subject to cross-examination as to other issues in the case.

True   15.   Issues involving the scope of direct examination are extremely unlikely to arise with respect to ordinary occurrence witnesses to a relevant event. Scope of direct examination issues arise most frequently in cases where many claims, counter-claims, cross-claims, etc., are being asserted by several parties.

B.   Modes of Impeachment; Collateral and Non Collateral Matters; Good Faith Basis

True   1.   Modes of impeachment, such as untrustworthy partiality and prior conviction, attack the sincerity component of credibility.

False   2.   Leading questions are employed to effectuate a mode of impeachment, such as asking an expert witness "You were paid over $5,000 to testify here today, weren't you," to raise an inference of untrustworthy partiality, but leading questions are not a mode of impeachment themselves.

True   3.   The factors are perception, recordation and recollection, narration and sincerity.

True   4.   In assessing the credibility of a witness, the trier of fact looks not only to the content of the witness' testimony on direct and his answers to questions asked on cross-examination, the trier of fact also assesses the demeanor of the witness throughout.

True   5.   While alcohol addiction as affecting personal knowledge is generally excluded, alcohol use at the time of perception of an event is a permitted subject of cross-examination.

False   6.   Defense counsel has a right to learn the name employed and residence occupied of all the prosecution witnesses at the time relevant in the litigation. If, however, the witness has acquired a new name and residence through, for example, participation in the witness protection program, such new name and address need not be disclosed.

False   7.   If a matter is considered collateral, the inquiry if otherwise proper is permitted but the answer of the witness on cross-examination must be accepted; extrinsic evidence, i.e., evidence offered other than through the witness himself, in contradiction is not permitted.

True   8.   Untrustworthy partiality, i.e., bias, interest, corruption, or coercion, is a non-collateral matter.

False   9.   Whether extrinsic evidence must as against may be introduced with respect to a non-collateral matter differs depending upon the particular attack on credibility involved. Thus, for example, prior conviction impeachment requires the introduction of extrinsic evidence if the witness denies having been convicted while cross-examination as to a fact raising the inference of bias denied by the witness permits, but does not require, the introduction of extrinsic evidence.

True   10.   A good faith basis as to the underlying matter contained in a question propounded to a witness on cross-examination is required.

C.   Prior Inconsistent Statements: Fed.R.Evid. 613

True   1.   Rule 613 governs the admissibility of prior inconsistent statements admitted as substantive evidence solely by virtue of operation of Rule 801(d)(1)(A).

False   2.   Rule 613(b) specifically states that it does not apply to admissions of a party-opponent as defined in Rule 801(d)(2).

False   3.   Rule 613(b) does not govern statements admissible pursuant to a hearsay exception contained in Rules 803, 804, or 807.

True   4.   Rule 613(a) provides that in examining a witness concerning a prior statement made by the witness, whether written or not, the statement need not be shown nor its contents disclosed to the witness at that time, but on request the same shall be shown or disclosed to opposing counsel.

True   5.   The rationale behind prior inconsistent statement impeachment is that a witness who testifies one way at trial while speaking inconsistently prior to trial is blowing hot and cold thereby raising doubts as to the truthfulness of both statements.

False   6.   Inconsistency may consist of the omission from a prior statement of a matter which would reasonably be expected to have been mentioned at that time if true.

True   7.   With respect to defining the requirement of inconsistency McCormick, Evidence § 34 at 127 (5th ed.1999) suggests the following: "[C]ould the jury reasonably find that a witness who believed the truth of the facts testified to would have been unlikely to make a prior statement of this tenor?" 3A Wigmore, Evidence § 1040 at 1048 (Chadbourn rev.1970) proposes a similar liberal test: "Do the two expressions appear to have been produced by inconsistent beliefs?" The liberal view of inconsistency has generally been applied in the federal courts.

False   8.   A witness who testifies to a fact at trail may be impeached with a prior statement of the witness claiming lack of recollection as to the fact; current recollection and prior lack of recollection are inconsistent.

True   9.   The formal insistence that the attention of the witness be directed to the statement on cross-examination is relaxed in Rule 613(b) in favor of simply providing the witness an opportunity to explain or deny and the opposite party an opportunity to examine on the statement, with no specification of any particular time or sequence. Rule 613(b) thus permits extrinsic proof to be introduced before the witness is provided an opportunity to admit, deny, and/or explain the prior statement.

True   10.   In practice, the traditional foundation is generally laid by counsel on cross-examination. Juxtaposition is the most effective form of impeachment. Counsel desiring primarily to impeach and not to highlight the prior statement to encourage substantive use by the trier of fact opts in favor of confronting the witness with the prior inconsistent statement on cross-examination. Custom and lack of appreciation of the change brought about by Rule 613(b) undoubtedly also play their part in maintaining the status quo.

False   11.   Where neither a cautionary nor limiting instruction is requested by counsel, if the prior inconsistent statement is extremely damaging if considered by the jury as substantive evidence and the proponent of such evidence is the prosecution in a criminal otherwise having a weak case, the court to avoid plain error must *sua sponte* give such an instruction, but not otherwise.

False   12.   Questions to the impeaching witness presenting extrinsic proof should state the time, place, circumstances of the statement and the subject matter of the statement but not its content. Leading questions are permitted as necessary to develop the witness' testimony, Rule 611(c).

True   13.   In practice, extrinsic evidence is rarely offered where a witness unequivocally admits making a non-collateral prior inconsistent statement.

True   14.   Extrinsic evidence establishing the existence of a collateral prior inconsistent statement is inadmissible.

True   15.   Neither prior practice at common law nor Rule 613(b) requires counsel to permit the witness to offer an explanation when examined on cross-examination as to an alleged prior inconsistent statement. The cross-examiner may require the witness to answer the questions whether he made the particular statement yes or no. As long as opposing counsel on redirect is permitted to elicit an explanation, the common law foundation requirement and Rule 613(b) are satisfied.

     D.   **Untrustworthy Partiality: Bias, Interest, Corruption, Coercion**

True   1.   Untrustworthy partiality is ordinarily initially explored on cross-examination prior to any extrinsic evidence being offered.

False   2.   Counsel may inquire on cross-examination as to the witness' feelings or beliefs as well as the witness' statements to establish untrustworthy partiality.

False   3.   Bias like other matters relevant to establishing untrustworthy partiality is a non-collateral matter. Extrinsic evidence is permitted but not required.

True   4.   Although the scope of such cross-examination is generally within the trial court's discretion, wide latitude must be afforded the defendant in cross-examination for the purpose of establishing partiality or otherwise challenging the credibility of a government witness. Where charges are dropped in exchange for testimony, where the witness is a co-indictee or has unrelated charges pending, is a paid informer, has been granted immunity, has been promised leniency, is awaiting sentence, is being held in protective custody, has been given special treatment at government expense, or has entered into a plea agreement, amongst others, foreclosure of the right to inquire may constitute reversible error.

True   5.   Counsel on cross-examination may inquire as to whether any deals were made with the witness by the prosecution pursuant to the right to explore potentially relevant matters on cross-examination but may not assert the existence of an actual deal in the form of a question absent a good faith basis as to the existence of the deal.

      E.   **Conviction of a Crime: Fed.R.Evid. 609**

False   1.   The trier of fact is already aware that self-interest may affect sincerity and that nobody has a greater interest in the outcome of a criminal case than the criminal defendant.

True   2.   Only misdemeanor convictions for crimes of dishonesty or false statement may ever be employed to impeach a witness' character for truthfulness; petty larceny is not a crime involving dishonesty or false statement, i.e., deceit, untruthfulness, or falsification—it does not involve some element of active misrepresentation.

False   3.   Shoplifting is not a crime involving dishonesty or false statement—a physical attempt to remain undetected does not make the crime one involving dishonesty or false statement—petty larceny does not involve some element of active misrepresentation.

False   4.   The trial court is not obligated to rule in advance of trial on a motion in limine as to the admissibility of a prior conviction. For example, the trial judge very well might wish to await actual introduction of evidence at trial before applying a discretionary balancing test.

False   5.   Evidence of a prior conviction is admissible under Rule 609 to establish that the witness has disobeyed a serious law of society evidencing a character that would lead the witness to lie under oath.

False   6.   Acts involving dishonesty or false statement, i.e., deceit, untruthfulness, or falsification—involves some element of active misrepresentation, are particularly probative of whether the witness will testify truthfully; acts of violence are not.

False   7.   Rule 609(e) provides that pendency of an appeal by any witness of the prior conviction is admissible, not just the criminal defendant.

False   8.   Unfortunately, the "mere fact" method has not generally found favor in the federal courts.

True   9.   Prior conviction impeachment does rest upon the premise that a person who has been shown to be willing to violate a serious law of society possesses a general character to be untruthful from which the jury may infer untruthfulness of the witness in testifying in the matter at hand.

True   10.   If a witness denies he was the one convicted, the prosecution must establish the fact of conviction and that the witness was in fact the person convicted through extrinsic evidence; prior conviction impeachment is a non-collateral matter requiring rather than permitting extrinsic proof if the witness denies the matter on cross-examination.

True   11.   Embezzlement, involving an element of active misrepresentation, is a crime of dishonesty or false statement.

False   12.   While all prior convictions subject to a discretionary balancing test under Rule 609 would be employed to impeach applying the mere fact method, thus initially giving the appearance that the mere fact method favors the prosecution, the mere fact method actually favors the accused. Almost all convictions are admitted already applying the discretionary balancing test. Most importantly, when the prior conviction is admitted against the criminal defendant anticipatorily on direct examination without the nature of the prior conviction being disclosed, the risk of unfair prejudice is significantly reduced. Such reduction becomes even more pronounced where the nature of the prior crime and the current charged offense are similar.

False   13.   Rule 609(b) provides that evidence of a conviction under this rule is not admissible if a period of more than ten years has elapsed since the date of the conviction or of the release of the witness from the confinement imposed for that conviction, whichever is the later date, unless the court determines that the probative value of the conviction supported   by   specific   facts   and   circumstances substantially outweighs its prejudicial effect.

True   14.   Although the jury is instructed that they are to consider the evidence of a prior conviction solely in determining the credibility of the defendant as a witness and not as evidence of guilt of the crime for which the defendant is on trial, Rule 105, it is rarely seriously asserted that the trier of fact is fully capable much less interested in making such a distinction:

"We accept much self-deception on this. We say that the evidence of the prior convictions is admissible only to impeach the defendant's testimony, and not as evidence of the prior crimes themselves. Juries are solemnly instructed to this effect. Is there anyone who doubts what the effect of this evidence in fact is on the jury? If we know so clearly what we are actually doing, why do we pretend that we are not doing what we clearly are doing?" Griswold, "The Long View," 51 A.B.A.J. 1017, 1021 (1965).

False   15.   As provided under Rule 609, successful completion of probation without incident alone does not preclude the prior conviction being employed to impeach; a finding of rehabilitation of the person convicted is required to make the prior conviction inadmissible, Rule 609(c)(1).

False   16.   Introduction by the criminal defendant on his direct examination of the fact of a prior conviction definitively ruled admissible to impeach by the trial court on a motion in limine waives the right to assert the error of the trial judge's motion in limine ruling on appeal; the opposing party must be given the choice as to whether or not to actually offer the prior conviction to impeach at trial.

False   17.   Rule 609(b) provides that evidence of a conviction, including a crime involving dishonesty or false statement, is not admissible if a period of more than ten years has elapsed since the date of the conviction or of the release of the witness from the confinement imposed for that conviction, whichever is the later date, unless the court determines that the probative value of the conviction supported by specific facts and circumstances substantially outweighs its prejudicial effect.

True   18.   Failure to give a limiting instruction is more likely to be plain error where the prior conviction and the current charge are similar.

True   19.   Rule 609(d) provides that evidence of a juvenile adjudication of the accused is not admissible to impeach the credibility of the accused if he testifies at the trial.

False   20.   Prior conviction impeachment is not only a non-collateral matter, if the witness denies the prior conviction on cross-examination, the cross-examining party *must* establish the fact of conviction and that the witness was in fact the person convicted through extrinsic evidence.

False   21.   Rule 609(c)(2) provides that a prior conviction is not admissible to impeach only if the prior conviction has been the subject of a pardon based upon a finding of innocence; pardons are based upon many other considerations such as health issues.

False   22.   Rule 609(a)(1) provides that the accused may be impeached with a prior conviction punishable by death or imprisonment in excess of one year if the court determines that the probative value of admitting the evidence outweighs the prejudicial effect to the accused, a discretionary balancing test different than the one incorporated into Rule 403.

False   23.   Armed robbery is not a crime involving dishonesty or false statement, i.e., deceit, untruthfulness or falsification—it does not involve some element of active misrepresentation.

False   24.   The more similar the prior conviction is to the crime for which the accused is on trial, the greater the risk of unfair prejudice arising that the jury improperly applying the bad man inference and thus greater the likelihood of the prior conviction being ruled inadmissible to impeach.

False   25.   The criminal defendant on anticipatory disclosure may testify to having been convicted of a particular offense in a particular court, on a particular date, following his plea of guilty; the accused's testimony that he pled guilty on the prior occasion suggests his willingness to "own up" to what he does for the further inference that he is innocent of the current charge as to which he pled not guilty.

F.   **Prior Acts of Misconduct: Fed.R.Evid. 608(b)(1)**

True   1.   Rule 608(b)(1) provides that the giving of testimony, whether by an accused or by any other witness, does not operate as a waiver of the accused's or the witness' privilege against self-incrimination when examined with respect to matters which relate only to credibility.

False   2.   Rule 608(b)(1) provides that specific instances of conduct of a witness may, in the discretion of the court, if probative of truthfulness or untruthfulness, be inquired into on *cross-examination* of the witness concerning the witness' character for truthfulness or untruthfulness.

False   3.   Specific instances of conduct sufficiently probative of untruthfulness—involves some element of dishonesty or false statement, i.e., deceit, untruthfulness, or falsification—some element of active misrepresentation—include conduct which constitutes commission of an offense not leading to a conviction as well as acts of misconduct not constituting a crime.

False   4.   Although filing of a false income tax return involves an element of misrepresentation and is thus sufficiently probative of untruthfulness to be the subject of inquiry, the witness must be asked about the underlying act and not whether he was arrested for the act. The fact of misconduct alone is relevant when cross-examining the alleged actor, not whether someone else might think that the witness committed the act.

True   5.   Extrinsic evidence with respect to the specific act of misconduct is not admissible; the matter is collateral, Rule 608(b). The cross-examiner must take the answer given by the witness.

G.   **Character for Truthfulness and Untruthfulness: Fed.R.Evid. 608**

False   1.   Evidence in the form of reputation or opinion in support of the character of a witness for truthfulness is permitted only if the character of the witness for truthfulness has been attacked by opinion or reputation evidence or otherwise, Rule 608.

False   2.   While the Advisory Committee's Note points out that whether contradiction constitutes a sufficient attack upon the character of the witness depends upon the circumstances, it has generally been held that mere contradiction by other evidence does not suffice.

False   3.   When a character witness testifies as to the reputation of the principal witness for truthfulness or untruthfulness, the proper question on cross-examination with respect to specific acts of conduct of the principal witness at common law is "Have you heard?"

False   4.   Extrinsic evidence with respect to specific acts of conduct of the principal witness not resulting in a conviction is not admissible; the cross-examiner must take the witness' answer. The prohibition against introduction of extrinsic evidence encompasses evidence establishing the existence of the act, arrest, indictment, report, rumor, etc., as well as evidence establishing that the character witness heard or knew about any of the foregoing.

True   5.   Opinion testimony must be based upon personal knowledge of the principal witness by the character witness; the extent of the relationship with the principal witness is a proper subject of inquiry on cross-examination.

True   6.   Rule 608(a) provides that the character of every witness may be attacked by testimony in the form of reputation or opinion testimony as to character for truthfulness.

False   7.   A showing of bias does not constitute a sufficient direct attack on character to permit introduction of evidence in support of the character of the witness for truthfulness.

True   8.   Upon testifying as to knowledge of the witness' reputation for truthfulness or untruthfulness, the witness may further be asked, "In view of that reputation, would you believe him under oath?"

True   9.   An opinion witness cross-examined as to specific instances of conduct may be asked whether knowledge of such instances, not including the incident at hand, would have resulted in the witness changing his testimony as to the character of the principal witness for truthfulness.

False   10.   Any character witness may be asked not only concerning the specific acts of the principal witness probative of truthfulness or untruthfulness, but may be cross-examined concerning familiarity with convictions as well as arrests, rumors, reports, indictments, etc., concerning the principal witness. Such facts have a natural bearing upon the reputation of the principal witness and the character witness' opinion of the principal witness. Lack of familiarity with such facts is relevant to an assessment of the basis for the character witness' testimony. Familiarity with such matters explores the character witness' standard of "truthfulness" or "untruthfulness." The specific instance of conduct probative of untruthfulness may have occurred either before or after the incident comprising the subject matter of the litigation.

False 11. If the witness' character for truthfulness has been attacked by means of opinion or reputation testimony "or otherwise," his character for truthfulness may then be supported but only in the form of opinion or reputation testimony, Rule 608(a)(2); specific instances of conduct in support of the witness' character for truthfulness remain inadmissible.

True 12. A reputation witness may not be cross-examined as to whether he had heard of an arrest or that the underlying specific existence of conduct occurred, unless the specific instance of conduct is probative of untruthfulness, i.e., involved dishonesty or false statement and thus some element of active misrepresentation. Armed robbery is not a crime involving dishonesty or false statement.

True 13. Testimony as to the reputation must be based upon the witness having discussed the reputation with others, having heard it discussed by others, or of never having heard it discussed although he would have heard contrary comments had they existed.

True 14. A question implying either coercion or corruption constitutes a sufficient direct attack on character for truthfulness to permit character evidence in the form of reputation or opinion evidence to be admitted to rebut.

False 15. Character for truthfulness at the time of witness' trial testimony is the relevant inquiry, not character for truthfulness at the time of event forming the subject matter of the litigation at hand.

12. **Relevant Evidence and Social Policy: Fed.R.Evid. 407–411**

False 1. Rule 407 bars in products liability litigation solely admission of evidence of subsequent remedial measures, i.e., measures taken with respect to the product occurring *after* the injury or harm allegedly caused by the product occurred.

False   2.   Evidence of a subsequent remedial measure may not be employed to impeach when the testimony introduced by a defendant goes no further than to maintain that nothing improper occurred. On the other hand, when the witness goes beyond what is necessary, i.e., "safe" or "not defective," and states on direct that this conduct was the "safest," "most reasonable," or "best designed product possible" then impeachment is in order.

True   3.   A change in an instruction manual after the event may be a subsequent remedial measure barred by Rule 407.

True   4.   See answer to question 2 supra.

True   5.   Evidence of agreeing to pay a valuable consideration and accompanying statement of fault are inadmissible to prove liability for the claim or its amount only if the person making the statement is disputing either the validity or amount of the claim; no dispute appears present here.

False   6.   Rule 408 bars the introduction of completed comprises when offered by any of the parties or a third party.

False   7.   Rule 408 provides that evidence of conduct or statements made in compromise negotiations are not admissible to prove liability for or invalidity of the claim or its amount.

True   8.   Rule 408 provides that statements made in settlement negotiations are not admissible to impeach through a prior inconsistent statement.

True   9.   Rule 409 provides that a statement offering to pay medical, hospital, or similar expenses occasioned by an injury is not admissible to prove liability for the injury.

True   10.   Statements of fault or fact accompanying an offer to pay medical expenses are not precluded; Rule 409 only precludes introduction of the payment of or offer to pay such expenses themselves.

True   11.   Rule 410 provides that in any civil or criminal proceeding evidence of (1) a plea of guilty later withdrawn; (2) a plea of nolo contendere; (3) any statement made in the course of any proceedings under Rule 11 of the Federal Rules of Criminal Procedure or comparable state procedure regarding either of the foregoing pleas; or (4) any statement made in the course of plea discussions with an attorney for the prosecuting authority which do not result in a plea of guilty or which result in a plea of guilty later withdrawn, is not admissible against the defendant who made the plea or was a participant in the plea discussions as either substantive evidence or for impeachment.

False   12.   Rule 410 applies to statements made in the course of discussions with an attorney for the prosecuting authority whenever the defendant in fact had exhibited a reasonable subjective expectation that plea negotiations were in progress. Accordingly, the trial court must apply a two-tiered analysis and determine, first, whether the accused exhibited an actual subjective expectation to negotiate a plea at the time of the discussion, and, second, whether the accused's expectation was reasonable given the totality of the objective circumstances. Where the defendant clearly manifested an intent to explore a plea in exchange for a concession, this determination creates little difficulty. On the other hand, where such a preamble is not stated, the totality of the circumstances may nevertheless evidence a reasonable subjective expectation that plea negotiations had been commenced. However, under a totality of the circumstances approach, an accused's subsequent account of his prior subjective mental impressions cannot be considered the sole determinative factor. Otherwise, every confession would be vulnerable to such subsequent challenge. Thus in order for the court to find "actual" and "reasonable" subjective expectation, the accused must have "exhibited" by expressing in some way the hope that a concession in exchange for his plea will come to pass. In short, hope of obtaining leniency is not enough; to have plea bargaining a discussion seeking a concession in exchange for a plea must occur. Unconditional, unbargained for, volunteered admissions or confessions by the accused are thus outside the scope of exclusion provided for in Rule 410.

False   13.   Rule 410 applies only to withdrawn pleas, nolo contendere pleas whether or not withdrawn, and statements made in the course of plea negotiations not resulting in a plea of guilty or resulting in guilty plea later withdrawn. A guilty plea not withdrawn is often admissible in a subsequent civil action arising out of the same facts, as well as sometimes in other situations, since an unwithdrawn plea of guilty admits all matters well pleaded in the indictment or information.

False   14.   An area of special significance in Rule 410 concerns the limitation of the rule as amended in 1980 to plea discussions between the attorney for the government and the attorney for the defendant or the defendant whether or not acting pro se. Excluded from the scope of Rule 410 are statements made during plea negotiations to law enforcement officers, unless the law enforcement officer is acting with express authority from a government attorney.

True   15.   When the authenticity of a statement employed at trial to impeach a plaintiff's witness is disputed, the fact that the statement was taken by an insurance investigator is admissible to show bias and interest.

13.   Privileges: Fed.R.Evid. 501

True   1.   Rule 501 states that in civil actions and proceedings with respect to an element of a claim or defense as to which State law supplies the rule of decision, the privilege of a witness, person, government, State, or political subdivision thereof shall be determined in accordance with State law.

False   2.   When two parties consult the same attorney their communications are protected by the attorney-client privilege as to third parties but not when offered in an action between the two of them, Standard 503(d)(5).

False 3. A law clerk is a representative of the lawyer, Standard 503(a)(3), whose presence does not destroy confidentiality, Standard 503(b)(1).

True 4. At a minimum, the lawyer-client privilege protects communications that constitute legal advice or tend directly or indirectly to reveal the substance of a client confidence.

True 5. The communication to the lawyer is not confidential in that it is intended by the client to be disclosed by the lawyer to a third person, Standard 503(a)(4).

False 6. The husband-wife testimonial privilege that exists solely in criminal cases belongs solely to the testifying spouse, in this case the wife.

True 7. The confidential communication privilege applicable in both civil and criminal cases survives termination of marriage by death or divorce.

False 8. Where an informer was neither a participant nor an eyewitness to the crime, discretion is normally exercised against disclosure.

False 9. Voluntary disclosure of a significant part of the confidential matter or communication waives the lawyer-client privilege only with respect to all other communications on the same subject matter.

True 10. Standard 513(b) provides that in jury cases, proceedings shall be conducted, to the extent practicable, so as to facilitate the making of claims of privilege without the knowledge of the jury.

False 11. The "subject matter test" refers to defining the representatives of a client other than an individual person, such as a corporation, falling within the umbrella of the lawyer-client privilege.

True   12.   A privilege is not waived if disclosure of a confidential communication occurred without the holder of the privilege having an opportunity to claim the privilege, Standard 512(b).

True   13.   Standard 503(b)(3) provides that the lawyer-client privilege applies to confidential communications made by the client or his lawyer to a lawyer representing another client in a matter of common interest in any dispute between the two clients. The presence of the other client does not obviate the privilege.

True   14.   Standard 503(d)(2) provides that the lawyer-client privilege does not apply as to a communication relevant to an issue between parties who claim through the same deceased client, regardless of whether the claims are by testate or intestate succession or by inter vivos transaction.

False   15.   Since the effect of a privilege is to suppress the truth, a privilege should be recognized only if the interest or relationship is of outstanding importance and would undoubtedly be harmed by denying the protection of privilege.

True   16.   Federal courts recognize a husband-wife confidential communications privilege in both civil and criminal cases. Both spouses are holders of the privilege.

False   17.   Standard 503(a)(1) provides that a "client" is a person, public officer, or corporation, association, or other organization or entity, either public or private, who is rendered professional legal services by a lawyer, or who consults a lawyer with a view to obtaining professional legal services from him.

True   18.   A claim of privilege against self-incrimination may be admitted and commented upon in a civil action.

False   19.   Rule 501 permits the federal courts to create additional privileges pursuant to the principles of the common law interpreted in light of reason and experience.

True   20.   An expert hired solely to assist in trial preparation, i.e., the expert will not testify at trial, is a representative of the lawyer, Standard 503(a)(3). Standard 503(b)(2) states that the lawyer-client privilege extends to confidential communications between the client's lawyer and the lawyer's representative.

True   21.   The United States Supreme Court in Jaffee v. Redmond, 518 U.S. 1, 116 S.Ct. 1923, 135 L.Ed.2d 337 (1996), recognized a privilege for confidential communications between psychotherapist and patient based upon the presence of a special need to maintain confidentiality.

False   22.   A document that is pre-existing does not acquire a privileged status by being conveyed to a lawyer as part of the process of a client obtaining legal advice.

False   23.   Federal courts do not recognize an accountant-client privilege.

False   24.   The trade secret privilege is a qualified privilege; the court can order disclosure if application of the trade secret privilege will tend to conceal fraud or otherwise work injustice, Standard 508.

True   25.   The known presence of a third party indicates a lack of intention that the communication be confidential thus precluding the statement from being protected by the lawyer-client privilege.

False   26.   The testimonial husband-wife privilege ceases to exist if the marriage becomes an utter sham.

True   27.   A statement to an attorney intended to be publicly disclosed is not confidential and thus not privileged.

False   28.   The scope of the lawyer-client privilege as applied to representatives of a corporate client extends beyond persons having authority to act upon advice rendered pursuant thereto, the "control group test," to those falling within the "subject matter test," adopted in principle if not name by the United States Supreme Court in Upjohn v. United States, 449 U.S. 383, 101 S.Ct. 677, 66 L.Ed.2d 584 (1981).

True   29.   Since the anti-marital facts testimonial privilege is not based primarily upon the notion of fostering confidential communications, it is not waived by prior voluntary disclosure by the spouse called at trial to testify.

True   30.   Standard 503(a)(2) provides that for purposes of determining the existence of a lawyer-client privilege, a "lawyer" is a person authorized, or reasonably believed by the client to be authorized, to practice law in any state or nation.

False   31.   The Federal Rules of Evidence in Rule 501 do not provide for any particular privilege. Privileges are to be recognized by the federal court as governed by the principles of the common law as they may be interpreted in light of reason and experience; application of the foregoing in fact led to recognition of a psychotherapist-patient privilege.

False   32.   Federal courts have refused to recognize a parent-child confidential communication privilege.

False   33.   The husband-wife testimonial privilege only applies in criminal cases.

True   34.   A parent of a minor child is a representative of the child. Standard 503(b)(1) provides that the lawyer-client privilege attaches to confidential communications between the client and his representative and his lawyer or his lawyer's representative.

True   35.   Federal Courts recognize a confidential communication to clergyman privilege, Standard 506.

14.   Burden of Proof and Presumptions: Fed.R.Evid. 301–302

True   1.   The party seeking assistance from the court, i.e., the plaintiff, is assigned the burden of pleading and the burden of proof.

True   2.   Once the state defines a crime, the burden of persuasion as to that element of that crime may not be shifted to the accused—each and every element of the crime as defined must be proved beyond a reasonable doubt by the prosecution. Moreover, since a directed verdict may not be entered against the accused, the burden of persuasion as to an element of the crime may not be shifted to the criminal defendant.

False   3.   The burden of going forward in the ordinary civil case, i.e., the burden of production, is satisfied by the introduction of evidence which would permit a reasonable jury viewing the evidence most favorable to the proponent to find that the matter sought to be established is more probably true than not true.

False   4.   The Morgan theory of presumptions shifts both the burden of production and the burden of persuasion to the party opposing operation of the presumption.

True   5.   A presumption is as a rule of law which requires that the existence of a fact (presumed fact) be taken as established when another fact or other facts (basic facts) are established, unless and until a certain specified condition is fulfilled. An inference is a conclusion as to the existence of a particular fact reached by considering other facts in the usual course of human reasoning. With respect to an inference, if fact A is established fact B may be deduced from fact A through reasoning and logic. An inference is thus a deduction the factfinder may in its discretion draw, but is not required to draw as a matter of law. Under certain circumstances an inference may be so strong that no other conclusion may reasonably be reached. However, this is because of the compelling nature of the particular factual circumstances rather than that, as is the case with a presumption, a rule of law requires the conclusion to be drawn.

True   6.   Insanity is a true affirmative defense in the federal court with the accused bearing the burden of persuasion of clear and convincing evidence.

False   7.   The introduction of prima facie evidence means only that the burdened party has satisfied its burden of production as to one element of the case.

True   8.   A conclusive presumption, otherwise called an irrebuttable presumption, would require that the trier of fact find the presumed fact. Since the jury may never be directed in a criminal case to find any fact against the criminal defendant, a conclusive presumption is unconstitutional in a criminal case.

False   9.   A presumption is as a rule of law which requires that the existence of a fact (presumed fact) be taken as established when another fact or other facts (basic facts) are established, unless and until a certain specified condition is fulfilled.

True   10. Burden of proof is a term used to encompass both the burden of production and the burden of persuasion.

True   11. Rule 301 adopts the Thayer bursting bubble theory of presumptions in all actions and proceedings not otherwise provided for by Act of Congress or by the Federal Rules of Evidence.

True   12. The Morgan theory of presumptions by shifting the burden of persuasion in addition to the burden of production which is alone shifted in applying the Thayer theory is more beneficial to the party who must establish the basic facts.

True   13.   A presumption is a rule of law for the handling of evidence, not a species of evidence.

True   14.   A criminal presumption operates completely differently than does a civil presumption. While the civil presumption creates a must unless situation, a criminal presumption is an instruction to the jury that they may but are not required to infer one fact from another.

True   15.   If the presumed fact is not adequately rebutted, i.e., the opposing party fails to satisfy its burden of production as to the non-existence of the presumed fact, the jury is instructed that it must find the presumed fact. If the party opposing the presumed fact does satisfy its burden of production, the effect of the presumption disappears. In either event, the jury is not instructed in terms of a presumption.

False   16.   The burden of persuasion in a civil case is best described as more probably true than not true. Preponderance of the evidence is not identical as evidence which preponderates over particular opposing evidence may nevertheless fail to establish the proposition to be more probably true than not true in light of all possibilities.

True   17.   Rule 302 states in civil actions and proceedings, the effect of a presumption respecting a fact which is an element of a claim or defense as to which State law supplies the rule of decision is determined in accordance with State law.

True   18.   The burden of producing evidence or going forward is satisfied by evidence which, viewed in the aspect most favorable to the burdened party, is sufficient to enable the trier of fact reasonably to find that the burden of persuasion has been satisfied.

True   19.   A criminal presumption, better called an instructed criminal inference, permits but does not require a jury to infer one fact from another.

False   20.   Burden of proof includes both the burden of production and the burden of persuasion. The Thayer "bursting bubble" theory of presumptions shifts solely the burden of production.

False   21.   The clear and convincing burden of persuasion, roughly 70–75%, lies between more probably true than not true, i.e., 50+%, and beyond a reasonable doubt, roughly 85 or 90 to 95%.

True   22.   The Thayer "bursting bubble" theory of presumptions provides that when the basic facts (A) are established, the presumed fact (B) must be taken as established unless and until the opponent introduces evidence sufficient to support a finding by a reasonable trier of fact of the nonexistence of the presumed fact. Upon introduction of such evidence, the presumption is overcome and disappears, without regard to whether the evidence is actually believed.

True   23.   A presumption as defined in Rule 301 must be rebuttable. A conclusive presumption is not rebuttable. A conclusive presumption is in reality a rule of substantive law.

False   24.   Rule 301 provides that in all civil actions and proceeding unless otherwise provided for by Act of Congress or by the Federal Rules of Evidence, the Thayer bursting bubble theory shall govern operation of the presumption.

False   25.   A prima facie case consisting of the introduction of prima facie evidence on each element of a claim, charge, a defense permits the case to proceed to be decided by the trier of fact. Introduction of evidence sufficient to constitute a prima facie case does not require as a matter of law, as distinguished from the weight of the evidence, that the opposing party introduce evidence to avoid a directed verdict; the burden of production is not shifted as a matter of law.

15.   Judicial Notice: Fed.R.Evid 201

True   1.   Rule 201(b) provides that an adjudicative fact to be judicially noticed must be one not subject to reasonable dispute in that it is either (1) generally known within the territorial jurisdiction of the trial court or (2) capable of accurate and ready determination by resort to sources whose accuracy cannot reasonably be questioned.

False   2.   Determination of foreign law, meaning a foreign country such as Albania, is governed by the provisions of Fed.R.Civ.Proc. 44.1 and Fed.R.Crim.Proc. 26.1, each of which provides both for the availability of judicial notice upon notice of intent and for the submission of evidence, including testimony.

False   3.   Judicial notice of a legislative fact does not require the insistence upon certainty, i.e., not subject to reasonable dispute, associated with judicial notice of an adjudicative fact.

True   4.   Rule 201(f) provides that in a criminal case, the court shall instruct the jury that it may, but is not required to, accept as conclusive any fact judicially noticed.

True   5.   Rule 201(e) provides that a party is entitled upon timely request to an opportunity to be heard as to the propriety of taking judicial notice and the nature of the fact to be noticed. In the absence of prior notification, the request may be made after judicial notice has been taken.

True   6.   Judicial notice may be taken of a fact not subject to reasonable dispute in that it is generally known within the territorial jurisdiction of the trial court, Rule 201(b)(1).

True   7.   A state is required to take judicial notice of the statutes of another state as well as Acts of Congress.

False   8.   Rule 201 only governs judicial notice of adjudication facts, Rule 201(a).

False   9.   The trial judge may not rely upon his or her own knowledge of particular facts in determining whether a fact may be judicially noticed. Rule 201(b) provides that for an adjudicative fact to be judicially noticed it must be one not subject to reasonable dispute in that it is either (1) generally known within the territorial jurisdiction of the trial court or (2) capable of accurate and ready determination by resort to sources whose accuracy cannot reasonably be questioned.

False   10.   Rule 201(d) provides that judicial notice may be taken at any stage of the proceeding, which includes on appeal.

True   11.   Rule 201(b)(2) provides for judicial notice of an adjudicative fact not subject to reasonable dispute because it is capable of accurate and ready determination by resort to sources whose accuracy cannot reasonably be questioned.

False   12.   Judicial notice of an adjudicative fact may be taken when the matter is solely to be determined by the trial court, Rule 104(a).

False   13.   The average rainfall in Miami, Florida is not a fact generally known within the territorial jurisdiction of the trial court, Rule 201(b)(1), but is a fact not subject to reasonable dispute because it is capable of accurate and ready determination by resort to sources whose accuracy cannot reasonably be questioned, Rule 201(b)(2).

True   14.   Rule 201(c)(1) provides that a court may take judicial notice, whether requested or not.

True   15.   Rule 201(f) provides that in a civil action or proceeding, the court shall instruct the jury to accept as conclusive any fact judicially noticed.

16.   Judge and Jury Participation: Fed.R.Evid. 611(a) and 614

True   1.   In practice, federal trial court judges hardly ever if ever sum up the evidence for the jury, Standard 107.

True   2.   The trial judge possesses wide discretion over the order of interrogating witnesses, Rule 611(a), which includes the calling of witnesses in the interests of justice outside the normal order of presentation.

False   3.   Rule 614(c) provides that objections to the calling of witnesses by the court or to interrogation by it may be made at the time or at the next available opportunity when the jury is not present.

False   4.   Federal trial court judges rarely exercise their discretion in favor of calling a lay witness to testify at trial.

True   5.   Under Rule 614(b), the trial court may question a witness to clarify confused factual issues, to correct inadequacies of direct or cross-examination, to aid an embarrassed witness, or otherwise to insure that the trial proceeds efficiently and fairly.

17.   Rulings on Admissibility: Fed.R.Evid. 103–106 and 602

False   1.   A formal exception is not required by Rule 103 to make any ruling of the court reviewable.

True   2.   While the general objection raises only the ground of relevancy, there is no point in reversing on appeal if a correct specific objection that could not be obviated could have been interposed at trial precluding the admission of the same evidence excluded by the judge in response to the general objection.

True   3.   There are a limited number of constitutional rights that are so basic to a fair trial that their infraction can never be treated as harmless, for example, complete lack of counsel, a biased trial judge, or a coerced confession, but not, for example, violation of the confrontation clause. Constitutional rights, the violation of which requires reversal automatically, are said to be "structural."

False   4.   A motion in limine refers to a motion addressing the admissibility of evidence made prior to trial as well as a motion made at trial prior to the introduction of the evidence.

True   5.   Rule 106 dealing with the remainder of related writings or recorded statements applies with equal face to writings and recordings introduced as substantive evidence or solely for the purpose of impeachment.

False   6.   Inadmissible evidence admitted by one party may open the door to otherwise inadmissible evidence being admitted in the discretion of the trial court to rebut.

False   7.   The objection "lack of foundation" applies to Rule 104(a) as well as Rule 104(b) determinations.

False   8.   The objection "lack of foundation" preserves solely the issue of lack of foundation for appeal.

True   9.   Motions in limine are employed with great frequency to clarify admissibility issues and thereby improve counsel's ability to prepare trial strategy.

False   10.   The examining counsel may have an unresponsive answer stricken even if it is otherwise admissible.

True   11.   A party in making a motion in limine may seek an order from the court requiring that the opposing party and his witnesses refrain from offering or mentioning before the jury the evidence constituting the subject matter of the ruling without first informing the court and obtaining the court's permission outside the hearing of the jury. This type of motion in limine is sometimes called preliminary or conditional.

False   12.   Transcripts of former testimony admitted into evidence will not normally be sent to the jury room.

False   13.   Counsel frequently will object and move to strike without requesting a curative instruction to the jury to disregard the struck evidence.

False   14.   Counsel opposing cross-examination is likely to object as to the form of the question if unsure of the appropriate specific objection.

True   15.   In both civil and criminal cases conditional relevancy, Rule 104(b), requires the introduction of evidence sufficient to support a finding when viewed most favorably to the proponent that the matter to be established is more probably true than not true, i.e., 50+%.

True   16.   Error that materially affected or substantially swayed the jury's deliberation affected a substantial right.

True   17.   A limiting instruction given to the jury as party of the judge's instruction to the jury on the law is, apart from co-defendant confession cases referred to as a *Bruton* problem, almost invariably assumed to be effective in limiting application of received evidence.

False   18.   A specific ground need not be stated to preserve error for appeal if the specific ground was apparent from the context, Rule 103(a)(1)(B).

True   19.   Rule 104(a) provides that the court in making its determination is not bound by the rules of evidence except those with respect to privileges.

False   20.   Rule 106, the "rule of completeness", applies solely to the remainder of a related writings or recorded statements; oral communications are not encompassed.

True   21.   The assertion of a specific ground of objection preserves solely that ground of objection for appeal.

False   22.   Counsel may employ narrative and/or specific questions in counsel's discretion; counsel is not required to commence each witness examination with narrative questions.

True   23.   Reversible error is defined as error affecting a substantial right of a party.

True   24.   Rule 104(b) specifically provides for the admission of evidence "subject" to the later introduction of evidence sufficient to support a finding of the fulfillment of the condition to admissibility.

True   25.   A motion to strike evidence may be accompanied by a request to the court to instruct the jury to disregard the objected to evidence, i.e., a curative instruction.

True   26.   Rule 103(b) provides that once the court makes a definitive ruling on the record admitting or excluding evidence, either at or before trial, a party need not renew an objection or make an offer of proof to preserve a claim of error for appeal.

False   27.   Rule 103(c) provides that the trial court may direct the making of an offer of proof in question and answer form.

False   28.   The determination of whether a statement satisfies the requirements of a hearsay exception such as an executed utterance is made by the court alone under Rule 104(a).

True   29.   The trial court has discretion to decide what, if anything, may be raised on cross-examination and/or established by extrinsic evidence once the opposing party introduces inadmissible evidence, i.e., opens the door.

True   30.   Offers of proof may ordinarily be made in other than question and answer form, although the trial court may direct the making of an offer in question and answer form, Rule 103(c).

True   31.   Rule 602, personal knowledge, is a specific application of Rule 104(b) conditional relevancy.

False   32.   Plain error which is applicable in both civil and criminal cases finds far greater application in criminal cases.

False   33.   Rule 901(a), authentication or identification, is a specific application of the concept of conditional relevancy, Rule 104(b).

True   34.   Apart from a confession of a co-defendant referred to as a *Bruton* problem, a limiting instruction is ordinarily considered sufficient to permit evidence admissible against less than all parties to be admitted into evidence.

False   35.   Counsel may eschew Rule 106 and develop the matter on cross-examination or as part of his own case.

False   36.   A curative instruction is given to the jury to advise them to disregard evidence stricken from the record pursuant to a motion to strike. A limiting instruction is given by the trial judge to the jury as part of his instructions to the jury as to the law governing the case.

False   37.   A general objection raises only the ground of relevancy.

True   38.   Rule 803(18) provides that if a learned treatise is admitted, the statements may be read into evidence but may not be received as an exhibit. A purpose of the proviso in Rule 803(18) is to prevent the learned treatise being provided to the jury during its deliberations.

False   39.   Even where the court's ruling is "definite", nothing prohibits the court from revisiting its decision when the evidence is actually offered at trial; the ruling remains a preliminary nonfinal ruling.

False   40.   Failure on the part of the court to give a limiting instruction, Rule 106, on its own motion with respect to other crime, wrong, or act evidence admitted under Rule 404(b) is not plain error.

True   41.   The trial court following the introduction of all evidence relevant to fulfillment of the condition must determine whether viewing the evidence most favorably a reasonable jury may find that this condition has been fulfilled. If not, the proponent's evidence will be struck. For example, a watch that says Rollex is self-authenticating under Rule 902(7) but if it's a cheap fake the evidence offered by Rollex will result in the proponent's evidence that the watch is a Rollex being struck.

True   42.   A party offering inadmissible evidence may very well have opened the door to the admissibility of otherwise inadmissible evidence in the form of the remainder of a related writing or recorded statement that ought in fairness be considered contemporaneously.

True   43.   The admission of evidence cannot be assigned as error if the trial court reserved ruling on the objection and never subsequently made a ruling.

True   44.   Determining the presence of sufficient assurances of trustworthiness, i.e., the testimony is the product of reliable principles and methods, required by *Daubert/Kumho*/Rule 702 is for the court alone under Rule 104(a).

False   45.   The trial objection "non responsive" is available solely to examining counsel; unresponsive is not a matter of concern to the opposite party if the answer is otherwise admissible. Opposing party may object on the ground of no question pending or that the answer is volunteered if the witness persists in continuing to give non responsive answers.

True   46.   Violation of certain constitutional rights are subject to harmless error analyses.

True   47.   Rule 103(a) provides that error may not be predicated upon a ruling excluding evidence unless a substantial right of a party is affected and the substance of the evidence was made known to the court by offer or was apparent from the content written which questions were asked, Rule 103(a)(1)(B).

True   48.   Rule 103(a) provides that only error affecting a substantial right of a party will result in reversal on appeal.

True   49.   Anticipatory disclosure on direct examination or otherwise of evidence "definitively ruled" admissible in advance of or earlier at trial on a motion in limine, for example a prior conviction, waives the right to claim error on appeal; the opposing party must be given the choice as to whether or not to actually offer the evidence at trial.

True   50.   Error not affecting a substantial right of a party is referred to as harmless error.

18.   **Confrontation Clause: *Crawford* to *Williams***

False   1.   The confrontation clause precludes admissibility of a hearsay statement in a criminal case only if that statement is "testimonial". According to *Bryant*, as set forth in Appendix C infra, an out-of-court statement is "testimonial" only if hearsay as defined in Rule 801(a)–(d) and the statement was made by, or made to, or elicited by a police officer, other law enforcement personnel, or a judicial officer, if upon objective evaluation of the statements and actions of both the declarant and interrogator, if any, involved in the interrogation or statement creation, along with the informality or formality of the interrogation or statement creation, considered in light of the circumstance in which the interrogation or statement creation occurred, the court concludes that the primary purpose of the interrogation or statement creation was to establish or prove past events relevant to a later criminal prosecution.

False   2.   The Supreme Court in *Davis* overruled *Roberts*. Statements, whether "testimonial" or "nontestimonial", are no longer subject to a reliability screening under the confrontation clause prior to admissibility against the criminal defendant if made by an unavailable declarant.

False   3.   See answer to question 1 above and Appendix C: Confrontation Clause Analysis, indicating that an objective evaluation from both the declarant's and law enforcement officer's perspective is required.

False   4.   A statement is "testimonial" if made to a police officer, other law enforcement personnel, or judicial officer only if made under circumstances objectively indicating that the primary purpose surrounding the statement's creation was to establish or prove past events relevant to a criminal prosecution.

False   5.   See answers to questions 3 and 4 above.

True   6.   The confrontation clause precludes the admissibility of "testimonial" statements in the absence of an opportunity on the part of the criminal defendant to cross-examine.

True   7.   A statement made to a friend is not made to a police officer, other law enforcement personnel, or judicial officer, and is thus always "nontestimonial". A "nontestimonial" hearsay statement is not subject to the confrontation clause.

True   8.   As occurred in *Davis*, a 911 call which began as an emergency, a cry for help, with respect to an ongoing incident and is thus "nontestimonial", became "testimonial" after the perpetrator fled the scene making all subsequent components of the 911 call elicited in a structured interrogation "testimonial" as objectively the primary purpose on the part of the government had turned to criminal investigation.

True   9.   See answer to question 8 above.

True   10.   The question restates the definition of "testimonial" contained in *Davis*.

False   11.   The supervisor lacks sufficient personal knowledge of the forensic test detailed in the laboratory report.

True   12.   A supervisor possesses sufficient personal knowledge of the forensic test detailed in the laboratory report when the supervisor signs the certification after observing the test reported.

False   13a.   Since John is not a government official, under the primary purpose testimonial/nontestimonial test, John may always testify to Sam's excited utterance as the testimonial prohibition applies solely to a government witness in court relating a nongovernment declarant's uncross-examined statement.

False   13b.   Bob, the police officer, may also testify to Sam's excited utterance statement. This completely volunteered statement, i.e., neither formality nor interrogation elicitation, is nontestimonial because the primary purpose of both Sam and Bob is a police emergency to protect Sam's mother from further harm by Sam's father.

False   13c.   As before, since John is not a government official, the *Bryant* definition version of testimonial, as was true for *Crawford/Davis* before the revision, is simply inapplicable. A nongovernment witness's in court testimony as to any out of court hearsay statement raises no currently recognized confrontation clause concern.

True   13d.   Statement two made by Sam does not indicate a current police emergency. Falling 51stories is certainly likely to result in instant death. Sam's dad is on the couch crying, obviously not a threat to anyone. As such, starting from the perspective of a police officer, Bob, the statement creation, still absent any aspect of formality or interrogation elicitation, occurred under circumstances indicating that the primary purpose of the statement was to establish or prove past events relevant to a later criminal prosecution. Given its content, viewing the statement from the declarant Sam's perspective, as *Bryant* says one must consider in part, the statement was made under circumstances indicating that the primary purpose of the statement was to establish or prove a past event relevant to a later criminal prosecution. Statement two is thus testimonial when testified to by Bob, a police officer.

19.   **Selected Federal Rules of Evidence Amendments: Fed.R.Evid. 404, 408, 606, 609, 801(d)(1)(B), 803(6), 803(7), 803(8), 803(10), 803(16) and 804(b)(3)**

False   1.   Rule 404(a)(1) never permits admissibility in a civil case of a person's character to prove the person acted in conformity with the character trait.

False   2.   Admissibility in a criminal case of evidence of the pertinent trait of the alleged victim is made subject in Rule 404(a)(2)(B) to the limitation imposed by the rape shield provisions of Rule 412.

True   3.   Rule 408(a)(1) excludes an offer of acceptance of a compromise of any civil claims when offered in a criminal case against the defendant as an admission of fault.

True   4.   Rule 408(a)(2) does not prohibit the introduction in a criminal case of statements or conduct during compromise negotiations provided such compromise negotiations related to a claim by a public officer or agency in the exercise if regulatory, investigative, or enforcement authority.

False   5.   Rules 408(a) and (a)(2) prohibit the use of statements made in compromise negotiations when offered to impeach through a prior inconsistent statement or contradiction.

False   6.   Corroboration of statements that tend to expose the declarant to criminal liability is required by Rule 804(b)(3)(B) with respect to both inculpatory and exculpatory statements.

True   7.   An express statement providing that Rule 408 does not require the exclusion of any evidence otherwise discoverable merely because it is presented in the course of compromise negotiations was recently deleted as superfluous.

False   8.   Jurors under Rule 606(b)(1) can testify neither that the jury misunderstood the consequences of their decision nor that they misapplied a jury instruction. Jurors can testify as to whether there was a mistake in entering the verdict onto the verdict form.

True   9.   Rule 609(a)(2) provides that a non remote crime can be employed to impeach regardless of punishment if it can be readily determined that establishing the elements of the crime required proof or admission of an act of dishonesty or false statement by the witness.

True   10.   Rule 609(a)(2) does not provide for admissibility of acts involving dishonesty or false statement when a statutory element of the crime did not require such proof.

False   11.   Rule 801(d)(B)(ii) provides that a statement consistent with the declarant's testimony is admissible as substantive evidence when relevant to rehabilitating the declarant's credibility as a witness when impeached with a prior inconsistent statement on a ground other than specified in Rule 801(d)(B)(i).

True   12.   Rule 803(6) places the burden on the opponent to show that the source of information or the method or circumstance of preparation indicate a lack of trustworthiness of the business record.

False   13.   Rule 803(7), with respect the evidence that a matter is not included in a business record, places the burden on the opponent to show that the source of information or circumstances of preparation indicate a lack of trustworthiness.

True   14.   The requirement of written notice by the prosecutor of intent to offer a certificate as to the absence of a public record or entry is as set forth in Rule 803(10)(B).

True   15.   Rule 803(16) provides that a statement in a document prepared before January 1, 1998 properly authenticated is admissible as an exception to the hearsay rule.

HEARSAY EXAMS
ANSWER KEY

HEARSAY EXAMS
TRUE-FALSE ANSWER KEY
WITH EXPLANATIONS

Exam I

True   1.   A car rental record, whether showing an act or the absence of an act, is being offered in evidence to prove the truth of the matter asserted, Rules 801(a)–(c),—all four hearsay risks are present.

True   2.   Rule 803(7) provides a hearsay exception for the absence of an entry in a business record upon introduction of a proper foundation which is assumed in the instructions.

False   3.   Looking around the car is nonverbal conduct not intended as an assertion—no intent to communicate—thus no sincerity risk.

True   4.   As structured, if the answer to question 1 of the set is False, the answer to question 2 is True.

False   5.   Rule 801(b) defines a declarant as a "person" who makes a statement. The rain gauge is not a statement by a person but rather the result of the mechanical processes of a machine.

True   6.   As structured, if the answer to Questions 1 of the set is False, the answer to question 2 is True.

False   7.   P's assertion of ownership of Beigeacre is relevant for the fact said—an operative act—the law attaches independent legal significance to the making of the statement, i.e., a claim of ownership, in an action for adverse possession.

True   8.   As structured, if the answer to question 1 of the set is False, the answer to question 2 is True.

True   9.   The confession is an out-of-court statement offered in evidence to prove the truth of the matter asserted, Rules 801 (a)–(c), i.e., the defendant is the head of a drug smuggling ring—all four hearsay risks are present. The statement does not meet the not hearsay by definition admission for a party-opponent provided in Rule 801(d)(2)(E) for several reasons but clearly because the statement is not in furtherance of the conspiracy.

False   10. The statement does not satisfy Rule 804(b)(3) or any other hearsay exception contained in Rules 803, 804, and 807.

False   11. The lecture on the application of calculus to the prediction of stock market performance is being offered to establish that the declarant was competent. It is relevant for that purpose for the fact said—an in court witness can testify that the lecture made sense. Clearly the lecture is not being offered to prove the truth of the matter asserted, Rules 801(a)–(c).

True   12. As structured, if the answer to question 1 of the set is False, the answer to question 2 is True.

True   13. The statement by D as to his health is an out-of-court statement being offered in evidence to prove the truth of the matter asserted, Rules 801(a)–(c), i.e., D is healthy.

True   14. Rule 803(3) provides a hearsay exception for statements of the declarant's then existing state of mind, or emotional, sensory, or physical condition.

True   15. This is a *Tatham* problem. See Appendix A A3(b) Basis for Nonasserted Inference or "Implied Assertion".

False   16. Statements that are hearsay applying *Tatham* hearsay analyses are not admissible through either being defined as not hearsay by Rule 801(d)(1) or (2) or pursuant to any hearsay exception contained in Rules 803, 804 or 807.

False   17.   The prior inconsistent statement is relevant for the fact said. The mere fact that a witness has previously maintained an inconsistent position is relevant in assessing the weight to be given to the witness' testimony.

True   18.   As structured, if the answer to question 1 of the set is False, the answer to question 2 is True.

False   19.   The confession is an out-of-court statement offered in evidence to prove the truth of the matter asserted, Rules 801(a)–(c),—all four hearsay risks are present. Rule 801(d)(2)(A) defines as not hearsay a party's own statement as an admission of a party-opponent when offered in evidence by an opposing party, here the prosecution.

True   20.   As structured, if the answer to question 1 of the set is False, the answer to question 2 is True.

False   21.   "Aaaaaaaagh" is verbal conduct not intended as an assertion—no intent to communicate—thus no sincerity risk.

True   22.   As structured, if the answer to question 1 of the set is False, the answer to question 2 is True.

True   23.   The bystander pointing to a nearby garage, i.e., nonverbal conduct, is being offered into evidence to prove the truth of the matter asserted, Rules 801(a)–(c),—all four hearsay risks are present. The pointing remains hearsay even though the truth of the matter asserted is confirmed when the police find the masked man in the garage. See Appendix A A3(a) *Personal knowledge of independently established facts.*

True   24.   The statement should be admitted under Rule 807, although under the facts of the case, Rules 807(A) and (B), the statement is more probative than other available evidence as to a material fact, are more problematic than with the other independently established fact statements discussed in the text.

False   25.   Promotion is nonverbal conduct not intended as an assertion—no intent to communicate by act—thus no sincerity risk.

True   26.   As structured, if the answer to question 1 of the set is False, the answer to question 2 is True.

True   27.   The statement, "[I believe] I am John Wayne," is relevant on the issue of commitment only if believed by the declarant to be true—the statement is being offered in evidence to prove the truth of the matter asserted, Rules 801(a)–(c),—the hearsay risks of sincerity and narration are present.

True   28.   Rule 803(3) provides a hearsay exception for statements of the declarant's then existing state of mind, emotion, sensation, or physical condition.

True.   29.   The statement by the wife to her husband that he has lost money betting on horses is being offered in evidence to prove the truth of the matter asserted, Rules 801(a)–(c), i.e., husband has lost money betting on horses—all four hearsay risks are present. The statement is not defined as not hearsay by any of the provision of Rules 801(d)(1) or (2).

False   30.   The statement does not meet the requirements of any hearsay exception contained in Rules 803, 804, and 807.

True   31.   The girlfriend's statement that the defendant forged a will is being offered in evidence to prove the truth of the matter asserted, Rules 801(a)–(c), i.e., the will is a forgery—all four hearsay risks are present. The statement is not an admission of a party-opponent by silence defined as not hearsay by Rule 801(d)(2)(B) because the defendant immediately denied forging the will. Nor is the statement admissible under any other not hearsay definition of Rule 801(d)(1) or (2).

False   32.   The statement does not meet the requirements of any hearsay exception provided in Rules 803, 804, and 807.

False   33.   The conduct of the employer is nonverbal conduct not intended as an assertion—no intent to communicate by act—thus no sincerity risk.

True   34.   As structured, if the answer to question 1 of the set is False, the answer to question 2 is True.

True   35.   The out-of-court statement by the testator's wife that her husband thinks he's the Pope is offered in evidence to prove the truth of the matter asserted, Rules 801(a)–(c), i.e., that Bob Harris thought he was the Pope—all four hearsay risks are present.

False   36.   This is a multiple level hearsay problem. While 803(3) would provide a hearsay exception for Bob Harris saying "I am the Pope", and no hearsay exception would be required if Bob Harris simply dressed and acted like the Pope, there is no hearsay exception for the wife's out-of-court statement repeating his statement or describing his conduct.

False   37.   The statement, "I'm alive," is relevant for the fact said—the mere uttering of coherent sounds makes the speech relevant on the issue of survival following the accident. She could have just as well said—"Don't forget to feed the dog." The statement would be not hearsay even if she instead had said, "I'm alive."

True   38.   As structured, if the answer to question 1 of the set is False, the answer to question 2 is True.

False   39.   The statement, "Joe ran the red light," is offered in evidence to prove the truth of the matter asserted, Rules 801(a)–(c), i.e., Joe ran the red light. By saying nothing, Joe however manifested adoption by silence of the truth of the matter asserted making the statement not hearsay by definition as an admission of a party-opponent, Rule 801(d)(2)(B), when offered by an opposing party, here the plaintiff.

True   40.   As structured, if the answer to question 1 of the set is False, the answer to question 2 is True.

True   41.   The statement, "Sam ran the red light," is an out-of-court statement offered in evidence to prove the truth of the matter asserted, Rules 801(a)–(c), i.e., Sam ran the red light. Rule 801(d)(1)(A) does not define the statement as not hearsay in that even though the out-of-court declarant is also in court subject to cross-examination, the prior inconsistent statement was not made under oath "at a trial hearing, other proceeding [grand jury], or in a deposition." The statement is not defined as not hearsay by any other provision of Rules 801(d)(1) or (2).

False   42.   The statement does not meet the requirements of any hearsay exception contained in Rules 803, 804, and 807.

False   43.   The transferring of money is nonverbal conduct not intended as an assertion—no intent to communicate—thus no sincerity risk.

True   44.   As structured, if the answer to question 1 of the set is False, the answer to question 2 is True.

False   45.   The statement at the deposition that the truck ran the red light is being offered in evidence to prove the truth of the matter asserted, Rules 801(a)–(c), i.e., the truck ran the red light—all four hearsay risks are present. Rule 801(d)(1)(A) however defines as not hearsay a prior inconsistent statement of a declarant who is also an in court witness testifying subject to cross-examination if the prior inconsistent statement was made under oath in a deposition. Lack of recollection when testifying and a prior statement are inconsistent for purposes of Rule 801(d)(1)(A). Finally a witness who testifies at trial to a lack of recollection as to the underlying event is nevertheless "subject to cross-examination" for purposes of Rule 801(d)(1)(A).

True   46.   As structured, if the answer to question 1 of the set is False, the answer to question 2 is True.

True   47.   The statement by Clifford to the police that Sarah, his wife, committed adultery is relevant in proving an intent to sell rather than give Sarah the ring only if Clifford "believed" Sarah committed adultery. Thus the hearsay risks of sincerity and narration are present. A person who believes another committed adultery is more likely to sell that person a ring than give it to her.

True   48.   Rule 803(3) provides a hearsay exception for a statement of the declarant's then existing state of mind, emotion, sensation, or physical condition. The statement is hearsay and not admissible if offered to prove that Sarah did in fact commit adultery.

False   49.   Rule 801(b) defines declarant as a "person" who makes a statement. A parrot is not a person.

True   50.   As structured, if the answer to question 1 of the set is False, the answer to question 2 is True.

Exam II

True   1.   The statement "D is going to kill me soon" is being offered in evidence to prove the truth of the matter stated, Rules 801(a)–(c), i.e., D is going to kill the declarant soon—all four hearsay risks are present. The statement does not meet the requirements to be defined as not hearsay under Rules 801(d)(1) or (2).

False   2.   The statement does not meet the requirements of any hearsay exception contained in Rules 803, 804, and 807. The declarant may be saying "I am afraid because D said he will kill me soon." If this were the statement, it would still be inadmissible. It is not admissible under Rule 803(3), current state of mind, because it would then be a statement of belief offered to prove the fact remembered or believed which is specifically precluded by Rule 803(3).

True   3.   The statement about warning the store concerning the slippery spot is being offered in evidence to prove the truth of the matter asserted, Rules 803(a)–(c), i.e., that the witness had so warned the store—all four hearsay risks are present.

False   4.   The statement is not an excited utterance, Rule 803(2), because it was not made under the stress of excitement caused by an event—the declarant was calm. Moreover Rule 803(1), present sense impression, is not satisfied even though the statement was made immediately after perceiving the event because the statement neither "explains" or "describes" the event but rather "relates" to the event.

False   5.   The conduct with the pistol and the snarl were nonverbal and verbal conduct intended as an assertion, being offered in evidence to prove the truth of the matter asserted, Rules 801(a)–(c), i.e., intent to shoot victim—the hearsay risks of narration and sincerity are present. The conduct and snarling of the defendant are defined as not hearsay as an admission of a party-opponent, Rule 801(d)(2)(A), when offered by an adverse party—here the State.

True   6.   As structured, if the answer to question 1 of the set is False, the answer to question 2 is True.

True   7.   The statement by the testator to the police that the defendant committed forgery is relevant in proving the testator's feeling toward the defendant only if the testator "believed" that the defendant committed forgery. Thus the hearsay risks of sincerity and narration are present.

True   8.   Rule 803(3) provides a hearsay exception for a statement of the declarant's then existing state of mind, emotion, sensation, or physical condition. The statement is hearsay and not admissible if offered to prove that the defendant did commit forgery.

False   9.   The statement that "[I know that] D has a vicious dog" is being offered in evidence to prove the truth of the matter asserted, Rules 801(a)–(c), i.e., that P knows D has a vicious dog. The hearsay risks of sincerity and narration are present. The statement of plaintiff is defined as a not hearsay admission of a party-opponent, Rule 801(d)(2)(A), when offered in evidence by an adverse party—here the defendant.

True   10.   As structured, if the answer to question 1 of the set is False, the answer to question 2 is True.

True   11.   The statement "D hates me" is being offered in evidence to prove the truth of the matter asserted, Rules 801(a)–(c), i.e., D hates Y—all four hearsay risks are present. The statement is not defined as not hearsay by any of the provisions of Rules 801(d)(1) or (2).

False   12.   The statement does not meet the requirements of any hearsay exception contained in Rule 803, 804, and 807.

True   13.   The settlement by the insurance company is an assertion by the insurance company that it believes that the defendant ran a red light offered in evidence to prove that the defendant ran a red light. Matter asserted includes both matters directly expressed and matters the declarant necessarily implicitly intended to assert. The statement is not defined as not hearsay by any of the provisions of Rule 801(d)(1) or (2).

False   14.   The statement does not meet the requirements of any hearsay exception contained in Rules 803, 804, and 807.

True   15.   For the statement to be relevant, M must have perceived, recorded and recollects that X failed to repay a loan of over $90,000 and be sincerely communicating an intent to pay $5,000 to have X killed. All four hearsay risks are present. The putting out of a contract possesses the same hearsay risks as the statement by M "X owes me over $90,000." The statement is not defined as not hearsay by any of the provisions of Rules 801(d)(1) or (2).

False   16.   The statement does not meet the requirements of any hearsay exception contained in Rules 803, 804, and 807.

True   17.   The statement "Call a priest" is relevant to establish that the victim had a settled hopeless expectation of death only if the victim truly wished to see a priest, i.e., believed that he was dying—a request to see a priest is an implicit assertion that the person believes they are dying—hearsay risks of sincerity and narration are present.

True   18.   Rule 803(3) provides a hearsay exception for statements of the declarant's then existing state of mind, emotion, sensation, or physical condition.

True   19.   The statement "My leg hurts" is offered in evidence to prove the truth of the matter asserted, Rule 801(c), i.e., the plaintiff's leg hurts.

True   20.   The statement is admissible under either Rule 803(3), then existing physical condition, as well as Rule 803(4), statements for purposes of medical diagnosis or treatment.

False   21.   Prescribing of high blood pressure pills is nonverbal conduct not intended as an assertion—no intent to communicate by act—thus no sincerity risk.

True   22.   As structured, if the answer to question 1 of the set is False, the answer to question 2 is True.

False   23.   The statement about needing the drugs for a medical purpose is relevant for the fact said—effect on listener. Determining whether a person is predisposed to sell cocaine is affected by what that person is told is the reason the purchaser wants the drugs.

True   24.   As structured, if the answer to question 1 of the set is False, the answer to question 2 is True.

True   25.   The statements to the narcotics officer that the defendant deals cocaine are being offered in evidence to prove the truth of the matter asserted, Rules 801(a)–(c), i.e., defendant deals cocaine—all four hearsay risks are present. If offered for its effect on listener to explain why the police targeted the defendant—not hearsay for this purpose—would exclude under Rule 403. The statement is not defined as not hearsay by any of the provisions of Rules 801(d)(1) or (2).

False   26.   The statement does not meet the requirements of any hearsay exception contained in Rules 803, 804, and 807.

False   27.   The statement that D was told Z forced D's daughter into prostitution is relevant for the fact said—effect on listener. A reasonable person being advised of such fact is more likely to kill the person who allegedly did that to his daughter than a person with no such advice. If offered to prove that Z forced the defendant's daughter into prostitution, the statement is hearsay and inadmissible.

True   28.   As structured, if the answer to question 1 of the set is False, the answer to question 2 is True.

False   29.   The statement concerning the weak front axle is relevant for the fact said—effect on listener. The reasonableness of taking the bus on the road is affected by having been told of a weak front axle. If the statement is offered to prove that the front axle was in fact weak and thus caused the accident, the statement is hearsay and inadmissible.

True   30.   As structured, if the answer to question 1 of the set is False, the answer to question 2 is True.

True   31.   The statement "No . . . Mike . . . don't shoot" is being offered in evidence to prove the truth of the matter implicitly being asserted, Rules 801(a)–(c), i.e., Mike intended to and thus did shoot the victim—all four hearsay risks are present.

True   32.   Rule 803(2) provides a hearsay exception for statements made while the declarant was under the stress of excitement caused by the event. Rule 803(1), providing for a hearsay exception describing an event made while perceiving the event, would also be satisfied.

True   33.   The statement to the plaintiff that the declarant heard the defendant saying the plaintiff stole footnotes is relevant on damages only if the declarant believes that the plaintiff stole footnotes—thus the hearsay risks of sincerity and narrative are present. Damage to reputation requires that the maker of a statement believe what he is saying to be true.

True   34.   Rule 803(3) provides a hearsay exception for statements of the declarant's then existing state of mind, emotion, sensation, or physical condition. The form of the statement being one of reporting and questioning and not being one of acceptance of truth on its face makes application of Rule 803(3) questionable but in a tight call most likely applicable.

True   35.   The conclusion of no sexual discrimination in the report is being offered in evidence to prove the truth of the matter asserted, Rules 801(a)–(c), i.e., that no sexual discrimination existed—all four hearsay risks are present.

False   36.   The only not hearsay by definition, Rules 801(d)(1) and (2), or hearsay exception, Rules 803, 804, and 807, possibly satisfied is Rule 803(6), records of regularly conducted activity, commonly called business records. However, the self-serving nature of the investigation report when offered by the V.A. to show no sexual discrimination argues strongly for exclusion because, as provided in Rule 803(6), "the source of information or the method or circumstances of preparation indicate lack of trustworthiness."

False 37. Scratching is nonverbal conduct not intended as an assertion—no intent to communicate by act—thus no sincerity risk.

True 38. As structured, if the answer to question 1 of the set is False, the answer to question 2 is True.

True 39. The police report containing the defendant's statement admitting fault is being offered in evidence to prove the truth of the matter asserted, Rules 801(a)–(c), i.e., defendant was at fault—all four hearsay risks are present.

True 40. The statement is admissible as multiple level hearsay, Rule 805, with Rule 803(8) admitting the statement for the fact said and Rule 801(d)(2)(A) admitting the statement itself as defined as not hearsay. All the requirements of Rule 803(8) are satisfied; the police report is being offered in a civil case and thus the Rule 803(8)(B) exclusion does not come into play.

False 41. In an action for adverse possession the law attaches independent legal significance to the fact that a party has over time openly maintained a claim of ownership to property—an operative act—thus the sign is relevant for the fact said.

True 42. As structured, if the answer to question 1 of the set is False, the answer to question 2 is True.

False 43. A declarant is defined in Rule 801(b) as a person who makes a statement. A dog is not a person.

True 44. As structured, if the answer to question 1 of the set is False, the answer to question 2 is True.

False 45. The statement is relevant for the fact said—effect on listener—whether D acted in good faith in discharging X is affected by what D had been told about X's conduct—X had been caught stealing in D's store.

True   46.   As structured, if the answer to question 1 of the set is False, the answer to question 2 is True.

True   47.   The statement that X had been caught stealing money from the store when offered to prove X had stolen money is an out-of-court statement offered in evidence to prove the truth of the matter asserted, Rules 801(a)–(c). The statement is not defined as not hearsay by any of the provisions of Rule 801(d)(1) or (2).

False   48.   The statement does not meet the requirements of any hearsay exception contained in Rules 803, 804, and 807.

False   49.   The picture depicts nonverbal conduct not intended as an assertion—no intent to communicate by act depicted—thus no sincerity risk. One can argue that the flashing is in fact an intent to communicate. If so perceived, the conduct is nevertheless properly classified as not hearsay because the inference that can be drawn from the conduct alone parallels the matter intended to be asserted. See Graham, Handbook of Federal Evidence § 801.3 n. 7 (8th ed. 2017).

Query: Is honking a horn nonverbal nonassertive conduct or is it nonverbal assertive conduct? Honking a horn is clearly an attempt to communicate something usually an apprehension of danger, but sometimes "hello" or an encouragement to move when a light turns green. Nevertheless, where an accident has occurred, the act of honking itself placed in such context is relevant as a warning to others as to the possibility of danger regardless of the presence or absence of an intent by the driver to assert. Moreover, the act of honking is itself a relevant act from which can be inferred the driver's awareness of danger once again regardless of the presence or absence of an intent by the driver to assert. In short, honking is nonhearsay for both purposes while being hearsay if offered to prove that the driver intended to warn others of his apprehension of danger. Similarly, stabbing someone 30 times is a relevant act from which can be inferred the perpetrator's hostility and intent to cause death regardless of the presence or absence of an actual intent on the part of the perpetrator to assert his feelings of hostility or intention to cause death. However, if the stabbing is offered to prove that the perpetrator intended to assert his hostility or intention to kill, the act of stabbing is hearsay. Since in both illustrations the nonhearsay relevance of honking and stabbing is substantial and sufficient alone for all practical litigation purposes, both acts are routinely admitted correctly as not hearsay. In fact a hearsay problem is rarely ever perceived to exist.

True   50.   As structured, if the answer to question 1 of the set is False, the answer to question 2 is True.

Exam III

True   1.   The statement "I hate P" is being offered into evidence to prove that testator hates P. Relevancy depends upon the testator actually believing the matter asserted—the hearsay risks of sincerity and narration are present.

True   2.   Rule 803(3) provides a hearsay exception for statements of the declarant's then existing state of mind, emotion, sensation, or physical condition. The concept of continuity of inference permits the trier of fact to infer that if testator hated P one week before his death, testator also hated P at the time of his death.

False   3.   The statement is relevant for the fact said—effect on listener—a person who hears a libelous statement about themselves is more likely to feel humiliated than a person who did not hear it and to feel so regardless of the statement's truth.

True   4.   As structured, if the answer to question 1 of the set is False, the answer to question 2 is True.

False   5.   The statement is relevant for the fact said—effect on listener—a person who hears on the radio that the sky is falling is more likely to think the sky is falling than one who has not so been advised regardless of the truth of the statement.

True   6.   As structured, if the answer to question 1 of the set is False, the answer to question 2 is True.

False   7.   A declarant is defined in Rule 801(b) as a person who makes a statement. A speedometer is not a person.

True   8.   As structured, if the answer to question 1 of the set is False, the answer to question 2 is True.

True   9.   The testimony at the deposition that the captain was drunk is being offered in evidence to prove the truth of the matter asserted, Rules 801(a)–(c), i.e., the captain was drunk—all four hearsay risks are present. The statement fails to satisfy Rule 801(d)(1)(A)'s not hearsay definition because the seaman was not available for cross-examination at trial.

True   10.   Rule 804(b)(1) provides a hearsay exception for former testimony including that given at a deposition. The captain's attorney was present and had an opportunity and similar motive to develop the seaman's testimony.

False   11.   A declarant is defined in Rule 801(b) as a person who makes a statement. A rooster is not a person.

True   12.   As structured, if the answer to question 1 of the set is False, the answer to question 2 is True.

False   13.   A confession by D—an acknowledgement of each and every element of the criminal charge—is an out-of-court statement offered in evidence to prove the truth of the matter asserted, Rule 801(c). Rule 801(d)(2)(A) defines as not hearsay admissions of a party-opponent made in an individual capacity when offered in evidence by an adverse party—here P.

True   14.   As structured, if the answer to question 1 of the set is False, the answer to question 2 is True.

False   15.   The statement is relevant for the fact said—effect on listener—a person's awareness of whether death is imminent is affected by having been told, "You have only a few minutes to live" regardless of the truth of the statement.

True   16.   As structured, if the answer to question 1 of the set is False, the answer to question 2 is True.

True   17.   The statement "I'm going fast" is relevant to show that the decedent believed his death was imminent only if he believed it to be true—the statement is being offered in evidence to prove the truth of the matter asserted, Rules 801(a)–(c),—the hearsay risks of sincerity and narration are present.

True   18.   Rule 803(3) provides a hearsay exception for a statement of declarant's then existing state of mind, emotion, sensation, or physical condition.

True   19.   The receipt is a memorialization of the transaction and not the transaction itself. As such it is an out-of-court statement offered in evidence to prove the truth of the matter asserted, Rules 801(a)–(c),—all four hearsay risks are present. The receipt at hand is similar to the receipt provided at the food store. The operative acts are the total from the items on the cash register followed by the payment—offer and acceptance. The receipt produced by the cash register is solely a memorialization.

True   20.   The receipt in the hands of the purchaser of a car is not a business record, Rule 803(6). However the receipt should be admitted, if more probative than other available evidence, as satisfying Rule 807—equivalent circumstantial guarantees of trustworthiness are present.

True   21.   This is a *Tatham* problem. See Appendix A A3(b).

False   22.   Statements that are hearsay applying *Tatham* hearsay analyses are not admissible through either being defined as not hearsay by Rules 801(d)(1) or (2) or pursuant to any hearsay exception contained in Rules 803, 804, and 807.

True   23.   The statement "my head" said while holding his head is being offered in evidence to prove the truth of the matter asserted, Rules 801(a)–(c), i.e., his head hurts.

True   24.   Rule 803(4) provides a hearsay exception for statements made for purposes of medical diagnosis or treatment. In addition, Rule 803(3) provides a hearsay exception for statements of the declarant's then existing physical condition.

True   25.   The statement that the brakes are shot is being offered in evidence to prove the truth of the matter asserted, Rules 801(a)–(c), i.e., the brakes are shot—all four hearsay risks are present. The statement is not defined as not hearsay by any of the provisions of Rules 801(d)(1) or (2). Defendant's silence does not rise to the level of an adoptive admission, Rule 801(d)(2)(B).

False   26.   The statement does not meet the requirements of any hearsay exception contained in Rules 803, 804, and 807.

False   27.   The statement is relevant for the fact said—effect on listener. Assumption of risk requires knowledge of the danger and being advised of the danger provides a reason to be aware regardless of the truth of the statement.

True   28.   As structured, if the answer to question 1 of the set is False, the answer to question 2 is True.

True   29.   The statement that the roller coaster is shaking is being offered in evidence to prove the truth of the matter asserted, Rules 801(a)–(c), i.e., the roller coaster is in bad condition—all four hearsay risks are present.

True 30. Rule 803(1) provides a hearsay exception for statements describing an event made while the declarant was perceiving the event or immediately thereafter. For Rule 803(2) to be satisfied, it would be necessary to show that the statement was made under the stress of excitement caused by an event, which may or may not be true as the problem is worded.

False 31. The statement is relevant for the fact said—the salesperson's affirmation of the plaintiff's question is an operative act—a warranty—the law attaches independent legal significance to the salesman's conduct.

True 32. As structured, if the answer to question 1 of the set is False, the answer to question 2 is True.

True 33. The investigator's report concluding that a traffic light is not needed is being offered in evidence to prove the truth of the matter asserted, Rules 801(a)–(c), i.e., a traffic light is not needed—all four hearsay risks are present.

False 34. The investigator's report fails to meet the requirements of Rule 803(8)(C)—the report appears to have been made in anticipation of litigation—thus the source of information or other circumstances indicate lack of trustworthiness.

True 35. The statement by P that she had just made a deal with D is being offered to prove the truth of the matter stated, Rules 801(a)–(c), i.e., P just made a deal with D—all four hearsay risks are present. P's statement to her secretary is not itself an operative act but rather the reporting of an operative act.

True 36. Rule 803(1) provides a hearsay exception for statements describing or explaining an event made while the declarant was perceiving the event or immediately thereafter. It is not necessary that the person spoken to also perceived the event.

False 37. The statement is relevant for the fact said. The fact that a statement was made, regardless of its content, is relevant to establish that the declarant was alive at that moment.

The fact that the statement was "I think Y is dead" rather than some other statement does not alter the foregoing analyses.

True   38.   As structured, if the answer to question 1 of the set is False, the answer to question 2 is True.

False   39.   Putting a sheet on someone's head is nonverbal conduct not intended as an assertion—no intent to communicate—thus no sincerity risk.

True   40.   As structured, if the answer to question 1 of the set is False, the answer to question 2 is True.

True   41.   The reputation of a person is an expressed collective community assessment being offered in evidence to prove the truth of the matter asserted, Rules 801(a)–(c), i.e., V is violent—all four hearsay risks are present.

True   42.   Rule 803(21) provides a hearsay exception for the reputation of a person's character among his association or in the community.

True   43.   The statement by the testator as to leaving C one-half of his estate in the will is being offered in evidence to prove the truth of the matter asserted, Rules 801(a)–(c), i.e., his will leaves C one-half of the estate—all four hearsay risks are present.

True   44.   Rule 803(3) provides a hearsay exception for statements of the declarant's memory or belief to prove the fact remembered or believed only when the statement relates to the execution, revocation, identification, or terms of declarant's will.

True   45.   The statement is relevant as to whether C was shortly thereafter left one-half of the declarant's estate in a will only if the declarant believed his statement that "C has treated me shamefully" to be true regardless of how C actually acted toward the declarant. The risks of sincerity and narration are present.

True 46. Rule 803(3) provides a hearsay exception for a statement of the declarant's then existing state of mind, emotion, sensation or physical condition.

False 47. The purchase of computers is nonverbal conduct not intended as an assertion—no intent to communicate by act—thus no sincerity risk.

True 48. As structured, if the answer to question 1 of the set is False, the answer to question 2 is True.

True 49. The prior criminal conviction is an out-of-court statement by the jury that D committed the assault offered in evidence to prove the truth of the matter asserted, Rules 801(a)–(c), i.e., that D committed the assault—all four hearsay risks are present.

True 50. Rule 803(22) provides a hearsay exception for a judgment of a prior conviction for a felony to prove any fact essential to sustain the judgment when offered in a civil case.

Exam IV

False 1. A prior inconsistent statement when offered to impeach credibility is relevant because it was said—the mere fact of failure to maintain the same position over time affects the credibility assessment made by the trier of fact.

True 2. As structured, if the answer to question 1 of the set is False, the answer to question 2 is True.

True 3. The statement by the psychiatrist as to the testator's progress on her emotional problems is being offered in evidence to prove the truth of the matter asserted, Rules 801(a)–(c), i.e., testator is well—all four hearsay risks are present. The statement is not defined as not hearsay by any of the provisions of Rules 801(d)(1) or (2).

False   4.   The statement does not meet the requirements of any hearsay exception contained in Rules 803, 804, and 807. Rule 803(4) does not encompass statements by the person providing medical diagnosis or treatment.

False   5.   The conducting of the second operation is nonverbal conduct not intended as an assertion—no intent to communicate by act—thus no sincerity risk.

True   6.   As structured, if the answer to question 1 of the set is False, the answer to question 2 is True.

False   7.   The statement to the officer that X had a gun is relevant for the fact said—effect on listener—a reasonable person would have their apprehension of danger affected by being told that X had a gun. If offered to prove X had a gun, the statement is hearsay and inadmissible.

True   8.   As structured, if the answer to question 1 of the set is False, the answer to question 2 is True.

False   9.   On the question of whether P was notified of the hazard, the announcement is relevant for the fact said—it is the notice.

True   10.   As structured, if the answer to question 1 of the set is False, the answer to question 2 is True.

False   11.   The statement is relevant for the fact said—the law attaches independent legal significance to the statement—applying the objective theory of contract the statement by P is an offer.

True   12.   As structured, if the answer to question 1 of the set is False, the answer to question 2 is True.

False 13. The "Owwwwww" is verbal conduct not intended as an assertion—no intent to communicate—thus no sincerity risk.

True 14. As structured, if the answer to question 1 of the set is False, the answer to question 2 is True.

True 15. The reputation of a person is an expressed collective community assessment being offered in evidence to prove the truth of the matter asserted, Rules 801(a)–(c), i.e., P was a womanizer—all four hearsay risks are present.

True 16. Rule 803(21) provides a hearsay exception for the reputation of a person's character among his associates or in the community.

False 17. Stopping a car is nonverbal conduct not intended as an assertion—no intent to communicate by act—thus no sincerity risk.

True 18. As structured, if the answer to question 1 of the set is False, the answer to question 2 is True.

False 19. The statement is relevant for the fact said. The fact that a statement was made, regardless of its content, is relevant to establish that the declarant was alive at that moment.

True 20. As structured, if the answer to question 1 of the set is False, the answer to question 2 is True.

True 21. The statement that the red car ran the red light is being offered in evidence to prove the truth of the matter asserted, Rules 801(a)–(c), i.e., the red car ran the red light—all four hearsay risks are present.

True   22.   Rule 803(2) provides a hearsay exception for statements relating to a startling event made while declarant was under the stress of excitement caused by the event.

True   23.   The business records of Dr. X indicating that there is no mention of P is offered in evidence to prove the truth of the matter asserted, Rules 801(a)–(c), i.e., that P was not treated by Dr. X—all four hearsay risks are present.

True   24.   Rule 803(7) provides a hearsay exception for business records to prove the nonoccurrence of a matter if the matter was of the kind of which a business record was regularly made and preserved.

True   25.   The statement is relevant to prove that V struck the first blow only when offered to prove the truth of the matter asserted, Rules 801(a)–(c), i.e., V killed six people in the past year—all four hearsay risks are present. The statement is not defined as not hearsay by any of the provisions of Rules 801(d)(1) or (2).

False   26.   The statement does not meet the requirements of any hearsay exception contained in Rules 803, 804, and 807.

False   27.   Doubling over and groaning is nonverbal conduct not intended as an assertion—no intent to communicate by act—thus no sincerity risk.

True   28.   As structured, if the answer to question 1 of the set is False, the answer to question 2 is True.

False   29.   The two white-coated gentlemen's action is nonverbal conduct not intended as an assertion—no intent to communicate by act—thus no sincerity risk.

True   30.   As structured, if the answer to question 1 of the set is False, the answer to question 2 is True.

False   31.   The statement "gigolo" is relevant because it was said—it has independent legal significance in an action for defamation constituting the utterance itself that was published that is asserted to be defamatory.

True   32.   As structured, if the answer to question 1 of the set is False, the answer to question 2 is True.

False   33.   Blowing of the foghorn is an act having independent legal significance in an action asserting negligence on the part of the lighthouse—blowing the foghorn constitutes the operative act of being a warning.

True   34.   As structured, if the answer to question 1 of the set is False, the answer to question 2 is True.

True   35.   The bedroom shade is conduct intended as an assertion offered in evidence to prove the truth of the matter asserted, Rules 801(a)–(c), i.e., D was home—all four hearsay risks are present.

True   36.   The leaving open of the bedroom shade should be admitted under Rule 807 being more probative than other available evidence while possessing equivalent circumstantial guarantees of trustworthiness to the denominated hearsay exceptions.

False   37.   Z is testifying in court on personal knowledge to a fact observed on the night in question, Rule 602. Z's testimony is admissible to prove that the shade was up. Of course, the fact testified to—shade up—is not itself relevant without the paramour's testimony.

True   38.   As structured, if the answer to question 1 of the set is False, the answer to question 2 is True.

True   39.   The statement is relevant only if the declarant believes that P is a no good slob—the statement is being offered to prove the truth of the matter asserted, Rules 801(a)–(c)—the hearsay risks of sincerity and narration are present.

True   40.   Rule 803(3) provides a hearsay exception for a statement of the declarant's then existing state of mind, emotion, sensation, or physical condition.

False   41.   Failure to communicate about a month to month tenancy is nonverbal conduct not intended as an assertion—no intent to communicate by act—thus no sincerity risk.

True   42.   As structured, if the answer to question 1 of the set is False, the answer to question 2 is True.

False   43.   The pronouncement of marriage is an operative act—the law attaches independent legal significance to the statement—the statement is thus relevant for the fact said.

True   44.   As structured, if the answer to question 1 of the set is False, the answer to question 2 is True.

False   45.   The statement is relevant for the fact said—effect on listener—whether the person acted in good faith in making the arrest is affected by what he had been told regardless of whether it is true.

True   46.   As structured, if the answer to question 1 of the set is False, the answer to question 2 is True.

False   47.   Acceptance of the offer is an operative act—the law attaches independent legal significance to the acceptance under the objective theory of contract—payment was most likely accompanied by a statement indicating the $10,000 was in full payment for the car—the payment would be an operative act and the statement relevant for the fact said as characterizing an independently relevant act.

True 48. As structured, if the answer to question 1 of the set is False, the answer to question 2 is True.

False 49. The statement is relevant for the fact said—effect on listener—the air traffic controller's statement provides notice relevant to determining the listener's actual knowledge at the time.

True 50. As structured, if the answer to question 1 of the set is False, the answer to question 2 is True.

MULTIPLE CHOICE ANSWER KEY WITH EXPLANATIONS

Exam I

D 1. What is being offered in evidence is the fact that the floor was mopped up ten minutes before the accident. No out-of-court statement is being offered—thus no hearsay risks present.

D 2. The statement is not made while perceiving an event nor under the stress of excitement. The statement is a backwards looking state of mind statement. The statement is admissible under Rule 804(b)(2)—statement under belief of imminent death.

C 3. The statement is being offered in evidence to prove that the car lights should have been turned on—offered in evidence to prove the truth of the matter asserted, Rules 801(a)–(c). This is the classic oral occurrence witness statement meeting neither a not hearsay definition nor a hearsay exception. Opinions are admissible if helpful. The declarant is available so not declaration against interest. Not a statement of a party at all.

A 4. Rule 803(1) provides a hearsay exception for statements describing an event made while the declarant was perceiving the event. The statement may be testified to by anyone with personal knowledge that it was made. Corroboration by another witness who observed the same event as to the truth of the matter asserted is not required. The Dead Man's Statute applies, when it does apply, only to preclude interested parties as witnesses.

B 5. The requirements of Rule 803(6), the business record hearsay exception, are satisfied. Rule 803(5) is unavailing as the witness does not claim insufficient recollection to enable the witness to testify fully and more importantly the nurse never herself had personal knowledge of the matter recorded. Since the nurse was operating within the business under a business duty to reduce the dictation to a business record, only one level of hearsay is involved.

A   6.   The statement is multiple level hearsay. While Rule 801(d)(2)(A), admission of a party-opponent, defines as not hearsay Ludtke's statements when offered by the prosecution, Rule 803(8) may not be utilized to establish that Ludtke actually made the statement because Rule 803(8)(A)(ii) specifically excludes public records memorializing matters observed by police officers or other law enforcement personnel from being admitted in criminal cases against the criminal defendant.

A   7.   Rule 803(3) provides a hearsay exception for the statements of a declarant's then existing state of mind. As interpreted by Mutual Life Insurance Co. v. Hillmon, 145 U.S. 285, 12 S.Ct. 909, 36 L.Ed. 706 (1892), the common law state of mind hearsay exception permits statements of intent to be admitted in evidence to prove the doing of the act intended—a principal accepted as well with respect to Rule 803(3).

D   8.   The statement is relevant for the fact said—effect on listener—a reasonable person's apprehension of danger is affected by being told that another has slashed three people.

D   9.   Confinement is nonverbal conduct not intended as an assertion—no intent to communicate by act—thus no sincerity risk.

A   10.   Rule 803(2) provides a hearsay exception for a statement relating to a startling event made while the declarant was under the stress of excitement caused by the event. The availability of the declarant is irrelevant in determining whether a statement is admissible under a Rule 803 exception. A declaration against interest, however, requires that the declarant be unavailable. *Res gestae* is a term having no application under the Federal Rules of Evidence.

B   11.   The statement "We hit him while he was in the crosswalk" is being offered in evidence to prove the truth of the matter asserted, Rules 801(a)–(c),—all four hearsay risks are present. The defendant by remaining silent under the circumstances adopted the statement as true making the statement admissible as defined as not hearsay as an admission of a party-opponent by Rule 801(d)(2)(B). There is only one out-of-court statement for hearsay analysis purposes and silence under the circumstances does not create an agency relationship.

A   12.   Rule 803(3) provides a hearsay exception for a statement by a declarant of then existing physical condition—ankle hurts so much; the declarant's opinion as to why he is in so much pain—ankle broken—is not encompassed within the exception.

D   13.   The statement is inadmissible under the excited utterance hearsay exception, Rule 803(2), because the declarant was no longer under the stress of excitement of the event when he made the statement—the statement is a product of reflection and deliberation. A declarant can't recreate the excitement that has passed by simply recalling an event and prefacing his statement with "Oh my God!!!"

B   14.   The statement is an out-of-court statement offered in evidence to prove the truth of the matter asserted, Rules 801(a)–(c), i.e., Driver was at fault. When offered by Walker, a party-opponent, Driver's statement is defined as a not hearsay admission of a party-opponent by Rule 801(d)(2)(A). Admissions of a party-opponent may include opinions and conclusions of law. The term res gestae has no application under the Federal Rules of Evidence.

B   15.   The statement is offered in evidence to prove the truth of the matter asserted, Rules 801(a)–(c), i.e., Adams intended to mooch off Frank that night. Rule 803(3) provides a hearsay exception for a statement of the declarant's then existing state of mind constituting an intention for the further inference that the declarant then acted in accordance with the expressed intention.

C   16.   The hearsay exception in Rule 803(3) has been interpreted to incorporate the concept enunciated in Mutual Life Insurance Co. v. Hillmon, 145 U.S. 285, 12 S.Ct. 909, 36 L.Ed. 706 (1892) that a statement of the existing state of mind is admissible not only for the inference of future conduct by the declarant (Adam) in accordance therewith but also to infer future conduct on behalf of another (Frank).

D   17.   The statement characterizes an independently relevant act, i.e., handing over the $20 bill with the driver's license, that constitutes an operative act under the criminal law—the law attaches independent legal significance to the statement—the statement is relevant for the fact said.

A   18.   The alleged statement that X alone committed the illegal act is a statement of an unavailable declarant offered in evidence to prove the truth of the matter asserted under the hearsay exception for statements against penal interest, Rule 804(b)(3). However the last sentence of Rule 804(b)(3) provides "A statement tending to expose the declarant to criminal liability and offered to exculpate the accused is not admissible unless corroborating circumstances clearly indicate the trustworthiness of the statement."

A   19.   The statement by Harnsberger that he fled the Faculty Lounge is being offered in evidence to prove the truth of the matter asserted, Rules 801(a)–(c), i.e., flight for the inference of consciousness of guilt. When offered by the prosecution, a party-opponent, the statement of Harnsberger is defined as a not hearsay admission of a party-opponent under Rule 801(d)(2)(A).

D   20.   The statement about the statute of limitations being one year is relevant for the fact said—effect on listener—whether a person knows or is aware of the law that the statute of limitations is one year is affected by the fact that the statement was made regardless of the truth of the statement.

B   21.   Harnsberger statement manifests an adoption or belief in the truth of the statement made to him that the statute of limitations is one year. When offered to prove the truth of the matter asserted, i.e., Harnsberger's knowledge that the statute of limitations is one year, when offered by a party-opponent, the statement is defined as a not hearsay admission of a party-opponent by Rule 801(d)(2)(B).

D   22.   The report is being offered in evidence to prove the truth of the matter asserted, Rules 801(a)–(c), i.e., the victim was knifed in the back. Rule 803(8) which provides a hearsay exception for public records and reports pursuant to Rule 803(8)(a)(ii) excludes reports of matters observed by law enforcement personnel and by Rule 803(8)(a)(iii) applicable here excludes investigative reports when offered by the government against a criminal defendant.

D   23.   The affidavit of Dr. Bond that plaintiff was suffering from a recently incurred back injury is being offered in evidence to prove the truth of the matter asserted, Rules 801(a)–(c), i.e., Rider has a new back injury. The affidavit does not conform to the regularity requirements to be admitted as a business record nor has the necessary foundation witness been called. The statement fails to meet the requirements for a statement for purposes of medical diagnosis, Rule 803(4), in that the affidavit is the doctor's statement while the exception covers solely the patient's statements to the doctor.

D   24.   The statement of X is being offered in evidence to prove the truth of the matter asserted, Rules 801(a)–(c), i.e., Blinky robbed the liquor store. The statement is not in furtherance of a conspiracy, nor is it otherwise in any way Blinky's own statement and thus not an admission of a party-opponent. The statement is not admissible as a statement against interest; Williamson v. United States, 512 U.S. 594, 114 S.Ct. 2431, 129 L.Ed.2d 476 (1994) states that non-self inculpatory collateral statements (Blinky robbed the liquor store) are not admissible under Rule 804(b)(3). Moreover, the admission of X's statement if X does not testify would violate the confrontation clause, see Appendix C.

B   25.   The statement by W is not part of the process of formation
                    of the contract and is thus not itself an operative act
                    relevant for the fact said. The statement of W, offered in
                    evidence to prove the truth of the matter asserted, Rules
                    801(a)–(c), i.e., there is a deal, is a statement explaining an
                    event made while the declarant was perceiving the event,
                    or immediately thereafter, Rule 803(1).

Exam II

B   1.   The statement written by Smith is relevant to establish
                    bias if Smith believes that Swartz is a fool—the hearsay
                    risks of sincerity and narration are present. The statement
                    "[I believe] Swartz is a fool" when offered in evidence to
                    prove the truth of the matter asserted, Rules 801(a)–(c), is
                    admissible under Rule 803(3) as a statement of the
                    declarant's then existing state of mind.

B   2.   Same analysis as prior question. Here the statement itself of
                    then existing state of mind if believed to be true shows bias
                    while in question 25 one must infer that a person who
                    believes another to be a fool is biased against them. Both
                    statements must be believed to be true to be relevant. Both
                    are admissible under Rule 803(3).

B   3.   This is a multiple level hearsay problem as there are two
                    out-of-court statements. The statement by defendant
                    promising plaintiff to sell the horse has independent legal
                    significance—is relevant for the fact said and thus not
                    hearsay. However the statement out-of-court by X that he
                    overheard defendant promise P to sell the horse, offered in
                    evidence to prove the truth of the matter asserted, Rules
                    801(a)–(c), i.e., the defendant made the statement, fails to
                    meet the requirements of any statement defined as not
                    hearsay by Rules 801(d)(1) and (2) nor the requirements of
                    any hearsay exception provided in Rules 803, 804, and 807.

C   4.   The statement by Y is an out-of-court statement offered in
                    evidence to prove the truth of the matter asserted, Rules
                    801(a)–(c), i.e., D ran red light, which meets the
                    requirements of the hearsay exception provided in Rule
                    803(2) for an excited utterance. The police report being
                    offered in evidence to prove that Y made the statement is
                    admissible for such purposes under Rule 803(8)(a)(ii),

public records and reports, in a civil case. Thus the multiple level statements are admissible, Rule 805.

B 5. The deposition testimony is being offered in evidence to prove the truth of the matter asserted, Rules 801(a)–(c), i.e., Lenich smashed into Works' car that was stopped at a red light. Rule 804(b)(1) provides a hearsay exception for depositions taken in the same case when the deponent is unavailable. The deponent, Kirst is unavailable under Rule 804(a)(5) in that Kirst is not subject to a subpoena and reasonable efforts to obtain his appearance proved fruitless.

D 6. The statement by X that W has a nice "ABM" is relevant to show confusion amongst the public only if X actually believed the machine was an "ABM"—the hearsay risks of sincerity and narration are present. Rule 803(3) provides a hearsay exception for statements of a declarant's then existing state of mind.

C 7. The statement by Passenger that Driver had been drinking is offered in evidence to prove the truth of the matter asserted, Rules 801(a)–(c), i.e., Driver had been drinking. The statement was not made by a party-opponent and was not against Passenger's interest. Nor is the statement otherwise defined as not hearsay by Rules 801(d)(1) or (2). Nor does the statement otherwise meet the requirements of any hearsay exception contained in Rules 803, 804, and 807.

A 8. The letter is being offered to refresh the witness' recollection. The witness will read the letter to himself and then after putting the letter down be asked if he now recalls the details of the accident. Counsel should not refer to the document as a letter—just ask him to read "this document." The witness now testifies as to the accident details on personal knowledge, Rule 602. Since the content of the letter is not being offered in evidence at all, there is no hearsay issue.

C   9.   The report is being offered in evidence to prove that Y committed the robbery—the truth of the matter stated, Rules 801(a)–(c). The report is admissible under the public records hearsay exception, Rule 803(8)(a)(iii)—results of an investigation made pursuant to authority granted by law—when offered *by the defendant in a criminal case.*

A   10.   The statement by Rider about having recently suffered a recurrence of an old back injury is being offered in evidence to prove the truth of the matter asserted, Rules 801(a)–(c), i.e., a recently recurring back injury—all four hearsay risks are present. The statement of Rider when offered by a party-opponent, here the Transit Company, is defined as a not hearsay admission of a party-opponent by Rule 801(d)(2)(B).

B   11.   The confrontation clause applies solely in criminal cases.

C   12.   The report of how the accident occurred is being offered in evidence to prove the truth of the matter asserted, Rules 801(a)–(c), i.e., Patty fell on her own. While the store, Mart, will argue that the report is admissible as a business record and was prepared in the ordinary course of business in its efforts to reduce accidents, the court will most likely exclude the report on the grounds that the report was made principally for purposes of litigation; "source of information or the method or circumstances of preparation indicate lack of trustworthiness."

D   13.   The statement by P two hours later to a nurse is offered in evidence to prove the truth of the matter asserted, Rules 801(a)–(c), i.e., D ran a red light. It is obviously not offered against P but by P. It is also clearly not admissible under Rule 803(3). It is a statement of belief offered to prove a past event. Rule 803(3) specifically precludes "a statement of memory or belief to prove the fact remembered or believed." The statement is not admissible under Rule 803(4) as going through a red light is not a statement of "inception or general character of the cause or external source thereof insofar as reasonably pertinent to diagnosis or treatment."

C 14. The most important criteria to be applied in determining whether to adopt a hearsay exception for a particular kind of statement is whether that kind of statement is typically accompanied by circumstantial guarantees of trustworthiness.

D 15. The police report is being offered to prove the truth of the statement contained therein by D that the "car must have slipped out of park" for the truth of the matter asserted, Rules 801(a)–(c). Multiple level hearsay is present, Rule 805. The police report is admissible in a civil case under Rule 803(8)(B) to prove that D made the statement while D's statement itself when offered by P is defined as a not hearsay admission of a party-opponent by Rule 801(d)(2)(A).

C 16. The statement by Miss Hood is being offered to prove the truth of the matter asserted, Rules 801(a)–(c), i.e., her intent to visit grandma. Rule 803(3) provides a hearsay exception for a statement of a then existing state of mind as evidence of that state of mind, here present intent, for the further inference that the person subsequently acted consistent with that present intent.

C 17. The statement that the light was yellow is a statement made out-of-court by a declarant under oath subject to the penalty of perjury at a deposition who testifies at the trial, subject to cross-examination, that is inconsistent with the declarant's trial testimony and is thus defined as not hearsay, Rule 801(d)(1)(A), making the statement admissible for impeachment (for which purpose relevancy only requires that the statement be said) and as substantive evidence.

D 18. The statement by Dr. Jenny A. Trick made to W is hearsay as to which there is no exception. If W in comparison testified on personal knowledge that the statement by Dr. Jenny A. Trick was made directly to A, it would be not hearsay as relevant for its effect on listener—a reasonable person is more likely to commit suicide having been told that he has an incurable disease than if not so told regardless of the truth of the statement; when a statement is relevant for the fact said no hearsay risks are present.

A   19.   The statement by the defendant Lyons that he poisoned his wife is being offered in evidence to prove the truth of the matter asserted, Rules 801(a)–(c), i.e., defendant poisoned his wife—all four hearsay risks are present. Rule 801(d)(2)(A) defines as a not hearsay admission of a party-opponent a statement by a party, here the defendant, when offered by the party-opponent, here the prosecution.

B   20.   The affidavit detailing Harry's observation of Joe is being offered in evidence to prove the truth of the matter asserted, Rules 801(a)–(c). The statement fails to meet the requirement of any of the not hearsay by definition provisions of Rules 801(d)(1) and (2) nor the requirements of any hearsay exception provided in Rules 803, 804, and 807. The statement being 15 years old, fails to satisfy Rule 803(16) which requires that the statements in the document be in existence 20 years or more.

D   21.   The statement of Lyons that he wants to borrow a gun "to commit a robbery" is being offered in evidence to prove the truth of the matter asserted, Rules 801(a)–(c), i.e., that Lyons intended to commit a robbery. The statement is defined as not hearsay by Rule 801(d)(2)(A)—the prosecution is offering a statement by the defendant. Since Lyons' own statement is being offered against him under Rule 801(d)(2)(A), it is unnecessary to explore whether the requirements of the coconspirator exception, Rule 801(d)(2)(E), are satisfied.

B   22.   The written judgment of conviction, bearing a signature of the clerk and the seal of the court, is self-authenticating under Rule 902(1). Rule 803(8)(A) provides a hearsay exception to prove the contents of the written judgment— that D was convicted of petty theft—the written judgment of conviction is a report of the activities of the office or agency.

B   23.   The crumpled paper bearing the number "ABC 666" is being offered in evidence to prove the truth of the matter asserted, Rules 801(a)–(c), i.e., that "ABC 666" is the number on the license plate of the getaway car. The hearsay exception for past recollection recorded is satisfied in this case. The witness testifies that I remember now remembering then but I don't remember now what I remembered then.

D   24.   The photograph does not contain an out-of-court assertion by a person offered in evidence to prove the truth of the matter asserted. The photograph's content is relevant when authenticated as fairly and accurately representing what it purports to represent—the car license number is "ABC 666." The license plate number itself is not being offered in evidence to prove what it asserts. It doesn't assert anything. The license number is in fact not relevant unless connected through other evidence to the defendant in some way, such as through a record of the state motor vehicle department showing such a license number as having been issued to the accused. A contrary situation would arise if the photograph showed a sign on the back of the truck saying "Ace Moving and Storage."

A   25.   A plea of nolo contendere is a statement that the accused is not contesting the entry of judgment against him. It is thus *not* a statement by D admitting committing the felony murder—a statement admitting the commission of the crime would be admissible. Moreover and in any event, Rule 410 bars the admission of a plea of nolo contendere against the defendant who made the plea in any civil or criminal case as an admission of a party-opponent defined as not hearsay by Rule 801(d)(2)(A). Finally, Rule 803(22) states that the hearsay exception for a judgment of a previous conviction is inapplicable where the conviction is upon a plea of *nolo contendere*.

COMPREHENSIVE EXAMS ANSWER KEY
TRUE-FALSE ANSWER KEY WITH EXPLANATIONS

Exam I

False 1. Rule 404(a)(1) and Rule 404(b)(1) both provide that evidence of crimes, wrongs, or other acts, i.e., specific instances of conduct, is not admissible to prove the character of a person in order to show action in conformity therewith. In addition, the evidence is not admissible for another purpose under Rule 404(b)(2).

False 2. Rule 404(a)(2)(A) permits the prosecution to introduce reputation testimony of a pertinent character trait of an alleged victim in a non-homicide case only to rebut such evidence offered by the defendant.

False 3. Rule 404(a)(1) and Rule 404(b)(1) provide that evidence of other crimes, wrongs, or acts, i.e., specific instances of conduct, is not admissible to prove the character of a person in order to show conformity therewith. In addition, the evidence is not admissible for another purpose under Rule 404(b)(2).

True 4. Rule 404(a)(2)(A) provides that the defendant in the first instance may offer evidence in the form of opinion testimony as to a pertinent trait of character of the victim.

False 5. Rule 404(a)(1), Rule 404(b)(1) and Rule 405(a) prohibit the use of prior instances of conduct on cross-examination to prove the character of a person in order to show he acted in conformity therewith.

True 6. Rule 609(a)(2) permits impeachment of a witness by means of a prior conviction involving dishonesty or false statement unless over 10 years old even if the prior conviction, as here, is for a misdemeanor, i.e., not punishable by death or imprisonment in excess of one year, otherwise called a felony, without application of a discretionary balancing test.

True   7.   Rule 608(a) provides that evidence in the form of reputation for character for untruthfulness is admissible to impeach the credibility of a witness.

True   8.   The testimony on personal knowledge is admissible to establish untrustworthy partiality, i.e., bias against the police.

True   9.   Rule 704(a) provides the testimony in the form of an opinion is not objectionable because it embraces an ultimate issue to be decided by the trier of fact, if otherwise admissible. To be otherwise admissible, the opinion of a lay witness must under Rule 701(b) be "helpful" which requires that the witness' testimony not invoke unexplored legal criteria, a requirement resolved favorably in the question.

False   10.   Rule 611(c)(2) permits leading questions when a party, here the plaintiff, calls a witness identified with an adverse party, here the site foreman of the defendant.

False   11.   Rule 407 precludes introduction of evidence of a subsequent remedial measure to prove negligence. However, here the evidence is offered for another purpose, impeachment, to show that the fence the witness says now surrounds the pit was not present when the accident occurred.

True   12.   Rule 411 provides that evidence that a person was insured against liability is not admissible upon the issue of whether the person acted negligently or otherwise wrongfully.

False   13.   No accountant-client privilege is recognized in the federal courts in a criminal case.

False   14.   The testimony is not hearsay. It is a statement that is relevant for the fact said for its effect on listener.

True   15.   All of the requirements provided for the admissibility of expert testimony by Rules 702–705 are met.

True   16.   Rule 803(3) permits introduction of a statement of current state of intention to do an act with another, Joe, to be introduced as evidence that the other person, Joe, acted in accordance with that intent—Joe went to the movies.

True   17.   Rule 803(3) permits introduction of a statement of current intent of the declarant to act as evidence that the declarant acted upon that intent—"I" went to the movies.

True   18.   An agreed stipulation is a judicial admission that conclusively withdraws a fact from contention in a case even if the fact is an ultimate fact constituting an essential element of a claim or defense.

False   19.   The statement is being offered to prove the truth of the matter asserted, Rules 801(a)–(c). It does not meet the requirements of the hearsay exception for state of mind provided in Rule 803(3). The statement "[I know that] yesterday I was in Crooked Creek" would fall within the inclusion in Rule 803(3) for statements of belief offered to prove the fact believed. Availability or unavailability does not affect a Rule 803 exception.

True   20.   Rule 803(3) permits introduction of a statement of current intent of the declarant to act as evidence that the declarant acted upon that intent—went to Crooked Creek on July 24. Availability or unavailability does not affect a Rule 803 exception.

False   21.   While the presence of the out-of-court declarant in court subject to cross-examination provides oath, demeanor, and cross-examination satisfies the testimonial concerns with respect to determining reliability underlying the rule against hearsay, trial concerns similar to those denominated in Rule 403 resulted in Rule 801(d)(1) being drafted by Congress to permit admissibility of some but by no means all prior statements of an in court witness.

False 22. A party may introduce evidence that contradicts evidence already received provided that the subject matter of the evidence is not collateral. The subject matter of the evidence is not collateral when relevant for a purpose other than contradiction. Whether the light was green or red is relevant for a purpose other than contradiction and is thus not collateral.

True 23. Rule 608(a) provides that evidence in the form of reputation for character for untruthfulness is admissible to impeach the credibility of a witness.

False 24. Under Rule 404(b)(2), the prosecution may offer evidence of a prior cocaine sale for the purpose of proving knowledge, intent and/or absence of mistake or accident. The government must introduce evidence sufficient to support a finding that the prior sale occurred—an arrest is an opinion of the police office inadmissible in evidence. If the police officer had personal knowledge of the prior cocaine sale, he needs to so testify in the current case.

False 25. The law is the sole province of the judge. Testimony by any witness defining the law to the jury is improper.

False 26. Under Rule 404(a)(1) evidence of a pertinent trait of character is not admissible in a civil case for the purpose of proving action in conformity therewith.

False 27. See id.

False 28. Testimony by an expert witness that another witness was not telling the truth is excluded as not of assistance to the trier of fact in understanding the evidence or determining a fact in issue, Rule 702.

False   29.   Rule 611(c)(1) provides that ordinarily leading questions are permitted on cross-examination. No reason exists not to permit a leading question here.

True   30.   Rule 803(18) provides a hearsay exception for statements from a learned treatise established as a reliable authority. Thus such statements when employed on cross-examination are admissible both to impeach and as substantive evidence. Such statements must be read into evidence—the learned treatise may not be received as an exhibit, Rule 803(18).

False   31.   Rule 803(18) provides a hearsay exception for statements from a learned treatise established as a reliable authority. Thus such statements when employed on cross-examination are admissible both to impeach and as substantive evidence. Such statements must be read into evidence—the learned treatise may not be received as an exhibit, Rule 803(18).

False   32.   Rule 705 provides that an expert may testify in terms of opinion or inference and give reasons therefor without first testifying to the underlying facts, data, and opinions, unless the court requires otherwise.

True   33.   Rule 501 provides that in civil actions and proceedings, with respect to an element of a claim or defense as to what State law supplies the rule of decision, the privilege of a witness, person, government, State, or political subdivision must be determined in accordance with State law.

True   34.   The same four dangers are also the hearsay risks.

True   35.   Rule 103(c) allows for the offer of proof to be made by avowal of counsel unless the court directs that the making of the offer be made in question and answer form.

True   36.   Rule 803(3) provides a hearsay exception for statements of the declarant's then existing physical condition.

False   37.   Rule 803(3) applies to then existing—current—only; statements expressing a prior physical condition are not encompassed.

True   38.   Evidence of specific instances of conduct offered to prove the character of a person in order to show action in conformity therewith meets the test for relevancy provided in Rule 401.

True   39.   An opinion by either a lay or expert witness that someone is negligent constitutes an unhelpful legal conclusion, Rule 701, that does not assist the trier of fact, Rule 702.

True   40.   Some common law courts failed to grasp that an opinion of a lay witness may be helpful even when the matter falls generally within an area of common knowledge of the jury.

False   41.   Rule 606(a) provides that a member of the jury may not testify as a witness before the jury in the trial of the case in which the juror is sitting.

True   42.   A prior conviction based upon a nolo contendere plea may be employed under Rule 609 to impeach to the same extent as if the particular conviction had followed a guilty plea or an adjudication of guilt.

True   43.   A party is not required to object until it becomes apparent that an objection is in order.

True   44.   Rule 901(a) states that authentication of a thing is satisfied by the introduction of evidence sufficient to support a finding that the matter in question is what its proponent claims.

True   45.   Rule 1003 provides for the admissibility of a duplicate in place of the original unless a genuine question is raised as to the authenticity of the original or under the circumstance it would be unfair to admit the duplicate in lieu of the original.

False   46.   The statement by Doody is admissible under Rule 803(3) as a statement by declarant of then existing state of mind—here an intent to keep fighting on.

False   47.   Rule 803(4) permits statements for medical diagnosis or treatment to be made to persons reasonably believed to be part of the process of obtaining diagnosis or treatment such as an ambulance driver or person eliciting intake information in an emergency room or doctor's office—anyone reasonably believed to have the responsibility to pass on the information to the person providing diagnosis or treatment.

False   48.   Whether racially segregated schools may ever be truly equal is a legislative fact not covered by Rule 201. While legislative judicial notice does not require that the fact not be subject to reasonable dispute, whether racially segregated schools can ever be truly equal is in fact not subject to reasonable dispute and could thus be judicially noticed if Rule 201 was deemed to apply.

True   49.   Rule 614(a) permits the court to call a witness on its own while Rule 614(b) permits the court to interrogate the witness, whether called by itself or a party.

False   50.   The trial judge pursuant to Rule 104(a) must decide whether the item of evidence under consideration has any tendency to make the existence of any fact that is of consequence to the determination of the action more probable or less probable than it would be without the evidence, Rule 401. The suggested jury instruction should not be given.

Exam II

False   1.   Rule 607 provides that the credibility of a witness may be attacked by any party, including the party calling the witness. The only limitation is that a prior inconsistent statement admissible solely to impeach may not be employed when the witness was called for the "primary purpose" as a "mere subterfuge" to place the inconsistent statement before the jury.

True   2.   Rule 608(b)(1) permits specific instances of conduct of a witness, if probative of untruthfulness, to be inquired of on cross-examination.

True   3.   Speed of a car is a matter of which most lay witness possess a sufficient personal knowledge foundation in order to perform the act of comparison "rationally" leading to the opinion, Rule 701(a).

False   4.   Most lay witnesses lack the personal knowledge foundation as to the sound of a .45 caliber pistol in comparison to other weapons and similar noises to "rationally" reach such a conclusion, Rule 701.

True   5.   Rule 602 states that a witness may not testify to a matter unless evidence is introduced sufficient to support a finding that the witness has personal knowledge of the matter.

True   6.   The defendant opened the door to evidence that he knows what marijuana looks like by voluntarily denying such knowledge on direct examination. Evidence of prior smoking of marijuana would have been admissible in any event on the government's case in chief under Rule 404(b)(2) to show knowledge of and intent to smoke marijuana.

True   7.   Rule 406 provides that the routine practice of an organization is admissible to prove that the conduct of the organization on a particular occasion was in conformity with the routine practice.

True   8.   Rule 411 precludes evidence of insurance when offered upon the issue of whether a person acted negligently. Rule 411 specifically provides the evidence of insurance is not made inadmissible when offered for another purpose. Here the party admitted having acted in the past negligently by saying something like, "I know it's my fault. My insurance company will pay for it."

True   9.   Inadmissible evidence may be admitted if the "door is opened" subject to application of Rule 403.

False   10.   The specific objection that is overruled preserves solely that specific objection for purposes of appeal.

True   11.   The requirement is abolished in Rule 613(a).

False   12.   Rule 603 permits a witness to declare that the witness will testify truthfully by either oath or affirmation. An affirmation is a promise to tell the truth making no reference to God.

True   13.   Surprise was not included in list of trial concerns incriminated in Rule 403, it being believed that when unfair surprise is asserted, enforcement of discovery sanctions or the granting of a continuance are more appropriate remedies than exclusion of the evidence on the basis of balancing harm against incremental probative value.

False   14.   Rule 610 only prohibits evidence of religious beliefs for the purpose of showing that by reason of their nature the witness' credibility is impaired or enhanced. Here association with the church is being offered for a different purpose to affect credibility, untrustworthy partiality in the form of interest and bias in favor of the church.

True   15.   Rule 404(a)(2))A) provides that in a criminal case evidence of a pertinent trait of character of the victim of the crime offered by the accused may be rebutted by the prosecution, all in the form of reputation or opinion character evidence, Rule 405(a).

False   16.   Use of the word "assaulted" is an unhelpful opinion. The lay witness must testify in this instance on personal knowledge to the details of what was perceived, not his or her evaluation of the conduct.

True   17. Here the testimony of the lay witness is helpful. It also represents a situation where accounting of the details alone would not accurately convey the total impression received by the witness.

True   18. Rule 702 provides that a witness may be qualified in an area of scientific, technical, or other specialized knowledge as an expert by knowledge, skill, experience, training, *or* education.

False   19. No such preference is provided in Rule 702.

False   20. The trial court has a gatekeeping responsibility, Rule 104(a), to determine whether the particular explanative theory employed is the product of reliable principles and methods, Rule 702(c), before permitting the expert witness to testify before the jury.

True   21. Rule 103(d) provides that the appellate court is not precluded from taking notice of plain errors affecting substantial rights although they were not brought to the attention of the trial court.

True   22. Rule 609(e) provides that the pendency of an appeal does not render evidence of a prior conviction inadmissible.

False   23. A prior consistent statement is admissible under Rule 801(d)(1)(B) only if offered to rebut an express or implied charge against the declarant of recent fabrication or improper influence or motive.

False   24. Whether to permit exhibits introduced in evidence to accompany the jury during deliberations rests primarily in the discretion of the trial court.

True   25. Rule 704(b) provides that no expert witness testifying with respect to the mental state or condition of a defendant in a criminal case may state an opinion or inference as to whether the defendant did or did not have the mental state or condition constituting an element of the crime charged or of a defense thereto. Such ultimate issues are matters for the trier of fact alone. Intent is an element of the crime charged.

<u>True</u>   26.   See id. Not knowing right from wrong constitutes a defense to the crime charged.

<u>True</u>   27.   An opinion that the defendant suffered from a particular mental disease which affected him in a certain way is not an opinion on the mental state or condition constituting an element of the crime charged or a defense thereto.

<u>False</u>   28.   It is the function of the jury not the judge to determine which of two witnesses is telling the truth. A more common example is a red light green light case.

<u>True</u>   29.   Rule 611(a) provides that the trial court shall exercise reasonable control over the order of interrogating witnesses and presenting evidence while Rule 611(b) provides that the trial court, in the exercise of discretion, may permit inquiries into matters beyond the scope of direct examination.

<u>False</u>   30.   The objection "incompetent, irrelevant and immaterial" raises only the objection of relevancy and only an objection on the ground of relevancy is preserved for appeal.

<u>True</u>   31.   The child has demonstrated that she understands the obligation to tell the truth, Rule 603. No obligation to believe in God is imposed.

<u>True</u>   32.   One of the trial concerns comprising Rule 403 is needless presentation of cumulative evidence.

<u>False</u>   33.   Psychotic is not an opinion that the defendant did or did not have the mental state or condition constituting an element of the crime charged or defense thereto.

False 34. There simply is no such rule. The case can go to the jury provided the circumstantial evidence constitutes a prima facie case.

True 35. Facts, data, or opinions not admitted in evidence satisfy the reasonably relied upon proviso of Rule 703 only if the facts, data, or opinions sought to be relied upon possess trustworthiness similar to that possessed by statements admitted pursuant to a hearsay exception.

True 36. All Rule 804(b) exceptions require that the declarant be unavailable as specified in Rule 804(a).

True 37. A great majority of jurisdictions prohibit polygraph evidence even upon stipulation of counsel based upon an assessment of reliability and danger of misleading the jury.

False 38. Rule 106 does not apply to oral conversation. Rule 106 states that when a writing or recorded statement or part thereof is introduced by a party, an adverse party may require the introduction at that time of any other part or any other writing or recorded statement which ought in fairness to be considered contemporaneously with it.

True 39. Once a person is arrested and given *Miranda* warning, it can no longer be said that failure to deny an accusation is an adoptive admission, Rule 801(d)(1)(B), as under the circumstance it is not only reasonable but advisable to simply remain silent.

False 40. Rule 803(5) states that with respect to a memorandum in recording admitted under the hearsay exception for recorded recollection, the memorandum or record may be read into evidence but may not itself be received as an exhibit *unless offered by an adverse party*.

True 41. The cross-examiner attacked W's credibility by inquiring about untrustworthy partiality, in this case bias.

Untrustworthiness partiality is a non collateral matter. Thus extrinsic evidence in the form of Y's testimony establishing facts from which bias may be inferred, i.e., W regularly dates D's sister, is admissible.

False 42. Rule 609(b) provides that evidence of a conviction is not admissible under Rule 609 if a period of more than ten years has elapsed since the date of the conviction or of the release of the witness from the confinement imposed for that conviction, whichever is the later date, unless the court determines, in the interests of justice, that the probative value of the conviction supported by specific facts and circumstances substantially outweighs its prejudicial effect.

True 43. Rule 901(a) provides that the requirement of authentication or identification as a condition precedent to admissibility is satisfied by evidence sufficient to support a finding that the matter in question is what its proponent claims. Rule 901(b) states that "[b]y way of illustration only, and not by way of limitation, the following are examples of authentication or identification conforming with the requirements of this rule:

(2) *Nonexpert Opinion on Handwriting.* A nonexpert's opinion that handwriting is genuine, based on a familiarity not acquired for the current litigation.

False 44. Rule 408 eliminates the common law requirement that statements made during compromise negotiations are to be excluded only if either they are inseparable or were accompanied by a qualifying phrase such as "hypothetically speaking" in favor of a blanket rule of exclusion.

False 45. A prior civil judgment is hearsay falling within no hearsay exception; Rule 803(22) provides a hearsay exception for certain final judgments in criminal cases.

False 46. Placing of the attorney's advice in issue waives the attorney-client privilege.

True   47.   Evidence of a subsequent remedial measure is admissible when the feasibility of precautionary measures is controverted.

True   48.   Rule 614(c) provides that objections to questions asked by the judge may be made at the time or at the next available opportunity when the jury is not present.

False   49.   As part of judicial gatekeeping as to explanative theories offered by an expert witness, Rule 702(d) requires that the trial court determine, Rule 104(a), whether the expert witness has applied the principles and methods reliably to the facts, data, and opinions of the case.

True   50.   Rule 702(c) requires that the trial court determine, Rule 104(a), whether the "testimony [explanative theory] is the product of reliable principles and methods."

Exam III

False   1.   *Daubert* and its follow up *Kumho* and Rule 702 apply solely in the federal court.

True   2.   Anyone with sufficient personal knowledge, Rule 602, may lay a foundation, Rule 901(b)(1), for the admissibility of a photograph; the photographer is not required.

False   3.   The objection made raises only the ground of relevancy; a ground other than relevancy, such as hearsay, is not preserved for appeal by the objection actually made at trial.

False   4.   A sufficient foundation for admission of a business record may be made by a custodian or other qualified witness as to regular, regular, at, personal knowledge. It is not required that the person who actually prepared the record testify.

True   5.   Prior similar accidents are relevant to establishing the dangerousness of the condition and the defendant's notice of such dangerousness.

True   6.   Rules 405(a) and (b), applicable to both civil and criminal cases, together provided that in cases in which a trait of character of a person is an essential element of a charge, claim, or defense, evidence of specific instances of that person's conduct as well as testimony in the form of reputation and opinion is admissible to prove the trait of character.

False   7.   Rule 609(a)(1)(B) provides that for purposes of attacking the credibility of a witness evidence that a witness other than an accused has been convicted of a crime shall be admitted, subject to Rule 403, if the crime was punishable by death or imprisonment in excess of one year under the law under which the witness was convicted, and evidence that an accused has been convicted of such a crime shall be admitted if the court determines that the probative value of admitting this evidence outweighs its prejudicial effect to the accused.

False   8.   Rule 407 precludes the introduction of a subsequent remedial measure to prove negligence.

False   9.   An argumentative question is improper on cross-examination.

True   10.   Rule 611(b) provides that cross-examination should be limited to the subject matter of the direct examination and matters affecting the credibility of the witness.

False   11.   Standard 503(a)(2), reflective of the common law, states that a "lawyer" is a person authorized, or reasonably believed by the client to be authorized, to practice law in any state or nation.

True   12.   Rule 706(a) provides that the trial court may appoint expert witnesses of its own selection on its own motion.

True   13.   Rule 404(a)(2)(B) permits the defendant in a criminal case to present character evidence in the form of opinion testimony as to a pertinent character trait of the victim.

False   14.   The attorney-client privilege applies regardless of whether the holder of the privilege is or is not a party to the action.

True   15.   An expert may be required to disclose facts, data, or opinions relied upon by the expert in forming an opinion, Rule 705, and generally cross-examined thereon.

False   16.   Photographs of the victim, no matter how bloody or otherwise gruesome, taken at the scene of the crime are very rarely excluded when an objection under Rule 403 on the grounds of unfair prejudice is interposed. The trial court generally believes the jury capable of distinguishing between the horrific nature of the crime and whether the defendant did it.

True   17.   Admissions of a party-opponent do not require a showing that the declarant had personal knowledge.

False   18.   Flight is nonverbal conduct not intended as an assertion and is thus not hearsay.

False   19.   Under the current interpretation of the confrontation clause, any prior inconsistent statement of the in court witness may be received as substantive evidence. Rule 801(d)(1)(A), however, for trial concern reasons limits admissibility to prior inconsistent statements given under oath subject to the penalty of perjury at a trial, hearing, or other proceeding, or in a deposition.

True   20.   When a doctor relies upon a laboratory report or an opinion of another doctor such reliance is reasonable—the laboratory report or opinion of the doctor possesses indicia of trustworthiness equivalent to that possessed by statements admitted pursuant to a hearsay exception.

False 21. Rule 703 provides that facts, data, or opinions reasonably relied upon that have not otherwise been admitted into evidence shall not be disclosed to the jury by the proponent of the opinion or inference unless the court determines that their probative value in assisting the jury to evaluate the expert's opinion substantially outweighs their prejudicial effect.

True 22. Rule 405(a) provides that in all cases in which evidence of character or a trait of character of a person is admissible, proof may be made by testimony as to reputation or by testimony in the form of an opinion.

False 23. Rule 804(a)(3) requires for unavailability lack of recollection of the subject matter of the declarant's statement, not lack of recollection of having made the statement.

True 24. A witness may be lead in open court before the jury on direct examination to refresh recollection provided that the content of the leading question is not itself critical in the context of the case.

True 25. Rule 615 requires that all witnesses, subject to four exceptions, are to be excluded from the courtroom when "The Rule" is invoked by a party.

False 26. Rule 704(a) provides that an opinion is not objectionable because it embraces an ultimate issue to be decided by the trier of fact. In fact, going through the red light is a fact rather than an opinion on the fact-opinion continuum.

False 27. Prior testimony by an expert on behalf of another client of the attorney raises the inference of bias through financial interest.

True 28. An opinion that a person is drunk is a lay witness opinion meeting the requirements set forth in Rule 701.

True   29.   An opinion that another person was nervous and afraid is a lay witness opinion meeting the requirements set forth in Rule 701.

False   30.   A present sense impression, Rule 803(1), consists of a statement describing or explaining an event or condition made while the declarant was perceiving the event or condition, or immediately thereafter.

False   31.   As illustrated by Rule 801(d)(2)(A), all that an admission of a party-opponent requires is that the statement is offered against a party and is a party's own statement—full stop, nothing else.

True   32.   Rule 804(b)(3) provides that if the declarant is unavailable, Rule 804(a), a statement that which was at the time of its making so far contrary to the declarant's proprietary interest that a reasonable person in the declarant's position would not have made the statement unless believing it to be true is not excluded by the hearsay rule.

True   33.   Rule 408(a)(1) provides that evidence of offering to furnish a valuable consideration in attempting to compromise a claim which was disputed as to either validity or amount is not admissible to prove liability for the claim or its amount.

False   34.   Rule 902(7) in providing that extrinsic evidence of authenticity as a condition precedent to admissibility is not required with respect to inscriptions, signs, tags, or labels purporting to have been affixed in the course of business and indicating origin, ownership, or control operates on the issue of authentication only as an exception to the hearsay rule.

False   35.   Standard 508, reflective of the common law, states that a person has a privilege, which may be claimed by him or his agent or employee, to refuse to disclose and to prevent other persons from disclosing a trade secret owned by him, if the allowance of the privilege will not tend to conceal fraud or otherwise work injustice.

False   36.   Use of the term "fact of consequence" in Rule 401 in place of materiality clarifies that the breadth of admissibility of relevant evidence extends to facts not in dispute.

False   37.   Rule 402 states that all relevant evidence is admissible, except as otherwise provided by the Constitution of the United States, by Act of Congress, by these rules, or by other rules prescribed by the Supreme Court pursuant to statutory authority. Evidence which is not relevant is not admissible.

True   38.   Rule 404(a)(1) permits the defendant to introduce evidence in the form of reputation testimony only as to a "pertinent trait" of character.

False   39.   Rule 702 permits a qualified expert to testify in the form of an opinion or otherwise.

True   40.   Expert witness testimony is subject to Rule 403.

True   41.   An opinion by a landowner as to value of his property is a lay witness opinion meeting the requirements set forth in Rule 701.

False   42.   An opinion in terms of "could" have been caused by X is permissible—absolute certainty that the event was caused by X is not required.

True   43.   The issue of whether particular evidence is relevant is ultimately one for the jury to decide.

False   44.   A trial judge may admit hearsay only if the trial judge determines, Rule 104(a), that the requirements of a hearsay exception contained in Rules 803, 804, or 807 have been satisfied.

False   45.   Pursuant to Rule 501, the principles of the common law as interpreted by the courts of the United States in the light of reason and experience recognize an attorney-client privilege.

True   46.   Rule 201(d) provides that judicial notice may be taken at any stage of the proceeding.

True   47.   Rule 404(b)(2) provides that evidence of crimes, wrongs, or other acts is admissible to prove identity or intent.

False   48.   Voice recognition is only one method of identification. Others include the reply doctrine, caller identification, and distinctive characteristics.

True   49.   Rule 1004(4)(d) provides that the original is not required, and other evidence of the contents of a writing, recording, or photograph is admissible, if the writing, recording, or photograph is not closely related to a controlling issue.

False   50.   Rule 706(d) provides that in the exercise of discretion the court *may* authorize disclosure to the jury of the fact that the court appointed the expert witness.

Exam IV

False   1.   Rule 703 requires that such facts, data, and opinions must be not "customarily" relied upon but "reasonably" relied upon which imposes a requirement that the facts, data, or opinions not admitted in evidence possess a trustworthiness similar to that possessed by statements admitted pursuant to a hearsay exception.

False   2.   A statement by a bystander relied upon by an accidentologist, not otherwise admitted in evidence, was employed as an illustration by the Advisory Committee of a situation where reliance by an expert is *not* reasonable—the occurrence witness' oral statement made well after an event is the classic hearsay statement not possessing sufficient trustworthiness to be admitted pursuant to a hearsay exception.

False   3.   Standard 503(d)(2), reflective of the common law, provides that there is no attorney-client privilege as to a communication relevant to an issue between parties who claim through the same deceased client, regardless of whether the claims are by testate or intestate succession or by inter vivos transaction.

False   4.   Standard 512, reflective of the common law, provides that the holder of a privilege will not be held to have waived the privilege where disclosure of the privileged confidential communication was made without the holder having any opportunity to claim the privilege.

True   5.   Since intent to disclose is of critical concern, the presence of an eavesdropper or person overhearing by accident does not destroy confidentiality, unless it is clear that the client knew that the communication was being overheard.

False   6.   Rule 1002 requires that, except as otherwise provided, to prove the content of a writing, the original writing must be introduced in court; oral testimony of its contents is not admissible unless the original writing is shown to be unavailable as provided in Rule 1004.

True   7.   Rule 411 does not apply to life insurance, only insurance against liability.

False   8.   Reputation admissible under Rule 405 is reputation where the person resides along with reputation among any substantial community of people with whom he constantly associated in his business, work, or other continued activity.

False   9.   Rule 702 states that a witness may be qualified as an expert by knowledge, skill, experience, training or education.

True   10.   During cross-examination of an expert, to show financial interest and thus bias an expert may be asked about the percentage of his income that comes from court related matters.

False   11.   The gatekeeping requirement of Rule 702 applies to scientific, technical or other specialized knowledge.

False   12.   The Supreme Court in *Daubert* held that Rule 702 does not incorporate *Frye*.

False   13.   The original writing rule only applies when a party seeks to prove the content of a photograph; it does not in any way affect the admissibility of testimony of a witness on personal knowledge relating what she observed.

False   14.   The prior consistent statement was made after the witness began to cooperate in connection with the plea agreement and thus does not rebut a charge of recent fabrication required by Rule 801(d)(2)(B); the prior consistent statement was made under and not *before* the improper influence leading to the alleged recent fabrication.

False   15.   The character of the victim for chastity is not an element in a rape case whether or not a consent defense is interposed and is thus not "in issue". Where the defense is consent to the charge of rape, if such evidence was not barred by Rule 412, character would be relevant only as a means of proving consent, not as an element itself.

False   16.   Intrusion on the notion that the jury must decide each and every element of a criminal charge and may not be instructed how to so find underlies Rule 201(g)'s requirement that in a criminal case the court shall instruct the jury that it *may, but is not required to*, accept as conclusive any fact judicially noticed.

False   17.   The Best Evidence Rule, now known as the Original Writing Rule, as stated in Rule 1002 provides solely that to prove the content of a writing, recording, or photograph, the original writing, recording, or photograph is required, except as otherwise provided in the Federal Rules of Evidence or by Act of Congress.

False   18.   Rule 403 provides that although relevant, evidence may be excluded if its probative value is substantially outweighed by the danger of unfair prejudice, confusion of the issues, or misleading the jury, or by considerations of undue delay, waste of time, or needless presentation of cumulative evidence.

False   19.   An opinion that the robber had a very high voice and seemed scared is a lay witness opinion meeting the requirements of Rule 701.

True   20.   Most courts preclude the defense offering expert testimony as to problems associated with eyewitness identification based upon the conclusion that such testimony is not helpful, i.e., the matter is one already within the common knowledge of the jury.

False   21.   Court appointment of an expert witness to testify before the jury under Rule 706 is an infrequent occurrence.

True   22.   Rule 405(a) provides that an opinion character witness may be cross-examined concerning relevant specific instance of conduct which includes under the facts of the problem an arrest for murder.

False   23.   The Federal Rules of Evidence are not applicable at depositions, Rule 1101(b).

False   24.   Rule 804(b)(1) contains additional requirements: "Testimony that:

(A) was given as a witness at a trial, hearing, or lawful deposition, Whether given during the current proceeding or a different one; and

(B) is now offered against a party who had—or, in a civil case, whose predecessor in interest hand—an opportunity and similar motive to develop it by direct, cross-, or redirect examination."

True   25.   D's ex-spouse waived her attorney-client privilege by her testimony on direct examination. Standard 511, reflective of the common law, states that a person upon whom the evidence rules confer a privilege against disclosure of the confidential matter or communication waives the privilege if he or his predecessor while holder of the privilege voluntarily discloses or consents to disclosure of any significant part of the matter or communication.

False   26.   Rule 612 provides that if a party uses a writing to refresh memory for purposes of testifying before testifying, an adverse party is entitled to have the writing produced at the hearsay, to inspect it, to cross-examine the witness thereon, and to introduce those portions which relate to the testimony *only if the court decides that justice requires the party to have those options.*

False   27.   The husband-wife testimonial privilege applicable in criminal cases belongs solely to the testifying spouse.

True   28.   Rule 803(4) encompasses medical history conveyed solely for the purpose of medical diagnosis which includes medical diagnosis provided by an expert hired solely to testify.

True   29.   Rule 804(a)(5) as well as the Confrontation Clause requires a showing by the prosecution, the party seeking to offer former testimony under Rule 804(b)(1), that the declarant is absent from the hearing and the proponent of the statement has been unable to procure the declarant's attendance by process or other reasonable means.

True   30.   An opinion that a driver was driving unsafely for conditions is a lay witness opinion meeting the requirements of Rule 701.

False   31.   Whether any statement is admissible in evidence pursuant to a hearsay exception, here Rule 804(b)(2), statement of belief in imminent death, is a determination to be made solely by the court pursuant to Rule 104(a).

True 32. A police officer may qualify as an expert witness on gang behavior; such testimony is often specialized knowledge that will assist the trier of fact to understand the evidence or to determine a fact in issue, Rule 702.

True 33. *Daubert/Kumho*/Rule 702 impose a gatekeeping requirement for the admissibility of all expert witness testimony where in practice the *Frye* test was simply not applied in product liability cases.

True 34. The attorney-client privilege, when applicable, is unconditional. See Standard 503 reflective of the common law.

False 35. Rule 804(b)(1) employs the term predecessor in interest which means community of interest (not limited to successor in interest) and is not limited to testimony offered *against* a party who had offered the testimony in evidence on his own behalf on the former occasion. For example, a deposition taken in the same matter is ordinarily admissible as former testimony when the declarant is unavailable; such deposition would ordinarily never have been previously offered into evidence by any party on any former occasion.

True 36. An opinion that something looked like blood is a lay witness opinion meeting the requirements of Rule 701.

False 37. This is double level hearsay. A's statement to the passenger is admissible under Rule 803(1), present sense impression, if testified to by A or the passenger. However A's later statement to W as to what A told the passenger is a hearsay statement that fails to meet any exception to the hearsay rule.

True 38. The hearsay exception provided in Rule 804(b)(2) for statements under belief in impending death requires that the declarant have personal knowledge of the matter related, Rule 602.

False 39. The gatekeeping test of *Daubert/Kumho*/Rule 702 is flexible; the five *Daubert* factors need not be applied.

True   40.   Rule 613(b) alters the common law by not requiring that the witness be confronted on cross-examination with the content of the statement and thus be given the opportunity either on cross-examination or redirect to admit, deny, and explain prior to the inconsistent statement being received in evidence.

False   41.   DNA evidence is admissible under both *Frye, Daubert* and Rule 702. Of course *Daubert* as interpreted by *Kumho* was incorporated into Rule 702. It is thus incorrect to treat *Daubert* and Rule 702 as separate concepts.

True   42.   While it is correct that a trial court can and should consider a party's willingness to stipulate to the fact the evidence is offered to prove, in light of *Old Chief* application of Rule 403 is extremely unlikely to result in the evidence being excluded as a result of the offer to stipulate.

True   43.   Hearsay may be received if the opponent fails to object.

False   44.   A witness who refuses to testify for any reason despite an order of the court to do so is unavailable, Rule 804(a)(2). His testimony at the preliminary hearing will most likely meet all of the requirements for former testimony, Rule 804(b)(1). It is also possible that the witness' preliminary hearsay testimony will be admissible pursuant to Rule 804(b)(6), forfeiture by wrongdoing.

True   45.   It is true that while lack of awareness of the rumor circulating in early 2003 as to D's arrest for assault is relevant to an assessment of the basis of the character witness' testimony as to D's reputation at that time for peacefulness, application of Rule 403 in such an instance leads to the requirement that the question about the rumor of an arrest for assault be permitted only if the prosecution has a good faith basis as to the underlying act, i.e., that D actually committed the assault (not the rumor nor the arrest) which is missing in this case.

True   46.   On cross-examination an expert witness may be asked to consider contrary versions of facts supported by the evidence and asked whether, if the contrary version was correct, her opinion would remain the same.

False   47.   Since the foundation facts relating to qualifying a witness as an expert, Rule 702, a decision made by the court under Rule 104(a), are also relevant to the jury's assessment of weight and credibility, ordinarily the foundational facts to qualify the expert are presented in the first instance before the jury, thus saving time.

False   48.   At early common law a party could not impeach any witness it called in any manner. Over time various different exceptions developed, one of which permitted impeachment with a prior inconsistent statement of the witness if both surprise and affirmation damage were shown.

False   49.   Improper admission of hearsay must be evaluated in the same manner as the improper admission of evidence for any other reason—while reversal is certainly possible reversal is certainly not always required. See generally Rule 103.

True   50.   Employment by an insurance company is relevant on the issue of bias. Bias is a non-collateral matter. Thus intrinsic evidence of X's employment by D's insurance company is permitted.

Exam V

False   1.   The improper influence or motive, love affair, existed when the prior consistent statement was made, i.e., after the accident, and thus does not rebut as required by Rule 801(d)(1)(B) because the prior consistent statement was not made *before* the love affair started.

False   2.   Under Rule 701 absolute certainty on the part of the lay witness is not required; opinions expressed with qualifications such as "I believe" or "I can't be positive, but" may be admitted as may opinions expressed in terms such as "could", "most probably", or "is similar to".

False   3.   A verbal act describes a statement to which the law attaches independent legal significance. A verbal act is relevant for the fact said and is thus not hearsay, Rules 801(a)–(c).

False   4.   A court may take judicial notice of legislative as well as adjudicative facts. However, the Federal Rules of Evidence through Rule 201 is only concerned with the judicial notice of adjudicative facts.

True   5.   The attorney-client privilege protects communications from the attorney to the client that would reveal confidential client communications at a minimum.

True   6.   Rule 501 provides that in civil actions and proceedings, with respect to an element of a claim or defense as to which State law supplies the rule of decision, the privilege of a witness, person, government, State, or political subdivision thereof shall be determined in accordance with State law.

True   7.   Rule 201(e) provides that in the absence of prior notification and an opportunity to be heard, the opportunity to be heard as to the propriety of taking judicial notice may be provided after judicial notice has been taken.

False   8.   The definition of hearsay contained in Rule 801 does not distinguish between direct and circumstantial evidence. Put another way, whether evidence is direct or circumstantial is irrelevant in the determination whether the evidence is or is not hearsay.

False   9.   A statement made in a deposition, such as the light was red, is an out-of-court statement offered in evidence to prove the truth of the matter asserted, Rules 801(a)–(c), i.e., red light.

False   10.   Rule 804(b)(3), providing a hearsay exception for statements against penal interest, requires as a prerequisite that the declarant be unavailable as a witness as described in Rule 804(a).

False   11.   Evidence of a prior conviction is not an express or implied charge against the declarant of recent fabrication or improper influence or motive as required by Rule 801(d)(1)(B) as a precondition for a prior consistent statement to be admitted to rebut.

True   12.   Rule 608(b)(1) provides that specific instances of conduct, other than conviction of a crime as provided in Rule 609, if probative of untruthfulness, may be inquired into on cross-examination of the witness.

True   13.   An opinion as to the height and weight of a person observed by the witness is a lay witness opinion meeting the requirements set forth in Rule 701.

False   14.   A police report certainly can qualify as a public record under Rule 803(8) unless the police report includes matters observed by police officers in an investigating posture offered against the criminal defendant, Rule 803(8)(A)(ii).

True   15.   A judicial determination of unavailability under Rule 804(a) is a Rule 104(a) determination; Rule 104(a) provides that the court in making such a determination is not bound by the rules of evidence except those with respect to privilege, i.e., can consider hearsay.

True   16.   Rule 803(18) provides that a learned treatise established as a reliable authority may be called to the attention of an expert witness on cross-examination.

False   17.   With respect to the taking of judicial notice of an adjudicative fact, actual knowledge of the trial judge of the matter is irrelevant. Rule 201(b) states for an adjudicative fact to be judicially noted, it must be one not subject to reasonable dispute in that it is either (1) generally known within the territorial jurisdiction of the trial court, or (2) can be accurately and readily determination by resort to sources whose accuracy cannot reasonably be questioned.

False   18.   Rule 404(a)(1) provides that in a civil case evidence of a pertinent trait of character, here peacefulness, is not admissible for the purpose of proving action in conformity therewith.

True   19.   The husband-wife testimonial privilege, applicable in criminal cases, does not survive divorce. Thus the state may call the spouse to testify over both her and the defendant's objection as to what she had observed.

False   20.   Rule 611(c)(1) provides that ordinarily leading questions should be permitted on cross-examination. Leading questions should not ordinarily be permitted on cross-examination that exceeds the scope of direct, Rule 611(b), or on cross-examination of a witness declared hostile as a matter of law when called by an opposing party under Rule 611(c)(2).

True   21.   True. Previously existing documents forming the basis of the confidential conversations do not become privileged by virtue of having been disclosed to an attorney for the purpose of securing professional legal services.

True   22.   With respect to statements admitted pursuant to the hearsay exception provided in Rule 803(2) for excited utterances and also for statements admitted pursuant to the hearsay exception provided in Rule 803(1) for present sense impressions, personal knowledge of the declarant may be established by reference to the content of the statement considered in light of surrounding circumstances, i.e., corroboration is not required.

False   23.   Leading questions on direct examination are frequently necessary to develop the witness' testimony, Rule 611(c), and thus properly permitted with respect to young children, a mentally retarded person, or a person with a poor memory.

False   24.   The traditional common law voucher rule precluded a party from impeaching a witness called by that party to testify.

True   25.   In performing its gatekeeping role under Rule 702(c), the trial court in determining whether the explanative theory possesses sufficient assurances of trustworthiness to be considered by the juror, i.e., is the product of reliable principles and methods, properly considers whether the particular explanative theory was developed solely for litigation purposes.

False   26.   An admission of a party-opponent, Rule 801(d)(2), is admissible as substantive evidence in its own right. Thus any witness who has sufficient personal knowledge that the statement was made may be employed to introduce the admission of the party-opponent. It is not necessary to attempt to elicit from the opposing party himself the fact that the out-of-court statement constituting an admission of a party-opponent was made.

True   27.   A business record, Rule 803(6) must be made by, or from information transmitted by, a person with personal knowledge under a business duty to do so.

False   28.   None of the provisions of Rule 902, self-authentication, are satisfied by a letter purporting to contain a person's signature on what purports to be the person's stationary.

False   29.   A plea of nolo contendere does not constitute an admission of a party-opponent in either a civil or criminal case, Rule 410(2)(a)(2).

False   30.   For example, Standard 506(c), reflective of the common law, states with respect to the confidential communication to clergyman privilege:

> **(c) Who May Claim the Privilege.** The privilege may be claimed by the person, by his guardian or conservator, or by his personal representative if he is deceased. The clergyman may claim the privilege on behalf of the person. His authority so to do is presumed in the absence of evidence to the contrary.

True   31.   Anything at all may be shown to a witness to refresh the witness' recollection, including items the witness never saw before and items created solely for the purpose of refreshing recollection. Of course, the opponent is then entitled to proceed as specified in Rule 612.

False   32.   Rule 605 provides specifically that no objection need be made in order to preserve error when the presiding trial judge testifies as a witness in the trial over which presiding.

False   33.   Rule 803(5) states that if a memorandum or record is admitted pursuant to the hearsay exception from recorded recollection, the memorandum or record may be read into evidence but may not itself be received as an exhibit unless offered by an adverse party.

False   34.   Specific instances of conduct, probative of untruthfulness, may only be inquired of on cross-examination of the witness, Rule 608(b)(1); the matter is considered collateral thus making extrinsic evidence, i.e., records of college suspension, inadmissible.

True   35.   Under Rule 806, when a hearsay statement has been admitted in evidence, the credibility of the declarant may be attached by any evidence that would be admissible for such purpose if declarant had testified as a witness—here a prior conviction for perjury admissible to impeach character for truthfulness pursuant to Rule 609(a)(2).

False   36.   Rule 701(c) specifically provides that a lay witness may *not* testify in the form of an opinion based upon scientific, technical or other specialized knowledge within the scope of Rule 702, here the law/fact question of defective and unreasonably dangerous in a design defect case.

False   37.   While still permitted, use of a hypothetical question is rarely seen today in federal court as a result of Rule 705 which provides that the expert may testify in terms of opinion or inference and give reasons therefor without first testifying to the underlying facts or data, unless the court requires otherwise.

False   38.   Rule 803(6) provides that a business record includes a memorandum, report, or data compilation in any form of acts, events, conditions, opinions, or diagnosis, here a physician's opinion.

True   39.   Nothing prevents a witness from wearing the hats of both a lay witness and expert witness in the same case. Care should be taken to be sure that the jury is clear as to which hat is on at every point in the trial.

False   40.   Rule 609(a)(2) states that for the purpose of attacking the credibility of a witness, evidence that any witness has been convicted of a crime shall be admitted if it involved dishonesty or false statement, regardless of the punishment.

False   41.   Rule 804(b)(3) provides a hearsay exception for a statement which was at the time of its making so far contrary to the declarant's pecuniary or proprietary interest, or so far tended to subject the declarant to civil or criminal liability, or to render invalid a claim by the declarant against another, that a reasonable person in the declarant's position would not have made the statement unless believing it to be true.

False   42.   Rule 1008 provides:

Ordinarily, the court determines whether the proponent has fulfilled the factual conditions for admitting other evidence of the content of a writing, recording, or photograph under Rule 1004 or 1005. But in a jury trial, the jury determines—in accordance with Rule 104(b)—any issue about whether:

(a) an asserted writing, recording, or photograph ever existed;

(b) another one produced at the trial or hearing is the original; or

(c) other evidence of content accurately reflects the content.

True   43.   Rule 608(a)(2) permits evidence in the form of reputation or opinion testimony as to character for truthfulness only after the character of the witness for truthfulness has been attacked by reputation or opinion testimony or otherwise. Impeachment by means of a prior conviction, Rule 609, is recognized as falling within the "or otherwise" component of Rule 608(a)(2).

False   44.   Rule 703 provides that the facts, data, or opinions in the particular case upon which an expert bases an opinion or inference may be those perceived by or made known to the expert at or before the hearing; if of a type reasonably relied upon by experts in the particular field in forming opinions or inferences upon the subject, the facts, data, or opinions need not be admissible in evidence in order for the opinion or inference to be admitted.

True   45.   Rule 405(a) provides that on cross-examination of a character witness, inquiry is allowable into relevant specific instances of conduct—here whether the reputation witness heard of D's arrest two years ago for extortion. Lack of familiarity with such matters is relevant to an assessment of the basis of the character witness' testimony. Familiarity with such matters explores the character witness' standard of peacefulness. The cross-examiner must possess a good faith basis that D committed the extortion inquired about.

False   46.   Rule 407 states that evidence of a subsequent remedial measure is not inadmissible when offered for a purpose other than to prove negligence, culpable conduct, etc., such as proving ownership, control, or feasibility of precautionary matters, if controverted, or impeachment.

False   47.   Evidence that D was never before involved in an accident, evidence of a specific instance of conduct offered to prove character of a person in order to show action in conformity therewith, is precluded by Rule 404(a)(1) and Rule 404(b)(1).

True 48. Impeachment by means of a prior conviction, Rule 609, is a non-collateral matter. However, not only is extrinsic evidence admissible with respect of prior conviction impeachment, extrinsic evidence establishing that the witness was in fact so convicted is required.

True 49. Rule 1002, the Original Writing Rule, provides that to prove the content of a writing, the original writing, or a duplicate if Rule 1003 is satisfied, when available must be produced; oral testimony of the contents of the writing is inadmissible.

True 50. Rule 613(b) provides:

(b) Extrinsic Evidence of a Prior Inconsistent Statement. Extrinsic evidence of a witness's prior inconsistent statement is admissible only if the witness is given an opportunity to explain or deny the statement and an adverse party is given an opportunity to examine the witness about it, or if justice so requires. This subdivision (b) does not apply to an opposing party's statement under Rule 801(d)(2).

MULTIPLE CHOICE ANSWER KEY WITH EXPLANATIONS

Exam I

C   1.   Rule 404(a)(2)(A) permits the prosecution to introduce character evidence in the form of reputation or opinion evidence as to the accused only if the accused has introduced such evidence as to a pertinent trait of his character in the first instance.

A   2.   Rule 404(a)(2)(A) permits the accused to introduce character evidence in the form of reputation testimony as to a pertinent trait of his character for the purpose of proving action in conformity therewith.

D   3.   Rule 405(a) permits a character witness to be cross-examined as to relevant specific instances of conduct of the witness whose character she is testifying about. The character witness may also be asked about whether he has heard from others that the principle witness did or did not commit relevant specific instances of conduct as such cross-examination explores the character witness's knowledge of reputation.

A   4.   Rule 404(a)(2)(B) permits the accused to introduce character evidence in the form of reputation or opinion testimony of the alleged victim in the first instance for the purpose of proving action in conformity therewith.

D   5.   Not paying for a hot dog is not relevant to determination of a self-defense claim; the pertinent character trait is peacefulness, not honesty. In any event Rule, 404(b)(1) provides that the evidence of a specific instance of conduct is not admissible to prove character of a person in order to show action in conformity therewith.

B   6.   How much Mutt cost does not have any tendency to make the existence of any fact that is of consequence to the determination of the action more probable or less probable than it would be without the evidence.

D   7.   Rule 406 provides that evidence of the habit of a person or of the routine practice of an organization, whether corroborated or not and regardless of the presence of eyewitness, is relevant to prove that the conduct of the person or organization on a particular occasion was in conformity with the habit or routine practice. Since habit rather than character is involved, the remaining answers are incorrect regardless of whether they state or do not state accurate principles of law dealing with the admissibility of character evidence.

C   8.   On direct examination leading questions should not be used except as necessary to develop the witness' testimony, Rule 611(c); no necessity is present here.

C   9.   Rule 403 provides that although relevant, evidence may be excluded if its probative value is substantially outweighed by the danger of unfair prejudice, confusion of the issues, or misleading the jury, or by considerations of undue delay, waste of time, or needless presentation of cumulative evidence. Here the unfair prejudice, i.e., the natural dislike of drug users and belief they steal to get money, substantially outweighs the probative value of the evidence that Brown robbed the bank to get money for drugs.

D   10.   The way the question was asked to Brown it was equivalent to "Who died and left you money?" Being such a general colloquial question, it is not natural to expect Brown to respond if the statement was not true. Thus Brown's silence is not an adoptive admission under Rule 801(d)(2)(B).

C   11.   Since Fidelity did not introduce evidence sufficient to support a finding that Mr. Works is alive, it did not satisfy its burden of production that would be placed upon it by either a Thayer or Morgan presumption. Thus the jury should be instructed that they must find Mr. Works is dead if they find he has not been heard from in 5 years.

D 12. A Morgan presumption shifts to the party opposing the presumption the burden of proving the nonexistence of the presumed fact, i.e., Mr. Works is alive, if the jury finds the existence of the basic fact, i.e., Mr. Works has not been heard from for 5 years.

C 13. Rule 407 provides:

When measures are taken that would have made an earlier injury or harm less likely to occur, evidence of the subsequent measures is not admissible to prove:

> *negligence;

> *culpable conduct;

> *a defect in a product or its design; or

> *a need for a warning or instruction.

But the court may admit this evidence for another purpose, such as impeachment or—if disputed—proving ownership, control, or the feasibility of precautionary measures.

C 14. Pursuant to Rule 404(a)(1) and Rule 404(b)(1) neither reputation or opinion testimony as to character nor specific instances of conduct may be introduced to prove character for the purpose of proving action in conformity therewith in a civil case.

C 15. Both prior identification of a person and past recollection recorded require that the witness testify at trial. An opinion contained in an out-of-court statement can only be admissible if the statement is admissible. Here the statement is hearsay that does not meet the requirements of any hearsay exception. The sketch is an out-of-court statement offered in evidence to prove the truth of the matter asserted, Rules 801(a)–(c), i.e., that sketch looks like the man who robbed me.

C 16. The statement is an out-of-court statement of a declarant who testifies in court offered in evidence to prove the truth of the matter asserted, Rules 801(a)–(c). The statement fails to meet the requirements to be admitted as a prior consistent statement, Rule 801(d)(2)(B), i.e., does not rebut, etc., nor does it meet the requirements for otherwise being defined as not hearsay, Rules 801(d)(1) and (2), or the requirements set forth with respect to any hearsay exception recognized in Rules 803, 804, and 807.

A   17.   Rule 609(2) permits for the purpose of attacking the character of a witness for truthfulness, evidence that the witness has been convicted of a crime involving dishonesty or false statement, regardless of punishment, not more than 10 years old.

D   18.   Contradiction by introduction of extrinsic evidence as to a collateral matter is not permitted. Evidence as to wearing a blue sweater is collateral because it is relevant in the lawsuit for no purpose other than to contradict the testimony of Claude's eyewitness that Bernie was wearing a green sweater.

B   19.   Bernie's statement is an admission of a party-opponent, Rule 801(d)(2)(A). Rule 613(b) specifically provides that the requirement that a witness be given at some time the opportunity to explain or deny an alleged prior inconsistent statement does not apply to admissions of a party-opponent as defined in Rule 801(d)(2).

B   20.   D's evidence does not include any direct evidence that P was drunk at the time of the accident. D's evidence amounts to evidence as to specific instances of conduct offered to prove character for the purpose of proving action in conformity therewith on a particular occasion offered in a civil case. Rule 404(a)(1) and Rule 404(b)(1) prohibit evidence of character in a civil case. D's evidence fails to meet the requirement for habit evidence, Rule 406, of extremely regular conduct, semi-automatic in nature.

D   21.   Rule 803(13) provides a hearsay exception for statements of fact concerning personal or family history contained in family Bibles, genealogies, charts, engravings on rings, inscriptions on family portraits, engravings on urns, crypts, or tombstones, or the like. Although the contents of a writing are sought to be proved, Rule 1002, the original is not required and other evidence of the contents of the writing is admissible since the original, the tombstones, cannot realistically be obtained in court by any available judicial process, Rule 1004(b).

A   22.   Standard 503(a)(3), reflective of the common law, provides that a "representative of the lawyer" is one employed to assist the lawyer in the rendition of legal services. An expert hired by the lawyer, here a doctor, to assist in the planning and conduct of litigation but will not testify at trial is a representative of a lawyer. Confidential communications to a representative of a lawyer are protected by the attorney-client privilege, Standard 503(b)(1).

B   23.   Rule 609(2) permits for the purpose of attacking the character of a witness for truthfulness, evidence that the witness has been convicted of a crime involving dishonesty or false statement, regardless of punishment, not more than 10 years old.

A   24.   Not only is impeachment by means of a prior conviction not a collateral matter, if the witness fails to admit the prior conviction when cross-examined, the examining party is obligated to introduce evidence establishing the prior conviction and that the witness is the same person who was convicted.

A   25.   With a Thayer presumption, once the party opposing the presumption satisfies a burden of production, here evidence sufficient to support a finding that it is more probably true than not that the letter was not received, the presumption of receipt of the letter disappears. The jury is then instructed without any reference being made at all to a presumption.

Exam II

D   1.   Rule 408(a)(1) provides that evidence of offering to furnish a valuable consideration in attempting to compromise a claim which was disputed as to validity or amount is not admissible to prove liability for the claim or its amount.

C   2.   Rule 608(b)(1) provides that specific instances of conduct of a witness, for purpose of attacking the witness' character for truthfulness, other than a conviction of crime as provided in Rule 609, if probative of untruthfulness, may be inquired into on cross-examination of the witness. The matter is considered collateral; extrinsic evidence is not admissible if the witness denies on cross-examination that the matter inquired of is true.

D   3.   Traditionally and logically, the proper form of a question to a reputation witness as to character is "Have you heard" while the proper form to an opinion witness as to character is either "Have you heard," "Are you aware" or "Do you know". Although it has been argued, albeit incorrectly, that such a distinction in form is no longer required, none of the foregoing forms of question were employed in the problem at hand.

C   4.   A lay witness may not be asked to perform a comparison of handwriting in support of the foundation authenticating a document. Rule 901(b)(3) provides that authentication may consist of comparison evidence by the trier of fact or by expert witnesses with specimens which have been authenticated; no mention is made of lay witness comparison evidence.

B   5.   How much the dog costs does not have any tendency to make the existence of any fact that is of consequence to the determination of the action more probable or less probable than it would be without the evidence.

D   6.   The fact that the dog has displayed a propensity to bite may be established by specific instances of conduct.

D   7.   Rule 406 provides that evidence of the habit of a person or of the routine practice of an organization, whether corroborated or not and regardless of the presence of eyewitness, is relevant to prove that the conduct of the person or organization on a particular occasion was in conformity with the habit or routine practice.

B   8.   The question, objectionable as leading, also calls for an unhelpful opinion of the witness as to whether another person might have mistaken another dog for the witness'. The trier of fact is in as good a position to decide that issue as the witness.

C   9.   The question is leading. Dixon's attorney by the question is suggesting the answer to Dixon. Dixon's attorney is not permitted under Rule 611(c) to ask a leading question to Dixon. Rule 611(c) states that leading questions should not be used on direct examination of a witness except as may be necessary to develop the witness' testimony and no showing of necessity has been made.

D   10.   Rule 404 prohibits the introduction of character evidence in the form of reputation or opinion testimony of character for the purpose of proving conduct in conformity therewith on a particular occasion in a civil case.

B   11.   Rules 404(a)(2)(A) and 405 permit the accused to offer evidence of a pertinent character trait in the form of reputation testimony for the purpose of proving action in conformity therewith on a particular occasion.

A   12.   Cross-examination with a good faith basis to raise an inference of bias is proper.

C   13.   The attorney-client privilege encompasses statements made in confidence by a client, Owner, to a lawyer representing another client, Driver, when offered in evidence by a third party, Litigant. See Standard 503(b)(3) reflective of the common law.

A   14.   Standard 503(d)(5), reflective of the common law, provides that the attorney-client privilege does not apply as to a communication relevant to a matter of common interest between two or more clients if the communication was made by any of them to a lawyer retained or consulted in common, when offered in an action between any of the clients.

A   15.   Rule 606(b)(2)(A) permits a juror to challenge a jury verdict on the ground that extraneous prejudicial information, i.e., something that was not admitted in evidence, was brought to the jury's attention.

A   16.   A witness testifying as to the reputation of the accused for honesty may be asked on cross-examination whether the witness had heard that the defendant was arrested for committing fraud—a crime of dishonesty, and thus a relevant specific instance of conduct, Rule 405(a). The cross-examiner needs a good faith basis as to the underlying act, i.e., D committed a fraud.

B   17.   The prosecution introduced Jackson's statement under the hearsay exception for statements of belief in imminent death, Rule 804(b)(2). Rule 806 provides that when a hearsay statement has been admitted in evidence, the credibility of the declarant may be attacked by any evidence which would be admissible for those purposes if declarant has testified as a witness, here impeachment by means of a prior inconsistent statement.

B   18.   Rule 608(b)(1) provides that specific instances of conduct of a witness, for purposes of attacking the witness character for truthfulness, other than a conviction of crime as provided in Rule 609, of probative untruthfulness may be inquired into on cross-examination of the witness provided, however, that the cross-examiner possess a good faith base for believing that the underlying act inquired of is true. Such a good faith basis is lacking here.

B   19.   The trial court applying Rule 602, which is a specific application of Rule 104(b), must decide whether a reasonable juror viewing the evidence most favorably can conclude that it is more probably true than not true that the witness has personal knowledge of the matter related.

C   20.   John's silence is not an adoptive admission, Rule 801(d)(2)(B), because it is not natural under the circumstances to expect John to deny the statement of Katie if it was not true—Katie was talking to the police, John was in custody.

B   21.   Rule 803(22) provides a hearsay exception for a judgment of conviction of a crime punishable by death or imprisonment in excess of one year based upon a plea of guilty to prove any fact essential to sustain the judgment when offered in a civil case.

D   22.   The evidence introduced by P is sufficient to support a finding that the photograph fairly and accurately represents what it purports to represent, Rule 901(b)(1), i.e., the condition of the box when it was returned by D to P. The fact that the daughter rather than P, the witness laying the foundation for the photograph, actually took the photograph does not affect admissibility.

A   23.   All of the requirements and none of the exceptions to applicability of the husband-wife confidential communication privilege are present. The husband-wife confidential communication privilege belongs to both spouses. Thus, H may invoke the husband-wife privilege to prevent W from testifying even though she has consented to do so.

A   24.   Rule 801(d)(1)(A) provides that a statement is not hearsay if the declarant testifies at the trial or hearing and is subject to cross-examination concerning the statement, and the statement is inconsistent with the declarant's testimony, and was given under oath subject to the penalty of perjury at a trial, hearing, or other proceeding, or in a deposition. "Other proceeding" includes the grand jury. The prior inconsistent statement is thus admissible as substantive evidence. It is also, of course, not hearsay as relevant for the fact said and thus admissible when offered to impeach.

D   25.   Evidence of the crimes, wrongs, or other acts constituting a prior instance of violence by the defendant against the victim is admissible under Rule 404(b)(2) as evidence of motive and intent.

Exam III

C   1.   The statement is not admissible as substantive evidence. It fails to meet the requirements of Rule 801(d)(1)(A), prior inconsistent statement, because the statement to the police was not given under oath subject to the penalty of perjury and a trial, hearing, or other proceeding, or in a deposition. A statement to the police is not an "other proceeding." The statement is admissible to impeach, assuming that witness is available to be recalled to explain or deny the prior inconsistent statement. Rule 613(b) abolishes the common law requirement that a proper foundation must be laid on cross-examination *prior* to extrinsic evidence of the prior inconsistent statement being introduced in favor of simply affording the witness at some time an opportunity to explain or deny.

D   2.   There is clearly no confidential communication privilege between husband and wife as John was present. As to the testimonial privilege, Standard 505(c)(2), reflective of the common law, provides that the testimonial husband-wife privilege does not apply as to matters occurring prior to the marriage.

C 3. The question on cross-examination lays a sufficient foundation of time, place, persons present, all liberally construed, and content of the statement for introduction of a prior inconsistent statement, i.e., provides opportunity for the witness to explain or deny, Rule 613(b). As presented, although the prior inconsistent statement is hearsay meeting neither a non hearsay definition nor the requirements of any hearsay exception, it has not been shown that the primary purpose of calling the witness was a mere subterfuge to place the prior inconsistent statement before the jury under the guise of impeachment. Impeachment of a witness by a party calling the witness is permitted, Rule 607.

A 4. Rule 801(d)(1)(C) defines as not hearsay a statement of identification of a person made after perceiving the person again made by a declarant who testifies at the trial and is subject to cross-examination concerning the statement. Rule 801(d)(1)(C) is *not* limited to criminal cases.

A 5. Rule 403 provides that although relevant, evidence may be excluded if its probative value is substantially outweighed by the danger of unfair prejudice, confusion of the issues, or misleading the jury, or by considerations of undue delay, waste of time, or needless presentation of cumulative evidence. The evidence is cumulated; each additional person adds very little incremental probative value while both wasting time and misleading the jury because of the total emphasis such time consuming testimony would have. Consider an alibi of being at a family reunion of 100 people. All 100 may have agreed to lie or not. In any event, listening to all 100 would certainly be cumulative.

A 6. The marriage certificate is admissible under Rule 803(16) as a statement in a document in existence 20 years or more the authenticity of which is established. Rule 901(b)(8) provides that a sufficient foundation is laid by evidence that a document or data compilation, in any form, (A) is in such condition as to create no suspicion concerning its authenticity, (B) was in a place where it, if authentic, would likely be, and (C) has been existence 20 years or more at the time it is offered.

D   7.   A conviction occurs when the jury returns its verdict. A conviction is thus an event that exists independent of the record of conviction made to memorialize the event. Thus Rule 1002, the Original Writing Rule, does not prevent a person from testifying on personal knowledge as to the three prior convictions.

D   8.   X's statement is an admission of a party-opponent under Rule 801(d)(2)(D); it is a statement of an employee of a party concerning a matter within the scope of his employment made during the existence of the employment relationship offered in evidence against the employer party. Authority to speak is not required.

D   9.   Rule 411 provides that evidence that a person was or was not insured against liability is not admissible upon the issue whether the person acted negligently or otherwise wrongfully.

C   10.   Rule 407 provides:

When measures are taken that would have made an earlier injury or harm less likely to occur, evidence of the subsequent measures is not admissible to prove:

   *negligence;

   *culpable conduct;

   *a defect in a product or its design; or

   *a need for a warning or instruction.

But the court may admit this evidence for another purpose, such as impeachment or—if disputed—proving ownership, control, or the feasibility of precautionary measures.

Here Dow is controverting ownership.

C 11. The Rule in Queen Caroline's case that a witness must first be permitted to see or be told of an inconsistent writing before being questioned about it is abolished by Rule 613(a) which provides that in examining a witness concerning a prior statement made by the witness, whether written or not, the statement need not be shown nor its contents disclosed to the witness at that time, but on request the same shall be shown or disclosed to opposing counsel.

D 12. Rule 408 provides:

(a) Prohibited Uses. Evidence of the following is not admissible—on behalf of any party—either to prove or disprove the validity or amount of a disputed claim or to impeach by a prior inconsistent statement or a contradiction:

(1) furnishing, promising, or offering—or accepting, promising to accept, or offering to accept—a valuable consideration in compromising or attempting to compromise the claim; and

(2) conduct or a statement made during compromise negotiations about the claim—except when offered in a criminal case and when the negotiations related to a claim by a public office in the exercise of its regulatory, investigative, or enforcement authority.

(b) Exceptions. The court may admit this evidence for another purpose, such as proving a witness's bias or prejudice, negating a contention of undue delay, or proving an effort to obstruct a criminal investigation or prosecution.

D 13. The statement is not hearsay; it is as relevant for the fact said—effect on listener—by providing notice or knowledge. The statement is not protected by the attorney-client privilege in that as provided in Standard 503(d)(2) which is reflective of the common law, no privilege applies to a communication relevant to an issue of breach of duty by the attorney to his client or the client to his attorney.

D   14.   Rule 103(a)(2) provides error may not be predicated upon a ruling which excludes evidence unless a substantial right of the party is affected, and in case the ruling is one excluding evidence, the substance of the evidence was made known to the court by offer or was apparent from the context within which questions were asked.

B   15.   The trial court clearly violated Rule 615 by not excluding from the courtroom prosecution witnesses except persons authorized by Rule 615 to remain such as a representative of the government under Rule 615(b), i.e., a law enforcement official. Rule 615 provides:

At a party's request, the court must order witnesses excluded so that they cannot hear other witnesses' testimony. Or the court may do so on its own. But this rule does not authorize excluding:

(a)   a party who is a natural person;

(b)   an officer or employee of a party that is not a natural person, after being designated as the party's representative by its attorney;

(c)   a person whose presence a party shows to be essential to presenting the party's claim or defense; or

(d)   a person authorized by statute to be present.

C   16.   Rule 803(2) provides a hearsay exception for a statement relating to a startling event made while the declarant was under the stress of excitement caused by the event. The fact that the declarant is unidentified does not preclude admissibility. Such statements are generally admitted if often after what the Advisory Committee called "hesitancy" properly called "reluctance." Here where the fact that such an unidentified declarant exists can be clearly established and where personal knowledge on the part of the unidentified declarant is also sufficiently established, the statement should and would be admitted.

A   17.   The witness' recollection has now been refreshed with a document, Rule 612. His subsequent testimony is based upon personal knowledge, Rule 602. Any document may be shown to the witness to refresh recollection. The document itself is not being offered into evidence; it thus need not be shown to be accurate which would be the case if the document was being offered as recorded recollection, Rule 803(5).

D   18.   Coercion is a form of untrustworthy partiality admissible to impeach. Coercion is a non collateral matter; extrinsic evidence is admissible—here the testimony of W2 as to D's threats to W.

D   19.   W's testimony is being offered under Rule 405(b) as a specific instance of conduct relevant to establish a character trait—child molester—which is itself an essential element of the claim in the case. Since W's testimony does not make reference to an out-of-court statement, it can't be hearsay.

B   20.   The evidence, relevant on the issue of bias, is not barred by Rule 610 which only precludes evidence of beliefs or opinions of a witness on matters of religion when offered for the purpose of showing that by reason of these matters the witness' credibility is impaired or enhanced.

D   21.   The inscription on the tombstone is being offered in evidence to prove the truth of the matter asserted, Rules 801(a)–(c). However, Rule 803(13) provides a hearsay exception for statements of fact concerning personal or family history contained in family Bibles, genealogies, charts, engravings on rings, inscriptions on family portraits, engravings on urns, crypts, or tombstones, or the like. Although the content of a writing is sought to be proved, Rule 1002, the original is not required and other evidence of the content of the writing is admissible since the original, the tombstone, cannot realistically be obtained by any available process or procedure, Rule 1004(b). Moreover, the photograph is a duplicate, Rule 1001(e), admissible to the same extent as an original under Rule 1003 unless a genuine question is raised as to the authenticity of the original or in the circumstances it would be unfair to admit the duplicate in lieu of the original, neither of which proviso appears applicable herein.

D   22.   The trial judge must act as a gatekeeper, Rule 104(a), under *Daubert/Kumho*/Rule 702 and thus determine as provided in Rule 702 if scientific, technical, or other specialized knowledge will assist the trier of fact to understand the evidence or to determine a fact in issue. A witness (a) qualified as an expert by knowledge, skill, experience, training, or education, may testify thereto in the form of an opinion or otherwise, if (b) the testimony is based upon sufficient facts, data, or opinions, (c) the testimony is the product of reliable principles and methods, and (d) the witness has applied the principles and methods reliably to the facts of the case. The trial court's decision will clearly be to exclude the testimony.

C   23.   No attorney-client privilege arose because Duncan's conversations with Berger were not confidential communications made for the purpose of facilitating the rendition of professional legal services to the client, Standard 503(b) (reflective of the common law).

B   24.   Rule 609(a)(2) provides that for the purpose of attacking the credibility of a witness evidence that the witness has been convicted of a crime is admissible if the crime involved dishonesty or false statement, regardless of punishment, provided not more than ten years has expired since the conviction. Forgery is a crime of dishonesty or false statement; no discretionary balancing test is to be performed.

B   25.   Rule 803(8)(A)(iii) permits the introduction of public records reflecting factual findings resulting from an investigation made pursuant to authority granted by law in civil cases, unless the sources of information or other circumstances indicate lack of trustworthiness. The fact that the report is a self-serving report prepared for purposes of litigation raises such indications of lack of trustworthiness. Moreover, it is not clear that such a report constitutes a regularly conducted business activity nor that the governmental agency is authorized by law to conduct such an investigation and issue such a report.

Exam IV

A   1.   Rule 404(b)(1) provides that while evidence of other crimes, wrongs, or acts is not admissible to prove the character of a person in order to show action in conformity therewith, it may, however, be admissible for other purposes, such as proof of motive, opportunity, intent, preparation, plan, knowledge, identity, or absence of mistake or accident, Rule 404(b)(2). Here the evidence is admissible to prove motive, intent, and the actual aggressive conduct, i.e., the actus reus.

D   2.   A "conclusive presumption" is not truly a presumption because it cannot be rebutted by evidence. A conclusive presumption is best thought of as a substantive rule of law.

D   3.   P is asserting negligent entrustment of the car which makes the character of X for recklessness an element of the claim. Rule 405(b) provides that where character is an element of a claim, proof may be made by specific instances of that person's conduct.

C   4.   D should be permitted to conduct an inquiry on cross-examination at that juncture limited to D's qualifications, often called voir dire. This permits the court to decide whether W is qualified as an expert before the jury hears his testimony on the merits. Thus if W is not qualified, the jury will not be exposed to inadmissible evidence.

A   5.   First of all, a statement to oneself alone is never admissible in evidence. Either the person must testify to a matter based upon personal knowledge or testify as to what was said to or by another as to that matter. If one were to permit statements made solely to oneself, the statement would still be excluded as hearsay in that it is an out-of-court statement offered in evidence to prove the truth of the matter asserted, Rules 801(a)–(c), falling within neither a not hearsay definition, Rules 801(d)(1) and (2), nor a hearsay exception, Rules 803, 804, and 807.

A   6.   Ascertainment of the governing law involves judicial notice of a legislative fact; only adjudication facts—the what, when, where, how, why, who aspects of the litigation—are encompassed by Rule 201.

D   7.   Rule 611(c)(2) permits a party to call an adverse party and interrogate by means of leading questions.

B   8.   The document is not only inadmissible hearsay, it is
                 irrelevant. The net worth of the defendant is not a fact of
                 consequence, i.e., in this case not a material proposition, to
                 the determination of the action. The defendant's net worth
                 would be an ultimate fact constituting a material proposition
                 and thus a fact of consequence if punitive damages were
                 alleged.

C   9.   Rule 803(2) provides a hearsay exception for a statement
                 relating to a startling event made while the declarant was
                 under the stress of excitement caused by the event. With
                 respect to the element of time, the standard of measurement
                 is the duration of the state of excitement. The amount of time
                 elapsed is but one factor to be considered by the court in
                 reaching a determination in the particular case. Other factors
                 include the nature of the condition or event, the age and
                 condition of the declarant, the presence or absence of self-
                 interest, and whether the statement was volunteered or in
                 response to a question.

C   10. Only the pre-existing books are not subject to the attorney-
                 client privilege. Communications, oral and written, between
                 the attorney and the attorney's representatives, here the
                 accountant, intended to be confidential made for the purpose
                 of facilitating rendition of legal services to the client are
                 protected by the attorney-client privilege. The accountant
                 will not be called as a witness by the defendant.

C   11. Rule 703 provides that facts, data, or opinions, if of a type
                 reasonably relied upon by experts in the particular field in
                 forming opinions or inference upon the subject, need not have
                 been admitted in evidence for the opinion or inference to be
                 admitted.

C   12. Rule 404(b)(1) provides that while evidence of other crimes,
                 wrongs, or acts is not admissible to prove the character of a
                 person in order to show action in conformity therewith, it is
                 admissible when offered for another purpose, here modus
                 operandi to prove identity, Rule 404(b)(2). Modus operandi,
                 which means literally "method of working", refers to a prior
                 crime or pattern of prior crimes so distinctive that the

separate crimes are recognizable as the handwork of the same wrongdoer, i.e., a signature.

C   13.   Standard 504(d)(3), reflective of the common law, states that there is no psychotherapist-patient privilege as to communications relevant to an issue of the mental or emotional condition of the patient in any proceeding in which the patient relies upon the condition as an element of his claim or defense.

A   14.   Pursuant to 609(b) provides:

(b) Limit on Using the Evidence After 10 Years. This subdivision (b) applies if more than 10 years have passed since the witness's conviction or release from confinement for it, whichever is later. Evidence of the conviction is admissible only if:

(1) its probative value, supported by specific facts and circumstances, substantially outweighs its prejudicial effect, and

(2) the proponent gives an adverse party reasonable written notice of the intent to use it so that the party has a fair opportunity to contest its use.

The 2005 misdemeanor stock fraud conviction involves dishonesty and false statement thus making it more probative on character for untruthfulness than the felony assault conviction and is less remote than the check forgery conviction. A civil judgment is not a conviction and thus fails to meet the requirement of Rule 609.

D   15.   Rule 605 states that the judge presiding at the trial may not testify in that trial as a witness and that no objection need be made in order to preserve the point.

B   16.   Rule 408 provides:

(a) Prohibited Uses. Evidence of the following is not admissible—on behalf of any party—either to prove or disprove the validity or amount of a disputed claim or to impeach by a prior inconsistent statement or a contradiction:

(1) furnishing, promising, or offering—or accepting, promising to accept, or offering to accept—a valuable consideration in compromising or attempting to compromise the claim; and

(2) conduct or a statement made during compromise negotiations about the claim—except when offered in a criminal case and when the negotiations related to a claim by a public office in the exercise of its regulatory, investigative, or enforcement authority.

(b) Exceptions. The court may admit this evidence for another purpose, such as proving a witness's bias or prejudice, negating a contention of undue delay, or proving an effort to obstruct a criminal investigation or prosecution.

D 17. The diary entry is admissible under Rule 803(16) as a statement in a document in existence 20 years or more the authenticity of which is established. Rule 901(b)(8) provides that a sufficient foundation is laid by evidence that a document or data compilation, in any form, (A) is in such condition as to create no suspicion concerning its authenticity, (B) was in a place where it, if authentic, would likely be, and (C) has been in existence 20 years or more at the time it is offered.

D 18. Rule 611(c) provides:

(c) Leading Questions. Leading questions should not be used on direct examination except as necessary to develop the witness's testimony. Ordinarily, the court should allow leading questions:

(1) on cross-examination; and

(2) when a party calls a hostile witness, an adverse party, or a witness identified with an adverse party.

Refreshing recollection is one of those circumstances referred to in Rule 611(c), first sentence, where leading questions are necessary to develop the witness' testimony.

D 19. Standard 503(d)(2), reflective of the common law, provides that while upon the death of the client, the attorney-client privilege survives in favor of his estate in regard to claims by outsiders against the estate, it does not apply to a communication relevant to an issue between parties who claim through the same deceased client, regardless of whether the claims were by testate or intestate succession or by inter vivos transaction. Thus Standard 503(d)(2) recognizes that will contests involve peculiar considerations, since the question of who succeeds to the interests of the decedent depends upon the outcome of the contest.

B   20.   The trial judge has discretion whether to permit a question that calls for a narrative response. The question will ordinarily be permitted unless the court foresees that the witness is likely to volunteer inadmissible evidence such as the content of an inadmissible hearsay statement.

D   21.   Rule 406 provides:

Evidence of a person's habit or an organization's routine practice may be admitted to prove that on a particular occasion the person or organization acted in accordance with the habit or routine practice. The court may admit this evidence regardless of whether it is corroborated or whether there was an eyewitness.

B   22.   The inquiry seeks to establish prejudice and is permissible if the cross-examiner possesses a good faith basis. Since the cross-examiner is not introducing evidence of religious beliefs for the purpose of showing that by reason of their nature the witness' credibility is impaired or enhanced, Rule 610 is inapplicable.

C   23.   General reliance by experts in the field does not mean that such reliance is reasonable; reasonable reliance by experts in the field is required by Rule 703. In fact, the accidentologist relying on a bystander statement is the illustration given in the Advisory Committee's Note to Rule 703 where reliance is not reasonable. For reliance to be reasonable, the statement not admitted into evidence relied upon by the expert must possess a trustworthiness similar to that possessed by statements admitted pursuant to a hearsay exception.

B   24.   The Illinois Dead Man's Act, made applicable by Rule 601 which states that in civil actions and proceedings with respect to an element of a claim or defense as to which State law supplies the rule of decision the competency of a witness shall be determined in accordance with State law, provides that an interested party is incompetent to testify to events that took place in the presence of the decedent.

A   25.   Rule 609(a)(1)(B) provides that for the purpose of attacking the credibility of a witness, evidence that an accused has been convicted of a crime punishable by death or imprisonment in excess of one year not more than ten years ago, shall be admitted if the court determines that the probative value of admitting the prior conviction evidence outweighs the prejudicial effect to the accused.

Exam V

A   1.   Whether or not a witness' recollection has been refreshed is a matter of conditional relevancy, Rule 104(b), with respect to personal knowledge, Rule 602. Pursuant to Rule 602 evidence must be introduced sufficient to support a finding by the jury viewing the evidence most favorable to the proponent that it is more probably true than not that the witness has personal knowledge of the matter related. Rule 612 provides that if a witness employs a document to refresh recollection while testifying, an adverse party is entitled to have the writing produced at the hearing, to inspect it, to cross-examine the witness thereon, and to introduce in evidence those portions which relate to the testimony of the witness.

A   2.   It is proper to cross-examine a witness, with a good faith basis, as to whether he was drunk at the time of observation. The cross-examiner is attacking the witness' capacity to acquire personal knowledge, Rule 602. A question on cross-examination may never be extrinsic as extrinsic refers to the introduction of evidence other than from the witness himself.

B   3.   Rule 410(a)(4) that any statement made in the course of plea discussions with an attorney for the prosecuting authority which do not result in a plea of guilty or which result in a plea of guilty later withdrawn is not admissible against the defendant in a subsequent criminal or civil case. While the defendant did not preface his attempt to enter into plea bargaining with something like, "Can we work something out here," his statement does sufficiently exhibit a reasonable subjective expectation of plea bargaining even though the prosecution at this point has said nothing.

D   4.   Since the prior incident did not lead to a conviction, the cross-examiner can only impeach the witness, character for truthfulness with a prior instance of conduct probative of untruthfulness, i.e., involves dishonesty or false statement, Rule 608(b)(1) robbery does not involve dishonesty or false statement. Moreover, in attacking character for truthfulness under Rule 608(b)(1), the proper procedure is to inquire as to the underlying act on cross-examination of the witness (no reference to the arrest may be made); extrinsic evidence is inadmissible.

B   5.   The clock itself is not hearsay as the clock showing time is not a statement by a person, Rule 801(b). The wife stating that the clock reads 1:00 A.M. is an out-of-court statement offered to prove truth of the matter asserted, Rules 801(a)–(c). The statement meets the requirement of the hearsay exception for present sense impressions, Rule 803(1), which provides a hearsay exception for a statement describing or explaining an event or condition made while the declarant was perceiving the event or condition, or immediately thereafter.

C   6.   The witness' recollection may be refreshed by means of a document, Rule 612 only if the witness first testifies to an inability to recall thus establishing that the witness' recollection needs refreshing.

A   7.   The statement is an out-of-court statement offered in evidence to prove the truth of the matter asserted, Rules 801(a)–(c), meeting neither a not hearsay definition provided in Rules 801(d)(1) and (2), nor a hearsay exception provided in Rules 803, 804, and 807. Habit testimony, Rule 406, may not be established by inadmissible hearsay.

A   8.   Rule 404(b)(1) provides that although evidence of other crimes, wrongs, or acts is not admissible to prove the character of a person in order to show action in conformity therewith, it may, however, be admissible for other purposes, such as proof of motive, opportunity, intent, preparation, plan, knowledge, identity, or absence of mistake or accident, Rule 404(b)(2). In this case, the prior theft is not relevant for any purpose other than proving character for conformity and is thus inadmissible.

D   9.   The photograph has been properly authenticated, Rule 901(a)(1). Evidence has been introduced sufficient to support a finding by a reasonable jury viewing the evidence most favorably that the photograph fairly and accurately represents the scene of the crime when first observed by the police officer. Photographs of crime scenes are rarely excluded when a Rule 403 objection is raised. Not only can the photograph be highly probative, trial judges believe juries are capable of separating the horrible nature of the crime from whether or not the accused committed the crime.

B   10. Rule 608(b)(1) provides that specific instance of conduct of a witness, for the purpose of attacking character for truthfulness, other than conviction of crime as provided in Rule 609, may be inquired into on cross-examination if probative of untruthfulness, i.e., involve dishonesty or false statement. A riot at a rock concert does not involve dishonesty or false statement.

D   11. No privilege applies. A previously existing document does not become privileged when the client provides the document to an attorney for the purpose of obtaining legal representation.

D   12. Rule 404(b)(1) provides that although evidence of other crimes, wrongs, or acts is not admissible to prove the character of a person in order to show action in conformity therewith, it may, however, be admissible for other purposes, such as proof of motive, opportunity, intent, preparation, plan, knowledge, identity, or absence of mistake or accident, Rule 404(b)(2). In this case, the prior act of flying in marijuana is relevant to show knowledge and intent on the part of the accused with respect to the flown in cocaine.

C   13. Rule 301 adopts the Thayer bursting bubble theory of presumptions. Under the Thayer bursting bubble theory if the party opposing the presumption offers no evidence as to the existence of the presumed fact, the jury should be instructed that if they find the basic facts, they must find the presumed fact.

B 14. Answer a tends to show bias, c is permitted under Rule 608(b)(1), while d is permitted under Rule 609(a)(2). Evidence of alcoholism, as distinguished from being drunk at the time of perception or testimony, is usually excluded. Moreover, the question asks the witness as to his reputation, not whether he is an alcoholic.

C 15. Answer a is barred by Rule 609, while b and d are collateral matters, i.e., not relevant in the litigation other than for contradiction. Extrinsic evidence is not admissible as to a collateral matter. Answer c, personal knowledge, is a non-collateral matter; extrinsic evidence is admissible.

D 16. W appears to be an expert qualified on the basis primarily of experience testifying as to a matter of assistance to the trier of fact in determining a fact in issue, Rule 702. That the expert witness testifies as to an ultimate fact is not objectionable under Rule 704(a).

C 17. The letter created as part of the process of obtaining legal advice falls within the lawyer-client privilege. Evidence of a privileged communication is not admissible when acquired under circumstances where the holder of the privilege is without an opportunity to assert the privilege, see Standard 512(b) which is reflective of the common law, here illegal copying.

B 18. The scope of redirect is limited to the subject matter of cross-examination. Where new matters are raised on cross-examination, the opposing party clearly must be permitted to conduct redirect examination, its first opportunity to address the new matter.

B 19. Rule 901(b)(2) provides that non-expert opinion as to the genuineness of handwriting, based upon familiarity not acquired for purposes of litigation, satisfies the requirement of authentication, i.e., evidence has been introduced sufficient to support a finding by a reasonable jury viewing the evidence most favorably to the proponent that it is more probably true than not that the matter in question is what the proponent claims, here that D signed the letter. Historically, remarkably little prior familiarity with handwriting has been found to be sufficient personal knowledge to permit a lay witness to authenticate a writing.

D   20.   Rule 406 provides:

Evidence of a person's habit or an organization's routine practice may be admitted to prove that on a particular occasion the person or organization acted in accordance with the habit or routine practice. The court may admit this evidence regardless of whether it is corroborated or whether there was an eyewitness.

C   21.   Once *Miranda* warnings are given, silence on the party of the defendant is not admissible as an admission of a party-opponent under Rule 801(d)(2)(B) or for purposes of impeachment as it is not natural under such circumstances for a person to respond to questions or volunteer information.

A   22.   Rule 608(b)(1) provides that specific instance of conduct of a witness, for the purpose of attacking character for truthfulness, other than conviction of crime as provided in Rule 609, may be inquired into on the cross-examination if probative of untruthfulness, i.e., involves dishonesty or false statement. Filing a false insurance claim involves dishonesty or false statement.

A   23.   A print from a negative is an original thus satisfying the Original Writing Rule. The photographer is not required to lay a sufficient foundation for the admission of a photograph. Rarely if ever will a photograph of a crime scene be excluded under Rule 403 on the grounds of being cumulative with eyewitness testimony. The photograph is sufficiently established to truly and accurately represent what it purports to represent thus satisfying the requirement of authentication, Rule 901(a)(1).

D   24.   This is a classic statement protected by the attorney-client privilege. An attorney has authority to assert the attorney-client on behalf of the client in the absence of evidence to the contrary.

D   25.   Rule 902(7) provides that extrinsic evidence of authenticity as a condition precedent to admissibility is not required with respect to inscriptions, signs, tags, or labels purporting to have been affixed in the course of business and indicating ownership, control, or origin.

Exam VI

C   1.   Answers b and c are in contention. Since sufficiently similar prior drug dealings offered to establish knowledge and intent are rarely excluded under Rule 403, the strongest argument, although very likely to be unsuccessful, is that the prior acts are not sufficiently similar to the present one on the issue of knowledge or intent.

B   2.   A testifying spouse, here the wife, has a privilege in a criminal case to refuse to testify against her husband as to matters she observed during the existence of a valid, non sham marriage.

C   3.   Rule 406 provides:

Evidence of a person's habit or an organization's routine practice may be admitted to prove that on a particular occasion the person or organization acted in accordance with the habit or routine practice. The court may admit this evidence regardless of whether it is corroborated or whether there was an eyewitness.

A   4.   The confidential communication privilege between husband and wife applicable in civil as well as criminal cases belongs to both spouses and survives divorce.

D   5.   The clergyman privilege applies whenever a clergyman receives a confidential communication in his or her capacity as spiritual advisor. The scope of the privilege is not limited to a confessional. The clergyman may claim the privilege on behalf of the person. The clergyman's authority to do so is presumed in the absence of evidence to the contrary. Here D did not waive the privilege, he simply did not assert it on his own. Notice that D also did not consent to the clergyman answering the question. See Standard 506 reflective of the common law.

A   6.   Rule 408(a), barring evidence of settlement to prove liability, does not require exclusion when the evidence is offered for another purpose, such as proving bias or prejudice of a witness, negating a contention of undue delay, or proving an effort to obstruct a criminal investigation or prosecution, Rule 408(b). Here the evidence is relevant to impeach by reason of bias.

D   7.   Rule 201(e) provides that a party is entitled upon timely request to an opportunity to be heard as to the propriety of taking judicial notice and the tenor of the matter noticed. When judicial notice is taken in a civil case, the jury is to be instructed to accept as conclusive any fact judicially noticed, Rule 201(f).

C   8.   W appears not to have declared by either oath or affirmation to testify truthfully. An oath must refer to God. An affirmation is a promise to tell the truth. Most importantly, the witness to satisfy Rule 603 must evidence a serious belief in the obligation to tell the truth which W has not.

D   9.   To show bias, an expert witness may be asked if she is being paid for her time.

B   10.   Rule 404(b)(1) provides that although evidence of other crimes, wrongs, or acts is not admissible to prove the character of a person in order to show action in conformity therewith, it may, however, be admissible for other purposes, such as proof of motive, opportunity, intent, preparation, plan, knowledge, identity, or absence of mistake or accident, Rule 404(b)(2). In this case, the evidence of the prior crime is not admissible for any other purpose. That being so, W's testimony is inadmissible period. The fact that Rule 801(d)(1)(C) is satisfied is a necessary but insufficient condition to admissibility as the only purpose for which the evidence is relevant is to show character for conformity which is precluded by Rule 404.

D   11.   The expert is reasonably relying upon the EEG under Rule 703. The Original Writing Rule does not apply to facts, data, or opinions not admitted in evidence reasonably relied upon by an expert in the particular field. Even if it were applicable, the original has been shown to be unavailable making secondary evidence admissible. Moreover a general objection only preserves lack of relevance for appeal.

B   12.   Rule 404(a)(2)(A) provides that the accused may introduce character evidence in the form of reputation or opinion testimony as to a pertinent trait of character of himself. The pertinent trait of character when charged with embezzlement is honesty while D's character witness sought to testify as to D's character of peacefulness.

D   13.   Rule 405 permits character evidence in the form of reputation and opinion testimony, Rule 405(a), as well as specific instances of conduct where character or a trait of character is an essential element of a charge, claim or defense, Rule 405(b). Rule 608 permits under limited circumstances evidence of character for truthfulness or untruthfulness for the purpose of attacking or supporting the witness' credibility while Rule 609 under limited circumstances permits admissibility of a prior conviction to impeach a witness' character for truthfulness.

D   14.   A child witness in the federal court is presumed competent, 18 USCA § 3509(c). D neither filed a written motion nor made an offer of proof as to the child's competency. A leading question is permitted under Rule 611(c) to a child witness when necessary to develop the child witness' testimony. Here the prosecution is attempting to elicit testimony from a child witness who either is frightened, nervous and upset, or lacks recollection. Leading questions are proper in either case.

A   15.   Rule 803(3) provides a hearsay exception for a statement of the declarant's then existing state of mind, emotion, sensation, or physical condition (such as intent, plan, motive, design, mental feeling pain, and bodily health).

C   16.   Rule 407 provides:

When measures are taken that would have made an earlier injury or harm less likely to occur, evidence of the subsequent measures is not admissible to prove:

     *negligence;

     *culpable conduct;

*a defect in a product or its design; or

*a need for a warning or instruction.

But the court may admit this evidence for another purpose, such as impeachment or—if disputed—proving ownership, control, or the feasibility of precautionary measures.

Here the feasibility of precautionary measures is being disputed.

D   17.   When the contents of a writing are sought to be proved, Rule 1004(c) provides that the original is not required and other evidence of the contents of the writing is admissible if at a time when an original was under the control of the party against whom offered, that party was put on notice, by the pleadings or otherwise, that the contents would be a subject of proof at the hearing, and that party does not produce the original at the hearing.

C   18.   The evidence is relevant as providing a motive for D making it more probable than without the evidence that D deliberately shot V.

A   19.   Rule 201(b)(1) the trial court may take judicial notice of an adjudicative fact not subject to reasonable dispute in that it is generally known within the territorial jurisdiction of the trial court. Rule 201(f) provides that in a criminal case, the court shall instruct the jury that it may, but is not required to, accept as conclusive any fact judicially noticed.

B   20.   All of the requirements for admissibility pursuant to the hearsay exception for business records, Rule 803(6), are satisfied. In this context, Madame X would also need to establish that she verifies the identity of persons visiting her establishment such as is done by an airline or car rental company, or in the alternative identify D in court as being the person who frequents her establishment.

B   21.   There are two statements involved—the statement by the patient to the admitting nurse and the statement by the nurse creating the intake form found in the hospital records. The admitting nurse's business duty under Rule 803(6) extends solely to matters pertinent to medical diagnosis or treatment. In addition Rule 803(4) provides a hearsay exception for the patient's statement to the extent it describes a general character of the cause or external source thereof insofar as reasonably pertinent to diagnosis in treatment.

Plaintiff's statement that an employee ran him down is a statement of fault, not a statement pertinent to medical diagnosis or treatment.

A   22.   Rule 806 provides that when a hearsay statement has been admitted in evidence, the credibility of the declarant may be attacked by any evidence which would be admissible for these purposes if declarant had testified as a witness. Rule 608(a) permits a party to introduce in the first instance evidence in the form of reputation or opinion testimony as to the character for untruthfulness of a witness to attack the credibility of the witness.

C   23.   Rule 606(b) provides that upon an inquiry into the validity of a verdict or indictment, a juror may not testify as to any matter or statement occurring during the course of the jury's deliberations or to the effect of anything upon that or any other juror's mind or emotions as influencing the juror to assent to or dissent from the verdict or indictment or concerning the juror's mental processes in connection therewith.

B   24.   Rule 803(22) permits introduction of evidence of a final judgment, entered after a trial or upon a plea of guilty (but not upon a plea of nolo contendere), adjudging a person guilty of a crime punishable by death or imprisonment in excess of one year, to prove any fact essential to sustain the judgment, but not including, when offered by the Government in a criminal prosecution for purposes other than impeachment, judgments against persons other than the accused. Since a judgment of conviction is an event that exists independently of the written record memorializing the judgment, i.e., the public record entered in the judgment roll of the conviction, a witness with personal knowledge may testify directly as to the judgment of conviction without violating the Original Writing Rule, 1002.

D   25.   P's prior statement when offered by D is an admission of a
                    party-opponent, defined as not hearsay by Rule 801(d)(2)(A),
                    admissible both as substantive evidence and for purposes of
                    impeachment. Rule 613(b), dealing with providing an
                    opportunity to explain or deny a prior inconsistent statement
                    employed to impeach, provides that it does not apply to
                    admissions of a party-opponent as defined in Rule 801(d)(2).

APPENDICES

APPENDIX A

HEARSAY AND NOT HEARSAY UNDER FEDERAL RULES OF EVIDENCE 801(a)–(d)

A. THE HEARSAY RULE

1. An Overview—Rule 802—Hearsay Rule—Hearsay is not admissible unless provided for by a federal statute, a Federal Rule of Evidence, or other rules prescribed by the Supreme Court.

As stated by McCormick, Evidence § 246 at 584 (Cleary ed. 1972), the common law defined hearsay as "testimony in court, or written evidence, of a statement made out of court, the statement being offered as an assertion to show the truth of matters asserted therein, and thus resting for its value upon the credibility of the out-of-court asserter." Absent an exception to the rule against hearsay, a hearsay statement is excluded on the ground that the trier of fact is not in a position to assess the accuracy of the statement, and with it the weight to be assigned to the matter asserted as true in the out-of-court statement: the hearsay statement was not made by the witness under oath, in the presence of the trier of fact observing the witness' demeanor, subject to contemporaneous cross-examination.

Article VIII of the Federal Rules of Evidence generally approaches hearsay in the traditional manner of a definition, Rules 801(a), (b) and (c), explored in detail in subsection 2 infra, and a rule excluding hearsay, Rule 802, subject to certain exceptions under which evidence is not required to be excluded. Hearsay is not admissible except as provided by "these rules" or by other rules prescribed by the Supreme Court pursuant to statutory authority or by Act of Congress, Rule 802. In some instances hearsay is admissible pursuant to an exception without regard to the availability of the declarant as a witness, Rule 803, while in other instances the hearsay exception requires that the declarant be unavailable, Rule 804. Rule 807 provides a residual exception for hearsay statements not otherwise admissible under either Rule 803 or Rule 804 but having equivalent circumstantial guarantees of trustworthiness. Provision is also made for hearsay within hearsay, Rule 805 and for attacking and supporting the credibility of the hearsay declarant, Rule 806. Article VIII departs from the common law in Rule 801(d)(1) by treating certain prior statements by a witness as defined as not hearsay, and in Rule 801(d)(2) by treating admissions of a party-opponent as defined as not hearsay rather than as a hearsay exception. Illustrative of non-evidence rules of the Supreme Court prescribed pursuant to statutory authority creating hearsay exceptions are Fed.R.Civ.Proc. 56, affidavits in support of motions for summary judgment and Fed.R.Crim.Proc. 4(a), affidavits to show grounds for issuing warrants. The admissibility of depositions continues in part to be governed by Fed.R.Civ.Proc. 32(a) and Fed.R.Crim.Proc. 15. Out-of-court statements that are either not hearsay pursuant to Rules 801(a)–(c) or are exempt from the bar of the rule against hearsay through definition as not hearsay, Rules 801(d)(1) and (2), or fall within a hearsay exception, Rules 803, 804, and 807, to be admitted into evidence must, of course, still meet other requirements for admissibility, such as relevance, authenticity, and when the contents of a document are sought to be proved, the Original Writing Rule, Rule 1002. While hearsay is not admissible except as provided, it is nevertheless incumbent upon the party opposing the introduction of an inadmissible hearsay statement to properly object, Rule 103(a). In the absence of an objection to hearsay, the jury may consider hearsay for whatever value it may have; such evidence is to be given its natural probative effect as if it were in law admissible.

The Introductory Note: The Hearsay Problem of the Advisory Committee describes the approach taken as follows:

> The factors to be considered in evaluating the testimony of a witness are perception, memory, and narration. Morgan, Hearsay Dangers and the Application of the Hearsay Concept, 62 Harv.L.Rev. 177 (1948), Selected Writings on Evidence and Trial 764, 765 (Fryer ed. 1957); Shientag, Cross-Examination: A Judge's Viewpoint, 3 Record 12 (1948); Strahorn, A Reconsideration of the Hearsay Rule and Admissions, 85 U.Pa.L.Rev. 484, 485 (1937), Selected Writings, supra, 756, 757; Weinstein, Probative Force of Hearsay, 46 Iowa L.Rev. 331 (1961). Sometimes a fourth is added, sincerity, but in fact it seems merely to be an aspect of the three already mentioned.

> In order to encourage the witness to do his best with respect to each of these factors, and to expose any inaccuracies which may enter in, the Anglo-American tradition has evolved three conditions under which witnesses will ideally be required to testify: (1) under oath, (2) in the personal presence of the trier of fact, (3) subject to cross-examination.

(1) Standard procedure calls for the swearing of witnesses. While the practice is perhaps less effective than in an earlier time, no disposition to relax the requirement is apparent, other than to allow affirmation by persons with scruples against taking oaths.

(2) The demeanor of the witness traditionally has been believed to furnish trier and opponent with valuable clues. Universal Camera Corp. v. N.L.R.B., 340 U.S. 474, 495–496, 71 S.Ct. 456, 95 L.Ed. 456 (1951); Sahm, Demeanor Evidence: Elusive and Intangible Imponderables, 47 A.B.A.J. 580 (1961), quoting numerous authorities. The witness himself will probably be impressed with the solemnity of the occasion and the possibility of public disgrace. Willingness to falsify may reasonably become more difficult in the presence of the person against whom directed. Rules 26 and 43(a) of the Federal Rules of Criminal and Civil Procedure, respectively, include the general requirement that testimony be taken orally in open court. The Sixth Amendment right of confrontation is a manifestation of these beliefs and attitudes.

(3) Emphasis on the basis of the hearsay rule today tends to center upon the condition of cross-examination. All may not agree with Wigmore that cross-examination is "beyond doubt the greatest legal engine ever invented for the

discovery of truth," but all will agree with his statement that it has become a "vital feature" of the Anglo-American system. 5 Wigmore § 1367, p. 29. The belief, or perhaps hope, that cross-examination is effective in exposing imperfections of perception, memory, and narration is fundamental. Morgan, Foreword to Model Code of Evidence 37 (1942).

> The logic of the preceding discussion might suggest that no testimony be received unless in full compliance with the three ideal conditions. No one advocates this position. Common sense tells that much evidence which is not given under the three conditions may be inherently superior to much that is. Moreover, when the choice is between evidence which is less than best and no evidence at all, only clear folly would dictate an across-the-board policy of doing without. The problem thus resolves itself into effecting a sensible accommodation between these considerations and the desirability of giving testimony under the ideal conditions.

> The solution evolved by the common law has been a general rule excluding hearsay but subject to numerous exceptions under circumstances supposed to furnish guarantees of trustworthiness. Criticisms of this scheme are that it is bulky and complex, fails to screen good from bad hearsay realistically, and inhibits the growth of the law of evidence.

> Since no one advocates excluding all hearsay, three possible solutions may be considered: (1) abolish the rule against hearsay and admit all hearsay; (2) admit hearsay possessing sufficient probative force, but with procedural safeguards; (3) revise the present system of class exceptions.

(1) Abolition of the hearsay rule would be the simplest solution. The effect would not be automatically to abolish the giving of testimony under ideal conditions. If the declarant were available, compliance with the ideal conditions would be optional with either party. Thus the proponent could call the declarant as a witness as a form of presentation more impressive than his hearsay statement. Or the opponent could call the declarant to be cross-examined upon his statement. This is the tenor of Uniform Rule 63(1), admitting the hearsay declaration of a person "who is present at the hearing and available for cross-examination." Compare the treatment of declarations of available declarants in Rule 801(d)(1) of the instant rules. If the declarant were unavailable, a rule of free admissibility would make no distinctions in terms of degrees of noncompliance with the ideal conditions and would exact no quid pro quo in the form of assurances of trustworthiness. Rule 503 of the Model Code did exactly that, providing for the admissibility of any hearsay declaration by an unavailable declarant, finding support in the Massachusetts act of 1898, enacted at the instance of Thayer, Mass.Gen.L.1932, c. 233 § 65, and in the English act of 1938, St.1938, c. 28, Evidence. Both are limited to civil cases. The draftsmen of the Uniform Rules chose a less advanced and more conventional position. Comment, Uniform Rule 63. The present Advisory Committee has been unconvinced of the wisdom of abandoning the traditional

requirement of some particular assurance of credibility as a condition precedent to admitting the hearsay declaration of an unavailable declarant.

> In criminal cases, the Sixth Amendment requirement of confrontation would no doubt move into a large part of the area presently occupied by the hearsay rule in the event of the abolition of the latter. The resultant split between civil and criminal evidence is regarded as an undesirable development.

(2)   Abandonment of the system of class exceptions in favor of individual treatment in the setting of the particular case, accompanied by procedural safeguards, has been impressively advocated. Weinstein, The Probative Force of Hearsay, 46 Iowa L.Rev. 331 (1961). Admissibility would be determined by weighing the probative force of the evidence against the possibility of prejudice, waste of time, and the availability of more satisfactory evidence. The bases of the traditional hearsay exceptions would be helpful in assessing probative force. Ladd, The Relationship of the Principles of Exclusionary Rules of Evidence to the Problem of Proof, 18 Minn.L.Rev. 506 (1934). Procedural safeguards would consist of notice of intention to use hearsay, free comment by the judge on the weight of the evidence, and a greater measure of authority in both trial and appellate judges to deal with evidence on the basis of weight. The Advisory Committee has rejected this approach to hearsay as involving too great a measure of judicial discretion, minimizing the predictability of rulings, enhancing the difficulties of preparation for trial, adding a further element to the already over-complicated congeries of pretrial procedures, and requiring substantially different rules for civil and criminal cases. The only way in which the probative force of hearsay differs from the probative force of other testimony is in the absence of oath, demeanor, and cross-examination as aids in determining credibility. For a judge to exclude evidence because he does not believe it has been described as "altogether atypical, extraordinary. * * * "Chadbourn, Bentham and the Hearsay Rule: A Benthamic View of Rule 63(4)(c) of the Uniform Rules of Evidence, 75 Harv.L.Rev. 932, 947 (1962).

(3)   The approach to hearsay in these rules is that of the common law, i.e., a general rule excluding hearsay, with exceptions under which evidence is not required to be excluded even though hearsay. The traditional hearsay exceptions are drawn upon for the exceptions, collected under two rules, one dealing with situations where availability of the declarant is regarded as immaterial and the other with those where unavailability is made a condition to the admission of the hearsay statement. Each of the two rules concludes with a provision for hearsay statements not within one of the specified exceptions "but having comparable [equivalent] circumstantial guarantees of trustworthiness." Rules 803(24) and 804(b)[(5)] [now Rule 807]. This plan is submitted as calculated to encourage growth and development in this area of the law, while conserving the values and experience of the past as a guide to the future.

For the convenience of the reader, the definition of hearsay, Rules 801(a), (b), and (c), and the two categories of statements exempt from the bar of the rule against hearsay, Rule 802, through definition as not hearsay, i.e. prior statement of witness, Rule 801(d)(1), and admission by party opponent, Rule

801(d)(2), are each treated separately in the sections which follow. With respect to each of the three segments comprising Rule 801, presentation of the text of the rule is followed by commentary addressed to the various subsections comprising the particular segment of Rule 801 under consideration.

2.   The Definition of Hearsay—Rules 801(a), (b), and (c)

(a)   Statement. "Statement" means a person's oral assertion, written assertion, or nonverbal conduct, if the person intended it as an assertion.

(b)   Declarant. "Declarant" means the person who made the statement.

(c)   Hearsay. "Hearsay" means a statement that:

(1)   the declarant does not make while testifying at the current trial or hearing; and

(2)   a party offers in evidence to prove the truth of the matter asserted in the statement.

Hearsay is defined in Rule 801(c) as a statement, other than one made by a declarant while testifying at the current trial or hearing, offered in evidence to prove the truth of the matter asserted in the statement. A statement, Rule 801(a), is a person's oral or written assertion, or nonverbal conduct, if the person intended it as an assertion. The term "assertion" includes both matters directly expressed and matters necessarily implicitly being asserted. A declarant is simply a person who makes a statement, Rule 801(b). Thus documentary evidence as well as the oral assertions of a witness, whether or not recorded, may fall within the definition of hearsay. The definition of hearsay contained in Rule 801 conforms with that of the common law. Specific applications of the definition of hearsay are presented in the sections that follow.

The four risks to be considered in evaluating the testimony of a witness are (1) perception in the sense of capacity and actuality of observation by means of any of the senses, (2) recordation and recollection (sometimes called memory), (3) narration (sometimes called ambiguity), and (4) sincerity (sometimes called fabrication).

> "When a witness testifies about an event he is saying that he perceived a particular fact, remembered it up to the moment of testifying and is now accurately expressing his memory in words. Error, deliberate or unconscious, can enter this process anywhere between the initial perception and the in-court narration. For instance, the witness may not have perceived the event at all, or he may have seen it without understanding, or his impression may have been affected by his emotional and intellectual condition at the moment, or he may have seen it so fleetingly that no accurate impression has remained. Or even if he accurately perceived the event when it occurred, the passage of time may have dulled his recollection or replaced the remembered facts with others. He may be deliberately lying in court, or be honestly mistaken, or be incapable of translating his memory into language that will have the same

meaning to his listeners." 4 Weinstein's Evidence ¶ 800[01] at 800–
9–800–10 (1984).

To encourage the witness to testify to the best of his ability regarding each of
the four risks, and to expose inaccuracies in the witness' testimony, a witness
possessing minimum credibility is required to testify at trial as to a matter
within his personal knowledge (1) under oath or affirmation, (2) in person, so
that the trier of fact may observe the witness' demeanor, and (3) subject to
contemporaneous cross-examination.

Each of the four risks associated with evaluating the accuracy of a witness' in-
court testimony are present as well when an out-of-court statement is offered
to prove the truth of the matter asserted. Thus the trier of fact must evaluate
risks of perception, recordation and recollection, narration, and sincerity when
determining the trustworthiness of a hearsay statement. When the statement
offered for the truth of the matter asserted was made out of court, however,
the trier of fact, where ascertaining inaccuracies, does not have the benefit of
having the declarant before it, under oath, and subject to contemporaneous
cross-examination. Hearsay is excluded because of the absence of these tests
for ascertaining trustworthiness.

> "An understanding of the hearsay rule requires an elementary
> consideration of the conditions which under our adversary system are
> imposed upon a witness testifying in open court and of the mental
> processes which the trier of fact must use in valuing testimony.
>
> If we assume that P, the proponent of the witness W, desires to
> persuade the trier T, to find the existence of fact A, P, through his
> attorney, will utter a series of sounds to which W will respond with
> another series of sounds. T must interpret these sounds and in doing
> so, must rely upon his sense of hearing aided by his sense of sight
> and his capacity for understanding and interpreting W's language.
> Suppose that he determines that the sounds uttered by W make up
> the sentence, 'I perceived A.' In order to put a proper value on this
> utterance as tending to prove the existence of A, T must either
> consciously or instinctively go through the following mental
> operations: (1) He must ask whether W by the use of this sentence
> means to convey to T what T would have meant if T had used the
> same words. If not, just what does he mean to convey? The answer
> will depend upon T's deduction as to W's use of language. (2) If T
> decides that W wants to have T believe that W perceived A, T must
> then ask whether W believes what he had said to be the truth. If not,
> T will not use the utterance as evidence of its truth. If so T has
> concluded that W believes that he now remembers that he perceived
> A. (3) But what about the validity of this belief? Does W really
> remember or is he deceiving himself by attributing to himself the
> experience of another? If he has had a personal experience, how much
> of what he relates is he remembering and how much is he
> reconstructing? T must determine to what extent, if at all, he can rely
> upon W's memory. (4) After determining how far W's memory is
> reliable, T must then decide to what extent W's mental impression at

the time of his perception corresponded to what was then open to his perception. T's decision will depend upon his conclusion as to W's capacity and opportunity for accurate perception, and the stimuli for using that capacity at the relevant time. All this means only that T must use his own capacity for accurate observation and his ability to interpret what is happening in his presence and must determine to what extent he can rely upon W's use of language, sincerity, memory and perception.

Now if T decides that the series of sounds uttered by W make up the sentence: 'Declarant told me that he perceived A,' it is obvious that T's mental operations will concern only W's auditory experience and will furnish no basis for a conclusion by T as to Declarant's use of language, sincerity, memory, or perception in his communication to W, except possibly what T can gather from W's description of the details of W's auditory experience. In a word, upon the issue of the existence or non-existence of A, Declarant is the witness and W is only the means by which Declarant's testimony is brought to T. W is telling only what he heard Declarant say, and W's testimony is hearsay.

Since we are assuming that the investigation as to the existence of A is in an Anglo-American court, Declarant, if present, would not be heard unless he spoke under oath or an equivalent sanction and subject to cross-examination. It would seem too close for argument that P cannot avoid the imposition of these conditions upon his witness by the device of transmitting Declarant's testimony through W. And, generally speaking, he cannot do so. Hearsay is prima facie inadmissible." Morgan, Basic Problems of Evidence 243–44 (1961).

The essential factor underlying the rule excluding hearsay is the inability to conduct cross-examination.

"The primary justification for the exclusion of hearsay is the lack of any opportunity for the adversary to cross-examine the absent declarant whose out-of-court statement is introduced into evidence." Anderson v. United States, 417 U.S. 211, 220, 94 S.Ct. 2253, 41 L.Ed.2d 20 (1974).

"Emphasis on the basis of the hearsay the rule today tends to center upon the condition of cross-examination. All may not agree with Wigmore that cross-examination is 'beyond doubt the greatest legal engine ever invented for the discovery of truth,' but all will agree with his statement that it has become a 'vital feature' of the Anglo-American system. 5 Wigmore, § 1376, p. 29. The belief, or perhaps hope, that cross-examination is effective in exposing imperfections of perception, memory, and narration is fundamental. Morgan, Foreword to Model Code of Evidence 37 (1942)." Advisory Committee's Introductory Note: The Hearsay Problem.

"Morgan ['Hearsay Dangers and the Application of the Hearsay Concept,' 62 Harv.L.Rev. 177, 186 (1948)] analyzed the protective function of cross-examination and concluded (1) that while the fear of exposure of falsehoods on cross-examination is a stimulus to truth-telling by the witness, actual exposure of willful falsehood is rarely accomplished in actual practice and (2) that the most important service of cross-examination in present day conditions is in affording the opportunity to expose faults in the perception and memory of the witness." McCormick, Evidence § 245 at 583 (Cleary ed. 1972).

The definition of hearsay contained in Rules 801(a)–(c) together with the four risks relating to trustworthiness of a statement with which the hearsay rule is concerned is depicted in the following "Stickperson Hearsay" diagrams. Figure A portrays the hearsay risks associated with an oral statement of an out of court declarant. Figure B portrays the hearsay risks associated with the introduction of a written or recorded statement of an out of court declarant.

STICKPERSON HEARSAY

Diagram A

In Court   **Out of Court**

Mickey   Marilyn

Recordation and Recollection   Recordation and Recollection

Narration and Sincerity   Narration and Sincerity

Perception   Perception

Testimony of In Court Witness   Out of Court Oral Statement   Event X

STICKPERSON HEARSAY

Diagram B

In Court   **Out of Court**

Mickey   Marilyn

Recordation and Recollection   Recordation and Recollection

Narration and Sincerity   Narration and Sincerity

Perception   Perception

Testimony of In Court Witness   Out of Court Written or Recorded Statement   Event X

Figure A represents Mickey testifying in court, under oath, subject to contemporaneous cross-examination repeating the contents of a conversation with Marilyn during which she described in detail what she had previously perceived-referred to in the diagram as Event X. Figure B represents Mickey authenticating in court a written or recorded statement of Marilyn detailing the same Event X. Thus the testimonial risks associated with in court testimony (Mickey) and the hearsay risks associated with an out of court statement (Marilyn) can be appreciated by beginning at the left of either diagram and following the dashed lines of Mickey and then Marilyn. The dashed lines of Mickey represent the risks associated with an in court declarant testifying as to a fact of which he has personal knowledge, in this case the *making* of the oral, written or recorded statement by Marilyn. The dashed lines of Marilyn represent the risks associated with an out of court declarant's hearsay statement, i.e., a statement that must either be believed by the declarant to be true or in fact be true in order to be relevant in the context of the particular litigation.

In both Figure A and Figure B, testimony of Mickey repeating or authenticating a statement by Marilyn relevant without regard to the truth of the matter stated, or Marilyn's belief in the truth of the matter stated, is represented by the movement from the left of the diagram along the dashed lines *to* the dotted line. Testimony of Mickey repeating or authenticating a statement by Marilyn relevant only if believed by her to be true or only if the matter asserted is in fact true is represented by movement from the left of the diagram along the dashed lines to the right of the dotted line. Only if relevance of the statement requires movement beyond the dashed lines of Mickey along the dashed lines of Marilyn either into her head alone (belief-two hearsay risks) or further down the other side (Event X-four hearsay risks) is the statement hearsay. Such statement is offered to prove the truth of the matter asserted, Rule 801(c). Thus anytime a statement's relevance depends upon movement along the dashed lines of the diagram from the in court testimony of Mickey to the right of the dotted line, the statement is hearsay. Conversely, to the extent that the statement is relevant simply by virtue of Mickey repeating his personal knowledge of the making of the oral statement (Figure A) or authenticating the written or recorded assertion of Marilyn (Figure B), since movement proceeds from the in court testimony of Mickey along the dashed lines only *to* the dotted line, the statement of Marilyn is not hearsay. Such statement is not being offered to prove the truth of the matter asserted but solely for the fact it was said.

Determining whether a statement offered at trial for a particular purpose is hearsay thus involves solely a search for the presence of hearsay risks (belief-two hearsay risks or Event X-four hearsay risks). If such hearsay risks are present the statement is hearsay. *No assessment of the magnitude of hearsay risks present is undertaken.* Magnitude of hearsay risks bears solely upon whether the hearsay statement is felt sufficiently trustworthy to be admitted pursuant to an exception to the rule against hearsay.

The term "matter asserted" as employed in Rule 801(c) and at common law includes both matters directly expressed and matters the declarant necessarily implicitly intended to assert. When the declarant necessarily intended to assert the inference for which the statement is offered, the statement is tantamount to a direct assertion and therefore is hearsay. The declarant necessarily intends to assert, i.e., implicitly asserts, matters forming the foundation for matters directly expressed in the sense that such additional matters must be assumed to be true to give meaning to the matters directly expressed in the context in which the statement was made. To illustrate, the question "Do you think it will stop raining in one hour?" contains the implicit assertion that it is currently raining. The fact that it is currently raining is a necessary foundation fact which must be assumed true for the question asked to make sense.

> With respect to the statement "it will stop raining in an hour," "[i]n addition to the express assertion, there is in that case a necessary implication of an assertion that it is now raining and will continue to rain for an hour. As far as the intent of the speaker is concerned, while it is principally to give his thought as to the cessation of the rain, it is incidentally without doubt to assert its present existence and continuance. It is due only to a chance use of words that he did not say 'the rain that is now falling will continue for an hour,' in which case the express and implied assertion would have been undoubtedly the same. It would seem, therefore, that . . . implied assertions are hearsay, ..." Seligman, "An Exception to the Hearsay Rule," 26 Harv.L.Rev. 146, 150–151 n.13 (1911).

Under the definition of hearsay contained in Rule 801(a)–(c) when a statement offered to prove the truth of the matter asserted is made "other than . . . by the declarant while testifying at the trial or hearing," the statement is hearsay without regard to whether or not the out of court declarant is available to testify or actually testifies at the trial or hearing at which the out of court statement is offered. Therefore the definition of hearsay in Rules 801(a)–(c) applies to all statements not made at the trial or hearing and thus not made subject to contemporaneous cross-examination before the trier of fact. When the out of court declarant does in fact also testify at trial, cross-examination, or direct and redirect examination, at that time provides an opportunity for the party opposing the truth of the out of court statement to explore the truth of the out of court statement before the trier of fact. Nevertheless, general admissibility of prior statements of in court witnesses is not provided for in the Federal Rules of Evidence. Rule 801(d)(1) does exempt from the operation of the rule against hearsay by definition as not hearsay certain prior inconsistent statements, Rule 801(d)(1)(A), and certain prior consistent statements, Rule 801(d)(1)(B). In addition statements of prior identification of a person after perceiving him are also exempted as not hearsay, Rule 801(d)(1)(C). The reasons for limiting the definition of not hearsay to only certain situations involving prior statements of an in court witness subject to later cross-examination are discussed in section B infra.

Notice that in deciding whether a statement falls within the definition of hearsay, it is irrelevant whether the statement was self-serving or disserving at the time of being either made or offered. It is similarly irrelevant in deciding whether a statement falls within the definition of hearsay as to whether the statement is being offered as direct or circumstantial evidence.

Occasionally, whether the party against whom a statement is offered was present when the statement was made has a bearing upon whether the statement is hearsay under Rules 801(a)–(c) or is defined by Rule 801(d)(2) as "not hearsay". Thus, an oral statement offered to show notice cannot have been effective as such unless it was made in the presence of the person sought to be charged with notice. Similarly, the presence of the party is essential if it is claimed that she admitted the truth of an oral statement by failing to deny it. In general, however, the presence or absence of the party against whom an extrajudicial statement is offered has no bearing upon either its status as hearsay or its admissibility, and an objection based on such absence betrays a basic lack of understanding of the nature of hearsay. Accordingly, in the great majority of situations, the objection "not in the presence of the defendant," and the converse in support of admissibility, "in the presence of the defendant," both frequently heard in criminal prosecutions, fail to address questions relevant to determining admissibility under the hearsay rule.

Under Rule 103, a party who does not make a timely objection cannot complain of the admission of hearsay. The question remains, however, of the weight and probative value of hearsay so admitted. The almost infinite variety which hearsay assumes precludes any answer except that hearsay will be considered and given its natural probative effect.

(a) Nonverbal Conduct Intended as an Assertion

Nonverbal conduct may on occasion clearly be the equivalent of an assertive statement, that is, done for the purpose of deliberate communication, and thus classified as hearsay, Rule 801(a). Nodding "Yes" or "No", pointing to identify the picture of the perpetrator in a mug shot book, pointing out the perpetrator in a lineup, and the sign language of the hearing impaired are as plainly assertions as are spoken words. So too is a videotape of the injured plaintiff recreating the accident which caused his injuries.

(b) Nonverbal Conduct Not Intended as an Assertion

Nonverbal conduct not intended as an assertion is not hearsay, Rule 801(a). The provision of Rule 801 declaring nonverbal conduct not intended as an assertion not hearsay resolves a long-time controversy among commentators. The controversy, however, has only been rarely the subject of judicial decision, frequently because the hearsay question has not been perceived. When the issue is whether an event happened, evidence of conduct from which the actor's belief may be inferred from which in turn the happening of the event may be inferred, bears at least a superficial resemblance to an out of court statement by the actor that he believed the event occurred. An analysis in terms of the principal danger which the hearsay rule is designed to guard against, i.e., lack of opportunity to test by cross-examination the capacity and actuality of his perception as well as his recordation, recollection, narration, and sincerity, however, leads to a rejection of the analogy between such an inference, sometimes called an "implied assertion," and an express allegation. When a person acts without intending to communicate a belief, his veracity is not involved. Furthermore there is frequently a guarantee of the trustworthiness of the inference to be drawn because the actor has based his actions on the correctness of his belief. Consider for example a person who is observed opening an umbrella, offered for the inference that it is raining. While the inference to be drawn from such nonverbal conduct is the same as in the case of a direct assertion that it is raining, the fact remains that the intent to assert is absent and thus the all-important danger believed to be inherent in hearsay with respect to sincerity is absent as well. While the risk of sincerity is removed, the objection still remains that the accuracy of the actor's perception and recollection are untested by cross-examination as to the possibility of honest mistake. However risks of error in these respects are more sensibly factors to be used in evaluating weight and credibility rather than grounds for exclusion. Practical necessity also supports treating nonverbal nonassertive conduct as falling outside the definition of hearsay. Consider the illustration of a car stopped at a traffic light offered for the inference that the light was red. Treatment of such conduct as hearsay would too often exclude highly trustworthy and probative evidence. Resort to the residual exception of Rule 807 is an inappropriate response to a frequently recurring situation.

The court must be satisfied of the probative value of the proffered proof in light of trial concerns. Thus the inference of belief drawn from the nonassertive conduct and/or the inference drawn from such belief when offered to prove the truth of the fact impliedly being asserted may be too ambiguous to warrant submitting the evidence to the jury; its probative value may be so slight in comparison with the possibility of confusing and misleading the trier of fact that exclusion pursuant to Rule 403 is proper. Thus if the person opening an umbrella was known to be both exiting a store that sells umbrellas and superstitious concerning the opening of umbrellas indoors, ambiguity associated with the offering of such evidence to establish that it was raining at the time would certainly be enhanced. Whether exclusion is warranted under Rule 403 of course would depend upon examination of all relevant circumstances.

When nonverbal conduct is at issue, it is not always perfectly clear whether an assertion was intended by the person whose conduct is in question. Consider the conduct of men and women during courting. If evidence of conduct is offered on the theory that it is not intended as an assertion and hence not hearsay, the burden of showing that an assertion was intended is on the party objecting to the evidence. The question of intention to assert is a preliminary one for the court, Rule 104(a). Even if the person intended to make an assertion, such as punching someone who insulted your companion, the person's conduct may itself be relevant to establish the same fact of consequence in the litigation and if so is not hearsay for such purpose.

Nonverbal conduct not intended as an assertion and thus not hearsay under Rule 801(a) is frequently, but incorrectly, treated as an admission of a party opponent. Illustrations include flight, silence, and the fabrication, destruction, or suppression of evidence. Such evidence may be excluded upon application of Rule 403.

(c) Oral or Written Conduct Not Intended as an Assertion

Considerations present with respect to nonverbal nonassertive conduct support the position taken in Rule 801(a)(1) that oral or written conduct not intended as an assertion is not hearsay. Examples of such conduct are screams of pain, outbursts of laughter, singing a song or uttering or writing an expletive. Of course any of the foregoing may be intended as an assertion.

(d) Statements Offered Other Than to Prove the Truth of the Matter Asserted; Verbal Act; Characterizing Act; Effect on Listener; Impeachment

Hearsay does not encompass all extrajudicial statements but only those offered for the purpose of proving the truth of matters asserted in the statement, Rule 801(c).

Therefore when the mere making of the statement is the relevant fact, i.e., tends to establish a fact of consequence, Rule 401, hearsay is not involved. Such statements are frequently said to be offered solely for the fact said and not for the truth of the matter asserted, i.e., the truth of their contents.

Verbal act. As to one group of extrajudicial statements falling outside the category of hearsay, the statement itself, the verbal act, has independent legal significance or gives rise to legal consequences, sometimes referred to as an operative act. Thus testimony by an agent as to a statement by the principal granting him authority to act as agent is not hearsay. Other illustrations include statements constituting contracts, canceling of an insurance policy, constituting an anticipatory breach, constituting the crime (e.g., selling drugs, solicitation, threatening someone's life, offering a bribe), directions issued by a police officer directing traffic, a stop sign at an intersection, statements offered as evidence of defamation, evidence offered that a statement has been made so as to establish a foundation for evidence showing the statement was made as part of a fraudulent scheme and is false, and statements offered to place in context other statements otherwise admissible made in a conversation.

Characterizing act. Also included in the group of statements comprising operative legal acts are assertions which relate to and characterize a particular act. Thus for example, where an instrument designating the executive's wife as his beneficiary was unclear as to whether she was to be the beneficiary of his insurance policy or of a six months gratuity payment, oral statements accompanying delivery of the instrument resolving the ambiguity were not hearsay.

Effect on listener. Another group falling outside the category of hearsay consists of statements made by one person which become known to another offered as a circumstance under which the latter acted and as bearing upon his conduct. For example a law enforcement official explains his going to the scene of the crime by stating that he received a radio call to proceed to a given location or to explain why an investigation was undertaken or other subsequent action, such testimony is not hearsay. However if he becomes more specific by repeating definite complaints of a particular crime by the accused, this is so likely to be misused by the jury as evidence of the fact asserted that the content of the statement, absent special circumstances enhancing probative value, such as the policeman shot a person leaving the bank after being advised that a bank clerk had been shot, should be excluded on the grounds that the probative value of the statement admitted for a non-hearsay purpose is substantially outweighed by the danger of unfair prejudice, Rule 403. Other illustrations of a statement being offered for the purpose of showing the probable state of mind of the listener include being placed on notice or having knowledge. Thus, in a negligence action to recover damages for personal injury sustained in a fall, a statement to a customer of a food store by the manager that the floor in aisle 2 is wet is not hearsay when it is offered to show the unreasonableness of the customer's conduct in skipping down aisle 2.

The same statement offered to show the floor was wet, of course, is hearsay. Similarly threats made to the defendant bearing on the reasonableness of his apprehension of danger or conversely providing a motive for action are not hearsay when offered for such purpose. In addition, the victim's fearful state of mind is an element in proving extortion. The testimony of victims as to what others say to them and the testimony of others as to what they said to the victim are admitted, not for the truth of the information in the statements but for the fact that the victim heard them from which one can infer the state of mind of a reasonable person having heard such statements. Similarly where the defendant alleges duress as a defense, statements threatening her and her two small children are not hearsay when offered to show her state of mind; in a prosecution for income tax violation, evidence as to advice received by the defendant at a tax protestors' meeting is not hearsay when offered to prove intent. Instructions to an individual to do something, such as a mother telling her son "Wait here, I'll be right back", are also not hearsay. Evidence relevant for its effect on the listener is subject to exclusion under Rule 403, after taking into consideration the giving of a limiting instruction.

A statement which is not hearsay when offered for its effect on listener is hearsay as defined in Rules 801(a)–(c) when offered to prove the truth of the matter asserted. The giving of a limiting instruction is appropriate. Thus a statement by Harry to John that Sam is the person who keyed John's car is not hearsay when offered as relevant to establish John's motive, and thus relevant to prove that John was the person who slashed Sam's tires, but hearsay when offered to prove that Sam in fact keyed John's car.

Impeachment. Prior statements of a witness inconsistent with the witness' in-court testimony offered solely to impeach, Rules 607 and 613, are not hearsay.

3.   Problem Areas in Defining Hearsay

(a)   Circumstantial Evidence

The employment of circumstantial evidence has occasionally over the years given rise to discussion of the application of the rule against hearsay. Such discussions have tended to be confusing and more often than not theoretically unsound. The reason for such inaccuracy may be attributed primarily to the fact that in most such instances while the evidence under consideration was highly probative, highly necessary and highly trustworthy, no applicable hearsay exception existed. Under such circumstances, it is not surprising that both the courts and commentators "squeezed" and thereby distorted the proper application of the definition of hearsay for the sake of admissibility of the evidence in the case at hand. With the enactment of the residual hearsay exception, Rule 807, resort to distortion of the hearsay definition in the interests of justice in the case at hand is no longer required. It should no longer be tolerated.

Hearsay questions arising with respect to evidence employed circumstantially, while varied, may for purpose of analysis conveniently be discussed in connection with certain relatively distinct and recurring situations. As will be developed, whether evidence is direct or circumstantial is irrelevant in determining whether the evidence falls within the rule against hearsay.

Mechanical traces. Presence of something upon a person or premises may constitute circumstantial evidence giving rise to an inference that a person did an act with which these circumstances are associated. Such items, referred to by 1A Wigmore, Evidence §§ 149–160 (Tillers rev.1983) as mechanical traces, include (1) the presence upon a person or premises of articles, fragments, stains, or tools, (2) brands on animals or timber, or (3) tags, signs and numbers on automobiles, railroad cars or other vehicles or premises and (4) postmarks, fingerprints and footmarks. Mechanical traces are frequently relevant as circumstantial evidence looking backwards to show that some act was or was not done. Hearsay questions arise only when the relevancy of the circumstantial evidence, such as a tag or sign, derives solely from the truth of the mechanical trace. Take for example the situation of a tag bearing the name "Bill Snow" on a briefcase containing narcotics. Since the relevancy of the tag to identify the defendant whose name is Bill Snow with the briefcase to which the tag is attached derives from the truth of the assertion made on the tag, i.e., this briefcase belongs to Bill Snow, the tag is hearsay. To say that the tag is a mechanical trace admissible as "circumstantial evidence of ownership" improperly ignores the definition of hearsay. To say that the tag is extremely probative and trustworthy evidence of ownership is simply to say that hearsay evidence may be extremely probative and trustworthy.

To be distinguished is the situation where the relevancy of the mechanical trace does not derive from the truth of the statement itself. Consider a book of matches bearing the name Red Fox Inn found on the defendant accused of a murder committed at the Red Fox Inn. If authenticated solely as having been taken off the person of the defendant, the matchbook is hearsay since its relevancy depends on the acceptance of the assertive statement on the matchbook that its origin is the Red Fox Inn. Now assume that the owner of the Red Fox Inn testifies that the matchbook found on the defendant is identical to the matchbooks he places on tables for use by customers. At this juncture, the relevancy of the matchbook is no longer dependent on the truth of the matter asserted but is based upon personal knowledge and the process of comparison. This point can be more easily appreciated by changing the cover of the matchbook to a modern design bearing no lettering at all. When the owner of the Red Fox Inn testifies that this matchbook is identical to those distributed at his bar, the nonhearsay nature of the physical evidence is highlighted.

Character of an establishment: McCormick, Evidence § 249 at 102 (4th ed. 1992) classifies as not hearsay situations where "the character of an establishment is sought to be proved by evidence of statements made in connection with activities taking place on the premises." The classic illustration involves the placing of telephone calls to an establishment accused of gambling. To enhance the probative value and trustworthiness of the statements under consideration, assume 20 policemen accompanied by 20 clergy of various denominations place tape recorders on 40 telephones and record 100 calls each answered by a police officer or clergy and each proceeding something like, "This is Tom, put $2 to win on Acne Pimple in the third at Belmont." While occasionally considered not hearsay as either a statement characterizing an act or as circumstantial evidence not being offered for the truth of the matter asserted but solely for the fact said, the plain and simple fact is that such statements fall clearly within the definition of hearsay. There is no independently relevant act, apart from the statements placing the bets themselves, for the statements to characterize. The statements are irrelevant if offered solely for the fact they were said. For any of the telephone calls to be relevant to establish that the establishment where the 40 telephones were located was a betting parlor, the declarant who placed the telephone call must have intended to call the number reached. Moreover, the declarant must have believed that the number dialed was a betting parlor. In addition, the declarant must have intended to place a bet, instead of, for example, playing a practical joke. Finally, and most importantly, the declarant's intention to place a bet must have been formed in reliance upon previously acquired personal knowledge that the number dialed is in fact a betting parlor. Thus the out-of-court statement placing a bet is relevant only when offered to prove the truth of the matter necessarily implicitly being asserted by the out-of-court declarant, i.e., that the establishment reached is in fact a betting parlor. As presented such statements also fall within the residual hearsay exception of Rule 807.

Notice that in the illustration the telephone calls were answered by the police officers and clergy. If a police officer had overheard a person working at the establishment respond to the statement, "This is Tom, put $2 to win on Acne Pimple in the third at Belmont," with, "You got it, settle up as usual," the situation would be entirely different. The statement of the out-of-court declarant need no longer be true to be relevant. Similarly, the statement of the person working at the establishment accepting the bet would be a verbal act possessing independent significance under applicable substantive criminal law.

Personal knowledge of independently established facts. On rare occasions, statements are offered into evidence to prove personal knowledge of the declarant as to the truth of the matter asserted when the truth of the matter asserted is firmly established by independent evidence. Personal knowledge of the declarant is relevant in such cases to establish the presence of the declarant at a particular location at a particular time. Consider, for example, the case of Bridges v. State, 247 Wis. 350, 19 N.W.2d 529 (1945). In *Bridges,* the defendant was convicted of taking indecent liberties with a seven year old girl named Sharon Schunk. She was abused by a man in an Army uniform at his house. The serious question was identification of the defendant as that person. This identification in part depended upon whether the house to which Sharon had been taken by her assaulter was the house at 125 East Johnson Street in which the defendant concededly resided at the relevant time. At trial, statements made by Sharon to her mother and police officers prior to discovery of the location of defendant's house as to the general appearance of the steps to the porch, the front door, and the room and articles therein of the house to which she had been taken by the perpetrator on February 26, 1945 were admitted. The Supreme Court of Wisconsin upheld admission of Sharon's statements as circumstantial evidence of personal knowledge not being offered to prove the truth of the matter asserted:

> Defendant contends the court erred also in admitting testimony by police officers as to matters stated by Sharon in defendant's absence. He claims these statements were hearsay evidence and therefore were not admissible. * * * There is testimony by police officers and also Mrs. Schunk as to statements which were made to them by Sharon on February 26 and 27, 1945, and also during the course of their subsequent investigations to ascertain the identity of the man who committed the offense and of the house and room in which it was committed. In those statements she spoke, as hereinbefore stated, of various matters and features which she remembered and which were descriptive of the exterior and surroundings of the house; and of the room and various articles and the location thereof therein. It is true that testimony as to such statements was hearsay and, as such, inadmissible if the purpose for which it was received had been to establish thereby that there were in fact the stated articles in the room, or that they were located as stated, or that the exterior features or surroundings of the house were as Sharon stated. That, however, was not in this case the purpose for which the evidence as to those statements were admitted. It was admissible in so far as the fact she had made the statements can be deemed to tend to show that at the time those statements were made,—which was a month prior to the subsequent discovery of the room and house at 125 East Johnson Street,—she had knowledge as to articles and descriptive features which, as was proven by other evidence, were in fact in or about that room and house. If in relation thereto Sharon made the statements as to which the officers and her mother testified, then those statements,—although they were extra-judicial utterances,— constituted at least circumstantial evidence that she then had such knowledge; and that such state of mind on her part was acquired by reason of her having been in that room and house prior to making the statements.

* * *

So in this case the proof that Sharon made the statements in question before there was any possibility of having what she stated she remembered about the house, and room, and articles therein, from her first contact therewith, affected or changed by what she learned after the discovery and location thereof, at 125 East Johnson Street, is material and significant in so far as it tended to show that she had knowledge of certain things in and about the house and room. The existence of those things in fact could not, however, be established by her hearsay statement, but had to be proven by other evidence which was competent. In other words, although proof of her extrajudicial assertions was competent to show such knowledge on her part, it could not be deemed to prove the facts asserted thereby. When, for instance, it was proven that Sharon stated during the evening after the alleged assault that there was a picture of the lady in the room, her statement did not constitute competent evidence to prove that there was such a picture in the room. But her statement was competent as evidence to prove that she had knowledge of such an object in the room and for this purpose the utterance is not inadmissible hearsay, but is a circumstantial fact indicating knowledge on the part of Sharon Schunk at a particular time.

Notwithstanding the court's holding, Sharon's statements are hearsay. Her statements were offered for the inference that she acquired her memory in a manner consistent with the events described in her statement. As so offered, all four hearsay risks are present. It is certainly possible, albeit unlikely, that Sharon created a description of the house out of whole cloth. More likely, she may have in good faith provided a description of a house where she had been on an occasion not connected to the assault. Finally, she may have described a house that was suggested to her earlier by the police or someone else as being the house where she had been taken. Admittedly, the magnitude of the hearsay risks are small. Nevertheless, because the risks of perception, recordation and recollection, narration, and sincerity are present with respect to Sharon's statements, the statements fall within the definition of hearsay when offered to prove Sharon's personal knowledge of objects in the defendant's house to establish that the assault took place in that house. Relevancy of Sharon's statements involves hearsay risks located in the "Stickperson Hearsay" diagram on the right of the dotted line. Sharon's statements are, however, admissible under the residual hearsay exception of Rule 807.

Circumstantial use of utterances to show state of mind. McCormick historically has asserted that while a direct declaration of the existence of a state of mind or feeling which it is offered to prove is hearsay, declarations which only impliedly, indirectly, or inferentially indicate the state of mind or feeling of the declarant are not hearsay. McCormick, Evidence § 249 at 590–91 (Cleary ed. 1972) employed the following illustration:

In a contested will case the proponent might seek to support the validity of testator's bequest to his son Harold against the charge of undue influence by showing that long before the time when the alleged influence was exerted, the testator had shown a special fondness for Harold. For this purpose evidence might be offered (a) that the testator had paid the expenses of Harold, and for none other of his children, in completing a college course, (b) that the testator said, "Harold is the finest of my sons," and (c) that he said, "I care more for Harold than for any of my other children." When offered to show the testator's feelings toward his son, under the suggested definition item (a) would present no hearsay question, item (b) would be considered a non-hearsay declaration raising a circumstantial inference as to the testator's feelings, and (c) a direct statement offered to prove the fact stated, and hence dependent for its value upon the veracity of the declarant, would be considered hearsay.

For McCormick the distinction, as artificial as it is, itself breaks down when one considers statements offered to show a person's mental incompetency. McCormick concluded that even the direct assertion "I believe that I am King Henry the Eighth," undeniably falling squarely within the definition of hearsay, may nevertheless be classified as nonhearsay on the theory of "verbal conduct offered circumstantially." Many years ago Professor Hinton correctly exposed the errors of McCormick's ways:

> It has sometimes been argued by judges and writers that, where the issue is the sanity of the testator, and some absurd statement by him is proved, e.g., "I am the Emperor Napoleon", no hearsay use is involved because we are not seeking to prove that he really was Napoleon, and hence that we are making a purely circumstantial use of his words to prove his irrational belief. The difficulty is that this view ignores the implied assertion of belief. If the statement had taken the form, "I believe that I am Napoleon", and were offered to prove that the testator so believed, it would be generally conceded [but not by McCormick] that the statement was hearsay, and receivable only because of an exception to the rule. The former assertion is simply a short method of stating the speaker's opinion or belief. Implied assertions seem to fall within the hearsay category as well as express assertions.

Hinton, State of Mind and the Hearsay Rule, 1 U.Chi.L.Rev.394, 397–98 (1934).

If the declarant must believe the matter asserted to be true for any inference to logically flow, whether the statement is "Harold is the finest of my sons", "I believe I am King Henry the Eighth," or "I am the Emperor Napoleon," the hearsay risks of sincerity and narration are present. Such statements are thus properly classified as hearsay. Consider the 8 year old boy shooting foul shots at the basket located on his garage who says "I'm Michael Jordan." Clearly his mental state does not come into question unless he believes the statement to be true. It is sometimes asserted that determining whether such statements are or are not hearsay is "limited to the realm of theory" in that a hearsay exception exists for statements of a declarant's then existing, mental, emotional or physical condition, Rule 803(3). Nevertheless the confusion that broad use of the concept of circumstantial evidence creates in the overall analysis of hearsay versus not hearsay remains. Moreover mechanical traces and character of an establishment statements do not conveniently fall within a common law hearsay exception. Characterizing assertive statements as circumstantial is simply utterly irrelevant in addressing the definitional framework of hearsay set forth in Rules 801(a)–(c). The practice should be discontinued.

(b) Basis for Nonasserted Inference or "Implied Assertion"

If a statement, although assertive in form, is offered as a basis for inferring something other than the truth of the matter asserted, the Advisory Committee's Note to Rule 801(a) indicates that the statement is "excluded from the definition of hearsay by the language of subdivision (c)." The Advisory Committee's assertion as to the non-hearsay nature of statements offered for a different inference rests on the assumption of a reduced sincerity risk alleged to be similar to that associated with nonverbal conduct not intended as an assertion at all.

> "Admittedly the uncross-examined statement is subject to all the hearsay dangers, except to the extent that deliberate falsification diminishes when a statement is not used to prove anything asserted therein. See Morgan, Basic Problems of Evidence 249 (1962)." McCormick, Evidence § 249 at 590 n.92 (Cleary ed. 1972).

It is extremely doubtful whether statements offered as a basis for inferring something other than the matter asserted possess a reduced sincerity risk, much less a reduced sincerity risk sufficient to warrant non-hearsay treatment. If a sufficiently reduced sincerity risk actually is not present, in spite of the implication in the Advisory Committee's Note, a statement offered as a basis for inferring something other than the matter asserted clearly must be considered hearsay under both the common law and Rules 801(a)–(c) definitions.

The famous English case of Wright v. Doe d. Tatham illustrates the problem under consideration. In *Tatham,* plaintiff's lessor claimed the right to inherit as heir of John Marsden. Defendant, Marsden's steward, claimed as devisee. The case hinged upon the testamentary capacity of Marsden. Defendant offered in evidence certain letters Marsden received from persons who had subsequently died. One of these letters from Marsden's cousin, dated October 12, 1784, recounted the details of a sea voyage, described conditions at the destination, and wished Marsden good health. Another from Rev. Marton, a vicar, dated May 20, 1786, requested Marsden to direct his attorney to propose some terms for a settlement of a dispute between Marsden and the parish or township. A third was a letter of gratitude dated October 3, 1799 from Rev. Ellershaw upon resigning a curacy to which Marsden had appointed him. The will and codicil were made in 1822 and 1824 respectively. At trial, three letters were excluded. A verdict was returned for plaintiff's lessor, and defendant sued out a writ or error to the Exchequer Chamber from the judgment entered thereon. The judgment was affirmed by an equally divided court. On further writ of error, the House of Lords also affirmed. 5 Cl. & F. 670, 47 Rev. Rep. 136 (1838). The following extract by Baron Parke in the Exchequer Chambers, 7

Adolph. & E. 313, 383–89, 112 Eng.Rep. 488 (1837), is selected from the
numerous opinions delivered in the two courts of review:

> PARKE, B. * * * It is argued that the letters would be admissible
> because they are evidence of the treatment of the testator as a
> competent person by individuals acquainted with his habit and
> personal character, not using the word treatment in a sense involving
> any conduct of the testator; that they are more than mere statements
> to a third person indicating an opinion of his competence by those
> persons; they are acts done towards the testator by them, which
> would not have been done if he had been incompetent and from
> which, therefore a legitimate inference may, it is argued, be derived
> that he was so.

Each of the three letters, no doubt, indicates that in the opinion of
the writer the testator was a rational person. He is spoken of in
respectful terms in all. Mr. Ellershaw describes him as possessing
hospitality and benevolent politeness; and Mr. Marton addresses him
as competent to do business to the limited extent to which his letter
calls upon him to act; and there is no question but that, if any one of
those writers had been living, his evidence, founded on personal
observation, that the testator possessed the qualities which justified
the opinion expressed or implied in his letters, would be admissible
on this issue. * * *

But the question is, whether the contents of these letters are evidence
of the fact to be proved upon this issue,—that is, the actual existence
of the qualities which the testator is, in those letters, by implication,
stated to possess: and those letters may be considered in this respect
to be on the same footing as if they had contained a direct and positive
statement that he was competent. For this purpose they are mere
hearsay evidence, statements of the writers, not on oath, of the truth
of the matter in question, with this addition, that they have acted
upon the statements on the faith of their being true, by their sending
the letters to the testator. That the so acting cannot give a sufficient
sanction for the truth of the statement is perfectly plain; for it is clear
that, if the same statements had been made by parol or in writing to
a third person, that would have been insufficient; and this is conceded
by the learned counsel for the plaintiff in error. Yet in both cases
there has been an acting on the belief of the truth, by making the
statement, or writing and sending a letter to a third person; and what
difference can it possibly make that this is an acting of the same
nature and sending the letter to the testor? It is admitted, and most
properly, that you have no right to use in evidence the fact of writing
and sending a letter to a third person containing a statement of
competence, on the ground that it affords an inference that such an
act would not have been done unless the statement was true, or
believed to be true, although such an inference no doubt would be
raised in the conduct of the ordinary affairs of life, if the statement
were made by a man of veracity. But it cannot be raised in a judicial

inquiry; and, if such an argument were admissible, it would lead to the indiscriminate admission of hearsay evidence of all manner of facts.

Further, it is clear that an acting to a much greater extent and degree upon such statements to a third person would not make the statements admissible. For example, if a wager to a large amount had been made as to the matter in issue by two third persons, the payment of that wager, however large the sum, would not be admissible to prove the truth of the matter in issue. You would not have had any right to present it to the jury as raising an inference of the truth of the fact, on the ground that otherwise the bet would not have been paid. It is, after all, nothing but the mere statement of that fact, with strong evidence of the belief of it by the party making it. Could it make any difference that the wager was between the third person and one of the parties to the suit? Certainly not. The payment by other underwriters on the same policy to the plaintiff could not be given in evidence to prove that the subject insured had been lost. Yet there is an act done, a payment strongly attesting the truth of the statement, which it implies, that there had been a loss. To illustrate this point still further, let us suppose a third person had betted a wager with Mr. Marsden that he could not solve some mathematical problem, the solution of which required a high degree of capacity; would payment of that wager to Mr. Marsden's banker be admissible evidence that he possessed that capacity? The answer is certain; it would not. It would be evidence of the fact of competence given by a third party not upon oath.

Let us suppose the parties who wrote these letters to have stated the matter therein contained, that is, their knowledge of his personal qualities and capacity for business, on oath before a magistrate, or in some judicial proceeding to which the plaintiff and defendant were not parties. No one could contend that such statement would be admissible on this issue; and yet there would have been an act done on the faith of the statement being true, and a very solemn one, which would raise in the ordinary conduct of affairs a strong belief in the truth of the statement if the writers were faithworthy. The acting in this case is of much less importance, and certainly is not equal to the sanction of an extrajudicial oath.

Many other instances of a similar nature, by way of illustration, were suggested by the learned counsel for the defendant in error, which, on the most cursory consideration, any one would at once declare to be inadmissible in evidence. Others were supposed on the part of the plaintiff in error, which, at first sight, have the appearance of being mere facts, and therefore admissible, though on further consideration they are open to precisely the same objection. On the first description are the supposed cases of a letter by a third person to any one demanding a debt, which may be said to be a treatment of him as a debtor, being offered as proof and that the debt was really due; a note, congratulating him on his high state of bodily vigor, being proposed as evidence of his being in good health; both of which are manifestly at first sight objectionable. To the latter class belong the supposed conduct of the family relations of a testator, taking the same precautions in his absence as if he were a lunatic; his election, in his absence, to some high and responsible office; the conduct of a physician who permitted a will to be executed by a sick testator; the conduct of a deceased captain on a question of seaworthiness, who, after examining every part of the vessel, embarked in it with his family; all these, when deliberately considered, are with reference to the matter in issue in each case, mere instances of hearsay evidence, mere statements, not on oath, but implied in or vouched by the actual conduct of persons by whose acts the litigant parties are not to be bound.

The conclusion at which I have arrived is, that proof of a particular fact, which is not of itself a matter in issue, but which is relevant only as implying a statement or opinion of a third person on the matter in issue, is inadmissible in all cases where such a statement or opinion not on oath would be of itself inadmissible; and, therefore, in this case the letters which are offered only to prove the competence of the testator that is the truth of the implied statement therein contained, were properly rejected, as the mere statement or opinion of the writer would certainly have been inadmissible. * * *

In *Tatham,* each of the three letters written to the testator, Marsden, and offered by the proponents of his will and codicil were not of a kind that would likely have been written to a mentally defective person. The inference suggested is that the writers believed him to be competent, which in turn justifies the inference that he was competent. Both the Exchequer Chamber and the House of Lords ruled the letters inadmissible hearsay as "implied assertion." The courts rejected the notion that since the out-of-court declarant did not intend to assert the matter for which the statement was being offered, i.e., the competency of the testator, there existed a sufficient reduction in the likelihood of conscious fabrication to warrant non-hearsay treatment.

The Advisory Committee's apparent attempted rejection of Wright v. Doe d. Tatham is as unfortunate as it is incorrect. Fortunately, it has not had significant impact on the courts which by and large continue to follow *Tatham.*

When a statement is offered to infer the declarant's state of mind from which a given fact in the form of an opinion or otherwise is inferred, because the truth of the matter asserted must be assumed in order for the nonasserted inference to be drawn, the statement is properly classified as hearsay under the language of Rules 801(a)–(c). Since the matter asserted in the statement must be true, a reduction in the risk of sincerity is not present. Thus, if Rev. Ellershaw were to testify in court, he would be required to lay a foundation establishing his personal knowledge of facts forming the basis of his opinion before rendering that opinion. If a sufficient foundation of personal knowledge was not established, Rev. Ellershaw would not be permitted to render his opinion as to Marsden's testamentary capacity. Similarly, for the letter of Rev.

Ellershaw to be offered in evidence for the further inference that Rev. Ellershaw believed Marsden possessed testamentary capacity, the existence of each of the facts which Rev. Ellershaw relied upon to support his expression of gratitude, whether or not expressed in the letter, must be within his personal knowledge in order for the opinion to be admissible. Moreover, the expression of gratitude itself must be sincerely felt for the inference of testamentary capacity to flow. Because the basis for Rev. Ellershaw's expression of gratitude, in addition to the expression itself, must be true for any inference as to testamentary capacity to flow from the matters asserted, all four hearsay risks are present. Finally because the matters asserted by the statement must themselves be true for any inference desired to be relevant, the sincerity risk is not reduced. The fact that the sincerity risk is fully present with respect to the matter asserted makes the statement hearsay even though the sincerity risk is arguably reduced with respect to the inference to be drawn once the truth of the matter asserted is assumed. Even this reduction in sincerity risk will not be present where the declarant intends that the nonasserted inference be drawn such as occurs with respect to statements made to accomplish a fraud.

The argument expressed below and accepted by the Advisory Committee, asserting a reduced risk of sincerity with respect to the inference to be drawn from the statement, fails to appreciate the risk of sincerity arising from the fact that the matter asserted must be true for any inference at all to arise.

"Reliance on an implied assertion involves the following reasoning process. The fact finder is informed by testimony that X engaged in certain conduct. This conduct is not a direct assertion of f, the disputed fact, but the fact finder is asked to infer from the conduct that X believes F to be true. Having made this inference the finder must then infer from X's belief in F that F is true. This inference from belief to truth will be sound only if X's belief faithfully reflects the fact and the reflection will be faithful only if X's perception of the fact and his recollection of that perception were accurate. Reliance on implied assertions, therefore, necessarily entails reliance on memory and perception. On the other hand, since an implied assertion by definition consists of conduct not intended as an assertion concerning F, there is no danger that the actor is being insincere about F. A person who did not intend to make any statement about F could not have intended to make a misleading statement about F. Similarly, since the actor's conduct does not consist of words expressly stating F, there is no danger that language apparently affirming or denying F, and so understood by the fact finder, was in reality intended to convey a different meaning. If brief, while reliance on uncross-examined express assertions would expose the fact finder to the dangers of faulty narration, insincerity, inaccurate perception, and erroneous memory, only the perception and memory dangers seem to be posed by uncross-examined implied assertions. Because implied assertions entail fewer dangers than express assertions—especially because implied assertions raise no problem of insincerity—it is argued that they should be classified as nonhearsay." Finman,

"Implied Assertions as Hearsay: Some Criticisms of the Uniform
Rules of Evidence," 14 Stan.L.Rev. 682, 685–86 (1962).

Realization that the argument of a reduced sincerity risk fails once it is
recognized that the matter asserted must be true for any inference to arise can
be appreciated by considering an example. Assume a statement by a company
president to his wife that he had a dull time on a weekend business cruise on
the company ship is offered to show that the ship, damaged by fire later in that
week, was believed by the company president to be seaworthy for the inference
that it was seaworthy. If the company president had really taken his secretary
with him that weekend by airplane to Las Vegas, where is the reduced risk of
sincerity? Compare the situation of the company president who, after
inspecting the ship, actually goes out to sea. The former is a statement offered
for a different inference, sometimes called an "implied assertion," where no
reduced sincerity risk is present. The latter is nonverbal nonassertive conduct,
where a reduction in the risk of fabrication is caused by a lack of an intent to
assert anything.

A statement made to Marsden may have no relevant content as to which truth
or falsity comes into question. Assume someone approaches Marsden and says
"Hi" or "Hope all is well with you." Such a statement may be offered for the
implied assertion that the declarant would not have spoken in such a manner
to someone who is not competent. Putting aside the relative weak probative
value of the implied assertion, the implied inference can be drawn only if the
declarant has previously acquired personal knowledge of Marsden through
prior contact. Thus the "implied assertion" is dependent upon the perception,
recordation and recollection, and narration of the declarant. It is also based
upon the declarant's sincerity in the sense of really intending to communicate
with Marsden. Thus the declarant could have made the statement to be polite
to someone in earshot knowing full well that Marsden was not capable of a
response. Therefore, even such statements possess all four hearsay risks and
are thus properly classified as hearsay.

In short, while the Advisory Committee was correct with respect to a reduced
risk of sincerity associated with nonverbal conduct not intended as an
assertion, it is suggested that the Advisory Committee did not sufficiently
consider the encouraged extension of the same concept to verbal statements
offered as a basis for inferring something other than the matter asserted. Since
the sincerity risk is fully present with respect to the matter asserted, the
statement is hearsay even though the sincerity risk is arguably reduced with
respect to the inference to be drawn once the truth of the matter actually
asserted is assumed. Even this reduction in sincerity risk would not be present
where the declarant intended that the nonasserted inference be drawn such as
occurs with respect to statements made to accomplish a fraud.

Even if one assumed that a reduced risk of sincerity did arise when an
assertive verbal statement is used to infer something other than the truth of
the matter asserted, the practical importance of the concept nevertheless is
small when compared to the analytical confusion the concept causes in the
minds of those attempting to apply the hearsay rule. Such confusion strongly
suggests rejection of the concept. Moreover, many statements potentially

falling within the category of statements offered for a different inference are admissible as a hearsay exception for then-existing state of mind, Rule 803(3). Thus, whenever the state of mind of the declarant is itself a fact of consequence in the litigation, discussion of whether the statement is hearsay is of no practical importance. However, where the inferred state of mind of the declarant is not an issue, but is itself used to infer the truth of a non-asserted fact, such as the competency of another in Wright v. Doe d. Tatham, the state of mind exception is not available. In such circumstances, if the statement possesses sufficient guarantees of trustworthiness, and is necessary in the context of the litigation, the statement may nevertheless be admissible under the residual hearsay exception of Rule 807.

The three letters in *Tatham* illustrate statements offered not for the truth of the matter asserted, but as a basis for drawing a nonasserted inference. The hearsay nature of such statements formed the basis of the foregoing discussion. Notice that not all statements offered in evidence for a further inference fall within the breadth of the concept of a statement offered as a basis for drawing a nonasserted inference. In the situation under discussion, the initial inference as to the state of mind of the declarant is inferred from the statement, not asserted by it. When the state of mind is directly asserted, the statement is clearly hearsay. Thus if Rev. Ellershaw had written Marsden's attorney stating that he believed Marsden possessed testamentary capacity, the letter would clearly be hearsay. Similarly, when the declarant also necessarily intended to assert, although he did not directly assert, the inference for which the statement is offered, the statement is hearsay. Matters that are implicitly being asserted are for hearsay analysis purposes tantamount to a direct assertion. Obviously, when the declarant also intends to assert the matter the statement is used to infer, the argument of a reduced risk of sincerity is a non sequitur. The closer the inference to be drawn is to the matter expressly asserted, the more likely the declarant intended to assert the inference the statement is offered to prove. Finally, the concept of a statement offered to infer something other than the truth of the matter asserted can be asserted by its supporters, albeit incorrectly, to apply solely to those situations where the actual statement of the declarant is used to infer the truth of an "implied assertion" being made by the declarant and not to inferences derived directly from assuming the truth of the matter actually asserted. Thus nothing in the nonasserted inference doctrine supports the notion, for example, that an out of court statement by a witness that a car was going 80 miles per hour five blocks from the site of the accident is not hearsay because the fact asserted is being used to infer speed at the time of the accident, a fact not itself being asserted.

4.   Interpreting the Definition of Hearsay

Courts and commentators have struggled with the definitional aspects of hearsay under the cloud that given the pigeonhole theory of class exceptions to the hearsay rule, many trustworthy and necessary statements if classified as hearsay would be excluded at trial. Attempts to expand admissibility through novel interpretations of the definition of hearsay naturally resulted. Such novel interpretations have taken the form, for example, of arguing that "I believe I am King Henry the Eighth" and statements offered to infer something other than the truth of the matter asserted are not hearsay. While novel, such interpretations are neither correct interpretations of the definition of hearsay nor do they comport with the analysis of risks the hearsay rule attempts to address. Such novel interpretations have at the same time greatly confused not only many practitioners and courts but thousands of law students each year. Whatever value these novel interpretations once had is no longer true today. With the availability of the residual hearsay exception of Rule 807, trustworthy and necessary hearsay will no longer be inadmissible simply because it fails to fit neatly into one of the pigeonhole hearsay exceptions.

It is therefore suggested that clarity would be fostered and confusion eliminated if once and for all the courts would declare that Rules 801(a)–(c) include (1) a statement to the extent relevant only if the declarant believes the matter asserted to be true, whether that statement be "I am Napoleon" or "I believe I am King Henry the Eighth" and (2) a statement whose relevance depends upon the matter asserted being true without reference to whether a further inference is then going to be drawn. Both of these novel approaches are in fact now recognized as hearsay by the text of Rules 801(a)–(c); any contrary suggestion in the Advisory Committee's Note with respect to statements forming the basis for a nonasserted inference is incorrect. What is needed is explicit court recognition thus putting the issue to rest. An alternative formulation of Rule 801(c), identical in content while highlighting the hearsay nature of statements offered as a basis for a nonasserted inference and all statements of state of mind, is as follows:

(c) Hearsay

> "Hearsay" is a statement offered in evidence, other than one made by the declarant while testifying at the trial or hearing, to the extent relevance depends upon (1) the truth of the matter asserted or (2) the declarant's belief in the truth or falsity of the matter asserted.

B.   PRIOR STATEMENT BY WITNESS

When the out-of-court declarant is also an in-court witness, the witness' prior statements, whether consistent or inconsistent with the witness' in court testimony, or constituting a prior statement of identification, can be explored on direct and redirect examination or cross-examination of the witness to the same extent as the witness's in court testimony on personal knowledge of the matters stated in such out-of-court statements. The witness is under oath throughout with his or her demeanor being observed throughout. Thus the truth assessing components of the ordinary system of oath, demeanor and cross-examination are satisfied wherever at the current trial or hearing the out-of-court declarant "testifies and is subject to cross-examination about a statement."

> "Considerable controversy has attended the question whether a prior out-of-court statement by a person now available for cross-examination concerning it, under oath and in the presence of the trier of fact, should be classed as hearsay. If the witness admits on the stand that he made the statement and that it was true, he adopts the statement and there is no hearsay problem. The hearsay problem

arises when the witness on the stand denies having made the statement or admits having made it but denies its truth. The argument in favor of treating these latter statements as hearsay is based upon the ground that the conditions of oath, cross-examination, and demeanor observation did not prevail at the time the statement was made and cannot adequately be supplied by the later examination. The logic of the situation is troublesome. So far as concerns the oath, its mere presence has never been regarded as sufficient to remove a statement from the hearsay category, and it receives much less emphasis than cross-examination as a truth-compelling device. While strong expressions are found to the effect that no conviction can be had or important right taken away on the basis of statements not made under fear of prosecution for perjury, Bridges v. Wixon, 326 U.S. 135, 65 S.Ct. 1443, 89 L.Ed. 2103 (1945), the fact is that, of the many common law exceptions to the hearsay rule, only that for reported testimony has required the statement to have been made under oath. [It should be noted, however, that Rule 801(d)(1)(A), as enacted by the Congress, requires that a prior inconsistent statement have been made under oath.] Nor is it satisfactorily explained why cross-examination cannot be conducted subsequently with success. The decisions contending most vigorously for its inadequacy in fact demonstrate quite thorough exploration of the weaknesses and doubts attending the earlier statement. State v. Saporen, 205 Minn. 358, 285 N.W. 898 (1939); Ruhala v. Roby, 379 Mich. 102, 150 N.W.2d 146 (1967); People v. Johnson, 68 Cal.2d 646, 68 Cal.Rptr. 599, 441 P.2d 111 (1968). In respect to demeanor, as Judge Learned Hand observed in Di Carlo v. United States, 6 F.2d 364 (2d Cir.1925), when the jury decides that the truth is not what the witness says now, but what he said before, they are still deciding from what they see and hear in court. The bulk of the case law nevertheless has been against allowing prior statements of witnesses to be used generally as substantive evidence. Most of the writers and Uniform Rule 63(1) have taken the opposite position." Advisory Committee's Note to Rule 801.

However not all prior statements of the in-court witness are defined as not hearsay by Rule 801(d)(1).

"The position taken by the Advisory Committee in formulating this part of the rule is founded upon an unwillingness to countenance the general use of prior prepared statements as substantive evidence, but with a recognition that particular circumstances call for a contrary result. The judgment is one more of experience than of logic. The rule requires in each instance, as a general safeguard, that the declarant actually testify as a witness, and it then enumerates three situations in which the statement is excepted from the category of hearsay. Compare Uniform Rule 63(1) which allows any out-of-court statement of a declarant who is present at the trial and available for cross-examination." Advisory Committee's Note to Rule 801(d)(1).

Consideration of trial concerns underlying Rule 403, i.e., the danger of unfair prejudice, confusion of the issues, misleading the jury, undue delay, waste of time and the needless presentation of cumulative evidence, result in only some prior inconsistent statements, Rule 801(d)(1)(A), and some prior consistent statements, Rule 801(d)(1)(B), being defined as not hearsay. On the other hand, as interpreted, all prior statements of identification of a person made after perceiving the person again, Rule 801(d)(1)(C), are defined as not hearsay.

A witness who testifies to a lack of recollection is nevertheless "subject to cross-examination" for purposes of Rule 801(d)(1).

1. Prior Inconsistent Statements—Rule 801(d)(1)(A)—Definitions

(d) Statements That Are Not Hearsay. A statement that meets the following conditions is not hearsay:

> **(1) A Declarant-Witness's Prior Statement.** The declarant testifies and is subject to cross-examination about a prior statement, and the statement:

>> **(A)** is inconsistent with the declarant's testimony and was given under penalty of perjury at a trial, hearing, or other proceeding or in a deposition;

* * *

At common law a witness could be impeached on a non-collateral matter by extrinsic proof that he made a statement out of court inconsistent with his in court testimony. The prior statement had to be inconsistent, and a proper foundation had to be laid during cross-examination of the witness. The inconsistent statement was hearsay and hence was not admitted as substantive evidence but rather was limited solely to its impeaching effect upon the credibility of the witness. Of course, prior inconsistent statements of a witness are not to be confused with an admission of a party-opponent, which has always been and continues to be regarded as substantive evidence, Rule 801(d)(2), requiring no preliminary foundation on cross-examination, Rule 613(b).

Rule 801(d)(1)(A) alters the common law to the limited extent of exempting from the bar of the rule against hearsay, Rule 802, through definition as not hearsay a prior statement of a declarant who testifies at trial and is subject to cross-examination concerning the statement, if the statement is inconsistent with his testimony, and was given under oath, subject to the penalty of perjury at a trial, hearing, or other proceeding, or in a deposition. Thus those prior inconsistent statements made under oath at formal proceedings are now substantively admissible. Grand jury testimony is included within the concept of "other proceeding," as are statements under oath at the witness's plea hearing. However, statements, whether oral or written, even if given under oath and videotaped, made to law enforcement officials fall outside the concept of "other proceedings." The foundation requirement of Rule 613 applies to prior inconsistent statements admitted as substantive evidence solely under Rule 801(d)(1)(A). The rationale behind the limited departure from the common law represented by Rule 801(d)(1)(A) is that expressed by the House Committee on the Judiciary that (1) unlike most other situations involving unsworn or oral statements, including for example oral statements by occurrence witnesses to a crime, there can be no dispute as to whether the prior statement was made, and (2) the context of a formal proceeding and an oath provide firm additional assurances of the reliability of the prior statement.

Critics of the common law prohibition against substantive use of a prior inconsistent statement have long contended that the declarant at trial is under oath, his demeanor may be observed, his credibility tested by cross-examination and that the timing of cross-examination is not critical. Rule 801(d)(1)(A) accepts the arguments of such critics only to the extent that the non-contemporaneous cross-examination relates to a prior inconsistent statement made under oath at a formal proceeding; substantive admissibility is allowed only for those statements possessing the highest degree of certainty of making made under circumstances conducive to truth telling.

Of course prior inconsistent statements not falling within the scope of Rule 801(d)(1)(A) may still be employed for the limited purpose of impeachment in accordance with Rules 607 and 613.

As the Advisory Committee's Note states, "If the witness admits on the stand that he made the statement and that it was true, he adopts the statement and there is no hearsay problem. The hearsay problem arises when the witness on the stand denies having made the statement or admits having made it but denies its truth."

2.   Prior Consistent Statements—Rule 801(d)(1)(B)—Definitions

The following definitions apply under this article:

(d) Statements That Are Not Hearsay. A statement that meets the following conditions is not hearsay:

> **(1) A Declarant-Witness's Prior Statement.** The declarant testifies and is subject to cross-examination about a prior statement, and the statement:

* * *

> > **(B)** is consistent with the declarant's testimony and is offered:
> >
> > > **(i)** to rebut an express or implied charge that the declarant recently fabricated it or acted from a recent improper influence or motive in so testifying; or
> > >
> > > **(ii)** to rehabilitate the declarant's credibility as a witness when attacked on another ground; or

* * *

Generally speaking, a witness cannot be corroborated on direct or redirect examination or rebuttal by proof of prior statements consistent with his in court testimony. Whatever inherent probative value such consistent statements may have is felt to be insufficient when viewed in light of trial concerns, Rule 403.

> "When the witness has merely testified on direct examination, without any impeachment, proof of consistent statements is unnecessary and valueless. The witness is not helped by it; for, even if it is an improbable or untrustworthy story, it is not made more probable or more trustworthy by any number of repetitions of it." 4 Wigmore, Evidence § 1124 at 255 (Chadbourn rev. 1972).

> "The introduction of a prior consistent statement on direct examination of a witness would often lead to cross-examination relating to circumstances surrounding the alleged making as well as possibly the calling of witnesses to support or deny the making of the statement. In short, one might have a mini-trial on the issue of whether the prior consistent statement was made and the circumstances surrounding its making." Graham, "Prior Consistent Statement: Rule 801(d)(1)(B) of the Federal Rules of Evidence, Critique and Proposal," 30 Hast.L.J. 575, 581 n.22 (1979).

> "The salutary nature and the necessity of such a rule are clearly apparent upon reflection in cases like the present, for without that rule a witness's testimony could be blown up out of all proportion to its true probative force by telling the same story out of court before a group of reputable citizens, who would then parade onto the witness stand and repeat the statement time and again until the jury might easily forget that the truth of the statement was not backed by those citizens but was solely founded upon the integrity of the said witness. This danger would seem to us to be especially acute in a criminal case ... when the ... previous out-of-court statement is repeated before the jury by ... law enforcement officers." Allison v. State, 162 So.2d 922, 924 (Fla. 1 DCA 1964).

However, under certain circumstances the probative value of a prior consistent statement clearly warrants introduction.

Rule 801(d)(1)(B)(i) provides that a prior consistent statement of a declarant testifying at trial and subject to cross-examination concerning the statement is admissible when offered "to rebut on express or implied charge that the declarant recently fabricated it or acted from a recent improper influence or motive in so testifying." Thus to rebut an express or implied charge that the witness is motivated or has been influenced to testify falsely or that his testimony is a recent fabrication, evidence is admissible that he told the same story *before* the motive or influence came into existence or before the time of the alleged recent fabrication.

> "A consistent statement, at a *time prior* to the existence of a fact said to indicate bias, interest, or corruption, will effectively explain away the force of the impeaching evidence; because it is thus made to appear that the statement in the form now uttered was independent of the discrediting influence." 4 Wigmore, Evidence § 1129 at 268 (Chadbourn rev. 1972) (emphasis in original).

The prior consistent statement is exempt from the bar of the rule against hearsay, Rule 802, through definition as not hearsay, Rule 801(d)(1)(B)(i), and thus is admitted as substantive evidence.

To illustrate, assume that John, while standing on the sidewalk, witnessed an automobile accident involving a car driven by Mary and a truck driven by Bill. The factual issue in dispute is the color of the traffic light at the intersection facing both parties. At trial, John testifies that the light facing Mary was green. On cross-examination, Bill's attorney brings out that four weeks after the accident John met Mary for the first time at her lawyer's office, that they dated thereafter, and that they are now engaged to be married. On redirect examination, John may testify that one day after the accident, and thus *before* the alleged improper influence or motive arose, he told his best friend Tim that the light facing the car driven by the woman was green. However, John may not testify that two weeks after John and Mary were engaged he told his mother that the light facing Mary was green.

Where admissible, the prior consistent statement may be testified to by either the witness himself or any other person with personal knowledge of the statement. Rule 801(d)(1)(B)(i) does require that the declarant testify at the trial and that he be subject to cross-examination concerning the prior statement, a requirement that is satisfied so long as the declarant is available to be recalled.

Rule 801(d)(1)(B)(ii). A prior consistent statement of the witness may be admitted without reference to Rule 801(d)(1)(B)(i), when relevant to rehabilitation in a manner other than refutation encompassed in Rule 801(d)(1)(B)(i), such as when the prior inconsistent statement serves to explain or modify a fragment thereof introduced by the opposite party for purposes of impeachment, or if it is otherwise related to or supportive of a denial or explanation offered in response to impeachment of a witness by an alleged self-contradiction, whether an inconsistent statement or a failure to speak when natural to do so, Rule 613, or to rebut a charge of faulty memory, Rule 801 (d)(1)(B)(ii).

> "A witness, Riley, testified that he participated in a bank robbery with the defendants. On cross-examination, Riley was impeached by a prior inconsistent statement he admitted having made in which he stated that he had perpetrated the robbery alone. Shortly after the inconsistent statement, however, Riley had made another statement consistent with his trial testimony. The witness explained that at the time of the inconsistent statement he shared a jail cell with the defendant and that he could not safely make the inculpating consistent statement until he was released from the cell. In admitting the consistent statement, the court stated: "[W]e think that in the situation where a key witness admittedly changes his story or his recital of important relevant events and admits that his former statements in regard to the proceedings in question were a fabrication, that he should be allowed to not only testify as to the reasons for his fabrication and the reasons why he decided to change his story; and all of the incidents and factors that shed light upon his

credibility, both pro and con, are admitted, subject to the Court's discretion, and left to the jury for its evaluation and determination. Naturally, a person who has made admittedly inconsistent statements stands impeached, but the court and the jury are still charged with the responsibility of ascertaining which evidence is to be credited and only by a full exposure of the relevant and pertinent facts in this difficult situation can the jury make an intelligent and reasonable attempt to ascertain the truth. In the case at bar there is no dispute about Riley's making either the consistent or the inconsistent statements. It is not a swearing match as to what was said, but presents the crucial issue of which statements constitute a correct recital of the events under consideration. In this posture, relevant evidence, particularly evidence which is subject to cross-examination, should in the discretion of the trial court be submitted to the jury for its evaluation." Hanger v. United States, 398 F.2d 91, 105 (8th Cir.1968).

With the 2013 amendment to Rule 801(d)(1), pursuant to Rule 801(d)(1)(B)(ii) which provides for the admissibility of prior consistent statements "to rehabilitate the declarant's credibility as a witness when attacked on another ground", i.e., one not encompassed in Rule 801(d)(1)(B)(i), such prior consistent statements are now admitted as substantive evidence in addition to rehabilitating the witness.

3. Prior Identification of a Person After Perceiving Him—Rule 801(d)(1)(C)—Definitions

(d) Statements That Are Not Hearsay. A statement that meets the following conditions is not hearsay:

(1) A Declarant-Witness's Prior Statement. The declarant testifies and is subject to cross-examination about a prior statement, and the statement:

* * *

(C) identifies a person as someone the declarant perceived earlier.

* * *

When a witness testifies and is subject to cross-examination, his prior statement identifying a person made after perceiving the person again earlier after an event, usually at a lineup, a one on one viewing often called a show-up, in a photograph or a sketch, or at a prior hearing, is exempt from the bar of the rule against hearsay, Rule 802, through definition as not hearsay, Rule 801(d)(1)(C). There is no requirement that the witness first be impeached. The theory is that courtroom identification is so unconvincing as practically to impeach itself thus justifying the corroboration. The purpose of the rule is to permit the introduction of more meaningful identifications made by a witness when memory was fresher and there had been less opportunity for influence to be exerted upon him.

> "[T]he earlier identification has greater probative value than an identification made in the courtroom after the suggestions of others and the circumstances of the trial may have intervened to create a fancied recognition in the witness' mind." Gilbert v. California, 388 U.S. 263, 273 n. 3, 87 S.Ct. 1951, 18 L.Ed.2d 1178 (1967).

> "We agree with the observation there made that 'Congress has recognized, as do most trial judges, that identification in the courtroom is a formality that offers little in the way of reliability and much in the way of suggestibility.'" quoting 4 Weinstein's Evidence ¶ 801 (d)(1)(C)[01] at 801–803. United States v. Lewis, 565 F.2d 1248, 1251 (2d Cir.1977).

The circumstances of the prior identification may, of course, be considered by the trier of fact in determining the weight to be accorded.

Rule 801(d)(1)(C) requires by its terms only that the person who made the identification testify at the trial or hearing and be subject to cross-examination. It seems reasonable to assume that the rule also contemplates that the declarant will testify in court on the subject of identification and not simply be available to be recalled to the stand by the defendant for cross-examination. The rule does not limit testimony as to the statement of identification made after perception solely to that of the identifying witness; testimony of any person who was present, for example a police officer, is also admissible. Of course overproof may unduly emphasize the prior identification to the extent of misleading the jury and consequently is subject to the court's discretionary control under Rule 403.

Rule 801(d)(1)(C) does not require on its face, nor has a requirement been imposed, that the identifying witness make a positive in court identification or identify the defendant in court at all. Similarly nothing in the text of the rule prohibits introduction of the out of court statement identifying the defendant made by a declarant who in court denies making or repudiates the identification and denies that the defendant is the person involved in the crime. Moreover while it can be argued that a witness who lacks recollection as to the identity of the individual, whether such lack of recollection is real or feigned, is not "subject to cross-examination concerning the statement" as provided in Rule 801(d)(1), legislative history indicates substantial support for applicability of Rule 801(d)(1)(C) in this context.

> "We are into the subject matter, and to highlight what I think the facts are. We have a robbery or a burglary, or some crime committed, and they are trying to decide who did it. They bring the victim down to the police station, and they put several people across the line-up, and the victim says, 'That is the guy who did it. That is the one.'

> So then they proceed on the basis of this, and when they get to trial, they call the same fellow who made positive identification within a week of the offenses and ask him, 'Is this the man? Is this the defendant?'

'Oh, I don't know. I don't know. I don't recognize him.'

What is suggested here is that in the field of organized crime—and in some of the even more unorganized crime—there are people of a more vicious nature who suggest to these witnesses that if they would ever like to see their children or their wives again, they had better not recognize this fellow. Or there may be financial reward.

The feeling of those who press for the law the way it came to the House and the way it would be now written is that this is protection for the public against the changing testimony of witnesses," Statement of Rep. Hungate on floor of House of Representatives reported in 4 Weinstein's Evidence 801–9–801–10 (1984).

Moreover the mere fact of lack of recollection itself impeaches the probative force of the prior statement of identification thus producing a greater effect on credibility than usually attained through cross-examination. Judicial opinion is in accord.

"It seems to us that the more natural reading of 'subject to cross-examination concerning the statement' includes what was available here. Ordinarily a witness is regarded as 'subject to cross-examination' when he is placed on the stand, under oath, and responds willingly to questions. Just as with the constitutional prohibition, limitations on the scope of examination by the trial court or assertions of privilege by the witness may undermine the process to such a degree that meaningful cross-examination within the intent of the rule no longer exists. But that effect is not produced by the witness's assertion of memory loss—which * * * is often the very result sought to be produced by cross-examination, and can be effective in destroying the force of the prior statement. Rule 801(d)(1)(C), which specifies that the cross-examination need only 'concer[n] the statement' does not on its face require more." United States v. Owens, 484 U.S. 554, 561, 108 S.Ct. 838, 98 L.Ed.2d 951 (1988).

In short, the text, the legislative history, as well as judicial opinion interpreting Rule 801(d)(1)(C) place no restrictions upon admissibility other than having the alleged out of court declarant in court on the witness stand subject to cross-examination concerning the statement.

C. ADMISSION BY PARTY—OPPONENT

1. An Overview

An opposing party's statement, whether an oral or written assertion, or nonverbal conduct offered in evidence by an adverse party to prove the truth of the matter asserted, falls within the definition of hearsay at common law and in Rules 801(a)–(c). Nevertheless, it has been universally accepted since the advent of the rule against hearsay that such a statement of an opposing party, referred to as an admission by a party-opponent, is admissible as substantive evidence to prove the truth of the matter asserted. While formerly considered an exception to the hearsay rule, in recognition of its position in the adversary system, Rule 801(d)(2) exempts admissions of a party-opponent from the operation of the rule against hearsay, Rule 802, by defining admissions of a party-opponent as "not hearsay".

> "Admissions by a party-opponent are excluded from the category of hearsay on the theory that their admissibility in evidence is the result of the adversary system rather than satisfaction of the conditions of the hearsay rule. Strahorn, A Reconsideration of the Hearsay Rule and Admissions, 83 U.Pa.L.Rev. 484, 564 (1937); Morgan, Basic Problems of Evidence 265 (1962); 4 Wigmore § 1048. No guarantee of trustworthiness is required in the case of an admission. The freedom which admissions have enjoyed from technical demands of searching for an assurance of trustworthiness in some against-interest circumstance, and from the restrictive influences of the opinion rule and the rule requiring firsthand knowledge, when taken with the apparently prevalent satisfaction with the results, calls for generous treatment of this avenue to admissibility." Advisory Committee's Note to Rule 801(d)(2).

Lack of opportunity to cross-examine is deprived of significance by the incongruity of the party objecting to his own statement on the ground that he was not subject to cross-examination by himself at the time.

> "If we define hearsay as an extra-judicial statement offered as tending to prove the truth of the matter stated, an admission clearly falls within it, and the most commentators so regard it. It must be conceded that the rule which makes admissions receivable is older than the hearsay rule and is a necessary concomitant of the accepted doctrine that evidence of any relevant conduct of a party is admissible against him, unless the subject of a claim of privilege. * * * Whatever may be true as to personal conduct of a party, there is no escape from the conclusion that a vicarious admission has all the essential characteristics of hearsay. For the practitioner the all-important fact is that evidence of an assertive admission is receivable for the truth of the matter asserted.

> The admissibility of an admission made by the party himself rests not upon any notion that the circumstances in which it was made furnish the trier means of evaluating it fairly, but upon the adversary theory of litigation. A party can hardly object that he had no opportunity to cross-examine himself or that he is unworthy of credence save when speaking under sanction of an oath. His adversary may use against him anything which he has said or done." Morgan, Basic Problems of Evidence 265–66 (1961).

In the nature of things, the statement is usually damaging to the party against whom offered, else it would not be offered. However neither Rule 801(d)(2) nor the common law cases lay down a requirement that the statement be against interest either when made or when offered, and the theory of the exception is not based thereon. The sometimes encountered label "admission against interest," is inaccurate, serves only to confuse, and should be abandoned.

Admissions are substantive evidence, as contrasted with mere impeaching statements, and no preliminary foundation need be laid by examining the declarant concerning the admission, Rule 613(b). Personal knowledge of the matter admitted is not required; nor is a requirement of mental capacity imposed. Admissions in the form of an opinion are competent, even if the opinion is a conclusion of law. The opinion rule, designed to elicit more concrete and informative answers, is a rule of preference as to the form of testimony. Since out-of-court statements are not made under circumstances in which alternative forms of expressions may be secured, this aspect of the opinion rule is inapplicable. Admissibility does not depend upon whether the declarant is unavailable, available, or actually testifies. Whether the specific requirements set forth in Rule 801(d)(2) not involving conditional relevancy, Rule 104(b), have been satisfied, such as whether a person is authorized to make a statement, Rule 801(d)(2)(C), or whether a statement concerns a matter within the scope of his agency or employment, Rule 801(d)(2)(D), are determined by the court, Rule 104(a). Admissions of a party-opponent may be excluded upon application of Rule 103.

2. Statements of Party Made in Individual or Representative Capacity, Rule 801(d)(2)(A)

* * *

(d) Statements That Are Not Hearsay. A statement that meets the following conditions is not hearsay:

* * *

(2) An Opposing Party's Statement. The statement is offered against an opposing party and:

* * *

(A) was made by the party in an individual or representative capacity;

(a) Individual Capacity; An Overview

A party's own statement made in his individual capacity when offered by an opposing party is defined as not hearsay, Rule 801(d)(2)(A).

As with all admissions by a party-opponent, no requirement of mental capacity of the declarant is imposed; the statement need not relate to a matter as to which the party had personal knowledge; it need not be against interest when made or when offered; it may contain opinions or conclusions of law; and it may be offered whether or not the party is unavailable, available, or actually testifies. If the party does testify, no foundation need be laid preliminary to its introduction in evidence, Rule 613(b).

(b) Plea of Guilty

The introduction into evidence of a guilty plea not later withdrawn, differs in theory though perhaps not in result from the introduction of a judgment resulting from it. The judgment may constitute a hearsay exception under Rule

803(22) when offered to prove any fact essential to sustain the judgment. The plea of guilty is offered not to prove that essential facts have been previously found to exist but rather to prove that the offender admitted facts constituting guilt. Thus a plea of guilty may be admissible as an admission of a party under Rule 801(d)(2)(A) or as a statement against interest of a non-party under Rule 804(b)(3).

Where evidence of a conviction on a plea of guilty is being offered against a party, the effect of proceeding pursuant to either Rule 803(22) or Rule 801(d)(2)(A) is identical. In both instances the facts admitted by the party by entering a plea of guilty, i.e., facts essential to sustain the conviction, may be admitted against him by a party-opponent as an evidentiary as distinguished from a judicial admission. The party's reason, if any, for pleading guilty may thus also be introduced.

A question is raised whether a plea of guilty may be introduced as either an admission of a party-opponent, Rule 801(d)(2)(A), or statement against interest, Rule 804(b)(3), in situations in which the judgment of conviction, Rule 803(22), could not be shown because the crime was not punishable by imprisonment in excess of one year. The question is not specifically addressed in either Rule 801(d)(2)(A) or Rule 804(b)(3). Similarly, neither Rule 803(22) nor its Advisory Committee's Note contains a specific reference to the admissibility of a guilty plea to an offense punishable by imprisonment for no more than one year. However the rationale expressed by the Advisory Committee in excluding convictions for crimes punishable by imprisonment for no more than one year from the operation of Rule 803(22) is extremely telling:

> Practical considerations require exclusion of convictions of minor offenses, not because the administration of justice in its lower echelons must be inferior, but because motivation to defend at this level is often minimal or nonexistent.

The rationale for excluding a prior conviction after trial for a minor offense applies with even greater force to a guilty plea entered to a minor offense. Accordingly, a plea of guilty to an offense punishable by imprisonment for no more than one year should be declared to fall outside the breadth of both Rules 801(d)(2)(A) and 804(b)(3).

> "In this type of case, particularly if a traffic violation is concerned, the accused typically pleads guilty, often without consulting counsel, 'as a matter of course or convenience.' 'The sensible citizen, even when in the right, pays his fine and goes about his business.' In order to effectuate the express policy of Rule 803(22) barring evidence of convictions punishable by imprisonment for less than one year, evidence of guilty pleas in non-felony cases should not be allowed as admissions under Rule 801(d)(2), or as statements against interest pursuant to Rule 804(b)(3)." 4 Weinstein's Evidence ¶ 803(22)(01) at 803–408 (1994).

Nevertheless, a majority of decisions admit the guilty plea under such circumstances with explanation.

(c) Statements of Party Made in a Representative Capacity

Rule 801(d)(2)(A) provides that if an individual has a representative capacity such as an administrator, executor, trustee, or guardian and the statement is offered against him in that capacity, the statement is admissible without reference to whether the individual was acting in a representative capacity in making the statement; all that is required is that the statement be relevant to representative affairs.

> "For purposes of Rule 801(d)(2)(A), it matters not whether a statement was made in the declarant's 'individual' or his 'representative' capacity. Thus where an executor, administrator, trustee, or guardian either sues or is sued, his own statement qualifies as an admission within the meaning of the Rule regardless whether made in his 'official' or his individual capacity, and inquiry into the surrounding circumstances is irrelevant for purposes of deciding the admissibility in question. The rationale appears to be that admissions are not received because trustworthy, so that the nature of the statement and the surrounding circumstances should not be important. What is important is the fact that the declarant is present and able to adduce whatever counterproof might exist in order to explain, deny, or refute the statement." 4 Louisell & Mueller, Federal Evidence § 423 at 258 (1980).

(d) Persons in Privity or Jointly Interested

At common law statements by a person in privity with a party were receivable in evidence as an admission of the party.

> "The term 'privity' denotes mutual or successive relationships to the same rights of property, and privies are distributed into several classes, according to the manner of this relationship. Thus, there are privies in estate, as donor and donee, lessor and lessee, and joint tenants; privies in blood, as heir and ancestor, and co-parceners; privies in representation, as executor and testator, administrator and intestate; privies in law, where the law, without privity of blood or estate, casts the land upon another, as by escheat." Metropolitan St. Ry. Co. v. Gumby, 99 F. 192, 198 (2d Cir.1900).

An admission by one jointly interested was also receivable at common law against others similarly interested.

Rule 801(d)(2) alters prior law by omitting any provision declaring either a statement by a person in privity with another or by one of persons jointly interested to be an admission by the other or others. Thus Rule 801(d)(2) in excluding such statements from the definition of admissions adopts the position advocated by Professor Morgan and the Model Code of Evidence that considerations of privity and joint interest neither furnish criteria of credibility nor aid in the evaluation of testimony. Statements formerly treated as a separate category of admission will, however, frequently qualify as representative admissions, Rule 801(d)(2)(C), or as statements against interest, Rule 804(b)(3), or fall within another hearsay exception. Other such statements will meet the requirements of the residual hearsay exception contained in Rule 807.

3. Manifestation of Adoption or Belief in Truth of Statement, Rule 801(d)(2)(B)

* * *

(d) Statements That Are Not Hearsay. A statement that meets the following conditions is not hearsay:

* * *

(2) An Opposing Party's Statement. The statement is offered against an opposing party and:

* * *

(B) is one the party manifested that it adopted or believed to be true;

* * *

Words or conduct. Excluded from the definition of hearsay by Rule 801(d)(2)(B) are statements to which a party has manifested his adoption or belief in their truth. However the party's words or conduct asserted to be a manifestation of assent to the truth of the statement may be susceptible of more than one interpretation. A party is held to have manifested an adoption or belief in the truth of a statement only if it appears that the person understood and demonstrably assented to its truth. Manifestation of adoption or belief in the truth of a statement by a party may be either expressed, such as "Yes, you're right," or implied from the party's reliance upon the contents of statements in related conversation, such as "Bet we won't get as much money from the next convenience store."

Whether a party has manifested his assent to another person's statement is a question of conditional relevancy under Rule 104(b). The burden of proof is on the proponent to show that adoption was intended; a mere statement that another person had made a particular statement is insufficient.

> "The mere fact that the party declares that he had heard that another person had made a given statement is not standing alone sufficient to justify a finding that the party has adopted the third person's statement. The circumstances surrounding the party's declaration must be looked to in order to determine whether the repetition did indicate an approval of the statement." McCormick, Evidence § 269 at 797 (3d ed. 1984).

To illustrate, if the contested matter in a civil action for damages is whether a visiting child tripped over her shoe laces or was pushed down the stairs by defendant homeowner's dog, a statement by the homeowner, after talking to his son, such as "I am very sorry. My son said that my dog jumped on your little girl," would be an admission. On the other hand, the statement "My son said that he thinks my dog jumped on your little girl," does not indicate approval of the reported assertion, and is thus not an admission. The statement of the homeowner is merely the reporting of another's assertion; it is not a manifestation of adoption or belief in the truth of its content.

Silence. Manifestation of belief in the truth of a statement may occur by silence, that is, a failure to respond when natural to do so.

> "[T]he courts have evolved a variety of safeguarding requirements against misuse, of which the following are illustrative. (1) The statement must have been heard by the party claimed to have acquiesced. (2) It must have been understood by him. (3) The subject matter must have been within his knowledge. At first glance, this requirement may appear inconsistent with the general dispensation with firsthand knowledge with respect to admissions, yet the unreasonableness of expecting a person to deny a matter of which he is not aware seems evident; he simply does not have the incentive or the wherewithal to embark upon a dispute. (4) Physical or emotional impediments to responding must not be present. (5) The personal makeup of the speaker, e.g., young child, or his relationship to the party or the event, e.g., bystander, may be such as to make it unreasonable to expect a denial. (6) Probably most important of all, the statement itself must be such as would, if untrue, call for a denial under the circumstances. The list is not an exclusive one, and other factors will suggest themselves. The essential inquiry in each case is whether a reasonable person would have denied under the circumstances, with answers not lending themselves readily to mechanical formulation." McCormick, Evidence § 270 at 800–01 (3rd ed. 1984).

If an oral or written statement is communicated by another person to a party in the litigation containing assertions of fact which if untrue the party would under all the circumstances naturally be expected to deny, his failure to speak is receivable against him in a civil case as an adoptive admission, Rule 801(d)(2)(B). With respect to a letter, while it is frequently stated that the general rule, subject to exception, is that failure to answer may not be introduced as an admission, the more acceptable view is that failure to reply to a letter containing statements which under all the circumstances one would expect the receiver to deny if felt untrue may be introduced in evidence as an admission by silence.

Silence under circumstances naturally calling for a denial has also been recognized as an admission in criminal cases. Evidence must be introduced sufficient to support a finding, Rule 104(b), that in light of the totality of the circumstances, a statement was made which the defendant heard, understood, had an opportunity to deny or object and in which the defendant by his silence acquiesced. Mere possession of a document standing alone does not constitute a manifestation of adoption or belief in its truth. In addition the court must pursuant to Rule 104(a) determine that it is more probably true than not true that the statement was such that under the circumstances it would naturally be expected that an innocent person would deny in some form the truth of the statement if he believed it to be untrue.

Various considerations, however, raise doubts as to the propriety of applying the rule in criminal cases when an accusation to the defendant is made under the auspices of law enforcement personnel. In addition to the inherently ambiguous nature of the inference itself, silence on the part of the defendant may be motivated by prior experience or prior advice of counsel. Treating silence as an admission also affords unusual opportunity to manufacture evidence. Moreover the accused would effectively be compelled to speak, either at the time or upon the trial by way of explaining his reasons for remaining silent, which, to say the least, crowds his privilege against self-incrimination uncomfortably. Nevertheless, silence of a witness, including the criminal defendant, that occurs post-arrest but prior to the actual giving of *Miranda* warnings has been held admissible to impeach. Whether prearrest silence may constitutionally be admitted as substantive evidence is unclear. Obviously once the *Miranda* warnings have been given advising the defendant of his right to remain silent, the defendant's failure to speak may no longer possibly be considered an admission, nor may his silence be employed for purposes of impeachment.

4. Vicarious Admissions, Rules 801(d)(2)(C) and (D)

* * *

(d) Statements That Are Not Hearsay. A statement that meets the following conditions is not hearsay:

* * *

(2) An Opposing Party's Statement. The statement is offered against an opposing party and:

* * *

(C) was made by a person whom the party authorized to make a statement on the subject;

(D) was made by the party's agent or employee on a matter within the scope of that relationship and while it existed; or concerning a matter within the scope of the agency or employment, made during the existence of the relationship, or. . . . The contents of the statement shall be considered but are not alone sufficient to establish the declarant's authority under subdivision (C), the agency or employment relationship and scope thereof under subdivision (D), or the existence of the conspiracy and the participation therein of the declarant and the party against whom the statement is offered under subdivision (E).

(a) Statement by Person Authorized to Speak—Rule 801(d)(2)(C)

Statements by a person authorized by a party to make a statement concerning the subject matter, such as the president of a corporation, the managing partner of a partnership, an attorney hired to represent the client before the I.R.S., or the sales manager of an automotive dealership, are admissions, Rule

801(d)(2)(C). The authority of the agent to speak as to a subject, which may be express or implied, must be established at trial.

As a matter of substantive agency law, neither the fact of authorization nor the scope of the subject matter of authority may be established by the agent's out of court statements. Nevertheless, Rule 801(d)(2) now provides that in determining whether a person was authorized at the time by the party to make a statement concerning the subject, the contents of the statement is to be considered but is not alone sufficient to establish the declarant's authority. Authorization to make a statement concerning the subject matter may, of course, be established by the acts or conduct of the principal or his statements to the agent or a third party.

Along with statements to other persons, statements by the authorized person to the principal himself are included in Rule 801(d)(2)(C). Accordingly a party's books or records are usable against him without regard to intent to disclose to third persons.

(b) Statement by Agent or Servant Concerning Matter Within Scope of His Agency or Employment—Rule 801(d)(2)(D)

A statement of an agent or servant concerning a matter within the scope of his employment, made during the existence of the relationship, is an admission of his employer, Rule 801(d)(2)(D). In determining whether an agency or employment relationship existed at the time of the statement and scope of such a relationship, the content of the statement is to be considered but is not alone sufficient.

Prior to Rule 801(d)(2)(D) courts applied the traditional agency test in determining admissibility of statements by agents or servants, i.e., whether the particular statement was authorized by the principal. Courts generally decided that damaging statements were not within the scope of authority, even of relatively high level employees. The obvious difficulty with applying strict agency principles is that agents or servants are very rarely authorized to make damaging statements—the truck driver is hired to drive, not to talk. However, as a result of the fact that it also seemed unreasonable to deny admission to inculpatory statements by the driver about the driving he was hired to do in light of the probable reliability of such statements, courts often stretched to find a basis for admissibility.

In recognition of the reliability and reasonableness of admitting such statements, Rule 801(d)(2)(D) declares statements of an agent or servant concerning a matter within the scope of his agency or employment to be defined as not hearsay if made during the existence of the relationship. Authority to speak is thus no longer of concern; all that is required is that the statement concern a matter within the scope of the agency or employment, and that the agent or servant still be employed at the time of making the statement. A statement meeting the requirement of Rule 801(d)(2)(D) is not made inadmissible simply because the statement was made to the employer and not a third person. However in a criminal prosecution, government employees are apparently not considered agents or servants of a party-opponent for the purpose of the admissions rules.

An attorney may, of course, act as an ordinary agent and as such make evidentiary admissions admissible against his principal, Rules 801(d)(2)(C) and (D). In addition, an attorney has authority in general to make judicial admissions for the client in all matters relating to the progress and trial of an action.

(c) The Requirement of Personal Knowledge

Admissions of a party-opponent are characterized by the Advisory Committee's Note to Rule 801(d)(2) as enjoying freedom from the restrictive influences of the rule requiring personal knowledge. However Weinstein's Evidence makes a strong argument that the rationale supporting elimination of the requirement of personal knowledge generally with respect to admissions fails to withstand analysis with respect to vicarious admissions, Rules 801(d)(2)(C) and (D).

> "Although commentators have suggested that an employee will not make a false statement damaging to his employer, both because he is interested in his employer's welfare and, because he does not wish to jeopardize his job, these reasons, while in part justifying the extension of the doctrine of vicarious admissions do not vindicate the unqualified admission of statements not based on personal knowledge. Such a statement may often consist of no more than gossip or speculation about the matter at issue. The mere fact that the agent heard it and repeated it does not remove any of the dangers against which the hearsay rule has traditionally guarded. * * * The danger is particularly apparent as regards intracompany reports. Certainly, even an employee well-disposed towards his employer may report rumors he had heard, not because of their truth, but because his employer may be interested in the fact that there are rumors. Allowing a report containing rumors not based on personal knowledge to be used indiscriminately against the employer amounts to a wholesale endorsement of the adage, 'where there's smoke, there's fire.' Moreover, it may be doubted, particularly in an era of widespread unionization, whether the theory that an employee would not spread unverified gossip because of fear for his job has much validity. Rather, it would seem a fact of human nature that rumor, unsubstantiated by fact, is at all times prevalent and virulent." 4 Weinstein's Evidence ¶ 801(d)(2)(C) [01] at 801–216–801–217 (1984).

Whatever the merits of the arguments for requiring personal knowledge in connection with any of the foregoing rules, the fact remains that lack of personal knowledge on the part of the declarant does not bar introduction of a statement as an admission of a party-opponent under Rule 801(d)(2). On the other hand, lack of personal knowledge may appropriately be considered in determining whether admissibility should be denied under Rule 403. An alternative resolution is to rest a finding of inadmissibility upon the notion that repetition of "rumor" lies outside the scope of a person's agency or employment, Rule 801(d)(2)(D). When the statement of the employee indicates reliance upon a statement from an unidentified source, most likely another employee, Rule 805 may serve to exclude the statement on the basis of an inadequate foundation that the unidentified person was a person authorized to make a statement concerning the subject, Rule 801(d)(2)(C), or that the person was an employee speaking concerning a matter within the scope of employment. Rule 801(d)(2)(D).

5.   Statements by Coconspirator, Rule 801(d)(2)(E)

* * *

(d) Statements That Are Not Hearsay. A statement that meets the following conditions is not hearsay:

* * *

(2) An Opposing Party's Statement. The statement is offered against an opposing party and:

* * *

(E) was made by the party's coconspirator during and in furtherance of the conspiracy.

A statement of one coconspirator is admissible against the others as an admission of a party-opponent in both civil and criminal cases, if made during the course of and in furtherance of the common objectives of the conspiracy, Rule 801(d)(2)(E).

Historical development. When a statement is offered under Rule 801(d)(2)(E), a foundation must be laid establishing both the conspiracy and defendant's and declarant's participation in the conspiracy. Two questions of interpretation of Rule 801(d)(2)(E) arose. First, whether in establishing the requisite foundation the content of the alleged coconspirator statement may itself be considered. A vast majority of federal decisions required that the foundation must be established solely by independent evidence, i.e., the content of the statement sought to be introduced could not be considered. The independent evidence could consist of the defendant's own statements or the in-court testimony of a coconspirator. The independent evidence could be circumstantial; hearsay evidence could be considered. Second, whether the sufficiency of the foundation with respect to the existence of the conspiracy and defendant's and declarant's participation are questions solely for the court under Rule 104(a), or questions in which both the court and jury participate under Rule 104(b). Several commentators advocated Rule 104(b) treatment. Other commentators supported application of Rule 104(a). Reported federal decisions clearly favored application of Rule 104(a).

Bourjaily v. United States. The Supreme Court in Bourjaily v. United States, 483 U.S. 171, 107 S.Ct. 2775, 97 L.Ed.2d 144 (1987) declared that determining the admissibility of a statement of a coconspirator is solely a matter for the court, Rule 104(a), and that the court in making its determination must apply the more probably true than not true standard of proof. In *Bourjaily*, the court also held as a matter of statutory interpretation that in reaching a determination as to whether there is a conspiracy and that the defendant and the declarant participated in the conspiracy, the content of the coconspirator's statement itself *may* be considered. Whether the existence of the conspiracy and the defendant's and the declarant's participation therein can be established to be more probably true than not true *solely* based upon the content of the coconspirator's statement sought to be admitted was expressly left undecided. A negative answer was provided by the lower federal courts; some independent evidence was required. Rule 801(d)(2)(E) was subsequently amended to codify the holding in *Bourjaily* by stating expressly that a court shall consider the contents of a coconspirator's statement in determining the existence of the conspiracy and the participation therein of the declarant and the party against whom the statement is offered. In addition amended Rule 801(d)(2)(E) now explicitly provides that the contents of the statement "must be considered but does not by itself establish" the existence of the conspiracy and the participation therein of the declarant and the party against whom the statement is offered. The independent evidence may consist of the circumstances surrounding the statement, such as the identity of the speaker, the context in which the statement was made, or evidence corroborating the contents of the statement.

In furtherance. The court must also decide under Rule 104(a) whether the statement was made by the declarant during the course of and in furtherance of the conspiracy. In making this determination it is also proper for the court to consider the content of the statement itself. The court applies the more probably true than not true burden of proof. Only if the court decides both of these issues in favor of the prosecution may the statement be admitted as a statement of a coconspirator, Rule 801(d)(2)(E). In reaching its decisions the court should take into account all relevant evidence, including evidence offered on behalf of the accused.

Statements made during the existence of the conspiracy must be more than casual statements. The statements must actually be in furtherance of the conspiracy. Statements in furtherance of the conspiracy include statements made to induce enlistment, induce further participation, prompt further action, reassure members, allay concerns or fears, keep conspirators abreast of ongoing activities, avoid detection, identify names and roles of conspiracy members while mere conversations or narrative declarations of past events are not in furtherance of the conspiracy.

The statement of the coconspirator in furtherance of the conspiracy is often made outside the defendant's presence. Similarly, it often does not refer to the defendant at all. Thus in a case of bank robbery, a statement by A to B to steal a car may be admissible against C even though C was neither present when the statement was made nor personally involved in stealing the car.

Statements made during the concealment phase fall within the scope of admissibility if in furtherance of the main objectives of the conspiracy, but not otherwise. Kidnappers in hiding waiting for ransom, or repainting a stolen car are illustrations of acts in furtherance of the main criminal objective of a conspiracy. Statements made in furtherance of these objectives are admissible. Statements made by a person after the objectives of the conspiracy have either failed or been achieved, or after the person against whom offered has withdrawn from the conspiracy, are not in furtherance of the conspiracy, and are thus not admissible under Rule 801(d)(2)(E). A conspiracy does not automatically terminate simply because the government, unbeknownst to some of the conspirators, has defeated its object.

Order of proof. With respect to the order of proof, the court has discretion to admit the coconspirator's statement subject to it being connected up later through introduction of sufficient evidence of the existence of the conspiracy and the declarant's or defendant's participation. Whenever it is reasonably practical, however, reported decisions prior to *Bourjaily* stressed that evidence of the conspiracy and the defendant's connection with it (at the time evidence independent of the coconspirator statement) should be admitted prior to the coconspirator's statement. At the conclusion of the presentation of evidence, the trial court on motion must determine on all the evidence including evidence offered by the defendant whether the government has established the requisite foundation to be more probably true than not true. The alternative of a "minihearing" in advance of trial has also been suggested. Either procedure avoids the danger of injecting into the record inadmissible hearsay in anticipation of proof of a conspiracy which never materializes.

The impact of *Bourjaily* on order of proof is substantial. Consideration of the content of the coconspirator's statement in determining its admissibility, even with some undefined and probably undefinable quantum of independent evidence being required, significantly eases the government's burden in many of its more difficult cases, cases very often involving drug trafficking. Assume, for example, that an informant or coconspirator now cooperating with the prosecution testifies that A told him that cocaine was being shipped to X, the defendant, by truck. Such a statement, in context, would strongly support a finding by the court that is more probably true than not true that a conspiracy existed and that A and X were participants in the conspiracy. With respect to the provision in Rule 801(d)(2)(E) that the content of the statement is not alone sufficient, even the slightest additional evidence of X's participation in the conspiracy would cement the court's determination. Given the ease with which the prosecution will be able to satisfy the court as to the admissibility of the coconspirator's statement given that the content of the statement may now be considered, prior concern that the jury not be exposed to the content of the coconspirator's statement lest it ultimately be excluded because of the absence of an adequate evidentiary foundation has all but completely disappeared.

While the crime of conspiracy need not be charged, the crime of conspiracy if charged may be submitted to the jury only if the evidence, including the statement of a coconspirator once admitted, viewed in the light most favorable to the government, could be accepted by a reasonably-minded jury as adequate to support a conclusion that appellant was guilty of conspiracy beyond reasonable doubt.

Jury instructions. In the process of instructing the jury, the court should not refer to its preliminary determination of facts leading to the introduction of the statement of a coconspirator under Rule 801(d)(2)(E).

6.   Judicial and Evidentiary Admissions

Judicial admissions must be distinguished from ordinary evidentiary admissions. A judicial admission is binding upon the party making it; it may not be controverted at trial or on appeal of the same case. Judicial admissions are not evidence at all but rather have the effect of withdrawing a fact from contention. Included within this category are admissions in the pleadings in the case, in motions for summary judgment, admissions in open court, stipulations of fact, and admissions pursuant to requests to admit. Ordinary evidentiary admissions, on the other hand, may be controverted or explained by the party. Within this category fall the pleadings in another case, superseded or withdrawn pleadings in the same case, stipulations as to admissibility, as well as other statements admissible under Rule 801(d)(2).

Occasionally, a party while testifying at trial or during a deposition or in response to an interrogatory admits a fact which is adverse to his claim or defense. A question then arises as to whether such a statement may be treated as a judicial admission binding the party and if so what circumstances must be present to justify such treatment. Of the various approaches followed in answering the question, treating a party's testimony or response to an interrogatory on all occasions as solely an evidentiary admission is preferable.

> "Three main approaches are reflected in the decisions, which to some extent tend to merge and do not necessarily lead to different results in particular situations. First, some courts take the view that a party's testimony in this respect is like the testimony of any other witness called by the party, that is, the party is free (as far as any rule of law is concerned) to elicit contradictory testimony from the same witness or to call other witnesses to contradict the statement. Obviously, however, the problem of persuasion may be a difficult one when the party seeks to explain or contradict his or her own words, and equally obviously, the trial judge would often be justified in ruling on motion for directed verdict that reasonable minds could only believe that the party's testimony against interest was true.
>
> Second, others take the view that the party's testimony is not conclusive against contradiction except when testifying unequivocally to matters in his or her 'peculiar knowledge.' These matters may consist of subjective facts, such as the party's own knowledge or motivation, or they may consist of objective facts observed by the party.
>
> Third, some courts adopt the doctrine that a party's disserving testimony is to be treated as a judicial admission, conclusive on the issue, so that the party may not bring other witnesses to contradict the admission, and if the party or the adversary does elicit such conflicting testimony, it will be disregarded. Obviously, this third rule demands many qualifications and exceptions. Among these are the following: (1) The party is free to contradict, and thus correct, his or her own testimony; only when the party's own testimony taken as a whole unequivocally affirms the statement does the rule of

conclusiveness apply. The rule is inapplicable, moreover, when the party's testimony (2) may be attributable to inadvertence or to a foreigner's mistake as to meaning, (3) is merely negative in effect, (4) is explicitly uncertain or is an estimate or opinion rather than an assertion of concrete fact, or (5) relates to a matter as to which the party could easily have been mistaken, such as the swiftly moving events just preceding a collision in which the party was injured.

Of these three approaches the first seems preferable in policy and most in accord with the tradition of jury trial. It rejects any restrictive rule and leaves the evaluation of the party's testimony and the conflicting evidence to the judgment of the jury, the judge, and the appellate court, with only the standard of reason to guide them." McCormick, Evidence § 258 at 153–55 (4th ed. 1992).

The trial court possesses discretion to relieve a party from the consequences of judicial admission. Fed.R.Civ.Proc. 8(e)(2) permits a pleader who is in doubt as to which of two or more statements of fact is true to plead them alternatively or hypothetically, regardless of consistency. When this is done, an admission in one alternative in the pleadings in the case does not nullify a denial in another alternative as a matter of pleading. Since the purpose of alternative pleadings is to enable a party to meet the uncertainties of proof, policy considerations demand that alternative pleadings not be admitted either as an admission of a party-opponent or for the purpose of impeachment.

Unequivocal admissions made by counsel during the course of trial are judicial admissions binding on his client. The scope of a judicial admission by counsel is restricted to unequivocal statements as to matters of fact which otherwise would require evidentiary proof; it does not extend to counsel's statement of his conception of the legal theory of a case.

———————

APPENDIX B

THE FEDERAL RULES OF EVIDENCE AS RESTYLED AND AMENDED AS OF DECEMBER 1, 2020

ARTICLE I.
GENERAL PROVISIONS

Rule 101.
Scope; Definitions

(a) Scope. These rules apply to proceedings in United States courts. The specific courts and proceedings to which the rules apply, along with exceptions, are set out in Rule 1101.

(b) Definitions. In these rules:

(1) "civil case" means a civil action or proceeding;

(2) "criminal case" includes a criminal proceeding;

(3) "public office" includes a public agency;

(4) "record" includes a memorandum, report, or data compilation;

(5) a "rule prescribed by the Supreme Court" means a rule adopted by the Supreme Court under statutory authority; and

(6) a reference to any kind of written material or any other medium includes electronically stored information.

Rule 102.
Purpose

These rules should be construed so as to administer every proceeding fairly, eliminate unjustifiable expense and delay, and promote the development of evidence law, to the end of ascertaining the truth and securing a just determination.

Rule 103.
Rulings on Evidence

(a) Preserving a Claim of Error. A party may claim error in a ruling to admit or exclude evidence only if the error affects a substantial right of the party and:

(1) if the ruling admits evidence, a party, on the record:

(A) timely objects or moves to strike; and

(B) states the specific ground, unless it was apparent from the context; or

(2) if the ruling excludes evidence, a party informs the court of its substance by an offer of proof, unless the substance was apparent from the context.

(b) Not Needing to Renew an Objection or Offer of Proof. Once the court rules definitively on the record—either before or at trial—a party need not renew an objection or offer of proof to preserve a claim of error for appeal.

(c) Court's Statement About the Ruling; Directing an Offer of Proof. The court may make any statement about the character or form of the evidence, the objection made, and the ruling. The court may direct that an offer of proof be made in question-and-answer form.

(d) Preventing the Jury from Hearing Inadmissible Evidence. To the extent practicable, the court must conduct a jury trial so that inadmissible evidence is not suggested to the jury by any means.

(e) Taking Notice of Plain Error. A court may take notice of a plain error affecting a substantial right, even if the claim of error was not properly preserved.

Rule 104.
Preliminary Questions

(a) In General. The court must decide any preliminary question about whether a witness is qualified, a privilege exists, or evidence is admissible. In so deciding, the court is not bound by evidence rules, except those on privilege.

(b) Relevance That Depends on a Fact. When the relevance of evidence depends on whether a fact exists, proof must be introduced sufficient to support a finding that the fact does exist. The court may admit the proposed evidence on the condition that the proof be introduced later.

(c) Conducting a Hearing So That the Jury Cannot Hear It. The court must conduct any hearing on a preliminary question so that the jury cannot hear it if:

(1) the hearing involves the admissibility of a confession;

(2) a defendant in a criminal case is a witness and so requests; or

(3) justice so requires.

(d) Cross-Examining a Defendant in a Criminal Case. By testifying on a preliminary question, a defendant in a criminal case does not become subject to cross-examination on other issues in the case.

(e) Evidence Relevant to Weight and Credibility. This rule does not limit a party's right to introduce before the jury evidence that is relevant to the weight or credibility of other evidence.

Rule 105.
Limiting Evidence That Is Not Admissible Against
Other Parties or for Other Purposes

If the court admits evidence that is admissible against a party or for a purpose—but not against another party or for another purpose—the court, on timely request, must restrict the evidence to its proper scope and instruct the jury accordingly.

Rule 106.
Remainder of or Related Writings or Recorded Statements

If a party introduces all or part of a writing or recorded statement, an adverse party may require the introduction, at that time, of any other part— or any other writing or recorded statement—that in fairness ought to be considered at the same time.

ARTICLE II.
JUDICIAL NOTICE

Rule 201.
Judicial Notice of Adjudicative Facts

(a) Scope. This rule governs judicial notice of an adjudicative fact only, not a legislative fact.

(b) Kinds of Facts That May Be Judicially Noticed. The court may judicially notice a fact that is not subject to reasonable dispute because it:

(1) is generally known within the trial court's territorial jurisdiction; or

(2) can be accurately and readily determined from sources whose accuracy cannot reasonably be questioned.

(c) Taking Notice. The court:

(1) may take judicial notice on its own; or

(2) must take judicial notice if a party requests it and the court is supplied with the necessary information.

(d) Timing. The court may take judicial notice at any stage of the proceeding.

(e) Opportunity to Be Heard. On timely request, a party is entitled to be heard on the propriety of taking judicial notice and the nature of the fact to be noticed. If the court takes judicial notice before notifying a party, the party, on request, is still entitled to be heard.

(f) Instructing the Jury. In a civil case, the court must instruct the jury to accept the noticed fact as conclusive. In a criminal case, the court must instruct the jury that it may or may not accept the noticed fact as conclusive.

ARTICLE III.
PRESUMPTIONS IN CIVIL CASES

Rule 301.
Presumptions in Civil Cases Generally

In a civil case, unless a federal statute or these rules provide otherwise, the party against whom a presumption is directed has the burden of producing evidence to rebut the presumption. But this rule does not shift the burden of persuasion, which remains on the party who had it originally.

Rule 302.
Applying State Law to Presumptions in Civil Cases

In a civil case, state law governs the effect of a presumption regarding a claim or defense for which state law supplies the rule of decision.

ARTICLE IV.
RELEVANCE AND ITS LIMITS

Rule 401.
Test for Relevant Evidence

Evidence is relevant if:

(a) it has any tendency to make a fact more or less probable than it would be without the evidence; and

(b) the fact is of consequence in determining the action.

Rule 402.
General Admissibility of Relevant Evidence

Relevant evidence is admissible unless any of the following provides otherwise:

- the United States Constitution;
- a federal statute;
- these rules; or
- other rules prescribed by the Supreme Court.

Irrelevant evidence is not admissible.

Rule 403.
Excluding Relevant Evidence for Prejudice, Confusion, Waste of Time, or Other Reasons

The court may exclude relevant evidence if its probative value is substantially outweighed by a danger of one or more of the following: unfair prejudice, confusing the issues, misleading the jury, undue delay, wasting time, or needlessly presenting cumulative evidence.

Rule 404.
Character Evidence; Other Crimes, Wrongs or Acts

(a) Character Evidence.

(1) Prohibited Uses. Evidence of a person's character or character trait is not admissible to prove that on a particular occasion the person acted in accordance with the character or trait.

(2) Exceptions for a Defendant or Victim in a Criminal Case. The following exceptions apply in a criminal case:

(A) a defendant may offer evidence of the defendant's pertinent trait, and if the evidence is admitted, the prosecutor may offer evidence to rebut it;

(B) subject to the limitations in Rule 412, a defendant may offer evidence of an alleged victim's pertinent trait, and if the evidence is admitted, the prosecutor may:

   (i) offer evidence to rebut it; and

   (ii) offer evidence of the defendant's same trait; and

(C) in a homicide case, the prosecutor may offer evidence of the alleged victim's trait of peacefulness to rebut evidence that the victim was the first aggressor.

(3) Exceptions for a Witness. Evidence of a witness's character may be admitted under Rules 607, 608, and 609.

(b) Other Crimes, Wrongs, or Acts.

(1) Prohibited Uses. Evidence of any other crime, wrong, or act is not admissible to prove a person's character in order to show that on a particular occasion the person acted in accordance with the character.

(2) Permitted Uses. This evidence may be admissible for another purpose, such as proving motive, opportunity, intent, preparation, plan, knowledge, identity, absence of mistake, or lack of accident.

(3) Notice in a Criminal Case. In a criminal case, the prosecutor must:

(A) provide reasonable notice of any such evidence that the prosecutor intends to offer at trial so that the defendant has a fair opportunity to meet it;

(B) articulate in the notice the permitted purpose for which the prosecutor intends to offer the evidence and the reasoning that supports the purpose; and

(C) do so in writing before trial—or in any form during trial if the court, for good cause, excuses lack of pretrial notice.

Rule 405.
Methods of Proving Character

(a) By Reputation or Opinion. When evidence of a person's character or character trait is admissible, it may be proved by testimony about the person's reputation or by testimony in the form of an opinion. On cross-examination of the character witness, the court may allow an inquiry into relevant specific instances of the person's conduct.

(b) By Specific Instances of Conduct. When a person's character or character trait is an essential element of a charge, claim, or defense, the character or trait may also be proved by relevant specific instances of the person's conduct.

Rule 406.
Habit; Routine Practice

Evidence of a person's habit or an organization's routine practice may be admitted to prove that on a particular occasion the person or organization acted in accordance with the habit or routine practice. The court may admit this evidence regardless of whether it is corroborated or whether there was an eyewitness.

Rule 407.
Subsequent Remedial Measures

When measures are taken that would have made an earlier injury or harm less likely to occur, evidence of the subsequent measures is not admissible to prove:

- negligence;
- culpable conduct;
- a defect in a product or its design; or
- a need for a warning or instruction.

But the court may admit this evidence for another purpose, such as impeachment or—if disputed—proving ownership, control, or the feasibility of precautionary measures.

Rule 408.
Compromise Offers and Negotiations

(a) Prohibited Uses. Evidence of the following is not admissible—on behalf of any party—either to prove or disprove the validity or amount of a disputed claim or to impeach by a prior inconsistent statement or a contradiction:

(1) furnishing, promising, or offering—or accepting, promising to accept, or offering to accept—a valuable consideration in compromising or attempting to compromise the claim; and

(2) conduct or a statement made during compromise negotiations about the claim—except when offered in a criminal case and when the negotiations related to a claim by a public office in the exercise of its regulatory, investigative, or enforcement authority.

(b) Exceptions. The court may admit this evidence for another purpose, such as proving a witness's bias or prejudice, negating a contention of undue delay, or proving an effort to obstruct a criminal investigation or prosecution.

Rule 409.
Offers to Pay Medical and Similar Expenses

Evidence of furnishing, promising to pay, or offering to pay medical, hospital, or similar expenses resulting from an injury is not admissible to prove liability for the injury.

Rule 410.
Pleas, Plea Discussions, and Related Statements

(a) Prohibited Uses. In a civil or criminal case, evidence of the following is not admissible against the defendant who made the plea or participated in the plea discussions:

(1) a guilty plea that was later withdrawn;

(2) a nolo contendere plea;

(3) a statement made during a proceeding on either of those pleas under Federal Rule of Criminal Procedure 11 or a comparable state procedure; or

(4) a statement made during plea discussions with an attorney for the prosecuting authority if the discussions did not result in a guilty plea or they resulted in a later-withdrawn guilty plea.

(b) Exceptions. The court may admit a statement described in Rule 410(a)(3) or (4):

(1) in any proceeding in which another statement made during the same plea or plea discussions has been introduced, if in fairness the statements ought to be considered together; or

(2) in a criminal proceeding for perjury or false statement, if the defendant made the statement under oath, on the record, and with counsel present.

Rule 411.
Liability Insurance

Evidence that a person was or was not insured against liability is not admissible to prove whether the person acted negligently or otherwise wrongfully. But the court may admit this evidence for another purpose, such as proving a witness's bias or prejudice or proving agency, ownership, or control.

Rule 412.
Sex-Offense Cases: The Victim's Sexual
Behavior or Predisposition

(a) Prohibited Uses. The following evidence is not admissible in a civil or criminal proceeding involving alleged sexual misconduct:

(1) evidence offered to prove that a victim engaged in other sexual behavior; or

(2) evidence offered to prove a victim's sexual predisposition.

(b) Exceptions.

(1) Criminal Cases. The court may admit the following evidence in a criminal case:

(A) evidence of specific instances of a victim's sexual behavior, if offered to prove that someone other than the defendant was the source of semen, injury, or other physical evidence;

(B) evidence of specific instances of a victim's sexual behavior with respect to the person accused of the sexual misconduct, if offered by the defendant to prove consent or if offered by the prosecutor; and

(C) evidence whose exclusion would violate the defendant's constitutional rights.

(2) Civil Cases. In a civil case, the court may admit evidence offered to prove a victim's sexual behavior or sexual predisposition if its probative value substantially outweighs the danger of harm to any victim and of unfair prejudice to any party. The court may admit evidence of a victim's reputation only if the victim has placed it in controversy.

(c) Procedure to Determine Admissibility.

(1) Motion. If a party intends to offer evidence under Rule 412(b), the party must:

(A) file a motion that specifically describes the evidence and states the purpose for which it is to be offered;

(B) do so at least 14 days before trial unless the court, for good cause, sets a different time;

(C) serve the motion on all parties; and

(D) notify the victim or, when appropriate, the victim's guardian or representative.

(2) Hearing. Before admitting evidence under this rule, the court must conduct an in camera hearing and give the victim and parties a right to attend and be heard. Unless the court orders otherwise, the motion, related materials, and the record of the hearing must be and remain sealed.

(d) Definition of "Victim." In this rule, "victim" includes an alleged victim.

Rule 413.
Similar Crimes in Sexual-Assault Cases

(a) Permitted Uses. In a criminal case in which a defendant is accused of a sexual assault, the court may admit evidence that the defendant committed any other sexual assault. The evidence may be considered on any matter to which it is relevant.

(b) Disclosure to the Defendant. If the prosecutor intends to offer this evidence, the prosecutor must disclose it to the defendant, including witnesses' statements or a summary of the expected testimony. The prosecutor must do so at least 15 days before trial or at a later time that the court allows for good cause.

(c) Effect on Other Rules. This rule does not limit the admission or consideration of evidence under any other rule.

(d) Definition of "Sexual Assault." In this rule and Rule 415, "sexual assault" means a crime under federal law or under state law (as "state" is defined in 18 U.S.C. § 513) involving:

(1) any conduct prohibited by 18 U.S.C. chapter 109A;

(2) contact, without consent, between any part of the defendant's body—or an object—and another person's genitals or anus;

(3) contact, without consent, between the defendant's genitals or anus and any part of another person's body;

(4) deriving sexual pleasure or gratification from inflicting death, bodily injury, or physical pain on another person; or

(5) an attempt or conspiracy to engage in conduct described in paragraphs (1)–(4).

Rule 414.
Similar Crimes in Child-Molestation Cases

(a) Permitted Uses. In a criminal case in which a defendant is accused of child molestation, the court may admit evidence that the defendant committed any other child molestation. The evidence may be considered on any matter to which it is relevant.

(b) Disclosure to the Defendant. If the prosecutor intends to offer this evidence, the prosecutor must disclose it to the defendant, including witnesses' statements or a summary of the expected testimony. The prosecutor must do so at least 15 days before trial or at a later time that the court allows for good cause.

(c) Effect on Other Rules. This rule does not limit the admission or consideration of evidence under any other rule.

(d) Definition of "Child" and "Child Molestation." In this rule and Rule 415:

(1) "child" means a person below the age of 14; and

(2) "child molestation" means a crime under federal law or under state law (as "state" is defined in 18 U.S.C. § 513) involving:

(A) any conduct prohibited by 18 U.S.C. chapter 109A and committed with a child;

(B) any conduct prohibited by 18 U.S.C. chapter 110;

(C) contact between any part of the defendant's body—or an object—and a child's genitals or anus;

(D) contact between the defendant's genitals or anus and any part of a child's body;

(E) deriving sexual pleasure or gratification from inflicting death, bodily injury, or physical pain on a child; or

(F) an attempt or conspiracy to engage in conduct described in paragraphs (A)–(E).

Rule 415.
Similar Acts in Civil Cases Involving Sexual
Assault or Child Molestation

(a) Permitted Uses. In a civil case involving a claim for relief based on a party's alleged sexual assault or child molestation, the court may admit evidence that the party committed any other sexual assault or child molestation. The evidence may be considered as provided in Rules 413 and 414.

(b) Disclosure to the Opponent. If a party intends to offer this evidence, the party must disclose it to the party against whom it will be offered, including witnesses' statements or a summary of the expected testimony. The party must do so at least 15 days before trial or at a later time that the court allows for good cause.

(c) Effect on Other Rules. This rule does not limit the admission or consideration of evidence under any other rule.

ARTICLE V.
PRIVILEGES

Rule 501.
Privilege in General

The common law—as interpreted by United States courts in the light of reason and experience—governs a claim of privilege unless any of the following provides otherwise:

- the United States Constitution;

- a federal statute; or

- rules prescribed by the Supreme Court.

But in a civil case, state law governs privilege regarding a claim or defense for which state law supplies the rule of decision.

Rule 502.
Attorney-Client Privilege and Work Product;
Limitations on Waiver

The following provisions apply, in the circumstances set out, to disclosure of a communication or information covered by the attorney-client privilege or work-product protection.

(a) Disclosure Made in a Federal Proceeding or to a Federal Office or Agency; Scope of a Waiver. When the disclosure is made in a federal proceeding or to a federal office or agency and waives the attorney-client privilege or work-product protection, the waiver extends to an undisclosed communication or information in a federal or state proceeding only if:

(1) the waiver is intentional;

(2) the disclosed and undisclosed communications or information concern the same subject matter; and

(3) they ought in fairness to be considered together.

(b) **Inadvertent Disclosure.** When made in a federal proceeding or to a federal office or agency, the disclosure does not operate as a waiver in a federal or state proceeding if:

> **(1)** the disclosure is inadvertent;

> **(2)** the holder of the privilege or protection took reasonable steps to prevent disclosure; and

> **(3)** the holder promptly took reasonable steps to rectify the error, including (if applicable) following Federal Rule of Civil Procedure 26(b)(5)(B).

(c) **Disclosure Made in a State Proceeding.** When the disclosure is made in a state proceeding and is not the subject of a state-court order concerning waiver, the disclosure does not operate as a waiver in a federal proceeding if the disclosure:

> **(1)** would not be a waiver under this rule if it had been made in a federal proceeding; or

> **(2)** is not a waiver under the law of the state where the disclosure occurred.

(d) **Controlling Effect of a Court Order.** A federal court may order that the privilege or protection is not waived by disclosure connected with the litigation pending before the court—in which event the disclosure is also not a waiver in any other federal or state proceeding.

(e) **Controlling Effect of a Party Agreement.** An agreement on the effect of disclosure in a federal proceeding is binding only on the parties to the agreement, unless it is incorporated into a court order.

(f) **Controlling Effect of this Rule.** Notwithstanding Rules 101 and 1101, this rule applies to state proceedings and to federal court-annexed and federal court-mandated arbitration proceedings, in the circumstances set out in the rule. And notwithstanding Rule 501, this rule applies even if state law provides the rule of decision.

(g) **Definitions.** In this rule:

> **(1)** "attorney-client privilege" means the protection that applicable law provides for confidential attorney-client communications; and

> **(2)** "work-product protection" means the protection that applicable law provides for tangible material (or its intangible equivalent) prepared in anticipation of litigation or for trial.

ARTICLE VI.
WITNESSES

Rule 601.
Competency to Testify in General

Every person is competent to be a witness unless these rules provide otherwise. But in a civil case, state law governs the witness's competency regarding a claim or defense for which state law supplies the rule of decision.

Rule 602.
Need for Personal Knowledge

A witness may testify to a matter only if evidence is introduced sufficient to support a finding that the witness has personal knowledge of the matter. Evidence to prove personal knowledge may consist of the witness's own testimony. This rule does not apply to a witness's expert testimony under Rule 703.

Rule 603.
Oath or Affirmation to Testify Truthfully

Before testifying, a witness must give an oath or affirmation to testify truthfully. It must be in a form designed to impress that duty on the witness's conscience.

Rule 604.
Interpreter

An interpreter must be qualified and must give an oath or affirmation to make a true translation.

Rule 605.
Judge's Competency as a Witness

The presiding judge may not testify as a witness at the trial. A party need not object to preserve the issue.

Rule 606.
Juror's Competency as a Witness

(a) At the Trial. A juror may not testify as a witness before the other jurors at the trial. If a juror is called to testify, the court must give a party an opportunity to object outside the jury's presence.

(b) During an Inquiry into the Validity of a Verdict or Indictment.

  (1) Prohibited Testimony or Other Evidence. During an inquiry into the validity of a verdict or indictment, a juror may not testify about any statement made or incident that occurred during the jury's deliberations; the effect of anything on that juror's or another juror's vote; or any juror's mental processes concerning the verdict or indictment. The court may not receive a juror's affidavit or evidence of a juror's statement on these matters.

  (2) Exceptions. A juror may testify about whether:

      (A) extraneous prejudicial information was improperly brought to the jury's attention;

      (B) an outside influence was improperly brought to bear on any juror; or

      (C) a mistake was made in entering the verdict on the verdict form.

Rule 607.
Who May Impeach a Witness

Any party, including the party that called the witness, may attack the witness's credibility.

Rule 608.
A Witness's Character for Truthfulness or Untruthfulness

(a) Reputation or Opinion Evidence. A witness's credibility may be attacked or supported by testimony about the witness's reputation for having a character for truthfulness or untruthfulness, or by testimony in the form of an opinion about that character. But evidence of truthful character is admissible only after the witness's character for truthfulness has been attacked.

(b) Specific Instances of Conduct. Except for a criminal conviction under Rule 609, extrinsic evidence is not admissible to prove specific instances of a witness's conduct in order to attack or support the witness's character for truthfulness. But the court may, on cross-examination, allow them to be inquired into if they are probative of the character for truthfulness or untruthfulness of:

(1) the witness; or

(2) another witness whose character the witness being cross-examined has testified about.

By testifying on another matter, a witness does not waive any privilege against self-incrimination for testimony that relates only to the witness's character for truthfulness.

Rule 609.
Impeachment by Evidence of a Criminal Conviction

(a) In General. The following rules apply to attacking a witness's character for truthfulness by evidence of a criminal conviction:

(1) for a crime that, in the convicting jurisdiction, was punishable by death or by imprisonment for more than one year, the evidence:

(A) must be admitted, subject to Rule 403, in a civil case or in a criminal case in which the witness is not a defendant; and

(B) must be admitted in a criminal case in which the witness is a defendant, if the probative value of the evidence outweighs its prejudicial effect to that defendant; and

(2) for any crime regardless of the punishment, the evidence must be admitted if the court can readily determine that establishing the elements of the crime required proving—or the witness's admitting—a dishonest act or false statement.

(b) Limit on Using the Evidence After 10 Years. This subdivision (b) applies if more than 10 years have passed since the witness's conviction or release from confinement for it, whichever is later. Evidence of the conviction is admissible only if:

(1) its probative value, supported by specific facts and circumstances, substantially outweighs its prejudicial effect; and

(2) the proponent gives an adverse party reasonable written notice of the intent to use it so that the party has a fair opportunity to contest its use.

(c) Effect of a Pardon, Annulment, or Certificate of Rehabilitation. Evidence of a conviction is not admissible if:

(1) the conviction has been the subject of a pardon, annulment, certificate of rehabilitation, or other equivalent procedure based on a finding that the person has been rehabilitated, and the person has not been convicted of a later crime punishable by death or by imprisonment for more than one year; or

(2) the conviction has been the subject of a pardon, annulment, or other equivalent procedure based on a finding of innocence.

(d) Juvenile Adjudications. Evidence of a juvenile adjudication is admissible under this rule only if:

(1) it is offered in a criminal case;

(2) the adjudication was of a witness other than the defendant;

(3) an adult's conviction for that offense would be admissible to attack the adult's credibility; and

(4) admitting the evidence is necessary to fairly determine guilt or innocence.

(e) Pendency of an Appeal. A conviction that satisfies this rule is admissible even if an appeal is pending. Evidence of the pendency is also admissible.

Rule 610.
Religious Beliefs or Opinions

Evidence of a witness's religious beliefs or opinions is not admissible to attack or support the witness's credibility.

Rule 611.
Mode and Order of Examining Witnesses and Presenting Evidence

(a) Control by the Court; Purposes. The court should exercise reasonable control over the mode and order of examining witnesses and presenting evidence so as to:

(1) make those procedures effective for determining the truth;

(2) avoid wasting time; and

(3) protect witnesses from harassment or undue embarrassment.

(b) Scope of Cross-Examination. Cross-examination should not go beyond the subject matter of the direct examination and matters affecting the witness's credibility. The court may allow inquiry into additional matters as if on direct examination.

(c) Leading Questions. Leading questions should not be used on direct examination except as necessary to develop the witness's testimony. Ordinarily, the court should allow leading questions:

(1) on cross-examination; and

(2) when a party calls a hostile witness, an adverse party, or a witness identified with an adverse party.

Rule 612.
Writing Used to Refresh a Witness's Memory

(a) Scope. This rule gives an adverse party certain options when a witness uses a writing to refresh memory:

(1) while testifying; or

(2) before testifying, if the court decides that justice requires the party to have those options.

(b) Adverse Party's Options; Deleting Unrelated Matter. Unless 18 U.S.C. § 3500 provides otherwise in a criminal case, an adverse party is entitled to have the writing produced at the hearing, to inspect it, to cross-examine the witness about it, and to introduce in evidence any portion that relates to the witness's testimony. If the producing party claims that the writing includes unrelated matter, the court must examine the writing in camera, delete any unrelated portion, and order that the rest be delivered to the adverse party. Any portion deleted over objection must be preserved for the record.

(c) Failure to Produce or Deliver the Writing. If a writing is not produced or is not delivered as ordered, the court may issue any appropriate order. But if the prosecution does not comply in a criminal case, the court must strike the witness's testimony or—if justice so requires—declare a mistrial.

Rule 613.
Witness's Prior Statement

(a) Showing or Disclosing the Statement During Examination. When examining a witness about the witness's prior statement, a party need not show it or disclose its contents to the witness. But the party must, on request, show it or disclose its contents to an adverse party's attorney.

(b) Extrinsic Evidence of a Prior Inconsistent Statement. Extrinsic evidence of a witness's prior inconsistent statement is admissible only if the witness is given an opportunity to explain or deny the statement and an adverse party is given an opportunity to examine the witness about it, or if justice so requires. This subdivision (b) does not apply to an opposing party's statement under Rule 801(d)(2).

Rule 614.
Court's Calling or Examining a Witness

(a) Calling. The court may call a witness on its own or at a party's request. Each party is entitled to cross-examine the witness.

(b) Examining. The court may examine a witness regardless of who calls the witness.

(c) Objections. A party may object to the court's calling or examining a witness either at that time or at the next opportunity when the jury is not present.

Rule 615.
Excluding Witnesses

At a party's request, the court must order witnesses excluded so that they cannot hear other witnesses' testimony. Or the court may do so on its own. But this rule does not authorize excluding:

(a) a party who is a natural person;

(b) an officer or employee of a party that is not a natural person, after being designated as the party's representative by its attorney;

(c) a person whose presence a party shows to be essential to presenting the party's claim or defense; or

(d) a person authorized by statute to be present.

ARTICLE VII.
OPINIONS AND EXPERT TESTIMONY

Rule 701.
Opinion Testimony by Lay Witnesses

If a witness is not testifying as an expert, testimony in the form of an opinion is limited to one that is:

(a) rationally based on the witness's perception;

(b) helpful to clearly understanding the witness's testimony or to determining a fact in issue; and

(c) not based on scientific, technical, or other specialized knowledge within the scope of Rule 702.

Rule 702.
Testimony by Expert Witnesses

A witness who is qualified as an expert by knowledge, skill, experience, training, or education may testify in the form of an opinion or otherwise if:

(a) the expert's scientific, technical, or other specialized knowledge will help the trier of fact to understand the evidence or to determine a fact in issue;

(b) the testimony is based on sufficient facts or data;

(c) the testimony is the product of reliable principles and methods; and

(d) the expert has reliably applied the principles and methods to the facts of the case.

Rule 703.
Bases of an Expert's Opinion Testimony

An expert may base an opinion on facts or data in the case that the expert has been made aware of or personally observed. If experts in the particular field would reasonably rely on those kinds of facts or data in forming an opinion on the subject, they need not be admissible for the opinion to be admitted. But if the facts or data would otherwise be inadmissible, the proponent of the opinion may disclose them to the jury only if their probative value in helping the jury evaluate the opinion substantially outweighs their prejudicial effect.

Rule 704.
Opinion on an Ultimate Issue

(a)   In General—Not Automatically Objectionable. An opinion is not objectionable just because it embraces an ultimate issue.

(b)   Exception. In a criminal case, an expert witness must not state an opinion about whether the defendant did or did not have a mental state or condition that constitutes an element of the crime charged or of a defense. Those matters are for the trier of fact alone.

Rule 705.
Disclosing the Facts or Data Underlying an Expert's Opinion

Unless the court orders otherwise, an expert may state an opinion—and give the reasons for it—without first testifying to the underlying facts or data. But the expert may be required to disclose those facts or data on cross-examination.

Rule 706.
Court-Appointed Expert Witnesses

(a)   Appointment Process. On a party's motion or on its own, the court may order the parties to show cause why expert witnesses should not be appointed and may ask the parties to submit nominations. The court may appoint any expert that the parties agree on and any of its own choosing. But the court may only appoint someone who consents to act.

(b)   Expert's Role. The court must inform the expert of the expert's duties. The court may do so in writing and have a copy filed with the clerk or may do so orally at a conference in which the parties have an opportunity to participate. The expert:

    (1)   must advise the parties of any findings the expert makes;

    (2)   may be deposed by any party;

    (3)   may be called to testify by the court or any party; and

    (4)   may be cross-examined by any party, including the party that called the expert.

(c) Compensation. The expert is entitled to a reasonable compensation, as set by the court. The compensation is payable as follows:

(1) in a criminal case or in a civil case involving just compensation under the Fifth Amendment, from any funds that are provided by law; and

(2) in any other civil case, by the parties in the proportion and at the time that the court directs—and the compensation is then charged like other costs.

(d) Disclosing the Appointment to the Jury. The court may authorize disclosure to the jury that the court appointed the expert.

(e) Parties' Choice of Their Own Experts. This rule does not limit a party in calling its own experts.

ARTICLE VIII.
HEARSAY

Rule 801.
Definitions That Apply to This Article; Exclusions from Hearsay

(a) Statement. "Statement" means a person's oral assertion, written assertion, or nonverbal conduct, if the person intended it as an assertion.

(b) Declarant. "Declarant" means the person who made the statement.

(c) Hearsay. "Hearsay" means a statement that:

(1) the declarant does not make while testifying at the current trial or hearing; and

(2) a party offers in evidence to prove the truth of the matter asserted in the statement.

(d) Statements That Are Not Hearsay. A statement that meets the following conditions is not hearsay:

(1) A Declarant-Witness's Prior Statement. The declarant testifies and is subject to cross-examination about a prior statement, and the statement:

(A) is inconsistent with the declarant's testimony and was given under penalty of perjury at a trial, hearing, or other proceeding or in a deposition;

(B) is consistent with the declarant's testimony and is offered:

(i) to rebut an express or implied charge that the declarant recently fabricated it or acted from a recent improper influence or motive in so testifying; or

(ii) to rehabilitate the declarant's credibility as a witness when attacked on another ground; or

(C) identifies a person as someone the declarant perceived earlier.

(2) An Opposing Party's Statement. The statement is offered against an opposing party and:

(A) was made by the party in an individual or representative capacity;

(B) is one the party manifested that it adopted or believed to be true;

(C) was made by a person whom the party authorized to make a statement on the subject;

(D) was made by the party's agent or employee on a matter within the scope of that relationship and while it existed; or

(E) was made by the party's coconspirator during and in furtherance of the conspiracy.

The statement must be considered but does not by itself establish the declarant's authority under (C); the existence or scope of the relationship under (D); or the existence of the conspiracy or participation in it under (E).

Rule 802.
The Rule Against Hearsay

Hearsay is not admissible unless any of the following provides otherwise:

- a federal statute;
- these rules; or
- other rules prescribed by the Supreme Court.

Rule 803.
Exceptions to the Rule Against Hearsay—Regardless of Whether the Declarant Is Available as a Witness

The following are not excluded by the rule against hearsay, regardless of whether the declarant is available as a witness:

(1) Present Sense Impression. A statement describing or explaining an event or condition, made while or immediately after the declarant perceived it.

(2) Excited Utterance. A statement relating to a startling event or condition, made while the declarant was under the stress of excitement that it caused.

(3) Then-Existing Mental, Emotional, or Physical Condition. A statement of the declarant's then-existing state of mind (such as motive, intent, or plan) or emotional, sensory, or physical condition (such as mental feeling, pain, or bodily health), but not including a statement of memory or belief to prove the fact remembered or believed unless it relates to the validity or terms of the declarant's will.

(4) Statement Made for Medical Diagnosis or Treatment. A statement that:

(A) is made for—and is reasonably pertinent to—medical diagnosis or treatment; and

(B) describes medical history; past or present symptoms or sensations; their inception; or their general cause.

(5) Recorded Recollection. A record that:

(A) is on a matter the witness once knew about but now cannot recall well enough to testify fully and accurately;

(B) was made or adopted by the witness when the matter was fresh in the witness's memory; and

(C) accurately reflects the witness's knowledge.

If admitted, the record may be read into evidence but may be received as an exhibit only if offered by an adverse party.

(6) Records of a Regularly Conducted Activity. A record of an act, event, condition, opinion, or diagnosis if:

(A) the record was made at or near the time by—or from information transmitted by—someone with knowledge;

(B) the record was kept in the course of a regularly conducted activity of a business, organization, occupation, or calling, whether or not for profit;

(C) making the record was a regular practice of that activity;

(D) all these conditions are shown by the testimony of the custodian or another qualified witness, or by a certification that complies with Rule 902(11) or (12) or with a statute permitting certification; and

(E) the opponent does not show that the source of information or the method or circumstances of preparation indicate a lack of trustworthiness.

(7) Absence of a Record of a Regularly Conducted Activity. Evidence that a matter is not included in a record described in paragraph (6) if:

(A) the evidence is admitted to prove that the matter did not occur or exist;

(B) a record was regularly kept for a matter of that kind; and

(C) the opponent does not show that the possible source of the information or other circumstances indicate a lack of trustworthiness.

(8) Public Records. A record or statement of a public office if:

(A) it sets out:

(i)   the office's activities;

(ii) a matter observed while under a legal duty to report, but not including, in a criminal case, a matter observed by law-enforcement personnel; or

(iii) in a civil case or against the government in a criminal case, factual findings from a legally authorized investigation; and

(B) the opponent does not show that the source of information or other circumstances indicate a lack of trustworthiness.

(9) Public Records of Vital Statistics. A record of a birth, death, or marriage, if reported to a public office in accordance with a legal duty.

(10) Absence of a Public Record. Testimony—or a certification under Rule 902—that a diligent search failed to disclose a public record or statement if:

(A) the testimony or certification is admitted to prove that

(i) the record or statement does not exist; or

(ii) a matter did not occur or exist, if a public office regularly kept a record or statement for a matter of that kind; and

(B) in a criminal case, a prosecutor who intends to offer a certification provides written notice of that intent at least 14 days before trial, and the defendant does not object in writing within 7 days of receiving the notice—unless the court sets a different time for the notice or the objection.

(11) Records of Religious Organizations Concerning Personal or Family History. A statement of birth, legitimacy, ancestry, marriage, divorce, death, relationship by blood or marriage, or similar facts of personal or family history, contained in a regularly kept record of a religious organization.

(12) Certificates of Marriage, Baptism, and Similar Ceremonies. A statement of fact contained in a certificate:

(A) made by a person who is authorized by a religious organization or by law to perform the act certified;

(B) attesting that the person performed a marriage or similar ceremony or administered a sacrament; and

(C) purporting to have been issued at the time of the act or within a reasonable time after it.

(13) Family Records. A statement of fact about personal or family history contained in a family record, such as a Bible, genealogy, chart, engraving on a ring, inscription on a portrait, or engraving on an urn or burial marker.

(14) Records of Documents That Affect an Interest in Property. The record of a document that purports to establish or affect an interest in property if:

(A) the record is admitted to prove the content of the original recorded document, along with its signing and its delivery by each person who purports to have signed it;

(B) the record is kept in a public office; and

(C) a statute authorizes recording documents of that kind in that office.

(15) Statements in Documents That Affect an Interest in Property. A statement contained in a document that purports to establish or affect an interest in property if the matter stated was relevant to the document's purpose—unless later dealings with the property are inconsistent with the truth of the statement or the purport of the document.

(16) Statements in Ancient Documents. A statement in a document that was prepared before January 1, 1998, and whose authenticity is established.

(17) Market Reports and Similar Commercial Publications. Market quotations, lists, directories, or other compilations that are generally relied on by the public or by persons in particular occupations.

(18) Statements in Learned Treatises, Periodicals, or Pamphlets. A statement contained in a treatise, periodical, or pamphlet if:

(A) the statement is called to the attention of an expert witness on cross-examination or relied on by the expert on direct examination; and

(B) the publication is established as a reliable authority by the expert's admission or testimony, by another expert's testimony, or by judicial notice.

If admitted, the statement may be read into evidence but not received as an exhibit.

(19) Reputation Concerning Personal or Family History. A reputation among a person's family by blood, adoption, or marriage—or among a person's associates or in the community—concerning the person's birth, adoption, legitimacy, ancestry, marriage, divorce, death, relationship by blood, adoption, or marriage, or similar facts of personal or family history.

(20) Reputation Concerning Boundaries or General History. A reputation in a community—arising before the controversy—concerning boundaries of land in the community or customs that affect the land, or concerning general historical events important to that community, state, or nation.

(21) Reputation Concerning Character. A reputation among a person's associates or in the community concerning the person's character.

(22) Judgment of a Previous Conviction. Evidence of a final judgment of conviction if:

(A) the judgment was entered after a trial or guilty plea, but not a nolo contendere plea;

(B) the conviction was for a crime punishable by death or by imprisonment for more than a year;

(C) the evidence is admitted to prove any fact essential to the judgment; and

(D) when offered by the prosecutor in a criminal case for a purpose other than impeachment, the judgment was against the defendant.

The pendency of an appeal may be shown but does not affect admissibility.

(23) Judgments Involving Personal, Family, or General History or a Boundary. A judgment that is admitted to prove a matter of personal, family, or general history, or boundaries, if the matter:

(A) was essential to the judgment; and

(B) could be proved by evidence of reputation.

(24) [Other exceptions.] [Transferred to Rule 807.]

Rule 804.
Exceptions to the Rule Against Hearsay—When the
Declarant Is Unavailable as a Witness

(a) Criteria for Being Unavailable. A declarant is considered to be unavailable as a witness if the declarant:

(1) is exempted from testifying about the subject matter of the declarant's statement because the court rules that a privilege applies;

(2) refuses to testify about the subject matter despite a court order to do so;

(3) testifies to not remembering the subject matter;

(4) cannot be present or testify at the trial or hearing because of death or a then-existing infirmity, physical illness, or mental illness; or

(5) is absent from the trial or hearing and the statement's proponent has not been able, by process or other reasonable means, to procure:

(A) the declarant's attendance, in the case of a hearsay exception under Rule 804(b)(1) or (6); or

(B) the declarant's attendance or testimony, in the case of a hearsay exception under Rule 804(b)(2), (3), or (4).

But this subdivision (a) does not apply if the statement's proponent procured or wrongfully caused the declarant's unavailability as a witness in order to prevent the declarant from attending or testifying.

(b) The Exceptions. The following are not excluded by the rule against hearsay if the declarant is unavailable as a witness:

(1) Former Testimony. Testimony that:

(A) was given as a witness at a trial, hearing, or lawful deposition, whether given during the current proceeding or a different one; and

(B) is now offered against a party who had—or, in a civil case, whose predecessor in interest had—an opportunity and similar motive to develop it by direct, cross-, or redirect examination.

(2) Statement Under the Belief of Imminent Death. In a prosecution for homicide or in a civil case, a statement that the declarant, while believing the declarant's death to be imminent, made about its cause or circumstances.

(3) Statement Against Interest. A statement that:

(A) a reasonable person in the declarant's position would have made only if the person believed it to be true because, when made, it was so contrary to the declarant's proprietary or pecuniary interest or had so great a tendency to invalidate the declarant's claim against someone else or to expose the declarant to civil or criminal liability; and

(B) is supported by corroborating circumstances that clearly indicate its trustworthiness, if it is offered in a criminal case as one that tends to expose the declarant to criminal liability.

(4) Statement of Personal or Family History. A statement about:

(A) the declarant's own birth, adoption, legitimacy, ancestry, marriage, divorce, relationship by blood, adoption, or marriage, or similar facts of personal or family history, even though the declarant had no way of acquiring personal knowledge about that fact; or

(B) another person concerning any of these facts, as well as death, if the declarant was related to the person by blood, adoption, or marriage or was so intimately associated with the person's family that the declarant's information is likely to be accurate.

(5) [Other exceptions.] [Transferred to Rule 807.]

(6) Statement Offered Against a Party That Wrongfully Caused the Declarant's Unavailability. A statement offered against a party that wrongfully caused—or acquiesced in wrongfully causing—the declarant's unavailability as a witness, and did so intending that result.

Rule 805.
Hearsay Within Hearsay

Hearsay within hearsay is not excluded by the rule against hearsay if each part of the combined statements conforms with an exception to the rule.

Rule 806.
Attacking and Supporting the Declarant's Credibility

When a hearsay statement—or a statement described in Rule 801(d)(2)(C), (D), or (E)—has been admitted in evidence, the declarant's credibility may be attacked, and then supported, by any evidence that would be admissible for those purposes if the declarant had testified as a witness. The court may admit evidence of the declarant's inconsistent statement or conduct, regardless of when it occurred or whether the declarant had an opportunity to explain or deny it. If the party against whom the statement was admitted calls the declarant as a witness, the party may examine the declarant on the statement as if on cross-examination.

Rule 807.
Residual Exception

(a) In General. Under the following conditions, a hearsay statement is not excluded by the rule against hearsay even if the statement is not admissible under a hearsay exception in Rule 803 or 804:

(1) the statement is supported by sufficient guarantees of trustworthiness—after considering the totality of circumstances under which it was made and evidence, if any, corroborating the statement; and;

(2) it is more probative on the point for which it is offered than any other evidence that the proponent can obtain through reasonable efforts.

(b) Notice. The statement is admissible only if the proponent gives an adverse party reasonable notice of an intent to offer the statement—including its substance and the declarant's name—so that the party has a fair opportunity to meet it. The notice must be provided in writing before the trial or hearing—or in any form during the trial or hearing if the court, for good cause, excuses a lack of earlier notice.

ARTICLE IX.
AUTHENTICATION AND IDENTIFICATION

Rule 901.
Authenticating or Identifying Evidence

(a) In General. To satisfy the requirement of authenticating or identifying an item of evidence, the proponent must produce evidence sufficient to support a finding that the item is what the proponent claims it is.

(b) Examples. The following are examples only—not a complete list—of evidence that satisfies the requirement:

(1) Testimony of a Witness with Knowledge. Testimony that an item is what it is claimed to be.

(2) Nonexpert Opinion About Handwriting. A nonexpert's opinion that handwriting is genuine, based on a familiarity with it that was not acquired for the current litigation

(3) Comparison by an Expert Witness or the Trier of Fact. A comparison with an authenticated specimen by an expert witness or the trier of fact.

(4) Distinctive Characteristics and the Like. The appearance, contents, substance, internal patterns, or other distinctive characteristics of the item, taken together with all the circumstances.

(5) Opinion About a Voice. An opinion identifying a person's voice—whether heard firsthand or through mechanical or electronic transmission or recording—based on hearing the voice at any time under circumstances that connect it with the alleged speaker.

(6) Evidence About a Telephone Conversation. For a telephone conversation, evidence that a call was made to the number assigned at the time to:

    (A) a particular person, if circumstances, including self-identification, show that the person answering was the one called; or

    (B) a particular business, if the call was made to a business and the call related to business reasonably transacted over the telephone.

(7) Evidence About Public Records. Evidence that:

    (A) a document was recorded or filed in a public office as authorized by law; or

    (B) a purported public record or statement is from the office where items of this kind are kept.

(8) Evidence About Ancient Documents or Data Compilations. For a document or data compilation, evidence that it:

    (A) is in a condition that creates no suspicion about its authenticity;

    (B) was in a place where, if authentic, it would likely be; and

    (C) is at least 20 years old when offered.

(9) Evidence About a Process or System. Evidence describing a process or system and showing that it produces an accurate result.

(10) Methods Provided by a Statute or Rule. Any method of authentication or identification allowed by a federal statute or a rule prescribed by the Supreme Court.

Rule 902.
Evidence That Is Self-Authenticating

The following items of evidence are self-authenticating; they require no extrinsic evidence of authenticity in order to be admitted:

(1) Domestic Public Documents That Are Sealed and Signed. A document that bears:

    (A) a seal purporting to be that of the United States; any state, district, commonwealth, territory, or insular possession of the United States; the former Panama Canal Zone; the Trust Territory of the Pacific Islands; a political subdivision of any of these entities; or a department, agency, or officer of any entity named above; and

    (B) a signature purporting to be an execution or attestation.

(2) Domestic Public Documents That Are Not Sealed But Are Signed and Certified. A document that bears no seal if:

    (A) it bears the signature of an officer or employee of an entity named in Rule 902(1)(A); and

(B) another public officer who has a seal and official duties within that same entity certifies under seal—or its equivalent—that the signer has the official capacity and that the signature is genuine.

(3) Foreign Public Documents. A document that purports to be signed or attested by a person who is authorized by a foreign country's law to do so. The document must be accompanied by a final certification that certifies the genuineness of the signature and official position of the signer or attester—or of any foreign official whose certificate of genuineness relates to the signature or attestation or is in a chain of certificates of genuineness relating to the signature or attestation. The certification may be made by a secretary of a United States embassy or legation; by a consul general, vice consul, or consular agent of the United States; or by a diplomatic or consular official of the foreign country assigned or accredited to the United States. If all parties have been given a reasonable opportunity to investigate the document's authenticity and accuracy, the court may, for good cause, either:

   (A) order that it be treated as presumptively authentic without final certification; or

   (B) allow it to be evidenced by an attested summary with or without final certification.

(4) Certified Copies of Public Records. A copy of an official record—or a copy of a document that was recorded or filed in a public office as authorized by law—if the copy is certified as correct by:

   (A) the custodian or another person authorized to make the certification; or

   (B) a certificate that complies with Rule 902(1), (2), or (3), a federal statute, or a rule prescribed by the Supreme Court.

(5) Official Publications. A book, pamphlet, or other publication purporting to be issued by a public authority.

(6) Newspapers and Periodicals. Printed material purporting to be a newspaper or periodical.

(7) Trade Inscriptions and the Like. An inscription, sign, tag, or label purporting to have been affixed in the course of business and indicating origin, ownership, or control.

(8) Acknowledged Documents. A document accompanied by a certificate of acknowledgment that is lawfully executed by a notary public or another officer who is authorized to take acknowledgments.

(9) Commercial Paper and Related Documents. Commercial paper, a signature on it, and related documents, to the extent allowed by general commercial law.

(10) Presumptions Under a Federal Statute. A signature, document, or anything else that a federal statute declares to be presumptively or prima facie genuine or authentic.

(11) Certified Domestic Records of a Regularly Conducted Activity. The original or a copy of a domestic record that meets the requirements of Rule 803(6)(A)–(C), as shown by a certification of the custodian or another qualified person that complies with a federal statute or a rule prescribed by the Supreme Court. Before the trial or hearing, the proponent must give an adverse party reasonable written notice of the intent to offer the record—and must make the record and certification available for inspection—so that the party has a fair opportunity to challenge them.

(12) Certified Foreign Records of a Regularly Conducted Activity. In a civil case, the original or a copy of a foreign record that meets the requirements of Rule 902(11), modified as follows: the certification, rather than complying with a federal statute or Supreme Court rule, must be signed in a manner that, if falsely made, would subject the maker to a criminal penalty in the country where the certification is signed. The proponent must also meet the notice requirements of Rule 902(11).

(13) Certified Records Generated by an Electronic Process or System. A record generated by an electronic process or system that produces an accurate result, as shown by a certification of a qualified person that complies with the certification requirements of Rule 901(11 or (12). The proponent must also meet the notice requirements of Rule 902(11).

(14) Certified Data Copied from an Electronic Device, Storage Medium, or File. Data copied from an electronic device, storage medium, or file, if authenticated by a process of digital identification, as shown by a certification of a qualified person that complies with the certification requirements of Rule 902(11) or (12). The proponent also must meet the notice requirements of Rule 902(11).

Rule 903.
Subscribing Witness's Testimony

A subscribing witness's testimony is necessary to authenticate a writing only if required by the law of the jurisdiction that governs its validity.

ARTICLE X.
CONTENTS OF WRITINGS, RECORDINGS, AND PHOTOGRAPHS
Rule 1001.
Definitions That Apply to This Article

In this article:

(a) A "writing" consists of letters, words, numbers, or their equivalent set down in any form.

(b) A "recording" consists of letters, words, numbers, or their equivalent recorded in any manner.

(c) A "photograph" means a photographic image or its equivalent stored in any form.

(d) An "original" of a writing or recording means the writing or recording itself or any counterpart intended to have the same effect by the person who executed or issued it. For electronically stored information, "original" means any printout—or other output readable by sight—if it accurately reflects the information. An "original" of a photograph includes the negative or a print from it.

(e) A "duplicate" means a counterpart produced by a mechanical, photographic, chemical, electronic, or other equivalent process or technique that accurately reproduces the original.

Rule 1002.
Requirement of the Original

An original writing, recording, or photograph is required in order to prove its content unless these rules or a federal statute provides otherwise.

Rule 1003.
Admissibility of Duplicates

A duplicate is admissible to the same extent as the original unless a genuine question is raised about the original's authenticity or the circumstances make it unfair to admit the duplicate.

Rule 1004.
Admissibility of Other Evidence of Content

An original is not required and other evidence of the content of a writing, recording, or photograph is admissible if:

(a) all the originals are lost or destroyed, and not by the proponent acting in bad faith;

(b) an original cannot be obtained by any available judicial process;

(c) the party against whom the original would be offered had control of the original; was at that time put on notice, by pleadings or otherwise, that the original would be a subject of proof at the trial or hearing; and fails to produce it at the trial or hearing; or

(d) the writing, recording, or photograph is not closely related to a controlling issue.

Rule 1005.
Copies of Public Records to Prove Content

The proponent may use a copy to prove the content of an official record—or of a document that was recorded or filed in a public office as authorized by law—if these conditions are met: the record or document is otherwise admissible; and the copy is certified as correct in accordance with Rule 902(4) or is testified to be correct by a witness who has compared it with the original. If no such copy can be obtained by reasonable diligence, then the proponent may use other evidence to prove the content.

Rule 1006.
Summaries to Prove Content

The proponent may use a summary, chart, or calculation to prove the content of voluminous writings, recordings, or photographs that cannot be conveniently examined in court. The proponent must make the originals or duplicates available for examination or copying, or both, by other parties at a reasonable time and place. And the court may order the proponent to produce them in court.

Rule 1007.
Testimony or Statement of a Party to Prove Content

The proponent may prove the content of a writing, recording, or photograph by the testimony, deposition, or written statement of the party against whom the evidence is offered. The proponent need not account for the original.

Rule 1008.
Functions of the Court and Jury

Ordinarily, the court determines whether the proponent has fulfilled the factual conditions for admitting other evidence of the content of a writing, recording, or photograph under Rule 1004 or 1005. But in a jury trial, the jury determines—in accordance with Rule 104(b)—any issue about whether:

(a) an asserted writing, recording, or photograph ever existed;

(b) another one produced at the trial or hearing is the original; or

(c) other evidence of content accurately reflects the content.

ARTICLE XI.
MISCELLANEOUS RULES

Rule 1101.
Applicability of the Rules

(a) **To Courts and Judges.** These rules apply to proceedings before:

- United States district courts;
- United States bankruptcy and magistrate judges;
- United States courts of appeals;
- the United States Court of Federal Claims; and
- the district courts of Guam, the Virgin Islands, and the Northern Mariana Islands.

(b) **To Cases and Proceedings.** These rules apply in:

- civil cases and proceedings, including bankruptcy, admiralty, and maritime cases;
- criminal cases and proceedings; and
- contempt proceedings, except those in which the court may act summarily.

(c) **Rules on Privilege.** The rules on privilege apply to all stages of a case or proceeding.

(d) **Exceptions.** These rules—except for those on privilege—do not apply to the following:

(1) the court's determination, under Rule 104(a), on a preliminary question of fact governing admissibility;

(2) grand-jury proceedings; and

(3) miscellaneous proceedings such as:

- extradition or rendition;

- issuing an arrest warrant, criminal summons, or search warrant;

- a preliminary examination in a criminal case;

- sentencing;

- granting or revoking probation or supervised release; and

- considering whether to release on bail or otherwise.

(e)   Other Statutes and Rules. A federal statute or a rule prescribed by the Supreme Court may provide for admitting or excluding evidence independently from these rules.

Rule 1102.
Amendments

These rules may be amended as provided in 28 U.S.C. § 2072.

Rule 1103.
Title

These rules may be cited as the Federal Rules of Evidence.

APPENDIX C
CONFRONTATION CLAUSE
ANALYSIS

§ 802.2 Rule 802: Hearsay Rule; Confrontation Clause Analysis

The Sixth Amendment provides in pertinent part that "[i]n all criminal prosecutions, the accused shall enjoy the right . . . to be confronted with witnesses against him. . . ." Confrontation clause cases fall into two broad categories: cases involving the admission of out-of-court statements and cases involving restrictions imposed by law or by the trial court on the scope or extent of cross-examination face to face with the accused.

With respect to out-of-court statements, the Advisory Committee to the Federal Rules of Evidence, in drafting the proposed rules and Congress, during the legislative process, both evidenced a clear intention to draft rules in such a way as to eliminate, if possible, any tension between the hearsay rule as embodied in Article VIII of the Federal Rules of Evidence and the confrontation clause. As explained herein, that was then and this is now.

Under the confrontation clause as currently interpreted, substantive admissibility of any prior statement of an in court witness testifying under oath subject to cross-examination is permissible. A witness is subject to cross-examination with respect to a prior inconsistent statement sufficient to satisfy the confrontation clause whenever the witness responds willingly to questions, even if the witness fails, for whatever reason, to recall an event or a statement relating to an event, or denies making the prior statement. Prior consistent statements admitted under similar circumstances also do not run afoul of the confrontation clause.

Historical overview. With respect to a witness who does not testify at trial under oath subject to cross-examination, the admissibility of the witness' hearsay statements was at one time governed by the United States Supreme Court opinion in Ohio v. Roberts, 448 U.S. 56 (1980):

> The Court has applied this "indicia of reliability" requirement principally by concluding that certain hearsay exceptions rest upon such solid foundations that admission of virtually any evidence within them comports with the "substance of the constitutional protection." Mattox v. United States, 156 U.S. at 244 * * * . This reflects the truism "hearsay rules and the Confrontation Clause are generally designed to protect similar values," California v. Green, 399 U.S. at 155, * * * and "stem from the same roots," Dutton v. Evans, 400 U.S. 74, 86, * * * (1970). It also responds to the need for certainty in the workaday world of conducting criminal trials.
>
> In sum, when a hearsay declarant is not present for cross-examination at trial, the Confrontation Clause normally requires a showing that he is unavailable. Even then, his statement is

admissible only if it bears adequate "indicia of reliability." Reliability can be inferred without more in a case where the evidence falls within a firmly rooted hearsay exception. In other cases, the evidence must be excluded, at least absent a showing of particularized guarantees of trustworthiness.

In *Roberts*, although declining to "map out a theory of the Confrontation Clause that would determine the validity of all hearsay exceptions," the Supreme Court stated without qualification that sufficient trustworthiness of hearsay statements of witnesses not called at trial, whether or not the declarant must be shown to be unavailable, can be "inferred without more" with respect to evidence falling squarely within a "firmly rooted hearsay exception." The Supreme Court also provided for the admission of statements not falling within a "firmly rooted" hearsay exception if such statement possesses "particularized guarantees of trustworthiness." Notably, the court's language exactly fits the requirements of Rule 807. Pursuant to Rule 807(a)(1), evidence can be admitted only if it possesses "equivalent circumstantial guarantees of trustworthiness" to the "firmly rooted" hearsay exceptions. Thus evidence properly admitted pursuant to Rule 807 also meets the requirements of the confrontation clause.

The quotation from *Roberts* presented above states that a hearsay statement falling within a hearsay exception contained in Rule 803 or an exemption through definition as "not hearsay" in Rule 801(d)(2) may be admitted against the criminal defendant in the normal case only if the government produces the declarant so he can be subjected to cross-examination at trial, or, if not produced, the government has made a sufficient showing that the declarant is not available to testify. Presumably, production would include making the declarant available to be called by the prosecution for direct examination at the option of the accused and subjected to cross-examination concerning the hearsay statement. In addition, if the declarant is not available for cross-examination at trial, the hearsay statement may be admitted only if it bears adequate "indicia of reliability." However, indicia of reliability "can be inferred without more in a case where the evidence falls within a firmly rooted hearsay exception." Taken literally, almost all hearsay exceptions in Rule 803 as well as statements defined as not hearsay in Rule 801(d)(2) could require a showing of unavailability or the production of an available declarant when a statement which is hearsay under Rules 801(a)–(c) is offered against the accused.

Several factors suggested that the Supreme Court had no such intention in mind. First, the foregoing indication in *Roberts* was made in the context of a discussion of the former testimony hearsay exception, Rule 804(b)(1), a hearsay exception which itself requires unavailability. Moreover, the casualness displayed in making the comment with respect to unavailability generally in the context of a hearsay exception requiring unavailability belied any intention to make a radical change in the law. As *Roberts* itself stated, while the confrontation clause "normally requires" a showing of unavailability, "competing interests" may warrant dispensing with confrontation at trial, and further relaxation of the hearsay rule in some cases depending on "considerations of public policy and the necessities of the case." The opinion also indicated that a demonstration of unavailability or production of the declarant is not required when the utility of confrontation is remote. In this context, it is interesting to note that generally speaking neither the state courts, the United States Courts of Appeals, nor the leading commentators on the Federal Rules of Evidence construed *Roberts* as ushering such a radical change. Finally, it is suggested that any reading of *Roberts* as mandating a requirement of unavailability or production with respect to almost all hearsay statements admissible pursuant to Rule 803 or Rule 801(d)(2) offered against the criminal defendant was completely out of character with other recent decisions of the Supreme Court, including Dutton v. Evans, 400 U.S. 74 (1970).

In United States v. Inadi, 475 U.S. 387 (1986), the Supreme Court addressed the question whether the statement in *Roberts* that "the Confrontation Clause normally requires a showing that [the declarant] is unavailable" applies to coconspirator hearsay statements. The Supreme Court held that considerations of reliability and necessity, benefit, and burden all support its conclusion that the confrontation clause does not mandate an initial showing of unavailability of the declarant before a statement of a coconspirator may be received in evidence. In White v. Illinois, 502 U.S. 346 (1992), the Supreme Court in the context of the "spontaneous declaration," see Rule 803(2), and the "medical examination," see Rule 803(4), hearsay exceptions being employed in a child sexual assault prosecution, went even further declaring that *Inadi* held that "*Roberts* stands for the proposition that unavailability analysis is a necessary part of Confrontation Clause inquiry only when the challenged out-of-court statements were made in the course of a prior judicial proceeding," Rule 804(b)(1).

The second question raised by *Roberts* with respect to the admissibility of a statement of a coconspirator under the confrontation clause whether a statement of a coconspirator admitted as a representative admission of a party-opponent falls within the notion of a "firmly rooted hearsay exception," or conversely whether such an admission of a party-opponent requires a "showing of particularized guarantees of trustworthiness," was answered by the Supreme Court in Bourjaily v. United States, 483 U.S. 171 (1987), in the affirmative: "We think the coconspirator exception to the hearsay rule is firmly enough rooted in our jurisprudence that, under this Court's holding in *Roberts*, a court need not independently inquire into the reliability of such statements." Interestingly, the majority opinion determines that the coconspirator hearsay exception satisfies the second prong of *Roberts*, not on the basis of an assessment of reliability, but rather on the basis that the coconspirator exception is of long standing tradition. The fact that an agency and adversary system plus necessity rationale are commonly asserted to support the common law coconspirator hearsay exception rather than an assessment of reliability was completely ignored. The fact that the adversary system rationale led the drafters of the Federal Rules of Evidence to provide that admissions of a party-opponent are not barred by application of the rule against hearsay by being defined in Rule 801(d)(2) as "not hearsay" rather than included as an exception in Rule 803 was completely overlooked. Thus, in *Bourjaily*, the court answered the question posed by the second prong of *Roberts* as to whether a statement of a nonappearing declarant admissible under the rules of evidence under a not hearsay definition or exception for a statement of a coconspirator "bears adequate 'indicia of reliability'" without ever exploring the reliability of statements of a coconspirator. In fact the court in *Bourjaily* may fairly be said to have gone so far as to restate *Roberts'* second prong so as to remove the concept of "firmly rooted" from being a means to infer "indicia of reliability" and reintroduce "firmly rooted" as an alternative method of satisfying *Roberts'* second prong, i.e., any statement of a nonappearing declarant meeting the requirements of a "firmly rooted hearsay" exception does not run afoul of the confrontation clause. Under such a gloss, the court would not examine a "firmly rooted" hearsay exception to determine whether it in fact possesses "adequate 'indicia of reliability'",—being of long standing tradition was all that was required. Other than with respect to statements against penal interest, Rule 804(b)(3), all of the hearsay exceptions and not hearsay definitions specifically denominated in Rules 801(d)(2), 803 and 804 were considered "firmly rooted."

In Lilly v. Virginia, 527 U.S. 116 (1999), a case without a majority opinion, the Supreme Court indicated, more or less explicitly, that the admission of custodial statements to law enforcement personnel against penal interest, i.e., testimonial material, such as oral statements regardless of whether tape recorded or videotaped, written statements, and affidavits, whether or not constituting a confession, that incriminate another person should ordinarily be found to have violated the confrontation clause when admitted against such other person in a criminal case; such evidence is "presumptively unreliable". It is clear that such a custodial statement to law enforcement personnel does not fall within a firmly rooted exception. However, because the various opinions employ different rationales and frequently refer to the facts surrounding the actual making of the statement, sometimes but not always mentioning that the declarant in the matter at hand was clearly attempting to shift blame to another, there existed ample wiggle room for lower courts to permit a custodial statement to law enforcement personnel into evidence if so inclined in spite of the clear tenor of the majority of the justices to the contrary. Thus, applying *Lilly*, it was not surprising to find some lower courts permitting a custodial statement to law enforcement personnel that incriminates another person to be admitted against such other person in a criminal case, not as a firmly rooted hearsay exception, but upon a finding of "particularized guarantees of trustworthiness".

Under *Lilly* it was clear that noncustodial incriminating collateral statements, while not firmly rooted, may be admitted against such other person in a criminal case pursuant to the confrontation clause if they satisfy the "particularized guarantees of trustworthiness" prong of *Roberts*.

Determining under what circumstances, a noncustodial (or possibly even a custodial statement) incriminating collateral statement in fact satisfies the "particularized guarantees of trustworthiness" prong of *Roberts* was unclear as *Lilly* did not contain a majority opinion outlining the factors appropriately considered in making such a determination. The foregoing question was of less concern in the federal court as Williamson v. United States, 512 U.S. 594 (1994) already declared non-self-inculpatory collateral statements inadmissible under Rule 804(b)(3). Former testimony, including depositions, meeting the requirements of Rules 804(a) and 804(b)(1) was unaffected by *Lilly* and continued to satisfy the requirements of the confrontation clause.

In short, *Inadi, White, Bourjaily* and *Lilly* interpreted the confrontation clause to mean that statements falling within any traditional firmly rooted common law hearsay exception (i.e., all provided except statements against penal interest under Rule 804(b)(3) and statements offered under the residual exception of Rule 807), were sufficiently reliable on their face to be admitted against the accused and that the imposition of a requirement of unavailability by the confrontation clause exists only when the challenged out-of-court statement was made in the course of a prior judicial proceeding, Rule 804(b)(1). If it was good enough for the Federal Rules of Evidence, it was good enough for the confrontation clause.

***Crawford* to *Clark*.** Well, along came Crawford v. Washington, 541 U.S. 36 (2004). In *Crawford*, the United States Supreme Court held that a "testimonial" statement is not admissible under the confrontation clause if the out of court declarant does not testify at the criminal trial subject to cross-examination unless the criminal defendant had a prior opportunity for cross-examination. The Supreme Court, however, stated, "[w]e leave for another day any effort to spell out a comprehensive definition of 'testimonial,'" while adding "[w]hatever the term covers, it applies at minimum to prior testimony at a preliminary hearing, before a grand jury, at a formal trial; and to police interrogations."

Justice Scalia, writing for the majority taking a historical approach, stated that with respect to the meaning of the confrontation clause the history of the Sixth Amendment supports two inferences. First, the principal evil at which the confrontation clause was directed was the civil-law mode of criminal procedure, and particularly its use of *ex parte* examinations as evidence against the accused. Second, the Framers would not have allowed admission of "testimonial" statements of a witness who did not appear at trial unless he was unavailable to testify and the defendant had had a prior opportunity for cross-examination.

With respect to defining "testimonial" statements, *Crawford* states:

> Various formulations of this core class of "testimonial" statements exist: *ex parte* in-court testimony or its functional equivalent that is, material such as affidavits, custodial examinations, prior testimony that the defendant was unable to cross-examine, or similar pretrial statements that declarants would reasonably expect to be used prosecutorially," Brief for Petitioner 23; "extrajudicial statements . . . contained in formalized testimonial materials, such as affidavits, depositions, prior testimony, or confessions," White v. Illinois, 502 U.S. 346, 365, 112 S.Ct. 736, 116 L.Ed.2d 848 (1992) (THOMAS, J. joined by SCALIA, J., concurring in part and concurring in judgment); "statements that were made under circumstances which would lead an objective witness reasonably to believe that the statement would be available for use

at a later trial," Brief for National Association of Criminal Defense Lawyers et al. as *Amici Curiae 3*. These formulations all share a common nucleus and thus define the Clause's coverage at various levels of abstraction around it. Regardless of the precise articulation, some statements qualify under any definition for example, *ex parte* testimony at a preliminary hearing.

Statements taken by police officers in the course of interrogations are also testimonial under even a narrow standard.

* * *

Where nontestimonial hearsay is at issue, it is wholly consistent with the Framers' design to afford the States flexibility in their development of hearsay law as does *Roberts*, and as would an approach that exempted such statements from Confrontation Clause scrutiny altogether. Where testimonial evidence is at issue, however, the Sixth Amendment demands what the common law required: unavailability and a prior opportunity for cross-examination. We leave for another day any effort to spell out a comprehensive definition of "testimonial." Whatever else the term covers, it applies at a minimum to prior testimony at a preliminary hearing, before a grand jury, or at a former trial; and to police interrogations. These are the modern practices with closest kinship to the abuses at which the Confrontation Clause was directed.

Given the absence in *Crawford* of a "comprehensive definition of 'testimonial'," it was not surprising that lower courts immediately employed a plethora of interpretations of "testimonial" leading to conflicting results. Of particular concern was the lack of coherence in the numerous decisions addressing whether 911 calls and statements made to police officers upon arrival at the scene were or were not "testimonial".

In Davis v. Washington, 547 U.S. 813 (2006), Justice Scalia, once again writing for the majority, stated:

Without attempting to produce an exhaustive classification of all conceivable statements or even all conceivable statements in response to police interrogation as either testimonial or nontestimonial, it suffices to decide the present cases to hold as follows: Statements are nontestimonial when made in the course of police interrogation under circumstances objectively indicating that the primary purpose of the interrogation is to enable police assistance to meet an ongoing emergency. They are testimonial when the circumstances objectively indicate that there is no such ongoing emergency, and that the primary purpose of the interrogation is to establish or prove past events potentially relevant to later criminal prosecution.

Davis continued that statements volunteered to a government official may also be testimonial if the primary purpose upon receipt of such statements is to establish or prove past events potentially relevant to later criminal prosecution. Whether the circumstances surrounding the making of the out-of-court statement were formal and solemn and whether the statement resulted from police interrogation or judicial examination, components of the concept of "testimonial" contained in *Crawford*, were completely abandoned as significant to confrontation clause analysis in *Davis*.

Pursuant to *Davis*, any statement made to or elicited by a police officer, other law enforcement personnel, or a judicial officer under circumstances objectively indicating at the time made that the primary purpose to which the statement will be used by the government is to establish or prove *past* events potentially relevant to later criminal prosecutions is "testimonial". Statements which are "testimonial" are not admissible under the confrontation clause if the out-of-court declarant does not testify at the criminal trial subject to cross-examination unless the criminal defendant had a prior opportunity for cross-examination. Conversely, any statement made to or elicited by a police officer, other law enforcement personnel, or a judicial officer under circumstances objectively indicating at the time made that the primary purpose to which the statement will be used by the government is other than prosecution of a past criminal event is nontestimonial. In addition to curtailment of an ongoing crime, the other primary purpose encompassed by the term "emergency" in *Davis*, protection of the police and third parties, as well as the victim from immediate further attack illustrate primary other purposes. While emergency as another primary purpose in *Davis* was not defined, emergency logically extends to circumstances requiring assistance from medical personnel, firefighters, or other government services such as those dealing with hazardous materials.

Very importantly, note that even though *Davis* like *Crawford* before it explicitly declined to present a comprehensive definition of "testimonial", *Davis* nevertheless clearly supports the proposition that *all other statements*, i.e., statements where the primary purpose to which the statement is employed at the time made does not relate to prosecuting a past criminal event, even when made to a government official, are not "testimonial." Thus, as occurred in *Davis*, a 911 call to an operator considered a government official, describing an ongoing emergency as to which the police will be called to act is not testimonial, while any statements made once the emergency has ceased are testimonial as the primary purpose on the part of the government viewed objectively shifted from responding to the emergency to proving past events relevant to later criminal prosecution. All statements made to someone other than a government official are always "nontestimonial"; unavailability of the declarant for cross-examination does not preclude admissibility against the criminal defendant.

Davis, both from what it states and does not state, clearly opines that the objective circumstance are to be considered from the perspective of the eliciting or receiving government agent and not the declarant in determining the primary purpose to which such statements are to be employed. Thus, consistent with the two historical inferences described in Crawford of consequence in determining the meaning of the confrontation clause, it is solely the conduct of police officers, other law enforcement personnel and judicial officers that is of concern.

In short, while *Davis* expressly states that it is not presenting a comprehensive definition of "testimonial", *Davis* may nevertheless in fact have done so or come very close to having done so and thus be the "another day" referred to in *Crawford*. *Davis* by its facts, considered together with what it said and didn't say, clearly rejects all three of the possible definitions of testimonial suggested in *Crawford* including in particular any focus upon whether hearsay statements made by the nontestifying out-of-court declarant "were made under circumstances which would lead an objective witness reasonably to believe that the statement would be available for use at a later trial." In *Davis* itself both the 911 statement by the declarant that Davis was then beating on her and the later statement that Davis had just run out the door after hitting her would both be statements an objective witness would reasonably believe would be available for use at a later trial. Yet no mention of such a fact was made in *Davis* whatsoever. Instead *Davis* focused its definition of testimonial solely upon the eliciting or receiving police officer, other law enforcement personnel, or judicial officer asking whether at the time made the primary purpose to which the statement will be used by the government is to establish or prove past events potentially relevant to a later criminal prosecution. In *Davis* the initial statement received for the primary purpose of responding to an emergency case declared nontestimonial while the subsequent statement was held to be testimonial in that the primary purpose to which the statement was employed by the police was "to establish or prove past events potentially relevant to later criminal prosecution." Similarly, a statement made by a doorman that Mr. Smith left by taxi at about 6:00 a.m. yesterday morning to a police officer would be testimonial regardless of the fact that since the statement is not accusatory in nature an objective witness would not reasonably expect the statement to be used in a later trial. On the other hand, a statement made to a police officer, "Call 911 and get an ambulance, my son just shot his father," would be nontestimonial according to *Davis* as the primary purpose upon receipt would be to respond to a medical emergency in spite of the fact that the declarant as an objective witness would reasonably believe that the statement would be used in a later trial. The declarant's expectations under *Davis* are irrelevant—only the primary purpose to which the police officer, other law enforcement personnel, or judicial officer puts the statement is of concern in determining if a statement is testimonial. Obviously, all statements not being testified to by a police officer, other law enforcement personnel or judicial officer are nontestimonial.

In Melendez-Diaz v. Massachusetts, 557 U.S. 305 (2009), the United States Supreme Court held that an analyst's affidavit that a substance was cocaine was "testimonial" and thus the admission of an analyst's affidavit in the absence of the testimony of the analyst herself who conducted the test violated the confrontation clause. Unfortunately in penning *Melendez-Diaz* Justice Scalia, continuing his one Justice rampage of supposed confrontation clause analysis, did not refer to the "primary purpose" test of *Davis*. Instead, Justice Scalia mischievously returned to *Crawford* stating that the analyst's affidavit fell within the "core class of testimonial statements." Since the sole purpose of the analyst's affidavit was to establish the identity in court of the substance removed from the accused as cocaine, the affidavit was "made under circumstances which would lead an objective witness reasonably to believe that the statement would be available for use at a later trial." Thus, in spite of the clear renunciation in *Davis* of the relevance of the declarant's expectation in favor of a focus solely upon the primary purpose of the government official, and only the government official, upon receipt of the out of court statement, Justice Scalia relied, fortunately in dicta, upon the clearly previously disregarded objective witness reasonable belief approach to determining whether a statement is "testimonial" or "nontestimonial". With any luck at all, the dicta in *Melendez-Diaz* would be recognized as simply another ill-advised attempt by Justice Scalia to fashion the confrontation clause in a manner only he, if anyone, is willing to accept as fundamentally sound and consistent in history, logic, and practice.

Such was not to be the case. In Michigan v. Bryant, 562 U.S. 344 (2011), Justice Sotomayor, writing for the majority, with Justice Scalia vehemently dissenting, the Supreme Court addressed the admissibility under the confrontation clause of a statement of a murder victim, i.e., "Rick shot me", made while then lying on the ground next to his car at a gas station about six blocks from the drug dealer's house to the police almost 25 minutes after having been shot in the back by the victim's drug dealer, Rick, at the drug dealer's home. The Supreme Court found the victim's statement to be nontestimonial; the primary purpose of the police interrogation of the victim was to enable assistance to meet an ongoing emergency. According to *Bryant*, a statement is testimonial, if upon objective evaluation of the statement and action of the parties involved in the interrogation, along with the formality or informality of the interrogation, considered in light of the circumstances in which the interrogation occurred, the court concludes that the primary purpose of the interrogation was to establish or prove past events relevant to a later criminal prosecution. Pursuant to the combined approach of *Bryant*, the court must consider the statements and actions of both the declarant and the interrogating government official, along with the formality or informality present, in determining objectively the "primary purpose" of the interrogation.

Following *Melendez-Diaz*, generally speaking, the testimony of a laboratory supervisor who did not perform but reviewed the analysis at issue, was familiar with laboratory procedures, rendered his own analysis or conclusion, and who signed the report, was found by lower courts to have satisfied the confrontation clause. In Bullcoming v. New Mexico, 564 U.S. 647 (2011), the United States Supreme Court, speaking through Justice Ginsburg agreed: the prosecution may introduce a laboratory or similar report only through a live witness competent to testify to the truth of the statements made in the report, i.e., a live witness who signed the certification or performed or observed the test reported in the certification.

Almost immediately following the *Bullcoming* opinion, the United States Supreme Court took certiorari in Williams v. Illinois, 567 U.S. 50 (2012), obviously based upon the hope of the dissenters in *Melendez-Diaz* and *Bullcoming* to bring about a change in result. *Williams* did not accomplish the goal. In fact, in a peculiar four one four opinion, the dissent written by Justice Kagan, coupled with the substance of Justice Thomas's concurrence in the judgment only, results in a five justice affirmation of both *Melendez-Diaz* and *Bullcoming*. *Williams*, in fact, extends the confrontation clause analysis of *Melendez-Diaz* and *Bullcoming* to the introduction of a forensic laboratory report ostensibly for basis only pursuant to Rule 703 of the Federal Rules of Evidence or a state law equivalent, i.e., the confrontation clause is satisfied only through a live witness competent to testify to the truth of the statements made in the report—a live witness who signed he certification or performed or observed the test reported in the certification.

Justice Kagan in ending her dissent opines initially that *Williams* leaves "significant confusion" in its wake only to conclude finally that "until a majority of this Court reverses or confines [*Melendez-Diaz* and *Bullcoming*], I would understand them as continuing to govern, in every particular, the admission of forensic evidence." Given the support in Justice Thomas's opinion in fact of the dissents reaffirmation of *Melendez-Diaz* and *Bullcoming*, Justice Kagan's later conclusion is correct—long live *Melendez-Diaz* and *Bullcoming*.

The plurality and concurring opinions in *Williams* clearly illustrate the observation that certain United States Supreme Court opinions simply serve to undermine the public's faith in our judicial system.

Justice Thomas's controlling concurring opinion, sharply criticized by the plurality and dissent, found the out of court laboratory statements nontestimonial solely on the basis of lack of the requisite "formality and solemnity", i.e., there is no certification or attestation that the statements contained in the report accurately reflect the DNA testing process used or the results obtained. Seriously!!!

The plurality opinion of Justice Alito that reasonable reliance by the testifying expert witness on a forensic laboratory report in *Williams* was for basis purposes only and not for its truth thus not violating the confrontation clause received only the weakest of support in the concurrence of Justice Breyer, i.e., "because the plurality's opinion is basically consistent with my views set forth, I join that opinion in full." In fact, nothing in the plurality opinion is "basically consistent" with Justice Breyer's position that forensic laboratory reports "lie" presumptively" "outside the perimeter of the clause as established by the Court's precedents."

Justice Alito's in reality three justice plurality opinion, comes on the heels of the Justices' statement during oral argument that the facts of *Williams*, i.e., Rule 703 reasonable reliance for basis only introduction of a DNA report of Cellmark, an outside accredited laboratory, were "worse" than *Bullcoming*. Nevertheless, Justice Alito for some reason felt compelled to uphold admission initially on the ground that *Williams* involved a bench trial, with the trial court better able than a jury to understand and apply the principle of evidence admitted for basis only. Justice Alito acknowledges that the risk of substantive employment increases with a jury trial and that "absent and evaluation of the risk of juror confusion and careful jury instruction, the testimony could not have gone to a jury."

Justice Alito's second ground for affirmance is no less disconcerting. The Cellmark DNA laboratory report is not testimonial since its primary purpose was not to accuse a "targeted individual" of engaging in criminal conduct. As Justice Thomas observes, "under this formulation, statements made 'before any suspect was identified' are beyond the scope of the confrontation clause." Justice Thomas further accurately observes that "there is no textual justification, however, for limiting the confrontation right to statements made after the accused's identity became known." While many commentators, including your author, have at one time or another supported an "accusatory" limitation interpretation of the confrontation clause, Justice Alito's particular identified accused version of the "accusatory" statement limitation is extremely unlikely to receive a better response in the literature that it received in Justice Thomas's and Justice Kagan's opinions.

In summary, the four dissenters in *Melendez-Diaz* and *Bullcoming* clearly chose the wrong vehicle in *Williams* to seek a fifth Justice for their position with respect to forensic laboratory reports.

It should be noted that the "significant confusion" anticipated by Justice Kagan has in fact shown its ugly head. The Seventh Circuit in United States v. Turner, 709 F.3d 1187 (7th Cir. 2013), found a DNA report prepared by a nontestifying laboratory technician presented in court by a supervisor who peer reviewed the report to be testimonial in part on the basis of satisfaction of the plurality opinions "targeted" accused approach and the fact *Turner* involved a jury trial. Both the California and Illinois Supreme Courts, based on completely different analyses, have concluded that an autopsy report is nontestimonial. See People v. Dungo, 286 P.3d 442 (Cal. 2012) (asserting that Justice Thomas's concurring opinion is controlling and that autopsy reports lack the "formality" and "solemnity" required to be considered testimonial); People v. Leach, 980 N.E.2d 570 (Ill. 2012) (relying on plurality opinion of Justice Alito, the autopsy report was not prepared for the primary purpose of accusing a particular targeted individual of a crime and did not link the already arrested defendant to the homicide.).

Of even more significance are the opinions of many recent state and federal courts, characterized as *"Forensic analyst independent review"* in the "Application Summary" infra, in clear conflict with the holdings of both *Melendez-Diaz* and *Bullcoming* in fact adopting the dissenter's opinions in both without attribution concluding that a forensic examiner who neither signed the certificate nor performed or observed the test reported in the certification, testifying to a so called "independent review" opinion, provides an opportunity to cross-examine satisfying the confrontation clause.

In Ohio v. Clark, 576 U.S. 237, 135 S.Ct. 2173 (2015), the United States Supreme Court applying the dual primary purpose approach of *Bryant* to statements by a child to his preschool teacher under a mandatory obligation to report suspected abuse to law enforcement authorities held that the child's statements were not testimonial, i.e., the statements were not made with the primary purpose of creating evidence for Clark's prosecution. A mandatory reporting obligation alone does not convert a conversation between a teacher and her student into a law enforcement mission aimed at gathering evidence for prosecution. In dicta, in *Clark* the United States Supreme Court declined to adopt a categorical rule excluding statements made to other than law enforcement personnel from operation of the confrontation clause.

"Testimonial" vs. "Nontestimonial": synthesis. Combining the *holding* of *Melendez-Diaz* confirmed in *Bullcoming* and possibly by *Williams* that an analyst's affidavit, i.e., a government created statement opining that a substance was cocaine is "testimonial", with the Supreme Court's jurisprudence in *Crawford/Davis/Bryant* and *Clark,* relating to informal or formal interrogations, when the declarant of the out of court statement is not and was not subject to cross-examination concerning the statement, the following defines the concept of "testimonial" for confrontation clause purposes:

> An out of court statement is "testimonial" only if hearsay as defined in Rule 801(a)–(d) and the statement was made by, or made to, or elicited by a police officer, other law enforcement personnel, or a judicial officer, if upon objective evaluation of the statement and actions of both the declarant and interrogator, if any, involved in the interrogation or statement creation, along with the informality or formality of the interrogation or statement creation, considered in light of the circumstance in which the interrogation or statement creation occurred, the court concludes that the primary purpose of the interrogation or statement creation was to establish or prove past events relevant to a later criminal prosecution.

An out of court statement includes not only verbatim recitation but also includes any outline, description, summary, etc., of the out of court statement that, fairly read, conveys to the jury the substance of the out of court assertion.

Out of court statements defined as not hearsay pursuant to Rule 801 do not present a confrontation clause issue. Thus, such statements may fairly be referred to as "nontestimonial". Out of court statements which are not hearsay under Rule 801 (a)–(c) because relevant for the fact said such as verbal act, effect on listener, or impeachment, do not rely upon the credibility of the out of court declarant. With respect to those prior statements of a declarant who testifies at trial and is subject to cross-examination about the prior statement admissible under either Rule 801(d)(1)(A), prior inconsistent statement, Rule 801(d)(1)(B), prior consistent statement, or Rule 801(d)(1)(C), prior statement of identification, the right to confront the witness against the criminal defendant has been provided. Finally, statements constituting an admission of a party opponent, Rule 801(d)(2), admissible pursuant to the adversary system theory of litigation, are also nontestimonial. Lack of opportunity to cross-examine is deprived of significance by the incongruity of the party objecting to his own statement on the ground that he was not subject to cross-examination by himself at the time.

In applying the foregoing combined approach to a particular interrogation, determining whether the primary purpose of an interrogation is to establish or prove past events relevant to a later prosecution or conversely for another primary purpose such as to enable police assistance to meet an ongoing emergency, the interrogator's purpose in logic and theory should be dominant as it is the interrogator who is asking the questions and it is the interrogator's conduct that ultimately determines how in fact the declarant's statement is ultimately in fact primarily employed. The informality or formality of the interrogations or statement creation and the primary purpose for which the declarant made the statement, objectively viewed, ultimately in fact should simply inform the decision by the governmental official as to the primary purpose to which the declarant's created statement or statement resulting from the interrogation will in fact be employed. While the foregoing is correct in logic and theory, *Bryant* itself found it unnecessary to decide how a conflict in primary purpose should be reached, rejecting in the process the suggestion by Justice Scalia dissenting of an apparent intent to give controlling weight to the "intentions of the police" as a misreading of the majority opinion. Justice Scalia counters by noting that the majority opinion fails to "provide an answer to this [conflict in primary purpose situation] glaringly obvious problem, probably because it does not have one" leaving judges free to pick an answer, i.e., "reach the 'fairest' result under the totality of the circumstances".

Any analysis, evaluation, prediction, etc., concerning *Crawford*, as narrowed in *Davis*, as interpreted in *Melendez-Diaz*, *Bullcoming*, and possibly in *Williams*, and as expanded in *Bryant*, and confirmed in *Clark,* must both begin and end with the caveat that given the variety of approaches taken by the lower courts to *Crawford/Davis* and its progeny, one should fully expect a tremendous diversity of interpretation of the confrontation clause to continue. Thus, for example, if a child describes an act of sexual abuse to a medical professional closely associated with law enforcement, since the primary purpose of the child declarant was presumably receiving medical assistance, even if the primary purpose of the recipient of the statement was to establish or prove past events relevant to a later criminal prosecution, following *Bryant* one can expect more and more decisions to focus on the declarant's primary purpose and find the statement to be nontestimonial. Similarly, as referenced in *Bryant*, if the domestic violence victim is perceived as "want[ing] the threat to her and to other potential victims to end, but that does not necessarily mean that the victim wants or envisions prosecution of the assailant," a court may emphasize the declarant's primary purpose and classify the statement as "nontestimonial", ironically thus making the statement admissible under the confrontation clause in the assailant's criminal prosecution in spite of the victim's lack of desire to see the assailant prosecuted. In short, as predicted by Justice Scalia, *Bryant* may usher in a new era of " 'fairest' result", which most likely will in fact be the interpretation favoring a nontestimonial determination and consequent admissibility.

Finally, what role is played by the confrontation clause, if any, in governing the admissibility of hearsay statements that are "nontestimonial" admitted pursuant to a hearsay exception made by a declarant who does not testify at the criminal trial subject to cross-examination? In other words, is the *Roberts* firmly rooted or particularized guarantees of trustworthiness requirement applicable to nontestimonial statements of nontestifying declarants? After *Crawford* failed to directly address this issue, lower courts almost unanimously concluded that *Roberts* did govern "nontestimonial statements. *Davis*, however, opines that the confrontation clause applies only to "testimonial" hearsay statements from which it follows that *Roberts* does not govern admissibility under the confrontation clause of "nontestimonial" statements. The fact that *Roberts* was in fact overruled in its entirety by *Crawford* was confirmed in Wharton v. Bockting, 549 U.S. 406 (2007), a decision holding that *Crawford* does not apply retroactively, but questioned somewhat in dicta in *Clark* where the United States Supreme Court declined to adopt a categorical rule excluding statements made to other than law enforcement personnel from operation of the confrontation clause.

Application summary. Supporting authority may be located on Westlaw in Graham, Handbook of Federal Evidence, § 808:7, supplemented annually.

"Subject to cross-examination" thus satisfying confrontation right

Bond hearing.

Depositions.

Closed-circuit television.

Forensic analyst available to be called at request of criminal defendant.

Forensic analyst had sufficient personal knowledge. It is very likely that many states have adjusted their forensic laboratory procedures to create forensic laboratory analysts with sufficient involvement with the underlying test and report preparation, i.e., signed the certification or performed or observed the test reported in the certification, to be declared by the court to possess sufficient personnel knowledge when called as a witness at trial. See, e.g., Galloway v. State, 122 So.3d 614 (Miss. 2013); State v. Deadwiller, 834 N.E.2d 362 (Wis. 2013); People v. Nelson, 994 N.E.2d 597 (Ill.App. 1 Dist. 2013).

Forensic analyst independent review opinion testimony. In spite of *Melendez-Diaz* and *Bullcoming,* approximately 22 state jurisdictions and 4 federal courts of appeal have found that the right of confrontation satisfied when a supervisor or other independent analyst, subject to cross-examination, renders an "independent" opinion following a "review" of the test results, testing procedures, etc., and objective evaluation of the raw data.

Impaired witness.

Lack of recollection. A refusal or inability of the witness to recall the events recorded in a prior statement does not render the witness unavailable for purposes of cross-examination and the confrontation clause.

Lack of testimony on direct as to content of statement.

Notice-and-demand.

Preliminary hearing.

Prior cross-examination.

"Not subject to cross-examination" thus not satisfying confrontation right

Appears but does not communicate.

Appears but recalcitrance precludes effective cross-examination.

Cross-examination precluded.

Cross-examination opportunity inadequate.

Debilitating health condition.

Written interrogatories.

Nontestimonial

Absence of record.

Admission by party-opponent, Rule 801(d)(2)(A).

Autopsy reports. Contra cases under **"Testimonial".**

Blood test certification.

Bruton redacted confession.

Business records.

Certificate of mailing.

Certified domestic and foreign business records, Rule 902(11) and (12), and similar authentications.

Chain of custody.

Co-conspirator statement. Co-conspirator statements have been found to be nontestimonial as verbal acts not being offered for their truth or simply because *Crawford* says so.

Defendant not suspect at time of statement.

Driving record; abstract.

Drug purchase log.

Dying declaration.

Fingerprint cards.

Gang expert testimony.

Immigration A-file documents.

Interpreter's statements. Contra cases under **"Testimonial".**

Intoxilyzer certificate of accuracy.

Not an element of crime.

Machine is not a witness.

Medical diagnosis or treatment primary purpose of statement even if person receiving statement associated with law enforcement.

Medical emergency.

Medical records.

Not hearsay statements. The confrontation clause does not apply to out-of-court statements offered in evidence for a purpose other than establishing the truth of the matter asserted as hearsay is defined in Rule 801(a) to (c), including statements offered for their effect on listener, to place other statements in context, and as reasonably relied upon pursuant to Rule 703. But see discussion supra with respect to *Williams* and Rule 703.

Police ongoing emergency; initial investigation.

Police ongoing emergency. 911.

Prior conviction records.

Prison recorded phone calls.

Public records.

Radar calibration.

Rule of completeness.

Search warrant.

Statement to confidential informant.

Statements to other than government officials.

Statements to police to initiate investigation of ongoing criminal activity.

Suppression hearing.

Warrants of deportation.

Testimonial

Absence of business or public record.

Autopsy reports. Contra cases under **"Nontestimonial".**

Confidential informant's statement.

Forensic analyst independent review. See cases under **"Subject to cross-examination."**

Forensic machine test results.

Future prosecution primary purpose of statement of alleged victim made to medical professional associated with law enforcement.

Guilty plea.

Guilty plea allocution.

Implied statements.

Interpreter's statements. Contra cases under **"Nontestimonial".**

Jury sentencing trial.

No police ongoing emergency; initial investigation.

Records prepared for criminal proceeding.

Sting operation.

Forfeiture/Waiver

Door opening.

Forfeiture by wrongdoing.

Rebuttal.

Rule of completeness.

Stipulation by counsel.

Waiver by counsel.

Waiver by failure to request appearance.

APPENDIX D
ANSWER SHEETS

SPECIFIC SUBJECT MATTER REVIEW

1. Relevance and the Exclusion of Relevant Evidence: Fed.R.Evid. 401–403

1. (T)   2. (T)   3. (T)   4. (T)   5. (T)
   (F)   (F)   (F)   (F)   (F)

2. Competency of Lay Witnesses: Fed.R.Evid. 601–606

1. (T)   2. (T)   3. (T)   4. (T)   5. (T)
   (F)   (F)   (F)   (F)   (F)

6. (T)   7. (T)   8. (T)   9. (T)   10. (T)
   (F)   (F)   (F)   (F)   (F)

3. Direct Examination: Fed. R. Evid. 106, 611(c), 612, 615

1. (T)   2. (T)   3. (T)   4. (T)   5. (T)
   (F)   (F)   (F)   (F)   (F)

6. (T)   7. (T)   8. (T)   9. (T)   10. (T)
   (F)   (F)   (F)   (F)   (F)

11. (T)   12. (T)   13. (T)   14. (T)   15. (T)
   (F)   (F)   (F)   (F)   (F)

4. Hearsay Definition: Fed.R.Evid. 801(a)–(d)

1. (T)   2. (T)   3. (T)   4. (T)   5. (T)
   (F)   (F)   (F)   (F)   (F)

6. (T)   7. (T)   8. (T)   9. (T)   10. (T)
   (F)   (F)   (F)   (F)   (F)

11. (T)   12. (T)   13. (T)   14. (T)   15. (T)
   (F)   (F)   (F)   (F)   (F)

16. (T)   17. (T)   18. (T)   19. (T)   20. (T)
   (F)   (F)   (F)   (F)   (F)

21. (T)   22. (T)   23. (T)   24. (T)   25. (T)
   (F)   (F)   (F)   (F)   (F)

26.	(T) (F)	27.	(T) (F)	28.	(T) (F)	29.	(T) (F)	30.	(T) (F)
31.	(T) (F)	32.	(T) (F)	33.	(T) (F)	34.	(T) (F)	35.	(T) (F)
36.	(T) (F)	37.	(T) (F)	38.	(T) (F)	39.	(T) (F)	40.	(T) (F)
41.	(T) (F)	42.	(T) (F)	43.	(T) (F)	44.	(T) (F)	45.	(T) (F)
46.	(T) (F)	47.	(T) (F)	48.	(T) (F)	49.	(T) (F)	50.	(T) (F)

5.   Hearsay Definition and Exceptions: Fed.R.Evid. 801–807

1.	(T) (F)	2.	(T) (F)	3.	(T) (F)	4.	(T) (F)	5.	(T) (F)
6.	(T) (F)	7.	(T) (F)	8.	(T) (F)	9.	(T) (F)	10.	(T) (F)
11.	(T) (F)	12.	(T) (F)	13.	(T) (F)	14.	(T) (F)	15.	(T) (F)
16.	(T) (F)	17.	(T) (F)	18.	(T) (F)	19.	(T) (F)	20.	(T) (F)
21.	(T) (F)	22.	(T) (F)	23.	(T) (F)	24.	(T) (F)	25.	(T) (F)
26.	(T) (F)	27.	(T) (F)	28.	(T) (F)	29.	(T) (F)	30.	(T) (F)
31.	(T) (F)	32.	(T) (F)	33.	(T) (F)	34.	(T) (F)	35.	(T) (F)
36.	(T) (F)	37.	(T) (F)	38.	(T) (F)	39.	(T) (F)	40.	(T) (F)
41.	(T) (F)	42.	(T) (F)	43.	(T) (F)	44.	(T) (F)	45.	(T) (F)
46.	(T) (F)	47.	(T) (F)	48.	(T) (F)	49.	(T) (F)	50.	(T) (F)
51.	(T) (F)	52.	(T) (F)	53.	(T) (F)	54.	(T) (F)	55.	(T) (F)
56.	(T) (F)	57.	(T) (F)	58.	(T) (F)	59.	(T) (F)	60.	(T) (F)

61.	(T) (F)	62.	(T) (F)	63.	(T) (F)	64.	(T) (F)	65.	(T) (F)
66.	(T) (F)	67.	(T) (F)	68.	(T) (F)	69.	(T) (F)	70.	(T) (F)
71.	(T) (F)	72.	(T) (F)	73.	(T) (F)	74.	(T) (F)	75.	(T) (F)
76.	(T) (F)	77.	(T) (F)	78.	(T) (F)	79.	(T) (F)	80.	(T) (F)
81.	(T) (F)	82.	(T) (F)	83.	(T) (F)	84.	(T) (F)	85.	(T) (F)
86.	(T) (F)	87.	(T) (F)	88.	(T) (F)	89.	(T) (F)	90.	(T) (F)
91.	(T) (F)	92.	(T) (F)	93.	(T) (F)	94.	(T) (F)	95.	(T) (F)
96.	(T) (F)	97.	(T) (F)	98.	(T) (F)	99.	(T) (F)	100.	(T) (F)

6. Authentication and Identification: Fed.R. Evid. 901–903

1.	(T) (F)	2.	(T) (F)	3.	(T) (F)	4.	(T) (F)	5.	(T) (F)
6.	(T) (F)	7.	(T) (F)	8.	(T) (F)	9.	(T) (F)	10.	(T) (F)

7. The Original Writing (Best Evidence) Rule: Fed.R. Evid. 1001–1008

1.	(T) (F)	2.	(T) (F)	3.	(T) (F)	4.	(T) (F)	5.	(T) (F)
6.	(T) (F)	7.	(T) (F)	8.	(T) (F)	9.	(T) (F)	10.	(T) (F)

8. Opinions and Expert Testimony: Fed.R.Evid. 701–706

1.	(T) (F)	2.	(T) (F)	3.	(T) (F)	4.	(T) (F)	5.	(T) (F)
6.	(T) (F)	7.	(T) (F)	8.	(T) (F)	9.	(T) (F)	10.	(T) (F)

11. (T)   12. (T)   13. (T)   14. (T)   15. (T)
    (F)   (F)   (F)   (F)   (F)

16. (T)   17. (T)   18. (T)   19. (T)   20. (T)
    (F)   (F)   (F)   (F)   (F)

21. (T)   22. (T)   23. (T)   24. (T)   25. (T)
    (F)   (F)   (F)   (F)   (F)

9. **Character, Habit, and Routine Practice: Fed.R.Evid. 404–406, 412–415**

1. (T)   2. (T)   3. (T)   4. (T)   5. (T)
    (F)   (F)   (F)   (F)   (F)

6. (T)   7. (T)   8. (T)   9. (T)   10. (T)
    (F)   (F)   (F)   (F)   (F)

11. (T)   12. (T)   13. (T)   14. (T)   15. (T)
    (F)   (F)   (F)   (F)   (F)

16. (T)   17. (T)   18. (T)   19. (T)   20. (T)
    (F)   (F)   (F)   (F)   (F)

21. (T)   22. (T)   23. (T)   24. (T)   25. (T)
    (F)   (F)   (F)   (F)   (F)

10. **Real and Demonstrative Evidence, Experiments, and Views**

1. (T)   2. (T)   3. (T)   4. (T)   5. (T)
    (F)   (F)   (F)   (F)   (F)

6. (T)   7. (T)   8. (T)   9. (T)   10. (T)
    (F)   (F)   (F)   (F)   (F)

11. (T)   12. (T)   13. (T)   14. (T)   15. (T)
    (F)   (F)   (F)   (F)   (F)

11. **Cross-Examination**

    A. **Leading Questions; Scope and Extent: Fed.R.Evid. 611(b)(c)**

1. (T)   2. (T)   3. (T)   4. (T)   5. (T)
    (F)   (F)   (F)   (F)   (F)

6. (T)   7. (T)   8. (T)   9. (T)   10. (T)
    (F)   (F)   (F)   (F)   (F)

11.   (T)   12.   (T)   13.   (T)   14.   (T)   15.   (T)
      (F)   (F)   (F)   (F)   (F)

B.   Modes of Impeachment; Collateral and Non Collateral Matters; Good Faith Basis

1.   (T)   2.   (T)   3.   (T)   4.   (T)   5.   (T)
     (F)   (F)   (F)   (F)   (F)

6.   (T)   7.   (T)   8.   (T)   9.   (T)   10.   (T)
     (F)   (F)   (F)   (F)   (F)

C.   Prior Inconsistent Statements: Fed.R.Evid. 613

1.   (T)   2.   (T)   3.   (T)   4.   (T)   5.   (T)
     (F)   (F)   (F)   (F)   (F)

6.   (T)   7.   (T)   8.   (T)   9.   (T)   10.   (T)
     (F)   (F)   (F)   (F)   (F)

11.   (T)   12.   (T)   13.   (T)   14.   (T)   15.   (T)
      (F)   (F)   (F)   (F)   (F)

D.   Untrustworthy Partiality: Bias, Interest, Corruption, Coercion

1.   (T)   2.   (T)   3.   (T)   4.   (T)   5.   (T)
     (F)   (F)   (F)   (F)   (F)

E.   Conviction of a Crime: Fed.R.Evid. 609

1.   (T)   2.   (T)   3.   (T)   4.   (T)   5.   (T)
     (F)   (F)   (F)   (F)   (F)

6.   (T)   7.   (T)   8.   (T)   9.   (T)   10.   (T)
     (F)   (F)   (F)   (F)   (F)

11.   (T)   12.   (T)   13.   (T)   14.   (T)   15.   (T)
      (F)   (F)   (F)   (F)   (F)

16.   (T)   17.   (T)   18.   (T)   19.   (T)   20.   (T)
      (F)   (F)   (F)   (F)   (F)

21.   (T)   22.   (T)   23.   (T)   24.   (T)   25.   (T)
      (F)   (F)   (F)   (F)   (F)

F.   Prior Acts of Misconduct: Fed.R.Evid. 608(b)(1)

1.	(T) (F)	2.	(T) (F)	3.	(T) (F)	4.	(T) (F)	5.	(T) (F)

G.   Character for Truthfulness or Untruthfulness: Fed.R.Evid. 608

1.	(T) (F)	2.	(T) (F)	3.	(T) (F)	4.	(T) (F)	5.	(T) (F)
6.	(T) (F)	7.	(T) (F)	8.	(T) (F)	9.	(T) (F)	10.	(T) (F)
11.	(T) (F)	12.	(T) (F)	13.	(T) (F)	14.	(T) (F)	15.	(T) (F)

12.   Relevant Evidence and Social Policy: Fed.R.Evid. 407–411

1.	(T) (F)	2.	(T) (F)	3.	(T) (F)	4.	(T) (F)	5.	(T) (F)
6.	(T) (F)	7.	(T) (F)	8.	(T) (F)	9.	(T) (F)	10.	(T) (F)
11.	(T) (F)	12.	(T) (F)	13.	(T) (F)	14.	(T) (F)	15.	(T) (F)

13.   Privileges: Fed.R.Evid. 501

1.	(T) (F)	2.	(T) (F)	3.	(T) (F)	4.	(T) (F)	5.	(T) (F)
6.	(T) (F)	7.	(T) (F)	8.	(T) (F)	9.	(T) (F)	10.	(T) (F)
11.	(T) (F)	12.	(T) (F)	13.	(T) (F)	14.	(T) (F)	15.	(T) (F)
16.	(T) (F)	17.	(T) (F)	18.	(T) (F)	19.	(T) (F)	20.	(T) (F)
21.	(T) (F)	22.	(T) (F)	23.	(T) (F)	24.	(T) (F)	25.	(T) (F)
26.	(T) (F)	27.	(T) (F)	28.	(T) (F)	29.	(T) (F)	30.	(T) (F)
31.	(T) (F)	32.	(T) (F)	33.	(T) (F)	34.	(T) (F)	35.	(T) (F)

14. Burden of Proof and Presumptions: Fed.R.Evid. 301–302

1.	(T) (F)	2.	(T) (F)	3.	(T) (F)	4.	(T) (F)	5.	(T) (F)
6.	(T) (F)	7.	(T) (F)	8.	(T) (F)	9.	(T) (F)	10.	(T) (F)
11.	(T) (F)	12.	(T) (F)	13.	(T) (F)	14.	(T) (F)	15.	(T) (F)
16.	(T) (F)	17.	(T) (F)	18.	(T) (F)	19.	(T) (F)	20.	(T) (F)
21.	(T) (F)	22.	(T) (F)	23.	(T) (F)	24.	(T) (F)	25.	(T) (F)

15. Judicial Notice: Fed.R.Evid. 201

1.	(T) (F)	2.	(T) (F)	3.	(T) (F)	4.	(T) (F)	5.	(T) (F)
6.	(T) (F)	7.	(T) (F)	8.	(T) (F)	9.	(T) (F)	10.	(T) (F)
11.	(T) (F)	12.	(T) (F)	13.	(T) (F)	14.	(T) (F)	15.	(T) (F)

16. Judge and Jury Participation: Fed.R.Evid. 611(a), 614

1.	(T) (F)	2.	(T) (F)	3.	(T) (F)	4.	(T) (F)	5.	(T) (F)

17. Rulings on Admissibility: Fed.R.Evid. 103–16, 602

1.	(T) (F)	2.	(T) (F)	3.	(T) (F)	4.	(T) (F)	5.	(T) (F)
6.	(T) (F)	7.	(T) (F)	8.	(T) (F)	9.	(T) (F)	10.	(T) (F)
11.	(T) (F)	12.	(T) (F)	13.	(T) (F)	14.	(T) (F)	15.	(T) (F)
16.	(T) (F)	17.	(T) (F)	18.	(T) (F)	19.	(T) (F)	20.	(T) (F)
21.	(T) (F)	22.	(T) (F)	23.	(T) (F)	24.	(T) (F)	25.	(T) (F)

26.	(T)	27.	(T)	28.	(T)	29.	(T)	30.	(T)
	(F)		(F)		(F)		(F)		(F)
31.	(T)	32.	(T)	33.	(T)	34.	(T)	35.	(T)
	(F)		(F)		(F)		(F)		(F)
36.	(T)	37.	(T)	38.	(T)	39.	(T)	40.	(T)
	(F)		(F)		(F)		(F)		(F)
41.	(T)	42.	(T)	43.	(T)	44.	(T)	45.	(T)
	(F)		(F)		(F)		(F)		(F)
46.	(T)	47.	(T)	48.	(T)	49.	(T)	50.	(T)
	(F)		(F)		(F)		(F)		(F)

18. Confrontation Clause: *Crawford* to *Clark*

1.	(T)	2.	(T)	3.	(T)	4.	(T)	5.	(T)
	(F)		(F)		(F)		(F)		(F)
6.	(T)	7.	(T)	8.	(T)	9.	(T)	10.	(T)
	(F)		(F)		(F)		(F)		(F)
11.	(T)	12.	(T)	13a.	(T)	13b.	(T)	13c.	(T)
	(F)		(F)		(F)		(F)		(F)
13d.	(T)
	(F)

19. Selected Federal Rules of Evidence Amendments: Fed.R.Evid. 404, 408, 606, 609, 801(d)(1)(B), 803(6), 803(7), 803(8), 803(10), 803(16) and 804(b)(3)

1.	(T)	2.	(T)	3.	(T)	4.	(T)	5.	(T)
	(F)		(F)		(F)		(F)		(F)
6.	(T)	7.	(T)	8.	(T)	9.	(T)	10.	(T)
	(F)		(F)		(F)		(F)		(F)
11.	(T)	12.	(T)	13.	(T)	14.	(T)	15.	(T)
	(F)		(F)		(F)		(F)		(F)

HEARSAY EXAMS
TRUE OR FALSE EXAM I

1.	(T) (F)	2.	(T) (F)	3.	(T) (F)	4.	(T) (F)	5.	(T) (F)
6.	(T) (F)	7.	(T) (F)	8.	(T) (F)	9.	(T) (F)	10.	(T) (F)

11. (T) (F) 12. (T) (F) 13. (T) (F) 14. (T) (F) 15. (T) (F)
16. (T) (F) 17. (T) (F) 18. (T) (F) 19. (T) (F) 20. (T) (F)
21. (T) (F) 22. (T) (F) 23. (T) (F) 24. (T) (F) 25. (T) (F)
26. (T) (F) 27. (T) (F) 28. (T) (F) 29. (T) (F) 30. (T) (F)
31. (T) (F) 32. (T) (F) 33. (T) (F) 34. (T) (F) 35. (T) (F)
36. (T) (F) 37. (T) (F) 38. (T) (F) 39. (T) (F) 40. (T) (F)
41. (T) (F) 42. (T) (F) 43. (T) (F) 44. (T) (F) 45. (T) (F)
46. (T) (F) 47. (T) (F) 48. (T) (F) 49. (T) (F) 50. (T) (F)

TRUE OR FALSE EXAM II

1.   (T) (F) 2.   (T) (F) 3.   (T) (F) 4.   (T) (F) 5.   (T) (F)
6.   (T) (F) 7.   (T) (F) 8.   (T) (F) 9.   (T) (F) 10. (T) (F)
11. (T) (F) 12. (T) (F) 13. (T) (F) 14. (T) (F) 15. (T) (F)
16. (T) (F) 17. (T) (F) 18. (T) (F) 19. (T) (F) 20. (T) (F)
21. (T) (F) 22. (T) (F) 23. (T) (F) 24. (T) (F) 25. (T) (F)
26. (T) (F) 27. (T) (F) 28. (T) (F) 29. (T) (F) 30. (T) (F)
31. (T) (F) 32. (T) (F) 33. (T) (F) 34. (T) (F) 35. (T) (F)
36. (T) (F) 37. (T) (F) 38. (T) (F) 39. (T) (F) 40. (T) (F)
41. (T) (F) 42. (T) (F) 43. (T) (F) 44. (T) (F) 45. (T) (F)
46. (T) (F) 47. (T) (F) 48. (T) (F) 49. (T) (F) 50. (T) (F)

TRUE OR FALSE EXAM III

1.   (T) (F) 2.   (T) (F) 3.   (T) (F) 4.   (T) (F) 5.   (T) (F)
6.   (T) (F) 7.   (T) (F) 8.   (T) (F) 9.   (T) (F) 10. (T) (F)
11. (T) (F) 12. (T) (F) 13. (T) (F) 14. (T) (F) 15. (T) (F)
16. (T) (F) 17. (T) (F) 18. (T) (F) 19. (T) (F) 20. (T) (F)
21. (T) (F) 22. (T) (F) 23. (T) (F) 24. (T) (F) 25. (T) (F)
26. (T) (F) 27. (T) (F) 28. (T) (F) 29. (T) (F) 30. (T) (F)
31. (T) (F) 32. (T) (F) 33. (T) (F) 34. (T) (F) 35. (T) (F)
36. (T) (F) 37. (T) (F) 38. (T) (F) 39. (T) (F) 40. (T) (F)

41.   (T) (F)   42.   (T) (F)   43.   (T) (F)   44.   (T) (F)   45.   (T) (F)
46.   (T) (F)   47.   (T) (F)   48.   (T) (F)   49.   (T) (F)   50.   (T) (F)

TRUE OR FALSE EXAM IV

1.   (T) (F)   2.   (T) (F)   3.   (T) (F)   4.   (T) (F)   5.   (T) (F)
6.   (T) (F)   7.   (T) (F)   8.   (T) (F)   9.   (T) (F)   10.   (T) (F)
11.   (T) (F)   12.   (T) (F)   13.   (T) (F)   14.   (T) (F)   15.   (T) (F)
16.   (T) (F)   17.   (T) (F)   18.   (T) (F)   19.   (T) (F)   20.   (T) (F)
21.   (T) (F)   22.   (T) (F)   23.   (T) (F)   24.   (T) (F)   25.   (T) (F)
26.   (T) (F)   27.   (T) (F)   28.   (T) (F)   29.   (T) (F)   30.   (T) (F)
31.   (T) (F)   32.   (T) (F)   33.   (T) (F)   34.   (T) (F)   35.   (T) (F)
36.   (T) (F)   37.   (T) (F)   38.   (T) (F)   39.   (T) (F)   40.   (T) (F)
41.   (T) (F)   42.   (T) (F)   43.   (T) (F)   44.   (T) (F)   45.   (T) (F)
46.   (T) (F)   47.   (T) (F)   48.   (T) (F)   49.   (T) (F)   50.   (T) (F)

MULTIPLE CHOICE EXAM I

1.   (A) (B) (C) (D)   2.   (A) (B) (C) (D)   3.   (A) (B) (C) (D)
4.   (A) (B) (C) (D)   5.   (A) (B) (C) (D)   6.   (A) (B) (C) (D)
7.   (A) (B) (C) (D)   8.   (A) (B) (C) (D)   9.   (A) (B) (C) (D)
10.   (A) (B) (C) (D)   11.   (A) (B) (C) (D)   12.   (A) (B) (C) (D)
13.   (A) (B) (C) (D)   14.   (A) (B) (C) (D)   15.   (A) (B) (C) (D)
16.   (A) (B) (C) (D)   17.   (A) (B) (C) (D)   18.   (A) (B) (C) (D)
19.   (A) (B) (C) (D)   20.   (A) (B) (C) (D)   21.   (A) (B) (C) (D)
22.   (A) (B) (C) (D)   23.   (A) (B) (C) (D)   24.   (A) (B) (C) (D)
25.   (A) (B) (C) (D)

MULTIPLE CHOICE EXAM II

1.   (A) (B) (C) (D)   2.   (A) (B) (C) (D)   3.   (A) (B) (C) (D)
4.   (A) (B) (C) (D)   5.   (A) (B) (C) (D)   6.   (A) (B) (C) (D)
7.   (A) (B) (C) (D)   8.   (A) (B) (C) (D)   9.   (A) (B) (C) (D)

10.	(A) (B) (C) (D)	11.	(A) (B) (C) (D)	12.	(A) (B) (C) (D)
13.	(A) (B) (C) (D)	14.	(A) (B) (C) (D)	15.	(A) (B) (C) (D)
16.	(A) (B) (C) (D)	17.	(A) (B) (C) (D)	18.	(A) (B) (C) (D)
19.	(A) (B) (C) (D)	20.	(A) (B) (C) (D)	21.	(A) (B) (C) (D)
22.	(A) (B) (C) (D)	23.	(A) (B) (C) (D)	24.	(A) (B) (C) (D)
25.	(A) (B) (C) (D)				

COMPREHENSIVE EXAMS
TRUE OR FALSE EXAM I

1.	(T) (F)	2.	(T) (F)	3.	(T) (F)	4.	(T) (F)	5.	(T) (F)
6.	(T) (F)	7.	(T) (F)	8.	(T) (F)	9.	(T) (F)	10.	(T) (F)
11.	(T) (F)	12.	(T) (F)	13.	(T) (F)	14.	(T) (F)	15.	(T) (F)
16.	(T) (F)	17.	(T) (F)	18.	(T) (F)	19.	(T) (F)	20.	(T) (F)
21.	(T) (F)	22.	(T) (F)	23.	(T) (F)	24.	(T) (F)	25.	(T) (F)
26.	(T) (F)	27.	(T) (F)	28.	(T) (F)	29.	(T) (F)	30.	(T) (F)
31.	(T) (F)	32.	(T) (F)	33.	(T) (F)	34.	(T) (F)	35.	(T) (F)
36.	(T) (F)	37.	(T) (F)	38.	(T) (F)	39.	(T) (F)	40.	(T) (F)
41.	(T) (F)	42.	(T) (F)	43.	(T) (F)	44.	(T) (F)	45.	(T) (F)
46.	(T) (F)	47.	(T) (F)	48.	(T) (F)	49.	(T) (F)	50.	(T) (F)

TRUE OR FALSE EXAM II

1.	(T) (F)	2.	(T) (F)	3.	(T) (F)	4.	(T) (F)	5.	(T) (F)
6.	(T) (F)	7.	(T) (F)	8.	(T) (F)	9.	(T) (F)	10.	(T) (F)
11.	(T) (F)	12.	(T) (F)	13.	(T) (F)	14.	(T) (F)	15.	(T) (F)
16.	(T) (F)	17.	(T) (F)	18.	(T) (F)	19.	(T) (F)	20.	(T) (F)
21.	(T) (F)	22.	(T) (F)	23.	(T) (F)	24.	(T) (F)	25.	(T) (F)
26.	(T) (F)	27.	(T) (F)	28.	(T) (F)	29.	(T) (F)	30.	(T) (F)
31.	(T) (F)	32.	(T) (F)	33.	(T) (F)	34.	(T) (F)	35.	(T) (F)
36.	(T) (F)	37.	(T) (F)	38.	(T) (F)	39.	(T) (F)	40.	(T) (F)
41.	(T) (F)	42.	(T) (F)	43.	(T) (F)	44.	(T) (F)	45.	(T) (F)

46.   (T) (F)   47.   (T) (F)   48.   (T) (F)   49.   (T) (F)   50.   (T) (F)

TRUE OR FALSE EXAM III

1.   (T) (F)   2.   (T) (F)   3.   (T) (F)   4.   (T) (F)   5.   (T) (F)

6.   (T) (F)   7.   (T) (F)   8.   (T) (F)   9.   (T) (F)   10.   (T) (F)

11.   (T) (F)   12.   (T) (F)   13.   (T) (F)   14.   (T) (F)   15.   (T) (F)

16.   (T) (F)   17.   (T) (F)   18.   (T) (F)   19.   (T) (F)   20.   (T) (F)

21.   (T) (F)   22.   (T) (F)   23.   (T) (F)   24.   (T) (F)   25.   (T) (F)

26.   (T) (F)   27.   (T) (F)   28.   (T) (F)   29.   (T) (F)   30.   (T) (F)

31.   (T) (F)   32.   (T) (F)   33.   (T) (F)   34.   (T) (F)   35.   (T) (F)

36.   (T) (F)   37.   (T) (F)   38.   (T) (F)   39.   (T) (F)   40.   (T) (F)

41.   (T) (F)   42.   (T) (F)   43.   (T) (F)   44.   (T) (F)   45.   (T) (F)

46.   (T) (F)   47.   (T) (F)   48.   (T) (F)   49.   (T) (F)   50.   (T) (F)

TRUE OR FALSE EXAM IV

1.   (T) (F)   2.   (T) (F)   3.   (T) (F)   4.   (T) (F)   5.   (T) (F)

6.   (T) (F)   7.   (T) (F)   8.   (T) (F)   9.   (T) (F)   10.   (T) (F)

11.   (T) (F)   12.   (T) (F)   13.   (T) (F)   14.   (T) (F)   15.   (T) (F)

16.   (T) (F)   17.   (T) (F)   18.   (T) (F)   19.   (T) (F)   20.   (T) (F)

21.   (T) (F)   22.   (T) (F)   23.   (T) (F)   24.   (T) (F)   25.   (T) (F)

26.   (T) (F)   27.   (T) (F)   28.   (T) (F)   29.   (T) (F)   30.   (T) (F)

31.   (T) (F)   32.   (T) (F)   33.   (T) (F)   34.   (T) (F)   35.   (T) (F)

36.   (T) (F)   37.   (T) (F)   38.   (T) (F)   39.   (T) (F)   40.   (T) (F)

41.   (T) (F)   42.   (T) (F)   43.   (T) (F)   44.   (T) (F)   45.   (T) (F)

46.   (T) (F)   47.   (T) (F)   48.   (T) (F)   49.   (T) (F)   50.   (T) (F)

TRUE OR FALSE EXAM V

1.   (T) (F)   2.   (T) (F)   3.   (T) (F)   4.   (T) (F)   5.   (T) (F)

6.   (T) (F)   7.   (T) (F)   8.   (T) (F)   9.   (T) (F)   10.   (T) (F)

11.   (T) (F)   12.   (T) (F)   13.   (T) (F)   14.   (T) (F)   15.   (T) (F)

16.   (T) (F)   17.   (T) (F)   18.   (T) (F)   19.   (T) (F)   20.   (T) (F)

21.   (T) (F)   22.   (T) (F)   23.   (T) (F)   24.   (T) (F)   25.   (T) (F)

26.   (T) (F)   27.   (T) (F)   28.   (T) (F)   29.   (T) (F)   30.   (T) (F)

31.   (T) (F)   32.   (T) (F)   33.   (T) (F)   34.   (T) (F)   35.   (T) (F)

36.   (T) (F)   37.   (T) (F)   38.   (T) (F)   39.   (T) (F)   40.   (T) (F)

41.   (T) (F)   42.   (T) (F)   43.   (T) (F)   44.   (T) (F)   45.   (T) (F)

46.   (T) (F)   47.   (T) (F)   48.   (T) (F)   49.   (T) (F)   50.   (T) (F)

MULTIPLE CHOICE EXAM I

1.   (A) (B) (C) (D)   2.   (A) (B) (C) (D)   3.   (A) (B) (C) (D)

4.   (A) (B) (C) (D)   5.   (A) (B) (C) (D)   6.   (A) (B) (C) (D)

7.   (A) (B) (C) (D)   8.   (A) (B) (C) (D)   9.   (A) (B) (C) (D)

10.   (A) (B) (C) (D)   11.   (A) (B) (C) (D)   12.   (A) (B) (C) (D)

13.   (A) (B) (C) (D)   14.   (A) (B) (C) (D)   15.   (A) (B) (C) (D)

16.   (A) (B) (C) (D)   17.   (A) (B) (C) (D)   18.   (A) (B) (C) (D)

19.   (A) (B) (C) (D)   20.   (A) (B) (C) (D)   21.   (A) (B) (C) (D)

22.   (A) (B) (C) (D)   23.   (A) (B) (C) (D)   24.   (A) (B) (C) (D)

25.   (A) (B) (C) (D)

MULTIPLE CHOICE EXAM II

1.   (A) (B) (C) (D)   2.   (A) (B) (C) (D)   3.   (A) (B) (C) (D)

4.   (A) (B) (C) (D)   5.   (A) (B) (C) (D)   6.   (A) (B) (C) (D)

7.   (A) (B) (C) (D)   8.   (A) (B) (C) (D)   9.   (A) (B) (C) (D)

10.   (A) (B) (C) (D)   11.   (A) (B) (C) (D)   12.   (A) (B) (C) (D)

13.   (A) (B) (C) (D)   14.   (A) (B) (C) (D)   15.   (A) (B) (C) (D)

16.   (A) (B) (C) (D)   17.   (A) (B) (C) (D)   18.   (A) (B) (C) (D)

19.   (A) (B) (C) (D)   20.   (A) (B) (C) (D)   21.   (A) (B) (C) (D)

22.   (A) (B) (C) (D)   23.   (A) (B) (C) (D)   24.   (A) (B) (C) (D)

25.   (A) (B) (C) (D)

MULTIPLE CHOICE EXAM III

1.	(A) (B) (C) (D)	2.	(A) (B) (C) (D)	3.	(A) (B) (C) (D)

1. (A) (B) (C) (D) 2. (A) (B) (C) (D) 3. (A) (B) (C) (D)

4. (A) (B) (C) (D) 5. (A) (B) (C) (D) 6. (A) (B) (C) (D)

7. (A) (B) (C) (D) 8. (A) (B) (C) (D) 9. (A) (B) (C) (D)

10. (A) (B) (C) (D) 11. (A) (B) (C) (D) 12. (A) (B) (C) (D)

13. (A) (B) (C) (D) 14. (A) (B) (C) (D) 15. (A) (B) (C) (D)

16. (A) (B) (C) (D) 17. (A) (B) (C) (D) 18. (A) (B) (C) (D)

19. (A) (B) (C) (D) 20. (A) (B) (C) (D) 21. (A) (B) (C) (D)

22. (A) (B) (C) (D) 23. (A) (B) (C) (D) 24. (A) (B) (C) (D)

25. (A) (B) (C) (D)

MULTIPLE CHOICE EXAM IV

1. (A) (B) (C) (D) 2. (A) (B) (C) (D) 3. (A) (B) (C) (D)

4. (A) (B) (C) (D) 5. (A) (B) (C) (D) 6. (A) (B) (C) (D)

7. (A) (B) (C) (D) 8. (A) (B) (C) (D) 9. (A) (B) (C) (D)

10. (A) (B) (C) (D) 11. (A) (B) (C) (D) 12. (A) (B) (C) (D)

13. (A) (B) (C) (D) 14. (A) (B) (C) (D) 15. (A) (B) (C) (D)

16. (A) (B) (C) (D) 17. (A) (B) (C) (D) 18. (A) (B) (C) (D)

19. (A) (B) (C) (D) 20. (A) (B) (C) (D) 21. (A) (B) (C) (D)

22. (A) (B) (C) (D) 23. (A) (B) (C) (D) 24. (A) (B) (C) (D)

25. (A) (B) (C) (D)

MULTIPLE CHOICE EXAM V

1. (A) (B) (C) (D) 2. (A) (B) (C) (D) 3. (A) (B) (C) (D)

4. (A) (B) (C) (D) 5. (A) (B) (C) (D) 6. (A) (B) (C) (D)

7. (A) (B) (C) (D) 8. (A) (B) (C) (D) 9. (A) (B) (C) (D)

10. (A) (B) (C) (D) 11. (A) (B) (C) (D) 12. (A) (B) (C) (D)

13. (A) (B) (C) (D) 14. (A) (B) (C) (D) 15. (A) (B) (C) (D)

16. (A) (B) (C) (D) 17. (A) (B) (C) (D) 18. (A) (B) (C) (D)

19. (A) (B) (C) (D) 20. (A) (B) (C) (D) 21. (A) (B) (C) (D)

22.   (A) (B) (C) (D)   23.   (A) (B) (C) (D)   24.   (A) (B) (C) (D)

25.   (A) (B) (C) (D)

MULTIPLE CHOICE EXAM VI

1.   (A) (B) (C) (D)   2.   (A) (B) (C) (D)   3.   (A) (B) (C) (D)

4.   (A) (B) (C) (D)   5.   (A) (B) (C) (D)   6.   (A) (B) (C) (D)

7.   (A) (B) (C) (D)   8.   (A) (B) (C) (D)   9.   (A) (B) (C) (D)

10.   (A) (B) (C) (D)   11.   (A) (B) (C) (D)   12.   (A) (B) (C) (D)

13.   (A) (B) (C) (D)   14.   (A) (B) (C) (D)   15.   (A) (B) (C) (D)

16.   (A) (B) (C) (D)   17.   (A) (B) (C) (D)   18.   (A) (B) (C) (D)

19.   (A) (B) (C) (D)   20.   (A) (B) (C) (D)   21.   (A) (B) (C) (D)

22.   (A) (B) (C) (D)   23.   (A) (B) (C) (D)   24.   (A) (B) (C) (D)

25.   (A) (B) (C) (D)

Table of Cases